INDIA IN...
European and ...
on India 1...–1...

INDIA INSCRIBED
European and British Writing
on India 1600–1800

KATE TELTSCHER

OXFORD
UNIVERSITY PRESS

OXFORD
UNIVERSITY PRESS

YMCA Library Building, Jai Singh Road, New Delhi 110 001

Oxford University Press is a department of the University of Oxford. It furthers the University's objective of excellence in research, scholarship, and education by publishing worldwide in

Oxford   New York

Athens   Auckland   Bangkok   Bogota   Buenos Aires   Calcutta
Cape Town   Chennai   Dar es Salaam   Delhi   Florence   Hong Kong   Istanbul
Karachi   Kuala Lumpur   Madrid   Melbourne   Mexico City   Mumbai
Nairobi   Paris   Sao Paulo   Singapore   Taipei   Tokyo   Toronto   Warsaw

with associated companies in Berlin Ibadan

Oxford is a registered trade mark of Oxford University Press
in the UK and in certain other countries

Published in India
By Oxford University Press, New Delhi

© Oxford University Press 1995

The moral rights of the author have been asserted
Database right Oxford University Press (maker)
First published 1995
Oxford India Paperbacks 1997
Second impression 1999

All rights reserved. No part of this publication may be reproduced, stored in a retrieval system, or transmitted, in any form or by any means, without the prior permission in writing of Oxford University Press, or as expressly permitted by law, or under terms agreed with the appropriate reprographics rights organization. Enquiries concerning reproduction outside the scope of the above should be sent to the Rights Department, Oxford University Press, at the address above

You must not circulate this book in any other binding or cover and you must impose this same condition on any acquirer

ISBN 019 564 2244

Printed by Pauls Press, New Delhi 110 020
Published by Manzar Khan, Oxford University Press
YMCA Library Building, Jai Singh Road, New Delhi 110 001

To the memory of
MRIDULA SHASTRI
Doctor, swimmer, Rhodes Scholar
Bombay 1964—Lockerbie 1988

Acknowledgements

This book owes much to the insight, guidance, and generous encouragement of John Carey and Jonathan Katz. A Senior North Scholarship at St John's College, Oxford, an Oxford University Frere Exhibition for Indian Studies, and study leave from Roehampton Institute enabled me to complete the work. For their help and many suggestions, I am very grateful to Rukun Advani, Christopher Bayly, Peter Marshall, Rudrangshu Mukherjec, Tapan Raychaudhuri, Andrew Topsfield, Joanna Thornborrow, Tom Trautmann, Sarah Turvey, Jenny Uglow and Robert Young. The staff at the Indian Institute Library—Elizabeth Krishnan, Simon Lawson, and Helen Topsfield—greatly eased the process of research. The friendship of Bhaswati and Swapan Chakravorty, Parul Dave-Mukherji, Tanvir Hasan, Robin Hicks, Carol Jackson, Srilata Müller, Philippa Park, Marian Rooney, Udayakumar and Maya Unnithan made all the difference. My family has been a great support, and Julian Loose, my best and most patient critic, has seen this project through from start to finish.

The illustrations are reproduced by permission of the Bodleian Library, Oxford; The India Office Library and Records, London; The British Library; The National Army Museum, London; and the Master and Fellows of University College, Oxford.

KATE TELTSCHER

Contents

	List of Figures	x
	Introduction	1
1	Compare and Contrast: Seventeenth-Century European Writing about India	12
2	Indian Women: The Seventeenth-Century European Fantasy	37
3	India on Europe's Conscience: Eighteenth-Century Missionary Accounts	74
4	'Foreign Conquerors' and 'Harmless Indians': British Representations of Company Rule	109
5	'Geographical Morality': The Trial of Warren Hastings and the Debate on British Conduct in India	157
6	Sir William and the Pandits: The Legal Researches, Poetry and Translations of William Jones	192
7	'Vocabularies of Vile Epithets': British Representations of the Sultans of Mysore	229
	Bibliography	259
	Index	275

List of Figures

end papers: Title page, *Les Hindous* by Baltazard Solvyns, Vol. 4 (1808–12), Bodleian Library, Oxford.

1. Title page of *Purchas His Pilgrimes* by Samuel Purchas (1625), Bodleian Library, Oxford (Lister. E. 53–4). — 13
2. Illustration of bathing woman from *Les Voyages* by François de la Boullaye le Gouz (1657) p. 153, Bodleian Library, Oxford (Med. AA. 2). — 40
3. Illustration of Mughal couple from *Les Voyages* by François de la Boullaye le Gouz (1657) p. 147, Bodleian Library, Oxford (Med. AA. 2). — 41
4. Title page of *La Porte Ouverte* by Abraham Roger (1670), Bodleian Library, Oxford (Douce. R. 552). — 57
5. Engraving of sati from *Itinerario Voyage ofte Schipvaert* by Jan Hughen Van Linschoten (1596), British Library (569.g.23). — 58
6. Memorial to Sir William Jones by John Flaxman (1796–8), University College, Oxford. — 203
7. Engraving of Ganesa from *Asiatick Researches*, vol. i (1789) between pp. 226–7, Bodleian Library, Oxford (Per. 17578 d.54). — 211
8. Engraving of Karttikeya from *Asiatick Researches*, vol. i (1789) between pp. 252–3, Bodleian Library, Oxford (Per. 17578 d.54). — 212
9. Painting of the reception of Tipu Sultan's sons as hostages by Robert Home (1793–4), National Army Museum, London. — 250
10. Mezzotint engraving by John Burnet (1843) after David Wilkie's painting of the discovery of Tipu Sultan's body (1838), India Office Library and Records, London (p. 430). — 254

Introduction

On 9 July 1994 Mark Tully announced his resignation from the post of BBC South Asia correspondent. For more than a quarter of a century, Tully's familiar tones had reported the subcontinent: the Bangladesh war, the State of Emergency, the storming of the Golden Temple, the televised *Ramayana*, the assassination of Rajiv Gandhi. Why, then, had the British voice of India fallen silent? In protest, said Tully, at new BBC management techniques. But another explanation was proposed by *Devil's Advocate*, an independent television programme broadcast the following month on Britain's Channel 4: Tully did not jump, he was pushed. The case against Tully was that he had become an embarrassment to the BBC, not because he publicly criticized the management, but through his excessive identification with Indian culture. However impartial in his reporting, Tully was too great an Indophile (or Hindophile) to continue as the BBC's man in Delhi. He had spoken in defence of the caste system and denounced the spread of consumerism in the subcontinent. Tully was invited to the London studio to answer both these charges and others made by members of a specially selected audience. The programme adopted a distinctly adversarial approach, with the presenter, Darcus Howe—writer, broadcaster and black rights activist—standing at a lectern, playing 'devil's advocate', and Tully the defendant sitting beside him, vulnerable on a dais, answering the cross-questioning. As the programme progressed it became increasingly apparent that it was not Tully alone who was on trial, but the whole issue of the representation of India. Who had the authority to speak for the subcontinent? Different, loudly contested versions of the current state of affairs were offered by the British reporter, the Trinidad-born presenter, and the South Asian audience of former untouchables, historians, industrialists, journalists and academics.[1] The programme, for me, offered a post-colonial staging of the long and contentious history of representing the subcontinent. The spectacle was full of resonances: Tully, called to account, was like some latter-day Warren Hastings; his trial, a forty-five-minute TV version of the nine-year-long impeachment. Speaking in his own defence, Tully assured viewers that Indians loved and esteemed him, echoing the claims made for Sir William Jones two centuries earlier. The origins of this passionate and long-lived debate over India in Europe and Britain lie in the seventeenth century, the historical point of departure for this book.

The year 1600 saw the initiation of Anglo-Indian trade contact with the foundation of the English East India Company. By 1800, the year following the defeat of Mysore, the concept of an Indian empire had entered British thought. The transition from trading partner to ruling power is charted in this book through a detailed analysis of a large number of textual (and some visual) representations of India. The opening chapters examine aspects of European writing of the seventeenth and eighteenth centuries. The main focus of the study, however, falls on British texts of the second half of the eighteenth century—the formative decades for the emergence of the discourse of colonialism. Or rather, discourses; for writing about India is, as I shall attempt to show, not monolithic or univocal. European and British texts create a network of intersecting and contending discourses about India. Claims to speak about India are as fiercely contested in eighteenth-century pamphlets as in the television studio today.

In analysing these competing discourses, I am centrally concerned with issues of colonial authority. How do these discourses enable the transition from the role of the merchant to the role of the state? Seventeenth- and early eighteenth-century European texts are preoccupied with a wide-ranging set of questions about authority in India: about the power of the Mughal empire, about the subjection of Indian women, about the spiritual authority of Jesuit and Lutheran missionaries. This concentration on issues of power provides a discursive framework that is particularly amenable to later colonial use. But at the same time, it must be stressed that representations of India are diverse, shifting, historically contingent, complex and competitive. Many of these texts are determined by national and religious rivalries, by domestic concerns—both cultural and political (just as the debate over Mark Tully's representation of India is linked to matters of BBC and, ultimately, government policy). The texts cannot be forced to tell a single narrative about colonial expansion or the British will to power.

It is of course essential to situate these works in their specific national, social and religious contexts. But it is equally important to recognize the elements shared by these texts, to note the way that they constantly refer to, reproduce, counter and build on one another. For the seventeenth and early eighteenth centuries it is possible to speak of a European tradition of writing about India. Travel accounts were frequently translated into several European languages and gathered into collections of voyages. François Bernier's hugely influential account of Mughal history, for instance, was published in France in 1670–1, and translated into English in 1671 and Dutch the year after, with German and Italian editions following in 1672–3 and 1675. In a study of the first European representations of the New World, Stephen Greenblatt has remarked that 'European mimetic capital, though diverse and internally competitive, easily crossed the boundaries of nation and creed'; the same can be said of the early representations of India and so, like Greenblatt, I have decided not to 'accord those boundaries an absolute respect'.[2]

If writing about India in the seventeenth and early eighteenth centuries can most appropriately be termed European, after 1765 when the British acceded to diwani—the Mughal grant to collect land revenues and administer civil justice in Bengal—a more specifically British tradition of writing about India emerges. A steady stream of travel accounts, military memoirs, scholarly journals and histories, together with some novels and poetry, were published both in London and Calcutta. In this study I draw on a wide range of texts, many of which have previously been ignored by scholars. I have largely excluded unpublished work from consideration, partly because there would simply be too much material, and partly in an attempt to build a network of intertextual relations, to show how one work informs another. Although I respect and highlight distinctions of genre, I have not separated the literary from the non-literary, nor rigidly isolated one genre from another. Individual authors themselves cross such divides: William Jones, for example, published legal texts, scholarly research, translations and poetry on India. All the texts that I consider are unified in their production of an India for a domestic or expatriate audience. They share certain assumptions, strategies and imagery. They influence, plagiarize, and attack one another. However, this book does not pretend to be an exhaustive examination of all possible sources; perhaps the most notable absence is the vast body of statistical and economic research produced during the early decades of Company rule. While this material is undoubtably central to the formulation of British policy on issues such as land tenure, it does not occupy a prominent position in public debate on India.

Of the many different kinds of texts discussed in this study, travel literature predominates. As G. R. Crone and R. A. Skelton have observed, by the start of the eighteenth century in Britain, 'the vogue of travel literature, which was outrun in popularity among the reading public only by theology, became firmly established and was to be sustained throughout the century'.[3] Crone and Skelton point to the large collections of travels published by Samuel Purchas (1625), Awnsham and John Churchill (1704), John Harris (1705), Campbell (1744-8) and Thomas Osborne (1747). They note the increasing numbers of merchants on the subscription lists for such collections as a sign of travel literature's increasing relevance to commercial enterprise.[4] From the 1730s an even larger public was reached when the periodical press started to reprint extracts from travel accounts.[5] The European market for travel literature was also extensive. *Les Six Voyages de Jean-Baptiste Tavernier*, for instance, went through seventeen editions and reprints in French from 1675 to 1724 and was included in Abbé Prévost's *Histoire Générale des Voyages* of 1755. Five English editions appeared between 1677 and 1688, two German editions in 1681, with Italian and Dutch translations the following year.[6] While Tavernier's work figures among the most popular accounts of India, its publishing history indicates the considerable readership for such texts right across Europe.

During the first half of the eighteenth century Europe viewed India largely through the medium of missionary letters. From 1702 to 1776 the French Jesuits published collections of letters from their missions all over the world, including India. Volumes of these *Lettres édifiantes et curieuses* appeared with varying frequency (about every second year from 1706 to 1743) and eventually built to a thirty-four volume collection. A second edition of 1780 rearranged the letters according to geographical region. In 1743 a selection was translated into English by Lockman, and a large German collection appeared over the years 1728 to 1755. Although clearly propagandistic—the *Lettres* were published to raise funds and justify Jesuit activities in the face of mounting opposition—contemporaries regarded them as an important source of information. Sylvia Murr has noted the significance of the collections to French intellectuals, citing by way of illustration, Montesquieu's numerous references to the *Lettres* in *L'Esprit des Lois*.[7]

Alongside popular travel and missionary genres, different types of writing about India flourished in particular periods. The mid-eighteenth-century Anglo-French struggle for power was recorded in numerous histories and military memoirs, while the four Anglo-Mysore wars which punctuated the latter half of the century furnished many more. The early decades of Company rule also saw the publication of a number of histories that answered specific demands of the administration, such as Alexander Dow's *History of Hindostan* which, Ranajit Guha has observed, focused on questions of land ownership. According to Guha, the colonial need to find out about land-holding practices for revenue collection provided the rationale for many of the first British studies of Indian history.[8]

Scholarly research into Indian culture reached a remarkably large readership. The proceedings of the Asiatic Society of Bengal, the *Asiatick Researches*, were first printed in Calcutta and London in 1789. In 1798 a pirated edition appeared in London, and two further editions were published within six years, with a French translation following in 1805.[9] More popular still was William Jones's 1789 translation of Kalidasa's drama, *Sakuntala*. Reprinted five times in England between 1790 and 1807, it was translated into German in 1791, to the loud acclaim of Herder and Goethe.[10]

Literary texts relating to India were published only occasionally over this period. A handful of novels were set in India, most notably the anonymous *Hartly House, Calcutta* (1789), and Elizabeth Hamilton's *Translation of the Letters of a Hindoo Rajah*, which ran to five editions from 1796 to 1811. Poetry was largely represented by William Jones's *Hymns* to Hindu deities, published in Calcutta in the *Asiatick Miscellany* of 1785, reprinted in Calcutta and London in 1787, and widely reviewed in the periodical press.[11] Criticism of the East India Company, widespread in the Britain of the 1770s and 1780s, resulted in a number of poetic protests against the injustice of British policy in India.

Anti-Company sentiment culminated in the impeachment of Warren Hastings over 1786–95. Reports of the proceedings of the trial and notable debates were printed in the daily press, periodicals and pamphlets. Later compilations and accounts of individual sessions or the whole impeachment were issued in book form.[12] Given the extensive reporting of the trial, it seems to me essential to include the rhetoric of the impeachment in a discussion of anti-Company texts. As I shall endeavour to show, the debate in print prepared the way for the trial, and the rhetoric of the impeachment in turn influenced the textual debate. Indeed authors and orators were often the same: Edmund Burke wrote pamphlets and journals as well as speaking on Indian matters in parliament and assuming responsibility for the prosecution of Hastings.

The many different kinds of text discussed in this study are considered primarily as representations. That is to say, they are neither evaluated on their supposed accuracy, nor assessed on the extent of knowledge of India which they display. My aim, like that of Natalie Zemon Davis, is not to 'peel away the fictive elements' in texts to 'get at the real facts', but to 'let the "fictional" aspects of these documents be the center of analysis', meaning by 'fictional' the 'forming, shaping and molding elements: the crafting of the narrative'.[13] To this end, the techniques of textual analysis are used on non-literary as well as literary texts. By concentrating on such aspects as narrative structure, style, images and tropes, I consider the ways that texts draw on literary models, how they influence and answer one another. In recent years, it is Stephen Greenblatt who has offered the clearest defence of such procedures in his comments on colonial discourse analysis: '[t]he problem is not that there is no truth or that we are forever doomed to ignorance—though considerable ignorance is certainly inescapable in these matters—but that the discourses of colonialism actually do much of the crucially important work of colonialism'.[14]

My methods are deeply indebted to Edward Said's *Orientalism*, the founding work in the study of colonial discourse. I share Said's basic contention that knowledge of the Orient is linked to the exercise of colonial power. But as several critics have observed, Said's concept of orientalist discourse is too monolithic and homogeneous.[15] Said's sense of an unbroken, unchanging tradition of European representation of the East, from the time of the ancient Greeks to the present day, pays insufficient regard to historical context (perhaps inevitably, because of its scope) and neglects inconsistencies, contradictions and instabilities. I have tried to be attentive to such issues in my work, and propose a much more conflictual model, one constructed from contending discourses. While Said asserts that the authority of orientalist representations goes unchallenged, I argue that writers who compete with one another, publishing rival accounts of India, inevitably foreground the textual nature of their writing.[16]

In *Orientalism* Said claims that European culture grows in strength and identity by setting itself off against an oriental Other. This book follows Said in examining the construction of European and British identities, for self-representation is everywhere implied in the representation of India. According to Said, orientalism produces an unshakeable assumption of European superiority, with the East always functioning as the West's negative foil. This study charts the emergence of a much less stable sense of European self; an identity that is shifting, various, and responsive to the demands of domestic politics and religious affiliation. It is however possible to distinguish broadly between pre-colonial and colonial self-representations. Early accounts generally (but by no means exclusively) confirm a sense of national prestige. For example, Sir Thomas Roe, the first English ambassador to the Mughal court, is preoccupied with the signs of respect due to an English ambassador. By refusing to perform customary obeisances and repeatedly describing Jahangir's court as a theatre, Roe implies the dignity and integrity both of his own sovereign and himself. Such proud assertions of national identity ring through the early literature, bolstered of course by a sense of the primacy of Christian faith. But with the accession to diwani in 1765, the British adopt the titles and structures of Mughal power themselves. What happens when the Self takes on the guise of the Other? The confident narratives of national identity continue to be told, but are now haunted by new anxieties and instabilities. The assumption of colonial power marks the emergence of a much more precarious sense of self.

In recent years, colonial discourse analysis has moved away from the Self/Other oppositions charted by Said in *Orientalism*, towards a more complex sense of the anxieties of colonial rule. Homi Bhabha, Sara Suleri and Nigel Leask have all, in their various ways, aimed (in Suleri's words) 'to break down the incipient schizophrenia of a critical discourse that seeks to represent domination and subordination as though the two were mutually exclusive terms' and to focus instead on the 'psychic disempowerment signified by the colonial encounter'.[17] For Suleri, the 'anxiety of empire' manifests itself everywhere: in the imperial attempt to classify the peoples of India, in homoerotic narratives of colonial encounter and the idiom of cultural migrancy. Suleri's study—like Bhabha's essays—is both sophisticated and highly suggestive, but tends to neglect distinctions of historical context and genre. While the insights of both these critics inform my work, a concern with the diversity and historical particularity of representations runs through this study. Thus I analyse the ways that the narratives of India articulate the vacillating confidence and insecurity of the early decades of Company rule. The tensions and contradictions of the newly assumed colonial role are played out in contending, historically contingent discourses.

My first chapter tests Said's thesis that the Orient is consistently represented as Europe's inferior Other by examining seventeenth-century European writing about India. As James Clifford and other critics of *Orientalism* have observed, Said tends to generalize and simplify— Clifford mischievously suggests that Said's 'critical manner sometimes appears to mimic the essentializing discourse it attacks'.[18] This chapter argues that texts about India are indeed more complex and contradictory than Said's view of such writing would allow. India is frequently represented as the antithesis, but occasionally as the analogue, of Europe. Narrative devices are generally used to distance and subordinate India, but at times they diminish Indian strangeness and challenge European assumptions of superiority.

The otherness of India is explored more fully in the second chapter which concentrates on seventeenth-century images of Indian women. Removed from the European travel writer by both race and gender, Indian women are typically represented as both dangerous and attractive. India is turned into the kind of exotic space described by G. S. Rousseau and Roy Porter:

> Containing an element of the forbidden, though without its correlate, the abominable, the exotic is that realm of the excluded which is not absolutely prohibited, but merely signposted by danger lights. It has equivalent status in the geo-cultural realm to the daydream in the psychodynamic. It is marked by frisson more than fear.[19]

This fantasy land is however disturbed by the presence of the sati—the widow who burns herself on her husband's funeral pyre—a troubling and ambiguous figure who becomes a central topos in the European literature of India.

In eighteenth-century representations of India, the oppositions posited by Said—East/West, Other/Self—are significantly fragmented and eroded. Both missionary and early colonial writers have specific reasons for constructing images of Indian collaboration. The third chapter discusses Jesuit and Lutheran letters to show how missionary writing tends to dismantle distinctions between India and Europe. Published with explicit fund-raising intentions, missionary letters portray Indians as financially dependent on Europe. Adherents to Europe's faith, Indian converts are admitted to a unified brotherhood of Christ. But the representations themselves are far from uniform; the doctrinal differences between Jesuits and Lutherans are played out in opposed images of India.

Early colonial writers, at pains to justify the Company's activities in the hostile climate of the 1770s and 1780s, were also eager to show Indian identification with British aims. The fourth chapter examines how British texts construct Indians as loyal colonial subjects who willingly submit to benign Company rule. It considers the ways that British authority is asserted through the depiction of subordinate Indians and the classification of diverse native 'types'. But it also shows how that authority is limited and challenged, locating sites of Indian defiance and resistance.

The chapter outlines the strategies by which texts articulate and attempt to resolve anxiety over the security and probity of Company rule.

Such complimentary representations of British rule are challenged by the debate over Company policy and the impeachment of Warren Hastings, discussed in the fifth chapter. The flattering images of British paternalistic care are here inverted so that the British take on the character of oriental despots—none more so than Hastings, as he appears in the rhetoric of Edmund Burke. Indians feature as pathetic, muted victims who must be championed and given a voice by the prosecution. These representations share many of the same terms as the pro-Company writing; a common stock of images circulates between the two sides of the debate. Anti-Company writing is perhaps the most obvious example of what Dennis Porter has termed 'counter-hegemonic thought', that is an alternative discourse that emerges 'within the given dominant hegemonic formation'.[20] As Porter has pointed out, such dissident voices are silenced by Said's unified, undifferentiated concept of orientalism.

The sixth chapter returns to one of the principal functions of British writing about India—self-justification. A discussion of the literary work, legal researches and reputation of Sir William Jones focuses on the political implications of Jones's association with Hindu tradition. His close identification with pandits implies an appropriation of their authority, and the *Hymns* to Hindu deities serve to relocate Indian culture within the English poetic tradition. These representations tend to obscure the violence and disruption of colonial intervention and make British authority in India appear natural and unproblematic. In a study of the institution and ideology of English studies in nineteenth-century India, Gauri Viswanathan argues that the 'English literary text, functioning as a surrogate Englishman in his highest and most perfect state, becomes a mask for economic exploitation'.[21] I assign a similar role to the long-lived image of Jones as a disinterested scholar: a projection of an ideal English self, far removed from the crude realities of colonial power.

The reassuring character of such images is, however, jeopardized by the Anglo-Mysore wars. The final chapter considers how the construction of British authority is undermined by Haidar Ali and Tipu Sultan. In the narratives of ex-captives, the power of Mysore is figured as a violation of national and religious identity: British soldiers are compelled to serve in slave battalions and forcibly converted to Islam. These representations invert images of willing Indian collaboration and imply that Tipu, like the British, has the power to erode distinctions between East and West. Tipu is typically (but not exclusively) cast as an oriental tyrant, as if to deny the similarities between Mysore's and Britain's policies and tactics, and, by re-erecting the barriers of difference, to contain the threat of Mysore. But with Tipu's defeat, the alarming spectre of native power is banished—at least for a while—and the British start to speak of their Indian empire.

NOTES

1. *The Devil's Advocate*, prod. Ambreen Hameed, LWT, Chanel 4, 17 August 1994. The participants in the studio debate were Harbans Virdee, Ram Murti Summan, Saraswati Dave, Prabhu Mohapatra, Swaraj Paul, Karan Thapar, and Akbar Ahmed.
2. Stephen Greenblatt, *Marvelous Possessions: The Wonder of the New World* (Oxford, 1991) 8.
3. G. R. Crone, R. A. Skelton, 'English Collections of Voyages and Travels 1625–1846', *Richard Hakluyt and his Successors*, ed. Edward Lynam (London, 1946) 78.
4. Crone and Skelton, 88–9.
5. Peter Marshall, Glyndwr Williams, *The Great Map of Mankind: British Perceptions of the World in the Age of Enlightenment* (London, 1982) 52–3.
6. William Crooke, ed., *Travels in India Jean-Baptiste Tavernier* (Oxford, 1925) i. lx–lxvi.
7. Sylvia Murr, 'Les Conditions d'emergence du discours sur l'Inde au Siècle des Lumières', *Purusartha* vii (1983) 239.
8. Ranajit Guha, *An Indian Historiography of India: A Nineteenth-Century Agenda and its Implications* (Calcutta, 1988) 7–9.
9. O. P. Kejariwal, *The Asiatic Society of Bengal and the Discovery of India's Past* (Delhi, 1988) 54, 89.
10. Raymond Schwab, *The Oriental Renaissance: Europe's Rediscovery of India and the East, 1680–1880*, trans. Gene Patterson-Black and Victor Reinking (New York, 1984) 51, 59.
11. Garland Cannon, *The Life and Mind of Oriental Jones: Sir William Jones, the Father of Modern Linguistics* (Cambridge, 1990) 233–7.
12. Peter Marshall, ed., *The Writings and Speeches of Edmund Burke* (Oxford, 1991) vi. 38–40.
13. Natalie Zemon Davis, *Fiction in the Archives: Pardon Tales and their Tellers in Sixteenth-Century France* (Cambridge, 1987) 3.
14. Stephen Greenblatt, ed., *New World Encounters* (Berkeley, 1993) xvi.
15. James Clifford, *The Predicament of Culture: Twentieth-Century Ethnography, Literature, and Art* (Cambridge, Mass., 1988) 262. See also Dennis Porter, '*Orientalism* and its Problems', *The Politics of Theory*, ed. Francis Barker *et al.* (Colchester, 1982) 181–2; Lata Mani and Ruth Frankenberg, 'The Challenge of *Orientalism*', *Economy and Society*, xiv, no. 2 (1985) 177; Robert Young,

White Mythologies: Writing History and the West (London, 1990) 128; Sara Mills, *Discourses of Difference: An Analysis of Women's Travel Writing and Colonialism* (London, 1991) 51.
16. See Mills, 73, for a related point.
17. Sara Suleri, *The Rhetoric of British India* (Chicago, 1992) 4. See also Homi Bhabha, *The Location of Culture* (London, 1994); Nigel Leask, *British Romantic Writers and the East: Anxieties of Empire* (Cambridge, 1992).
18. Clifford, 262.
19. G. S. Rousseau and Roy Porter, eds, *Exoticism and the Enlightenment* (Manchester, 1990) 4.
20. Dennis Porter, 181.
21. Gauri Viswanathan, *Masks of Conquest: Literary Study and British Rule in India* (London, 1989) 20.

CHAPTER ONE

Compare and Contrast: Seventeenth-Century European Writing about India

The peculiarly ostentatious title page of *Purchas His Pilgrimes* proclaims the grandiose aims of Samuel Purchas's scheme. Published in 1625, Purchas's four folio volumes were to form *A History of the World in Sea Voyages and Lande Travells*. The title page (Fig. 1) is dominated by the figures of Prince Charles, to whom the work is dedicated, and King James, enthroned and backed by a map of Britain. Balancing this is an image of the tombs of their predecessors, Elizabeth I and Prince Henry. Two of the illustrations between the monarchs represent the suppression of the Gunpowder Plot and the defeat of the Armada: unequivocal symbols of the assertion of English authority. Below, thirty medallion portraits plot a genealogy of travel from Noah to Purchas's contemporaries. Purchas's own portrait appears at the bottom, flanked by two hemispheres. The visual impression is one of immense detail and variety, neatly contained: each portrait is encircled twice, named and set within a square. The whole page suggests that the world is being mapped and charted by a succession of travellers, all for the greater glory of England. It is dominated by images of authority and control: the figures of the monarchs and their triumphs, the lineage of voyagers, and the two hemispheres.[1]

Such an impression of ordered authority is central to the aims of seventeenth-century travel literature on India. The Indian travels collected by Purchas and his predecessor, Richard Hakluyt, are among the most influential accounts of India to appear in the period that saw the foundation and growth of the English East India Company. A clear relation exists between these accounts and the developing trade links with India.

FIG. 1: Title page of *Purchas His Pilgrimes* by Samuel Purchas (1625) Bodleian Library, Oxford.

Such narratives generally confirm a sense of national prestige. Accounts of India typically rely on Europe as a constant parallel, either through explicit analogy or implied reference. Cultural difference is generally elided through comparison, or registered in terms of deviation from a European norm. Much of this writing then serves to validate the home culture; but, as I hope to show, not all. I try to pay particular attention to moments which unsettle the confident narratives of cultural description, particularly in the writing of Sir Thomas Roe, the first English ambassador to the Mughal court, and in the work of François Bernier, whose account of contemporary Mughal history was published in 1670–1. Bernier's *History*, which ran to eight editions in the French original (over the period 1670–1725), and three in English translation (from 1671 to 1684), was to exert a lasting influence over later authors. Bernier constructed a comprehensive critique of Mughal government based on the misconception that the Mughal nobility held land only for life, and that at the landholder's death the property reverted to the emperor. This indictment of Mughal government was, however, contained in a text which at other moments renounced any claim to absolute knowledge of the East. I shall try to identify such tensions both within and between texts, and trace the 'competing and fluctuating logics of similarity and difference' (to borrow Lisa Lowe's phrase) which mark the early discourse of India.[2]

Trade and Authority

If we return to Purchas's collection, we find that the impression of order conveyed by the title page is reinforced by the division of the work into twenty books, arranged geographically and chronologically. But unlike the neat containment proposed by the title page, these divisions keep slipping. In his preface to the reader, Purchas explains his problems: 'NOW for the Method, I confesses I could not be therein exact . . . because I had such a confused Chaos of printed and written Bookes, which could not easily be ordered. . . . Yet are we not altogether without Order.'[3]

This editorial struggle to impose order is paralleled by the attempts of the individual writers to organize their material. The travel accounts collected by Purchas fall within a discipline, 'cosmography', which Francis Bacon describes as a 'kind of history manifoldly mixed'. Discussing the branches of civil history in *The Advancement of Learning* of 1605, Bacon defines cosmography as a compound of 'natural history, in respect of the regions themselves; of historic civil, in respect of the habitations, regiments, and manners of the people; and the mathematics, in respect of the climates and configurations towards the heavens'.[4] In addition to the complexities suggested by Bacon's diverse categories, the travel author must find a way of marrying 'cosmographic' observations with personal narrative.

One of the most basic methods of combining the two can be observed in Ralph Fitch's account of his Eastern travels of 1583 to 1591, included in Hakluyt's *Voyages*. Fitch hangs his observations haphazardly on the geographical framework provided by his travels. A typical extract will illustrate this technique:

From Bannaras I went to Patenaw downe the river of Ganges: where in the way we passed many faire townes, and a countrey very fruitfull: and many very great rivers doe enter into Ganges, and some of them as great as Ganges, which cause Ganges to bee of a great breadth, and so broad that in the time of raine you cannot see from one side to the other. These Indians when they bee scorched and throwen into the water, the men swimme with their faces downewards, the women with their faces upwards, I thought they tied something to them to cause them to doe so: but they say no. There be very many thieves in this countrey, which be like to the Arabians: for they have no certaine abode, but are sometime in one place and sometime in another. Here the women bee so decked with silver and copper, that it is strange to see, they use no shooes by reason of the rings of silver and copper which they weare on their toes. Here at Patanaw they finde gold in this maner. They digge deepe pits in the earth, and wash the earth in great bolles, and therein they finde the gold . . .[5]

The reader is presented with a series of apparently unrelated observations about the country through which Fitch is passing. This technique conveys a sense of verisimilitude—the indiscriminate flow of observations mimicking the flood of the traveller's varied impressions. However, Fitch breaks with this haphazard arrangement to append a summary of Indian trading commodities, so that his account also functions as a kind of commercial reference work.

The effect of verisimilitude seems less important than establishing an authoritative text, for Fitch actually copies both the form and substantial sections of his account from an earlier Italian narrative by Caesar Frederici. What is interesting about this is its blatancy. Hakluyt places the two narratives close together in his collection, and so it is rapidly apparent that Fitch lifts whole sections of Frederici's account piecemeal. The startling transparency of this plagiarism indicates the lack of any pressure on travel writers of the period to produce original material. If anything, familiar passages of description seem desirable, for both Hakluyt and Purchas generate a similar sense of duplication with their marginal comments which point out when travellers record the same things, or how similar observations have been made in different parts of the world.[6] Such repetition bolsters the sense of a report's authenticity: if different individuals notice the same things, it is more likely that they are telling the truth. This editorial preoccupation with veracity can also be seen in the second edition of Hakluyt's *Voyages* (1599) which omitted the fanciful *Travels* of Mandeville on grounds of implausibility.

This desire to produce a credible text causes one of Purchas's authors, William Hawkins, to divide the account of his Indian travels of 1608 to 1613 into two halves.[7] The first contains his personal narrative, the story of dealings with the Mughal emperor; the second, his 'cosmological' observations. By separating the personal from the factual, Hawkins seems to endow the second part of his work with the status of unchallengeable truth.[8] To maintain his authoritative tone, Hawkins makes use of previous writers, like Hakluyt and Purchas, with their marginal notes. Describing the Hindu practice of cremation, Hawkins reminds his readers that it is a custom of which they have 'read in other Authors'.[9] He thus appeals to an authenticating body of knowledge, referring, as it were, to a succession of travellers like that pictured on Purchas's title page. This sense of a voyaging tradition is encapsulated by an incident recorded in the journal of Hawkin's companion, William Finch, also included in *Purchas His Pilgrimes*. Breaking their outward voyage at Sierra Leone, the sailors take water at a spring where, carved on the rocks, they find 'the names of divers English men which had bin there; amongst the rest, of Sir Francis Drake, which had bin there seven and twentie yeeres before . . .'[10] The English are, quite literally, leaving their mark on the world; staking their claim through the act of inscription.

These writers are not only conscious of a continuity with the travels of the past, they also confidently predict a voyaging future. Hawkins imagines a succession of future travellers when he cuts short a description of the customs of the 'Heathen Communality': 'They use many other fopperies and superstitions, which I omit, leaving them for other Travellers, which shall come from thence hereafter.'[11] Hawkins, discriminating as to what he should include in his account, places himself in a position of authority, reminding us of his power to regulate the flow of information from East to West. At the same time, because he does not specify the 'fopperies and superstitions', he manages to suggest that the range of heathen delusion is infinite. This device of witholding information seems to be a favourite means of both staking a claim to authorial power and scorning non-Christian belief. Another narrative collected by Purchas, Edward Terry's account of his travels in India as chaplain to Sir Thomas Roe, refers equally dismissively to Hindu festivals:

It were easie to enlarge, but I will not cast away Inke and Paper in farther description of their stupid Idolatries, the summe is, that both Mahometans and Gentiles ground their opinions upon tradition, not Reason, and are content to perish with their Fore-fathers, out of a preposterous zeale, and loving perversenesse never ruminating on what they maintayne, like to uncleane beasts which chew not the Cud.[12]

Here Terry's indignation is focused on what he considers the irrationality of Islam and Hinduism. To adhere to 'tradition, not Reason' is backward looking and, he suggests in his final simile, bestial. Conversely, Terry himself displays the faculty of reason to the full, delighting in providing hypothetical explanations for the phenomena that he observes. Describing the ferocity of the monsoon, he suggests that 'The reason in Nature may be the subtiltie of the Aire, wherein there are fewer Thunder-stones made, then in such Climates where the Aire is grosse and cloudy'.[13] The scientific language adds a certain weightiness to the explanation; here, as elsewhere, the tone strives to be both informed and reliable.

All these writers were, directly or indirectly, involved in exploring trading possibilities with India. Their accounts had to convey a sense of dependable authority since they were written to indicate commercial opportunities to their employers or patrons, to function as sources of practical information. Hakluyt's *Voyages*, in fact, became standard issue on all East India Company expeditions.[14] Some of these accounts could well be termed merchant guide books. Finch provides detailed descriptions of towns and routes with precise directions and Baedeker-like asides: commenting that the inhabitants of a town 'are very friendly to the English',[15] and advising his readers to 'Note that', in mosques, 'you may not enter of these places but bare-foot'.[16] The travel accounts are so closely identified with trade in Purchas's mind that, when he refers to Terry's narrative, all his metaphors have their origin in commerce: Terry's descriptions are 'rich Cates of Sea and Land varieties farre fetched and deere bought by him, and here imparted gratis'. Purchas uses a second image of consumption when he describes the report as a 'good fare-well draught of English-Indian liquor', and finally depicts it as the type of trading commodity for which India was famed: 'a Gemme' or 'Precious-stone'.[17]

Purchas's metaphors draw upon the popular conception of India as a land of great riches; we may recall Barabas's description in *The Jew of Malta* of 'the Merchants of the Indian Mynes, / That trade in metall of the purest mould'.[18] This notion of Indian wealth is one that he travel writers help to perpetuate. Finch describes the city of Ahmedabad as a tempting mercantile prospect:

The buildings comparable to any Citie in Asia or Africa, the streets large and well paved, the Trade great (for almost every ten dayes goe from hence two hundred Coaches richly laden with Merchandise for Cambaya) the Merchants rich, the Artificers execellent for Carvings, Paintings, Inlayd Workes, imbroydery with Gold and Silver: at an houres warning it hath in readinesse sixe thousand Horse; the gates perpetually strong guarded . . .[19]

He depicts a well organized, secure, wealthy city with an established trade in an abundance of desirable commodities. Equally alluring is Finch's description of the lifestyle of that other great symbol of Indian wealth, the Mughal emperor. He is describing the imperial mansion at Allahabad:

In the waters side within the Moholl [mansion] are divers large Devoncans [halls], where the King with his Women often passe their times in beholding Gemini, paying his tribute to Ganges. Betweene them and the waters side at the foote of the wall is a pleasant Garden shaded with Cypresse Trees, and abounding with excellent fruits and flowres, having in the midst a faire Banquetting House, with privie staires to take Boate.[20]

This is a seductive image of luxury and languor made more exotic by the use of unfamiliar architectural terms. The enclosed idyll with its wall, 'privie staires' and fruitful gardens, is pervaded by a sense of timeless indolence as the emperor and his harem watch the rivers flow by.

Both these images of India—the land of trade and the sensuous idyll—are combined by Terry. In one paragraph, he enumerates the country's trading commodities and continues:

For places of pleasure they have curious Gardens, planted with fruitfull Trees and delightfull Flowers, to which Nature daily lends such a supply as that they seeme never to fade. In these places they have pleasant Fountaynes to bathe in, and other delights by sundrie conveyances of water, whose silent murmure helps to lay their senses with the bonds of sleepe in the hot seasons of the day.[21]

This is a quite conscious evocation of what was only implicit in Finch's garden: the image of the earthly paradise, ever fruitful, careless and timeless. But Terry's next paragraph disrupts the dreams of both the sleepers by the fountain and his readers:

But lest this remote Countrey should seeme like an earthly Paradise without any discommodities: I must needes take notice there of many Lions, Tygres, Wolves, Jackals . . . and many other harmefull beasts. In their Rivers are many Crocodiles, and on the Land over-growne Snakes, with other venimous and pernicious Creatures. In our houses there we often meete with Scorpions, whose stinging is most sensible and deadly, if the patient have not presently some Oyle that is made of them, to anoint the part affected, which is a present cure. The aboundance of Flyes in those parts doe likewise much annoy us, for in the heate of the day their numberlesse number is such as that we can be quiet in no place for them, they are ready to cover our meate assone as it is placed on the Table, and therefore wee have men that stand on purpose with Napkins to fright them away when as we are eating: in the night likewise we are much disquieted with Musquatoes . . . and in their great Cities, there are such aboundance of bigge hungrie Rats, that they often bite a man as he lyeth on his bed.[22]

I quote at some length to convey the strikingly forceful and determined nature of Terry's destruction of the idea of the paradisal idyll. In fact, the onslaught continues with a description of the trying rigours of the Indian climate.

Launching his attack with a list of dangerous wild animals which his readers would only have met in books or plays, Terry rapidly moves beyond the kind of representation of Indian horrors familiar from emblem books. He situates his description in place (in houses, cities, bed), and in time (at meals and in the night), and depicts more familiar hazards such as flies and rats: the reader is thrust into a grim reality where sleepers are more likely to be bitten by mosquitoes than doze by fountains. It is for an explicitly Christian purpose that such emphasis is laid on India's 'discommodites' to counter the excitement generated by the idyll and trade 'commodities' of the previous paragraph. Terry explains: 'there is no Countrey without some discommodities, for therefore the wise Disposer of all things hath tempered bitter things with sweet, to teach man that there is no true and perfect content to be found in any Kingdom, but that of God.'[23]

Despite this suggestion of divine balance, Terry's insistence on the horrors of Indian fauna—the numerous 'venimous and pernicious Creatures' and the 'aboundance of Flyes'—implies that he regards Indian wildlife as an aberration from the norm set by England. The descriptions of harmful Indian animals carry an implicit comparison with the harmless creatures at home; Terry is, in a sense, moralizing geography. He seems to have derived his narrative technique from an allegorical genre, and his account itself has interesting affinities with the 'Bowre of Blisse' episode in The *Faerie Queene*.

Acrasia's garden of sensual indulgence shares several features with the emperor's: it is 'the most daintie Paradise on ground' with 'painted flowres' and 'trees vpshooting hye'.[24] It also possesses

> A gentle streame, whose murmuring waue did play
> Emongst the pumy stones, and make a sowne,
> To lull him soft a sleepe, that by it lay;
> The wearie Traueiler, wandring that way,
> Therein did often quench his thristy heat,

> And then by it his wearie limbes display,
> Whiles creeping slomber made him to forget
> His former paine, and wypt away his toylsom sweat.[25]

Seductive as these images are, like Terry's, they are deceptive. It is Guyon's task to destroy the Bowre, and, when all is razed, he learns that Acrasia's sexual charms turn men to hideous beasts. Terry's narrative then functions much as a Christian allegory: he builds up the image of an earthly paradise only to destroy it and demonstrate its shortcomings. The parallels between the two passages indicate not so much that Terry is consciously adapting Spenser's imagery, but that travel writers inevitably find themselves drawing upon literary tropes. In following an allegorical model, Terry casts the strange and unknown in a reassuringly familiar pattern.

Analogies with Home

Some authors draw explicit comparisons with the familiar. This is the technique adopted by Sir Thomas Roe in the journal, published by Purchas, which he kept as ambassador to Jahangir's court from 1615 to 1619. As the anthropologist and historian Bernard Cohn has observed, 'Roe read the political world in which he found himself in terms of his own system of meanings'.[26] One metaphor which Roe uses repeatedly to describe the formal arrangement of the emperor's throne room is that of the theatre: 'This sitting out hath so much affinity with a Theatre, the manner of the King in his Gallery; the great men lifted on a Stage as Actors; the Vulgar below gazing on, that an easie description will enforme of the place and fashion.'[27] Roe's confidence that his metaphor effortlessly conveys the scene to his reader is significant. The spectacle of Mughal power is displayed for the ambassador, who in turn stages it for his domestic audience. The image of the theatre, which Roe claims to be an exact representation of the court, is itself most commonly used as a symbol of unreality or feigning. Indeed Roe's whole conception of the Mughal court is shot through with a sense of unreality. Recording Jahangir's birthday ceremony, when the emperor was himself weighed against various commodities which were then distributed to his subjects, Roe doubts the authenticity of the entire show: the so-called riches are only stage props in the spectacle. Jahangir sits on the scales opposite bags in which 'they say was silver', and then is weighed against gold and jewels, and precious stones, but I saw none, it being in bagges might bee Pebbles; then against cloth of Gold, Silke, Stuffes, Linnen, Spices, and all sorts of goods, but I must beleeve, for they were in fardles. Lastly, against Meale, Butter, Corne, which is said to be given to the Beniani [Hindus], and all the rest of the Stuffe: but I saw it carefully carryed in, and none distributed.[28]

Given Roe's perception, central to his description, of the court as a theatre, it follows that the Mughals are staging a play: *Tamburlaine the Great*—appropriately enough, given that Tamburlaine (properly Taimur) was Jahangir's ancestor. Roe refers to Marlowe's play when he receives a sign of favour from the emperor's son, Sultan Khurram; and the allusion is no doubt informed by Roe's suspicion of the prince's integrity, his fear that he is only feigning good will:

By and by came a Cloath of gold Cloake of his owne, once or twice worne, which hee caused to be put on my backe, and I made reference very unwillingly. When his Ancestor Tamerlane was represented at the Theatre, the garment would well have become: but it is heere reputed the highest favour to give a garment worne by a Prince. . . .[29]

Roe's distrust of ostentation and the ceremonial gestures of the Mughal court transforms the genuine cloth of gold cloak into a tawdry stage imitation. Cohn comments that Roe misunderstands the presentation of the khilat, or robe of honour, 'as a sign of debasement, rather than an act of incorporation in a substantive fashion which made him a companion of the ruler'.[30] Roe reads the signs of an Eastern court through the conventions of English theatrical representation. Equipped with the wrong cultural script, Roe turns a compliment into an insult.

From his assumed vantage point of a spectator at a play, Roe can comment wryly on the stage action. He is particulary interested in the performance of a fellow ambassador from Persia:

he appeared rather a Jester or Jugler, then a person of any gravity, running up and downe and acting all his words like a Mimicke Player (now indeed the Atachikanne [audience chamber] was become a right Stagge) . . . his tongue was a great advantage to deliver his owne businesse, which he did with so much flattery and obsequiousnesse, that it pleased asmuch as his gift, even calling his Majesty King and Commander of all the World (forgetting his owne Master had a share in it) and on every little occasion of good acceptation hee made his Tessilims [obeisance]. When all was delivered for that day, hee prostrated himselfe on the ground, and knocked with his head as if hee would enter in.[31]

These extravagant gestures are indeed reminiscent of *Tamburlaine*. If we compare the ambassador's behaviour to that of Theridamas, king of Argier, when he greets Tamburlaine, we can better understand the origins of Roe's theatrical conceit:

> My Lord, the great and mighty Tamburlain,
> Arch-monarke of the world, I offer here,
> My crowne, my selfe, and all the power I have,
> In all affection at thy kingly feet.[32]

Given Marlowe's obvious attachment to striking stage images of dominance—captive kings pulling Tamburlaine's chariot or imprisoned in an iron cage—Theridamas would surely deliver these lines literally humbled at Tamburlaine's feet.

Roe finds such shows of self-abasement abhorrent; the comic picture of the Persian knocking his head on the floor masks a deeper repugnance. From the very first, Roe emphasizes his refusal to perform these obeisances. In fact, part of the humour of the passage stems from the contrast between the Persian's antics and his own more dignified deportment. Roe's refusal to participate in this custom marks him off as different, defiantly independent from the court. He remains an observer of the spectacular display of excess, a mediator between the Eastern fiction and the Western audience. While the whole court is engaged in the 'flattery and obsequiousnesse' of false theatrical spectacle, Roe represents sincerity and sober reality. Faced with this opposition between the Mughal court and Roe, the reader inevitably fixes Roe as the norm by which to judge the deviation of the court. And Roe's representation of the Mughal court as a theatrical sham presided over by 'Mock Kings',[33] does not so much raise doubts about the nature of kingship, as legitimate the court of Roe's own sovereign—King James. Following Said, we might say that Roe's denigration of the Mughal court, reinforces a sense of European superiority by implying a positive Western counterpart. Such an argument effectively reformulates ideas contained in Montaigne's famous essay, 'Of the Caniballes', translated into English by John Florio in 1603. Montaigne, arguing against the widespread perception of Brazilian Indians as barbarous, reasons that: 'men call that barbarisme which is not common to them. As indeed, we have no other ayme of truth and reason, than the example and *Idea* of the opinions and customes of the countrie we live in. There is ever perfect religion, perfect policie, perfect and compleat use of all things.'[34] Such reflex acts of cultural condemnation are apparent in the travel accounts on India, particularly in the first area specified by Montaigne: religion.

This is most obviously demonstrated by the common depiction of Hindu gods as monsters or devils. The development of this Indian god/monster tradition in Western pictorial representation has been traced by Partha Mitter and is equally evident in the written accounts.[35] Fitch observes that 'their chiefe idoles bee blacke and evill-favoured, their mouthes monstrous . . .',[36] and Finch writes of temples housing 'stone images of monstrous men feareful to behold, but adored by the Indians with flowers and offerings'.[37] By stressing the incongruity of worshipping an image that is 'fearful to behold', of adoring a monster, Finch implies that Hinduism is strangely illogical and perverted. Also pervading his account is the sense that Hindu ritual is incomprehensible. He notes that 'though it be never so cold, they will wash themselves in cold water or in warme',[38] and describes ceremonies by the Ganges where devotees 'kisse the ground twentie or thirtie times. . . . And some of them will make their ceremonies with fifteene or sixteene pots . . . they make their mixtures tenne or twelve times . . . and say divers things over their pots many times'.[39] Such passages imply, through their sustained vagueness and imprecision, that these actions are both unintelligible and completely inconsequential.

Another typical response to Hinduism is caricature: humour acts as an outlet for the anxiety created by the threat of the unknown. Fitch dispels any fear caused by such reports as monster worship with a crude parody of Hinduism:

They have a very strange order among them, they worshippe a cowe, and esteeme much of the cowes doung to paint the walles of their houses. They will kill nothing not so much as a louse: for they hold it a sinne to kill any thing. . . . They say if they should be buried, it were a great sinne, for of their bodies there would come many wormes and other vermine, and when their bodies were consumed, those wormes would lacke sustenance, which were a sinne, therefore they will be burned.[40]

Designed to disgust, this passage draws on images from the repertoire of bad jokes and graveyard humour: dung, lice, decomposing bodies and worms; but its main aim, with its absurdly tortuous explanation of Hindu cremation, is to depict Hindu belief as laughably illogical. As always with satire, readers are left with a comforting sense of their own superiority: when ridicule is cast on Hindu beliefs and logic, Protestantism appears supremely reasonable.

Of course, following the Reformation, writers would be well used to the practice of condemning and ridiculing Catholicism and its superstitious rituals to affirm Protestantism; and we need only think of the two illustrations on Purchas's title page of English triumphs over Catholic aggression and conspiracy—the Armada and the Gunpowder Plot—to realize the extent to which religion was identified with national pride. It is interesting to note that some writers combine attacks on heathens with anti-papist jibes, hitting, as it were, two targets at once. This technique is by no means exclusive to writing on India; Stephen Greenblatt notes that the sixteenth-century Huguenot pastor Jean de Léry draws an analogy with the Catholic mass to condemn the rituals of the Tupinamba of Brazil.[41] In the context of India, where the English were competing with the Portuguese for trade concessions, verbally sparring with them at the Mughal court and physically skirmishing at sea, the attractions of a double attack against infidel and Catholic rival were irresistible. Consider, for example, Terry's description of Muslim worship:

The Priests doe neither reade nor preach in their Churches, but there is a set forme of prayer in the Arabian tongue, not understood by most of the common people, yet repeated by them as well as by the Moolaas. They likewise rehearse the Names of God and Mahomet certayne times every day upon Beads, like the misse-led Papist, who seemes to regard the number, rather then the weight of Prayers.[42]

In this passage, Terry notes the absence from the Muslim form of worship of those elements which were central to the Protestant church service: readings, sermons and liturgy in the vernacular, and so implies a comparison with the Latin Catholic mass, an analogy made explicit when he likens Muslim prayer beads to rosaries.

Looking more closely at Terry's technique, we see that he keeps as his basic premise the familiar concept of Christian ritual, and everything that he notices is as a discrepancy from, or analogy to, the Protestant and Catholic forms. It is only through his preconceptions that he can observe the scene: abroad can be represented only in terms familiar from home. This is, inevitably, the common predicament of all travellers; a fact acknowledged by François Hartog in his study of Herodotus. For Hartog, the 'fundamental question' about travel writing is 'in the last analysis, what does a traveler talk about? About what is "the same" or about what is the "other"? The traveler's procedure comes down to constructing an image of what is other that will be a "telling" one for the audience from the world of the same.'[43]

Such a strategy is apparent throughout Terry's account. Describing the use of land, for example, he observes 'Their ground is not enclosed'[44] and that deer are 'nowhere imparked: the whole Kingdome is as it were a Forrest, for a man can travell no way but he shall see them, and (except it bee within a small distance off the King) they are every man's Game'.[45] Terry is noting the differences between Indian and English landholding practice. At the same time, he is also commenting on social issues: in England, deer parks numbered among aristocratic privileges and the enclosure of common land was regarded by many as a major cause of poverty. If what Terry notices in India is determined by English current concerns, it follows that travel accounts can be read as much for what they reveal about home as about abroad; a fact which writers of that genre so closely related to travel literature—utopian fiction—have long perceived.

Equally evident in their descriptions of society abroad are the authors' personal social preoccupations. Terry observes that the caste system, which determines that Hindus only marry within their own 'Tribe, Sect, and Occupation', means that 'they never advance themselves'.[46] It is surely significant that Terry, who as chaplain to Sir Thomas Roe would have expectations of preferment, should note the impossibility of self-betterment in Hindu society. It is just as telling that his employer, Roe (Esquire of the Body to Elizabeth, knighted by James in 1605) is troubled by the apparent absence of class distinctions in the proceedings of the Mughal court, where 'the common base people knew as much as the Councell, and the newes every day, is the Kings new resolutions, tossed and censured by every rascall'.[47] Roe's concept of a properly ordered society is also shaken by the emperor's custom of presenting himself daily to his subjects:

This course is unchangeable, except sicknesse or drinke prevent it, which must be knowne: for as all his Subjects are slaves, so is hee in a kind of reciprocall bondage, for hee is tyed to observe these houres and customs so precisely, that if he were unseene one day, and no sufficient reason rendred, the people would mutinie . . .[48]

It appears to Roe that the common people control the emperor, so upending the social hierarchy, and raising the ugly spectre of popular power. Roe is even more troubled by Mughal landholding customs. According to Roe, the emperor owns all the land in the country and parcels it out to the aristocracy; but when a lord dies, all his land reverts to the emperor. This is an idea which François Bernier would subsequently develop, as we shall see later. It is this lack of inheritance—the means by which the English aristocratic and merchant classes maintained and increased their power—that particularly disturbs Roe:

he [the emperor] heires all mens goods that dye, as well as those gained by industry, as Merchants, as those that lived by him, and takes all their money;

leaves the Widow and Daughters what he pleaseth; gives the sonnes some little Signiorie, and puts them anew to the World, whose Fathers die worth two or three Millions.[49]

Roe heightens the sense of the injustice of this system with pathetic appeals for the vulnerable widows and daughters, the ill-provided-for sons, thrust, like babies, 'anew to the World'. Noting his particular indignation on behalf of the merchants, it is worth remarking that Roe himself came from a wealthy trading family; his grandfather, Sir Thomas Roe, had been Lord Mayor of London.

Both Terry and Roe are typical in projecting images of English society onto Indian society and recording the differences. For most part, the representations follow Said's model of binary opposition: India is presented negatively, as the inverse of England; but there are exceptions. Terry remarks, of the Muslims, that 'many amongst them, to the shame of us Christians, what impediment soever they have either by pleasure or profit, pray five times every day'.[50] Terry uses Muslim devotion to censure Christian laxity; the infidel reprimands the faithful. This positive image has so much force precisely because of the general practice of depicting India negatively. Terry seems to envisage a kind of competition of devotion between East and West which Europe is losing, 'to the shame of us Christians'. He manipulates the tradition to make his moral point and exhort his readers to greater piety; he is, after all, a chaplain.

Roe also records an instance of heathen virtue, but, unlike Terry, not solely as an incitement to increased Christian virtuousness. Roe is at court when the emperor receives a 'professed poore holy' beggar. His account of the meeting is unusually detailed and long:

This miserable wretch cloathed in rags; crowned with feathers, covered with ashes, his Majestie talked with about an houre, with such familiaritie and shew of kindnesse, that it must needs argue an humilitie not found easily among Kings. The Begger . . . gave the King a Present, a Cake, asht, burnt on the coales, made by himselfe of course graine, which the King accepted most willingly, and brake one bit and eate it, which a daintie mouth could scarce have done. After he tooke the clout, and wrapt it up, and put in the poore mans bosome, and sent for one hundred Rupias, and with his owne hands powred them into the poore mans lap, and what fell besides, gathered up for him; when with his collation of banquetting and drinke came, whatsoever he tooke to eate, he brake and gave the Begger halfe, and after many strange humiliations and charities, rising, the old Wretch not being nimble, he tooke him up in his armes, which no cleanly body durst have touched, imbracing him, and three times laying his hand on his heart, calling him father, he left him, and all of us and me in admiration of such a vertue in a heathen Prince.[51]

Roe's description, with its endlessly extended syntax, piling one precise observation upon another, reflects a mounting incredulity at Jahangir's 'many strange humiliations and charities'. The emperor's actions take on a symbolic significance, so that Jahangir almost turns into an emblem of charity. At succesive stages in his description, Roe draws inferences from the emperor's actions: Jahangir's kindness 'must needs argue an humilitie not found easily among Kings', his acceptance of the cake is something which 'a daintie mouth could scarce have done' and the beggar whom he helps to his feet 'no cleanly body durst have touched'. The encounter obviously repels Roe: his physical distaste for the dirty beggar is evident, and the pairing of the king with the pauper offends his sense of social propriety. But his fascination with the encounter derives, I think, from its proverbial and biblical resonances. The king is linked with the beggar: wealth and power with poverty and impotence. Tilley's *Dictionary of Proverbs* supplies the pairing, 'A king or a beggar',[52] but the first book of Samuel contains a more significant passage: 'He raiseth up the poore out of the dust and lifteth up the beggar from the dunghill, to set them among princes, and to make them inherit the throne of glory.'[53] Roe is watching a biblical ideal being acted out before him; little wonder that he is left 'in admiration of such a vertue in a heathen Prince'.

Stephen Greenblatt has observed that in *Mandeville's Travels*, Indian religious rituals—self-mutilation and child-sacrifice—are represented 'as an extreme version of Christian practices'. He adds that Indian rituals are depicted

as if the language of religious adoration were now literalized, as if the homiletic force of saints' lives were acted out in the pilgrimages of the devout, as if the Indians took seriously, in their bodies as well as their souls, the Christian cult of suffering love. The effect is less to commend Christian moderation or to confirm the universal truth of Christian rituals than to translate those rituals, in the face of such martyrdom, into half-hearted metaphors.[54]

Greenblatt suggests that such descriptions induce in the reader a sense of self-estrangement; that Christian rituals are defamiliarized by their literal Indian enactment.[55] In the case of Roe's narrative, the biblical resonances of the emperor's behaviour also unsettle Christian certainties: if a heathen can realize biblical truths, then Christendom's most basic premises of superiority are thrown into question. Perhaps it is this submerged challenge that accounts for the passage's peculiar intensity.

While Roe's suggestion that a heathen could be equally or more virtuous than a Christian is disturbing, it does follow the familiar rhetorical pattern of comparison and contrast between East and West which we have traced throughout this chapter. Roe finds it more problematic to relate a historical narrative which does not fit this comparative framework, a story interesting in and of itself. Roe introduces this particular anecdote—a story of a foiled plot to poison a sultan—with a preface claiming its universal applicability. The story, Roe asserts, will 'shew wisdome and patience in a father, faith in a servant, falshood in a brother, impudent boldnesse in a faction that dare attempt any thing, when the highest Majesty gives them liberty, either beyond the law of their owne condition, or the limits of policie and reason.'[56]

Roe turns the characters—actually the same imperial family with which the rest of his account has been concerned—into types or stock figures, and presents the action as an enactment of political truths. But Roe is, apparently, not confident that this is adequate reason for the anecdote's inclusion. When he has related the story, he also provides a more pragmatic justification: the court factions that he has described might affect trading practice. He explains: 'This [the story] I insert to this end, that you may beware scattering your goods in divers parts and engaging your stocke and servants farre into the Countrey: for the time will come, when all in these Kingdomes will be in combustion.'[57] The anecdote is represented as a different kind of narrative from the rest of the text, one which it is necessary to 'insert'. This lengthy and apologetic framing of the story argues that, for Roe, travel writing cannot easily contain narratives which concede a degree of autonomy to the East.

In fact, this particular anecdote forms part of a projected history of Mughal India that Roe, although he deems it 'not unworthy committing to writing', never produces.[58] He reasons that the public would be unreceptive: 'because they [the historical narratives] are of so remote parts, many will despise them: and because the people are esteemed barbarous, few will beleeve them.'[59] Here he sounds more like Montaigne. It is clear that the process of representing the Eastern other is more self-conscious than Said would allow. Roe is well aware of the conditions which govern the reception of travel writing. Readers judge the authenticity of reports of foreign lands by their preconceptions. They only believe what they want to be told; they want to hear of the strangeness, difference and barbarity of abroad to flatter their own sense of civilization at home.

Bernier's *History*

It fell to the French doctor and intellectual François Bernier to write the kind of history which Roe had envisaged, around half a century later. Published in French in 1670–1 and translated into English in 1671–2,

Bernier's *History of the Late Revolution of the Empire of the Great Mogol* is made up of a historical narrative with appended letters on the economy and government of the Mughal empire, on the cities of Delhi and Agra and on Hinduism. The letters are addressed to named individuals— to Jean-Baptiste Colbert, Louis XIV's finance minister and founder of the *Compagnie des Indes Orientales*, to François La Mothe Le Vayer, tutor to the royal family, and to Jean Chapelain, the poet. The fruit of a twelve-year-long stay at the Mughal court, the *History* devotes more serious attention to Indian history than any preceding work. During his time at the Mughal court, Bernier first worked as physician to Prince Dara Shukoh, and was then employed to inform Daneshmand Khan, the secretary of state for foreign affairs, of recent developments in European science and philosophy. He was well qualified for both jobs. Trained in medicine, Bernier belonged to the French intellectual circle known as the sceptics, and had been secretary to the philosopher Pierre Gassendi, whose work he popularized.

Bernier's philosophical background is evident in his ambition to formulate universal rules about mankind. He devotes a considerable section of the 'Letter to the Lord Colbert' to the exposition of his economic theories, which centre on the damage to the individual and the state caused by the crown ownership of all land. In Bernier's account, as in Roe's earlier formulation, the abuses of the Mughal empire are attributed to the fact that the emperor owned all the land and distributed it for life tenure among the nobles. This was a misconception which was to have a long life: Montesquieu developed the influential theory of oriental despotism from Bernier's work, and Marx turned to the same source as the basis for his ideas on the Asiatic mode of production. According to Bernier, there were no great landed families, nor any system of inheritance in the Mughal empire. This resulted in a complete absence of loyalty to the state or sense of duty towards the people; self-interest predominated. The landholders were only concerned with the immediate accumulation of wealth, having no care to maintain or improve the land, since they could not pass it down to their children. The peasantry, trading and artisan classes were exploited and tyrannized. With no prospect of making any money themselves, they in turn lost interest in the standard of their work: the land was badly cultivated, commerce flagged, buildings were poorly maintained and the quality of art and crafts suffered. There was no proper system of education because the nobles did not bother to endow institutions; and without a well-educated administrative class, the country was badly governed.[60]

Not unexpectedly, Bernier's theories reflect contemporary European trends in political thought; what one historian has called 'the great question of the century, the problem of the origin and nature of the state and society'.[61] What is interesting is the way that he extrapolates from his view of India's ills to generalize about the human condition:

> this *Meum* and *Tuum*, accompanied with the hopes that every one shall keep, what he works and labours for, for himself and his children as his own, is the main foundation of whatever is regular and good in the World: Insomuch that whosoever shall cast his Eyes upon the different Countries and Kingdoms, and taketh good notice of what follows upon this Propriety of Sovereigns, or that of the People, will soon find the true source and chief cause of that great difference we see in the several States and Empires of the World, and avow, that this, is in a manner that, which changes and diversifyeth the Face of the whole Earth.[62]

His rule applies to all humanity; it is only the varying economic structures of countries that determine the differences between peoples. Bernier depicts India languishing under tyrannical rule, setting Asia in opposition to Europe; but at the same time, he suggests a sense of similarity by imagining a Europe mismanaged under the Mughal economic system. Bernier's text deploys both the 'rhetoric of difference' and the 'rhetoric of identification', the competing discourses which, for Lisa Lowe, disrupt Said's monolithic notion of orientalism.[63] The text first asserts European superiority, then undermines it by imagining what would happen if European monarchs also owned all the land:

> Their kingdoms would be very far from being so well cultivated and peopled, so well built, so rich, so polite and flourishing as we see them. Our Kings are otherwise rich and powerful; and we must avow that they are much better and more royally served. There would soon be Kings of deserts and solitudes, of beggars and barbarians, such as those are whom I have been representing. . . . We should find the great Cities and the great Burroughs rendred inhabitable because of the ill Air, and to fall to ruin, without any bodies taking care of repairing them; the hillocks abandon'd, and the fields overspread with the bushes, or fill'd with pestilential marishes, as hath been already intimated.[64]

Europe is equally susceptible to the evils which afflict India; crown ownership of the land would spread a similar dereliction over the country as in Asia. In a study of Marx's theory of the Asiatic mode of production, Brendan O'Leary suggests that Bernier's account of Mughal land ownership contained a half-disguised warning to its addressee, Colbert. O'Leary argues that Bernier was obliquely commenting on the French nobility's anxiety that Louis XIV intended to claim all French land as royal property.[65] Acknowledging this parallel, the contemporary reader would recognize the similarities between the two systems of government, but at the same time, Bernier's transference of the conditions of 'abroad' to 'home', would induce an unsettling sense of self-estrangement.

Bernier extends his notion of a flawed economic system to help explain an episode in the section of his work devoted to the history of the Mughal empire. When the old emperor, Shah Jahan, was imprisoned by one of his sons, Aurangzeb, in the latter's attempt to secure the throne, none of the great lords went to Shah Jahan's aid. Bernier is at first outraged at this disloyalty:

> and (which is almost incredible) there was not one that had the courage to stir, or to attempt the least in the behalf of his King, and for him that had made them what they were, and raised them from the dust, and perhaps from slavery it self ... to advance them to riches and honour. ... 'Tis not withstanding to be noted what I said, that they were necessitated to do what they did. For 'tis not in the *Indies*, as in *France*, or other States of Christendom, where the Grandees and Nobles have large possessions of Land and great Revenues, which enables them for a while to subsist of themselves. *There* they have nothing but pensions ... which the King can take away from them at all hours, and thus ruine them in an instant; so that they shall be considered no more than if they never had been, nor have any credit to borrow a farthing.[66]

Bernier modifies his initial response to the lords' ingratitude with a reflection on the demands of political expediency under the Mughal system. He first judges the nobles' behaviour from a Western standpoint, then from an Eastern: cowardly inconstancy is reinterpreted as inevitable caution. Each view is given equal rhetorical force: the emotive attack on the lords' unfaithfulness is balanced against the pathetic image of the nobles reduced to penury.

The ability to interpret one event in two different ways is characteristic of Bernier. He acknowledges that there is no such thing as absolute judgement; that chance may determine the course of events, and that the haphazard outcome of an action may influence the interpretation of motive. Bernier's sense of the contingency of judgement is exemplified in his description of Aurangzeb's capture of his father and the fortress at Agra. Bernier first points out a tactical error of Shah Jahan's; then acknowledges that some other commentators consider it a prudent move, for

> men almost always judge of things by the event; that often very foolish Enterprises have been observed to suceed, and which therefore are approv'd by all; that if *Chah-Iehan* had prosper'd in his design, he would have been esteem'd the most prudent and most able man in the World; but now being taken, he was

nothing but a good Old Man, that suffer'd himself to be led by a Woman, his daughter *Begum* . . .[67]

In his willingness to admit the validity of contradictory interpretations, Bernier momentarily renounces the claim to authorial omniscience; he is not the only privileged interpreter of events. Bernier is also aware that the process of writing history may distort the truth, or that the truth may be impossible to ascertain.

Bernier's interest in historiography may well have derived from his friend and fellow-sceptic La Mothe Le Vayer, to whom one of the letters in the *History* was addressed. In an essay of 1668, 'Du Peu de Certitude qu'il y a dans l'Histoire', La Mothe argues that history is fraught with uncertainty, that the historian can be misled by informants, by his own prejudices, by national loyalties or self-interest. Entirely different accounts of the same battle, for instance, are produced by historians of victorious and vanquished nations. For La Mothe, historical knowledge is inevitably partial and biased.[68]

In acknowledging the limitations of historiography, Bernier seems to renounce the exclusive claim of the West to interpret the East, to give up the attempt, which Said finds in all orientalist scholarship, to make the East 'systematically . . . knowable by Western laymen'.[69] At the same time as Bernier formulates universal economic rules to explain the condition of mankind, as an historian, he does not pretend to absolute knowledge. He allows his characters' motives to remain mysterious and mixed. When Emir Jemla lets Aurangzeb, his one-time ally, trick him into being imprisoned, Bernier presents the reader with a variety of possible interpretations:

Emir, whether it were by reason of the Friendship he had sworn to *Aureng-Zebe,* or for the great promises made to him, or the apprehension he had, of seeing near him *Sultan Mazum* [Aurangzeb's second son], who stood by, very pensive and well Armed, and *Sultan Mahmond* (Aurangzeb's first son], who looked grim upon him . . . and had at his very entrance lift up his Foot as if he would have hit him; whatever of these considerations might induce him, consented to all what *Aureng-Zebe* desired, arid approved of the Expedient to suffer himself to be imprison'd.[70]

While this passage is in part a narrative ploy to demonstrate how circumstances conspire against Emir Jemla, Bernier's refusal to single out a motive endows Emir Jemla with a degree of autonomy. Bernier does not completely dominate his Eastern subjects, but acknowledges their ultimately unknowable and independent existence.

But this is not to say that Bernier is consistent in his depiction of character. While at times the protagonists may appear both complex and mysterious, on occasion he will simplify the presentation and turn them into stock figures—heroes and villains. When Dara Shukoh (Bernier's sometime employer and Shah Jahan's eldest son) is defeated in the battle for the succession by Aurangzeb, Bernier begins the process of turning Dara into a tragic hero. Betrayed in battle by 'one of the blackest Treacheries that ever was imagined', Dara, previously a complex political figure, simply becomes 'the good Prince'.[71] Bernier, as we have seen earlier, is quite conscious of the techniques of historical writing; here he is using the outcome of events to determine the judgement of character as a means of enlisting the reader's sympathy. As Dara's plight worsens, Bernier launches a great empathic appeal on his behalf:

And now what could this poor Prince *Dara* do? He seeth himself abandoned, and frustrated of his hopes. He considers, that to turn back safe to *Amadevad* was impossible, in regard that it was a march of thirty and five daies; that it was in the heat of Summer; that water would fail him; that they were all the Lands of *Raja's*, Friends or Allies of *Iesseigne* or *Iessomseigne*; that the Army of *Aurenge-Zebe*, which was not harassed like his, would not fail to follow him. 'Tis as good, *saith he*, to perish here; and although the match be altogether unequal, let us venture all, and give battel once more. But alas! what does he mean to do? He is not only abandon'd by all, but he hath yet with him *Chah-Navaze-kan*, whom he trusts, and who betrays him, and discovers all his designs to *Aureng-Zebe*.[72]

By listing the many hazards—natural rigours, hostile territory, military inferiority and personal treachery—Bernier invites the reader to put himself in Dara's position, to share his desperate perplexity. This kind of reader participation is further encouraged by the rhetorical questioning: the reader is forced to consider Dara's options, only to find that there is no suitable response. This direct identification between reader and character helps to decrease the distance between East and West.

At such moments, Bernier disrupts the strict opposition of Orient and Occident, inviting the reader to adopt instead a range of shifting positions with regard to the Indian protagonists—to identify with them, to revise initial opinions of them, to concede their autonomy. Said's thesis cannot accommodate such plurality of tone; nor can it account for the central paradox of Bernier's career: as the originator of the theory of oriental despotism, Bernier is responsible for one of the most abiding constructions of the East as Europe's Other, yet his flexible narrative technique works against the reductive logic of binary opposition. A site of competing economic, political and historiographic discourses, Bernier's *History*

34 / *India Inscribed*

displays in microcosm the characteristic tensions of the many heterogeneous European discourses of India.

Notes

1. See J. B. Hartley, 'Maps, Knowledge, and Power', *The Iconography of Landscape*, eds Denis Cosgrove and Stephen Daniels (Cambridge, 1988) 277–312.
2. Lisa Lowe, *Critical Terrains: French and British Orientalisms* (Ithaca, New York, 1991).
3. Samuel Purchas, *Hakluytus Postumus or Purchas His Pilgrimes*, 20 vols (Glasgow, 1905–7) i. xliv–xlv.
4. Francis Bacon, *The Advancement of Learning and New Atlantis* (Oxford, 1974) 77.
5. Richard Hakluyt, *The Principle Navigations Voyages Traffiques & Discoveries of the English Nation*, 12 vols (Glasgow, 1904) v. 480.
6. See Margaret T. Hodgen, *Early Anthropology in the Sixteenth and Seventeenth Centuries* (Philadelphia, 1964) 345.
7. Purchas, iii. 1–51.
8. In much the same way, modern anthropologists have tended to publish the formal account of their field experience separately from the personal account. See Mary Louise Pratt, 'Fieldwork in Common Places', *Writing Culture: The Poetics and Politics of Ethnography*, eds James Clifford and George E. Marcus (Berkeley, 1986) 31.
9. Purchas, iii. 49.
10. Ibid., iv. 1.
11. Ibid., iii. 50.
12. Ibid., ix. 40.
13. Ibid., 19.
14. James A. Williamson, 'Richard Hakluyt', *Richard Hakluyt and his Successors*, ed. Edward Lynam (London, 1946) 39.
15. Purchas, iv. 28–9.
16. Ibid., 61.
17. Ibid., ix. 1.
18. Christopher Marlowe, *The Jew of Malta*, I. i. 19–20.
19. Purchas, iv. 63.
20. Ibid., 68.
21. Ibid., ix. 24.
22. Ibid., 24.
23. Ibid., 25.
24. Edmund Spenser, *The Faerie Queene*, eds Thomas P. Roche and C. Patrick O'Donnell (Harmondsworth, 1978) II, xii, 58. 1; 5.
25. Spenser, II, v, 30.
26. Bernard S. Cohn, 'The Command of Language and the Language of Command', *Subaltern Studies IV* (1985), 278.

27. Purchas, iv. 328.
28. Ibid., 405.
29. Ibid., 381.
30. Cohn, 279. See also M. N. Pearson, ed., *Legitimacy and Symbols in the South Asian Writings of F. W. Buckler* (Ann Arbor, 1985) 24–6, 179.
31. Purchas, iv. 370.
32. Christopher Marlowe, *Tamburlaine the Great.* Part II, I. iii. 113–16.
33. Purchas, iv. 325.
34. Michel de Montaigne, *The Essayes of Michel Lord of Montaigne*, trans. John Florio, ed. Thomas Seccombe (London, 1908) 257.
35. Partha Mitter, *Much Maligned Monsters: History of European Reactions to Indian Art* (Oxford, 1977).
36. Hakluyt, v. 480.
37. Purchas, iv. 48.
38. Hakluyt, v. 475.
39. Ibid., 478.
40. Ibid., 470–1.
41. Stephen Greenblatt, *Marvelous Possessions: The Wonder of the New World* (Oxford, 1991) 14–15.
42. Purchas, ix. 38.
43. François Hartog, *The Mirror of Herodotus: The Representation of the Other in the Writing of History*, trans. Janet Lloyd (Berkeley, 1988) 256.
44. Purchas, ix. 20.
45. Ibid., 17.
46. Ibid., 43.
47. Ibid., iv. 327.
48. Ibid., 327–8.
49. Ibid., 444.
50. Ibid., ix. 38–9.
51. Ibid., iv. 386.
52. M. P. Tilley, *A Dictionary of Proverbs in England in the Sixteenth and Seventeenth Centuries* (Ann Arbor, 1950) K 67.
53. I Samuel ii. 8.
54. Greenblatt, 47–8.
55. Ibid., 47.
56. Purchas, iv. 361.
57. Ibid., 362.
58. Ibid., 361.
59. Ibid., 361.
60. François Bernier, *The History of the Late Revolution of the Empire of the Great Mogul*, 6 parts (London, 1671) 'A Letter to the Lord Colbert', 68–102.
61. Stephan Skalweit, 'Political Thought', *New Cambridge Modern History: The Ascendancy of France 1648–88*, ed. F. L. Carsten (Cambridge, 1961) 100.
62. Bernier, 'A Letter to the Lord Colbert', 101–2.
63. Lowe, 45.
64. Bernier, 'A Letter to Lord Colbert', 86, 88.

36 / India Inscribed

65. Brendan O'Leary, *The Asiatic Mode of Production* (Oxford, 1989) 57.
66. Bernier, i. 153-5.
67. Ibid., 147.
68. Peter Burke, 'Bernier's Orient: An Occidentalist's Perspective' (unpublished seminar paper) 2; François La Mothe Le Vayer, 'Du Peu de Certitude qu'il y a dans l'Histoire', *Oeuvres*, 7 vols (Dresden, 1756-9) v. ii. 442-68.
69. Edward W. Said, *Orientalism* (1978; rpt Harmondsworth, 1985) 65.
70. Bernier, i. 61-2.
71. Ibid., 121, 124.
72. Ibid., 203-4.

CHAPTER TWO

Indian Women: The Seventeenth-Century European Fantasy

In 1699 in the English town of Sherborne, the Rev. John Sprint preached a wedding sermon on the duties of a wife. Published subsequently as *The Bride-Woman Counseller*, the sermon attempts to justify female subordination in marriage and suggests that wives should follow the practice of 'Persian Ladies who have the resemblance of a Foot worn on top of their Coronets' to show that 'the height of their Glory, Top-Knot and all, does stoop to their Husband's feet'.[1] The oriental example is cited in what is, by then, a well-worn argument that rehearses many commonplace reproaches against the female sex. The sermon takes its small place in the long-running debate over the nature and status of women, the so-called 'Woman Question' or 'Querelle des Femmes', which commenced in Europe in the fifteenth century and was pursued intermittently for some four centuries. It reached a climax in England and France in the period 1550–1640 with the publication of numerous pamphlets and treatises, serious and scurrilous, that either praised feminine virtue or condemned feminine vice.[2] The controversy provides a set of feminine types for writers to discover in other cultures, and travel accounts themselves contribute to the discussion (as with Sprint's sermon). Seventeenth-century writing on India is strikingly preoccupied with issues familiar from the debate: questions of Indian women's virtue or vice, their chastity and wifely submission or sexual appetite and depravity.

IMAGES OF INDIAN WOMEN

Unlike the 'Woman Question' polemicists, travel writers only occasionally generalize about the sex as a whole, tending rather to categorize Indian women according to their religious affiliation, Muslim or Hindu.

Writers frequently represent Muslim and Hindu women as complementary opposites, ignoring any distinctions between different Hindu castes. The jealously guarded Muslim woman in purdah is set against the Hindu woman, ostentatiously bejewelled, freely on show. John Fryer, surgeon to the East India Company from 1672 to 1681, contrasts the two:

The *Moors* are by Nature plagued with Jealousy, cloistring their Wives up, and sequestring them the sight of any besides the *Capon* that watches them. When they go abroad, they are carried in close *Palenkeens*, which if a Man offer to unvail it is present death; the meanest of them not permitting their Women to stir out uncovered; of whom they are allowed as many as they can keep. . . . The *Gentues* observe not that strictness, both Sexes enjoying the open Air. Their Women are manacled with Chains of Silver (or Fetters rather) and hung with Earrings of Gold and Jewels, their Noses stretched with weighty Jewels, on their Toes Rings of Gold, about their Waste a painted Clout, over their Shoulders they cast a Mantle; their Hair tied behind their Head . . . a-top a Coronet of Gold beset with Stones; compleatly bodied, and so flexible that they are excellent Dancers, and good at feats of Activity: I having seen them hold Nine Gilded Balls in play with their Hands and Feet, and the Muscles of their Arms and Legs . . .[3]

The invisible Muslim in the inviolable privacy of her 'close Palankeen' is opposed to the minutely observed Hindu in the 'open Air'. To unveil the Muslim women's litter (let alone her body) is to court execution. Fryer emphasizes the difference in the women's lifestyles by employing the language of imprisonment, more obviously applicable to Muslim women, as a metaphor for the heavy jewellery of the Hindus: 'Their Women are manacled with Chains of Silver (or Fetters rather)'. This language seems not to imply restraint—the women are capable of 'feats of Activity'—but rather emphasizes their subordination to men, a sense reinforced by the use of the possessive pronoun, '[t]heir Women'. Equally subject to masculine control as Muslim women, Hindus are represented as all body, physical specimens on display for a male audience.

The seclusion of the Muslim woman deprives the travel writer of his essential role as observer, and also denies him his customary masculine prerogative of visual (and implied sexual) possession of women; the Muslim woman very obviously belongs to another man. The travel writer's exclusion provides the space for speculation and fantasy. Writers are divided over Muslim purdah: does this confinement indicate chastity or is it merely an attempt at preventing promiscuity? Hindu women elicit equally contradictory responses: does their freedom reflect their husbands' confidence or their sexual availability? Either way, the writers invariably assume that all women of the same religion behave in the same way, and often contrast the sexual conduct of Hindu women with that of Muslim.

Jean de Thévenot, a French traveller and nephew of Melechisedech de Thévenot, editor of a collection of voyages, champions the chastity of the Hindus: 'The Women of *Dehly* are handsome, and the Gentiles very chast; insomuch, that if the *Mahometan* Women did not by their wantonness dishonour the rest, the Chastity of the *Indians* might be proposed as an example to all the Women of the *East*.'[4] Here Thévenot carefully distinguishes the sexual mores of oriental women from those of Europeans, offering Hindu women as models of Eastern chastity. But Muslim women find a defender in an earlier French writer, François de la Boullaye le Gouz. In an account first published in Paris in 1653, le Gouz writes that he would seem to disparage Mughal women by describing the sweet-smelling oils with which they anoint themselves after bathing.[5] By mentioning the massage at all, Le Gouz is of course suggesting something of the sensuality he affects to dismiss; but this gives only the slightest glimpse of Muslim sexuality. A few pages on, an illustration reveals a naked Hindu woman bathing and anointing herself with oil, in exactly the pose that le Gouz censured out of respect for Muslim women (Fig. 2). The Hindu woman is obviously being defined in contrast to the Muslim; she is represented as sexually available. The illustration itself is unusual: the woman covers herself with a cloth so fine, the accompanying text explains, that her flesh is still visible. The cloth is a kind of sexual tease, both covering and revealing, almost a parody of the Muslim female garment, the burka. She is like one of those tantalizing figures whom Suzanne Rodin Pucci describes as populating the oriental harem in eighteenth-century European fiction; women

who dance, speak, write and figure sexual desire before the eyes of the 'oriental' sultan and Western observer, reader, voyeur, provide a focus for the simultaneous profusion and disappearance, veiling and unveiling, of sexual as well as cultural differences that constitute the charms of the exotic.[6]

In fact Le Gouz complains that his engraver ignored some of these 'charms of the exotic'. Indian women, he writes, are physically different to Europeans, but the engraver would not reproduce their unfamiliar proportions:

Elles ... ont les cuisses, & les iambes fort longues, le corps assez court, au rebours de celles d'Europe; Le Graueur n'a pas en tout poinct imité l'Original de

40 / *India Inscribed*

FIG. 2: Illustration of bathing woman from *Les Voyages* by François de la Boullaye le Gouz (1657), Bodleian Library, Oxford.

mon dessein, de peur que le corps ne parut disproportionné par de trop longues cuysses, il a cru faire vn sacrilege de dessigner vne femme nuë faitte autrement que celles de son païs . . .[7]

(They . . . have very long thighs and legs and a quite short body, the opposite of European women. The engraver did not imitate the original of my drawing in all points, for fear that the body would appear out of proportion with overlong thighs, he thought it sacrilegious to draw a naked women formed any other way to those of his country . . .)

By ridiculing the engraver's provincial assumption that all naked women look like the French, le Gouz both flatters the reader by implying the shared perspective of the well-travelled sexual connoisseur, and strengthens the authority of his claim to identify Indian women's difference.

This sense of Indian female otherness, both Muslim and Hindu, is heightened by their respective areas of sexual mythology: the secret harem and Hinduism's occult sexual practices. Rana Kabbani has argued that, by the Renaissance, the luxurious harem had already become a standard topos of European writing about the East.[8] Le Gouz's engraver serves him better in conveying something of the exclusivity of the seraglio. Le Gouz explains that a picture will be a clearer representation of Mughal dress than a written description, but the illustration that follows unexpectedly reveals a Muslim couple embracing (Fig. 3).[9] This engraving, while based on motifs taken from Mughal painting, is less a faithful copy than a Western construct. The woman being embraced holds a chowry, a yak-tail fan, the sign of an attendant; in Mughal painting a prince would not be depicted in such an indecorous liaison. The serving woman should be situated on the other side of the couple, at a respectful distance, looking towards them. The discrepancy in the size of the Muslim pair and Hindu servant, although a feature of Mughal painting, is overemphasized.[10] The engraver seems to distinguish deliberately between Muslim and Hindu, and construct his own pictorial narrative by averting the servant's gaze. The reader's voyeuristic sense of enjoyment at happening upon a private scene is reinforced by the figure of the servant turning away from the couple 'pour leur donner toute liberté' (to give them complete freedom);

FIG. 3: Illustration of Mughal couple from *Les Voyages* by François de la Boullaye le Gouz (1657), Bodleian Library, Oxford.

the reader is both excluded—as in Mughal painting, all the faces are in profile, none looking out—and also the only observer of the scene.

The furtive glimpse of harem life permits the reader of le Gouz to re-enact accounts of travel writers' own experiences. Sir Thomas Roe, the ambassador to Jahangir's court, catches sight of two of the emperor's wives, or more exactly, parts of the emperor's wives:

> at one side in a window were his two principall Wives, whose curiositie made them break little holes in a grate of Reed that hung before it, to gaze on me. I saw first their fingers, and after laying their faces close, now one eye now another sometime I could discerne the full proportion, they were indifferently white, blacke haire smooth up, but if I had no other light, their Diamonds and Pearles had sufficed to shew them: when I looked up they retyred and were so merry, that I supposed they laughed at me.[11]

Unlike le Gouz's reader, Roe himself is being watched, but he is also surreptitiously observing the women in a kind of illicit game of peek-a-boo. The little holes picked in the window screen afford brief views of the riches of the harem. Still excluded, Roe eagerly observes tiny details. While Roe can see hardly anything of the women, they can of course see all of him. Normal visual relationships are overturned: the women are in the dominant position, looking at the man; for once the travel writer, more observed than observing, is made aware of his own exoticism.

François Bernier, in spite of his twelve years' service to Mughal nobles, saw even less than Roe. In his description of the fort at Delhi, he has to omit the harem: 'I now wish I could lead you about in the *Seraglio*, as I have done in the rest of the Fortress: but who is the Traveller that can speak of that as an eye-witness?'[12] Since the claim of being an eyewitness is crucial to the authority of a travel writer, this is an expression of authorial impotence. Significantly, the sole occasion Bernier entered the seraglio, his eyes were covered with a scarf and he was led 'like a blind man' by a eunuch.[13] The only way to avoid the disabling rules of the harem was to be admitted as a doctor. Both John Fryer and Niccolao Manucci, 'a Venetian, and Chief Physitian to *Orangzeb* for above Forty Years', claimed this privileged medical access 'to the Knowledge of the Mysteries of the *Seraglio*, which are carefully conceal'd from the Eyes of the Publick'.[14]

Fryer, sent to bleed one of the wives of a Mughal commander, was conducted to a room partitioned by a curtain, with an arm extended through a hole in the material. Initially, Fryer's contact with the harem resembles Roe's glimpses of the emperor's wives through the broken screen: the partially breached barrier between the man and the women. But the curtain falls down:

> this was a slight fence for such Animals, who leaning too hard as they peeped, pulled it down, and discovered the whole Bevy, fluttering like so many Birds when a Net is cast over them; yet none of them sought to escape, but feigning a shamefacedness, continued looking through the wide Lattice of their Fingers . . .[15]

As soon as the curtain falls and the traveller can see, he resumes his dominant position as a male observer of women. This sense of superiority is particularly evident in Fryer's characterization of the women as animals and trapped birds. The women are fascinated by their hunter and only feign modesty. Roe's image of the wives spying on him through the blind is transmuted to a coy picture of women peeping through the useless screen of their fingers.

Fryer observes that the women seem to be engaged in normal household tasks:

> In this interview they appeared to me not altogether unimployed, there lying pared Mangoes, and other Fruits for Confection, and Achars, or Pickles; some Samples of good Housewifry in Needleworks; and no indecent decorum in managing their Cloystered way of living, making it agreeable to the choice of Custom rather than Restraint . . .[16]

Although Fryer asserts the women's housewifely conduct, he undermines his statement by couching it in negative terms: 'not altogether unimployed', 'no indecent decorum'; he is playing on his readers' expectations of harem idleness and debauchery. These expectations are first denied, then fulfilled immediately after when he quotes Homer on the brutality and wickedness of women, a phrase that the dead Agamemnon uses in Hades of Clytemnestra, his adulterous wife and murderer.[17] Fryer does not fully endorse 'foulmouthed' Homer's condemnation 'that Stigmatize them [women]', adding the qualification 'how deservedly I dare not say', but he goes on to suggest that circumstantial evidence probably proves Homer right: 'And a Man would guess no less, to see the number of Spies upon them, of Toothless Old Women, and Beardless Eunuchs, that they are incontinent in their Desires, for which reason they debar them the sight of any thing Male, but their Lord.'[18] Although, as an eyewitness, Fryer can only report the boring respectability of the harem, he still manages to confirm the myth of wicked dissipation. Interestingly, he appeals to the authority of the *Odyssey* to effect this extraordinary volte-face. Fryer wrests a quote from a canonical Western text to substantiate his speculations about Muslim female sexuality. The appeal to Homeric authority reveals the framing perspective of the European debate about female morality.

Fryer is not the only writer to fantasize about the 'incontinent' desires of harem women. Denied regular sex, they are supposed to be driven by lust. We find stories of lovers smuggled into the harem and salacious comments about banned objects of phallic shape (particularly vegetables).[19] The construction of the harem woman seems to be related to that of the European widow; both are represented as sexually experienced, but frustrated. The widow is invariably portrayed (both in medical treatises and in literary texts) as lascivious and predatory. Of course harem women do not enjoy the freedom and financial power which, Lisa Jardine has convincingly argued, constitute the widow's particular threat. But narratives of their desperate attempts at sexual gratification recall the strategems of fictional widows. Both types are indebted to anti-feminist arguments which see proof of feminine fraility and imperfection in the triumph of sensuality over reason.[20]

Sensuality reigns supreme in the account of the Mughal emperor's seraglio offered by Manucci. He luxuriates in a description of the women's fine clothes and extravagent jewellery, commenting: 'The Reader will doubtless here fancy himself transported into a Fairy Land where all is Pearl and Diamonds. But the Description we have given, comes very much short of the Truth.'[21] In this other world, the emperor gives names to his possessions : his jewels, his slaves, his wives. Like Adam, he names a new universe for himself: 'They [the jewels] have all their particular Names. One is called the *Sun*, another the *Moon*, another the *Bull's Eye* or the *Bear star*. 'Tis by these Names the Mogol distinguishes and calls for 'em.'[22] The alternative world of the harem also enjoys its own climate: 'The Appartments of those Queens are Magnificent and Delightful. The Heats of that burning Climate don't in the least incommode them. They are every where furnish'd with purling Streams, Shades, *Jet D'eaus* and Subterranean Grotto's to take the fresh Air in.'[23] In this watery, sensual region, inside and out are confounded: fountains and streams run through apartments, fresh air is found in underground caves; the seraglio is like an inverted world.

Manucci's description of harem debauchery follows this pattern of inversion. The favouritism that the emperor shows his daughters extends to 'a Connivance at their keeping Gallants', the opposite of paternal duty and unusual even for the travel accounts. The emperor's laxity corrupts the whole harem: 'the Rigours of the Cloister are often dispens'd with in their Favour.... Idleness together with a delicious way of living and reading wanton Books, must needs be a Source of Vice in Cloisters, where the Power of true Religion restrains to no Rules.'[24] This image of the corrupt convent (hinted at also in Fryer's description of the harem as a 'Cloystered way of Living'[25]) is such a staple of male sexual fantasy precisely because it transgresses boundaries and turns convention on its head.

But Manucci's account is not just a sexual reverie. The female superintendents of the harem also have important state functions: each is paired with a minister at court, shares his official title, supervises his work and reports to the emperor. They, not the male nobles, are the real sources of power:

All intreagues of State are carry'd on, War and Peace are made, Vice-Royships and Governments obtain'd by their Means: In fine, they have the principal distribution of the Court Favors.... They are properly speaking the Cabinet Council of the *Mogol*... 'Tis easily conceiv'd that the principal care of each great Officer of the Empire is to keep himself in the good Graces of his Court Lady. The least rupture with her is attended with inevitable Ruin. Happy is the Man whose Lot has not condemn'd him to a dependance on a capricious Correspondant![26]

Customary political and gender hierarchies are completely overturned in the seraglio: men sue for favours from the women. Military power also lies in female hands:

what seems most extraordinary is his [the Emperor] being always guarded within the *Seraglio* by a Company of *Tartarian* Virago's, consisting of a Hundred in Number, arm'd with Bows and Arrows, a Poynard and Cimeter. Madam their Captain has the Rank and Pay of an *Omhra* of the Army.[27]

The hyperbolic reference to 'Madam their Captain', like the earlier quip on the 'capricious Correspondant', suggests the nervous humour of anxiety. The harem, locus of many a male fantasy of dominance, is here policed by a force of viragos. The lure of female sexuality is never far from the threat of female power.

The menacing aspect of female sexuality is even more apparent in the accounts of Hindu women. These narratives centre on strange religious practices, ceremonies which would have been even more mysterious to Westerners than the harem. The accounts offer a threatening, perverted version of worship and tap fears of witchcraft and couplings with the devil. The decade of the 1620s saw European witchcraft trials at their height, and the persecution of women as witches continued throughout the

46 / *India Inscribed*

seventeenth century. The identification of women with the devil therefore readily suggested itself to travel writers.

It is the alliance of religion and sex that most disturbs and titillates. The French diamond merchant Tavernier describes a Hindu temple frequented by temple dancers:

> This Pagod is full of a great number of naked Images, among the rest is a large Figure of one that seems to resemble *Apollo*, with his privy parts all uncover'd. When the old Curtisans have got together a good sum of Money in their Youth, they buy young Slaves, whom they teach to Dance, and sing wanton Songs, and instruct in all the mysteries of their infamous Art. And when these young Girls are eleven or twelve years old, their Mistresses send them to this Pagod, believing it will bring them good fortune, to offer and surrender up themselves to this Idol.[28]

Tavernier seems to leave it deliberately ambiguous whether the young dancers surrender themselves up spiritually or sexually to the idol. Certainly, the wedding day custom of brides being penetrated by idols becomes a favourite horror story for travel writers. Linschoten makes it into something of a joke, imagining the bridegroom 'being verie ioyfull and proud, that their *Pagode* hath honored him so much and eased him of so much labour', and Philip Baldaeus, a Dutch minister, decides 'for modesty's sake' to 'relate [it] in *Latin*', a language inaccessible to most women and those of the lower classes.[29] Both these devices—humour and scholarly translation—mask anxiety. It is the English traveller Sir Thomas Herbert who reveals his fascination:

> Their vilest ceremony is this. That at the marriage of a Virgin, the Bridegroome, to honour the Deuillish Idoll, brings her afore the *Pagode*, or Idoll; who commonly is of a tall stature, and shaped vgly, in his privy parts he has a bodkin of gold or siluer, an intended Jnstrument, to violate her chastitie. Which, they suppose obtained, by the Pagotha, such time, as she is forcably put vnto his Engine, the sharpnesse being such, that the bloud issues not only thence, but from other parts of her wounded body, this done, with great ioy and applause he returnes to her Pagan husband, and if shee be with childe that yeare, tis supposed the Pagod got it.[30]

The obscene details in this description are presented as part of an exposé of the horrors of paganism (and the laughable ignorance of pagans) in a distant land. The woman is raped by her religion. Sex and violence clearly guaranteed sales: Herbert's account went into several editions, and it was revised and expanded twice over a period of more than thirty years.

Travel writing grants considerable licence to its authors; its quasi-scientific status confers authority, while the public expectation of foreign outlandishness ensures that sensational stories are happily consumed. Tales of the sexual activities involved in lingam worship, brahmanic sexual privileges and religious prostitution (often in connection with lurid descriptions of religious suicide at the Jagannath festival) abound in Indian travel literature.[31] Hindu female devotees are represented as deluded by the devil or, like European witches, copulating with him.[32] The accounts map out a very alien region of occult sexual practices, the dark side of paganism from which travellers are excluded.

Europeans are, however, said to be included in the sexual customs of the inhabitants of the Malabar coast. Here the male dream, at least as old as Marco Polo, of the traveller having free access to another man's wife, persists.[33] Authors tend to claim knowledge of specific encounters between wives and foreigners, thus authenticating the fantasy and emphasizing the sense of inclusion. John Ovington, chaplain to the East India Company, records one such instance:

> the Husbands, even the prime Nobility, to compleat the Welcom of their Entertainments, offer the Familiarity of their Wives; and esteem the rejecting this Civility as an Affront. Two *English* Merchants some time before I came to *India*, were invited abroad, and after Dinner were tempted with this kind of Treat; but the Piety of one of them kept him from it, whilst the immodest Frolicks of the other intic'd him on to the use of an unlawful Pleasure. And many of the Women by their usual Custom in these cases, quite contrary to that of other Nations, have gained the Name of *Malabar Quills*.[34]

Although Ovington apparently condemns the merchant who took advantage of the offer (as a clergyman must), his actual language mitigates the sense of sin. Ovington pairs negative moral vocabulary with positive terms of enjoyment: 'tempted' with 'treat', 'immodest' with 'Frolicks' and 'unlawful' with 'Pleasure'; as though admitting that the merchant's failings were understandable. In fact, the dominant Western reaction to this custom embodies a sense of transgression extraordinarily absolved: the husband, incredibly, gives the stranger permission to cuckold him. Customary notions of propriety are upended, the conduct is 'quite contrary to that of other Nations'. But this sense of utter foreignness is coupled with an unusual feeling of intimacy: the travellers are being entertained by the husbands, and even more familiarly, by the wives.

It is just this mixture of strangeness and intimacy that the early sixteenth-century traveller Ludovico di Varthema expresses in his account of the custom.[35] Varthema and his travelling companion are invited to a merchant's home:

When we had arrived at his house, he gave us a collation, and then he said to us: 'My friends, Patanci nale banno gnan penna periti in penna orangono panna panni cortu', that is, 'Fifteen days hence I wish to bring home my wife, and one of you shall deflower her for me'. We remained quite ashamed at hearing such a thing. Then our interpreter said: 'Do not be ashamed, for this is the custom of the country'. Then my companion hearing this said: 'Let them not do us any other mischief, for we will satisfy you in this;' but we thought that they were mocking us. The merchant saw that we remained undecided, and said: 'O langal limaranconia ille ocha manezar irichenu', that is, 'Do not be dispirited, for all this country follows this custom.' Finding at last that such was the custom in all this country, as one who was in our company affirmed to us, and said that we need have no fear, my companion said to the merchant that he was content to go through this fatigue. . . . Fifteen days from that time this merchant brought home his wife, and my companion slept with her the first night. She was a young girl of fifteen years, and he did for the merchant all that he had asked of him. But after the first night, it would have been at the peril of his life if he had returned again, although truly the lady would have desired that the first night had lasted a month.[36]

Varthema's merchant speaks (phoney) Malayalam; a device that both generates a sense of verisimilitude—recording his actual words—and emphasizes his foreignness. The translation renders the merchant's request comprehensible, but it sounds so bizarre that the Europeans do not believe it; they are dealing with alien concepts as well as a foreign language. At first they feel shamed by the suggestion, but their sense of guilt is absolved by the merchant's reassurances and finally dispelled by humour—they can refer to the wedding night as a 'fatigue'. The strange, sinful proposal has been assimilated and turned into a joke. Lasting only one night, the encounter is strictly circumscribed, and the danger of the transgressive alliance thus contained. The concluding, knowing remark about the bride's enjoyment of the night implies both the lasciviousness of the woman once deflowered, and the superior sexual prowess of European men.

François Pyrard de Laval, an early seventeenth-century traveller, also comments on the sexual preferences of Goanese women, Hindu and Christian, for European men. He is discussing the slaves/prostitutes who form liaisons with Portuguese men:

Toutes ces Indiennes, tant Chrestiennes que autres, ou metisses, desirent plustost avoir la co[m]pagnie d'vn homme de l'Europe vieil Chrestien que des Indiens . . . car elles ayment fort les hommes blancs de deçà, & encores qu'il y ait des Indie[n]s fort blancs, elles ne les ayment pas tant.[37]

(All these Indian women, as much the Christians as the others or those of mixed race, prefer the company of a Christian man from Europe to that of the Indians . . . for they adore white men from here, and even though there are some very fair-skinned Indians, they do not love them as much.)

Europeans may easily win a prostitute's heart, but this love is not without its hazards. Pyrard de Laval explains that many Portuguese soldiers set up house with Indian prostitutes and live openly as man and wife; but if the men become involved with other women, the prostitutes will poison them. Pyrard de Laval offers this as a warning to travellers against such involvement:

Mais c'est vn gra[n]d mal-heur pour vn soldat ou autre Portugais & estranger, de faire amitié auec ces femmes Mestices ou Indien[n]es impudiques, car l'on voit fort peu d'hom[m]es qui en sortent sans peril.[38]

(But it is a great misfortune for a soldier or other Portuguese man or foreigner to take a liking to one of these immodest mixed race or Indian women, for one sees very few men who can extricate themselves without danger.)

The prostitutes are credited with knowledge of a poisonous drug, which will lie dormant for months inside the body before killing.[39] Sexually available women, like the mysterious female Hindu devotees, are endowed with threatening, secret powers.

Encounters with Indian prostitutes can be represented as frightening challenges to a traveller's sense of identity. John Albert de Mandelslo, a young German noble, describes how he often stayed at lodges belonging to the East India Company, where the English, to show their hospitality, laid on dancing girls:

they made the greatest entertainment imaginable; and to come to the the height of that Country's endearments, they sent for some *Benjan* women, who were very desirous to to see my cloaths, which I still wore after the *Germane* fashion, though the *English* and *Dutch* who are settled in the *Indies*, go ordinarily according to the mode of the Country, and would have oblig'd me to put them off; but perceiving I was unwilling to do it, and withal that I made some difficulty to accept of the profers they made me to strip themselves naked, and to doe any thing I would expect from persons of their sex and profession, they seem'd to be very much troubled, and so went away.[40]

Mandelslo makes a point of distinguishing between his style of dressing and that of the expatriates. He keeps his German clothes, while the resident Europeans adopt Indian dress; he retains a sense of his national decorum, while the others identify themselves with the Indians. This distinction seems in part to explain his reluctance to undress for the prostitutes: he refuses to remove his clothes because without them he would shed his German character; the loss of self in sex with a foreigner would become a loss of national identity. Of course, he is also concerned to protect his personal reputation: like other travel writers, he claims intimate knowledge of such activities rather than actual participation. On another occasion, Mandelslo records that he refused an English merchant's offer of dancing women for fear of compromising his Christian self: he 'made some scruple to meddle in that kind.with a *Pagan*'.[41]

Indian prostitutes even threaten the foreigner's sexual identity. Outside Kotta-Kunnu on the Malabar coast, John Fryer records that prostitutes live among the *mestico* (Portuguese-Indian) community:

> Beyond the Outworks live a few *Portugals Mustezoes* or *Misteradoes*; among whom are Stews and Brothels; the Women of this Coast being the most professedly Lewd of any; being said to instruct the Men to be Patients, while they act the Masculine Part in their Lascivious Twines.[42]

Marginalized, living outside the town among people of mixed race and no certain nationality, the prostitutes take the sexual initiative, and so deprive their clients of their masculinity. These prostitutes embody male fears of female domination, but are also the stuff of male sexual fantasy: women greedy for 'their Lascivious Twines'.

From the travel literature, we can build up a composite picture of Hindu women as dangerously exciting, attracted to Europeans, available on their wedding night and involved in occult sexual practices. This image makes India the perfect setting for pornographic literature. In 1664 or 1665 Richard Head published a picaresque novel, *The English Rogue*, which was suppressed on grounds of obscenity but immediately republished. Most of the novel follows the adventures of the hero, Latroon, through the criminal underworld, but about two-thirds of the way through he embarks on a ship bound for the East Indies. In India, the book concentrates almost exclusively on sexual encounters and strange sexual practices drawn from the repertoire of images provided by travel literature. Head sometimes elaborates on the travel accounts, but often either paraphrases or practically reproduces them. Mandeville and Linschoten have been suggested as Head's sources, and I would add Thomas Herbert, whose account of sexual encounters at the Jagannath festival is very closely followed in Head's own description.[43] The novel is full of familiar scenes: Latroon spends a wedding night with a Malabar virgin and is pursued by a lustful Indian woman who finds her way into his bed, while the ship's bo'sun selects a prostitute who would poison him if he were unfaithful.[44] The images of travel literature are re-presented as pornography. That the gap between the two genres is so easily bridged suggests that India has become a playground for sexual fantasy.

THE SATI

There is one striking exception to the representation of Hindu women solely in terms of sexual activity: the sati. The rite of widow burning is an absolute denial of the widow's physical self. Sati is the ultimate expression of wifely subservience which, while it flatters the sense of masculine superiority in its affirmation of patriarchal authority, also functions as a rejection of all other men. As an erasure of the widow's sexuality, sati bears a distant affinity with the ideal life of chastity and fidelity to the memory of a deceased husband prescribed for (though rarely practised by) seventeenth-century English widows.[45] The sati is therefore a potent image of conjugal fidelity that often acts as a counter to the construct of Hindu female sexuality. The complex and contradictory representations of sati by European travel writers reflect the highly ambivalent masculine responses to the act.

The faithfulness and courage of the sati set her apart from Hindu men who, according to the travel writers, are invariably unfaithful cowards. Fryer and Manucci are two of the many who report the untrustworthiness of the Hindus:

> The chief Pleasure of the *Gentiles*, or *Banyans*, is to Cheat one another, conceiving therein the highest Felicity, though it be Cuckolding, which they are expert at. The being born in the *Indies*, is enough to be born Inconstant.[46]

Terry is among those who depict the Hindus as cowardly; he excepts the warrior Rajputs, but 'all the rest in the Countrey are in general Pusilanimous'.[47] The sati is thus exempt from the most common criticisms levelled at Hindus. She might be close to becoming a type of female courage and fidelity, respected for those qualities that Hindus revere in her, were it not for Christian hatred of paganism and abhorrence of suicide. Just how close she comes is demonstrated by a reference to sati in Pierre Le Moyne's *La Gallerie des Femmes Fortes*, a compilation of stories of exemplary female courage published in 1667. In this contribution to the 'Woman Question' debate, Le Moyne takes issue with Torquato Tasso who had argued that chastity and courage were gendered virtues, that the dominant virtue for women was chastity, and for men courage.[48] Le

Moyne finds both these virtues united in his chaste heroines drawn from the annals of Jewish, 'Barbarian', Roman and Christian history. He argues that married love can produce instances of worthy and virtuous death, but feels it necessary to discount sati from consideration, together with Greek and Roman tragic suicides, because it contravenes Christian teaching: 'Ie sçay bien que cette cruaté superstitieuse & reguliere des Indiennes: & cet autre desespoir tumultuaire & precipité des Romaines & des Grecques, sont également reprouuez par les loix du Christiainisme.'[49] (I know well that this superstitious and regular cruelty of Indian women: and that other tumultuous and precipitate despair of the Romans and Greeks, are equally condemned by the laws of Christianity.) Le Moyne's definition of sati as a superstitious and regular cruelty condenses the three main Christian arguments against the heroic status of the sati. 'Cruelty' refers to the view that the widow is forced to burn herself against her wishes, 'superstitious' implies that her religious motives are pagan delusions, and 'regular' denies any individual heroism by suggesting that sati is merely customary. I shall consider all three interpretations, starting with the view that sati is no more than a custom.

In *Life's Preservative against Self-killing*, a treatise against suicide published in 1637, John Sym argues that '*law and custome* prevaile against the light of *nature* among the *Heathen*; because they knew no higher rule to examine and try their lawes by, and therefore submit to *humane ordinances* absolutely, bee they good or bad'.[50] He cites sati as an example of misguided custom:

Lawes and *Customes* in some places seeming to require and warrant people in some cases to kill themselves. As among the *Heathens* and *Indians*; where by *custome* or *law*, *servants* and *wives*, in testimony of love to their *Masters* and *Husbands*, were wont to cast themselves into the fire to bee burnt, with the corps of their dead *masters* and *husbands*: but the true cause of that Law was, to restraine the frequent *poysoning* of masters and husbands, by their servants and wives; *and* that *law* and *custome* was practised to avoide suspition, and ignominie that they lived in, if they did not so kill themselves.[51]

Sym picks up on the reason generally offered by travel writers to explain sati: an ancient law passed as a deterrent to wives who poisoned their husbands in order to take lovers; once instituted, sati became a devoted wife's duty demanded by a society which ostracized and humiliated the widow if she remained alive. Sym's reference to these explanations implies their widespread acceptance and indeed we find them in many of the travel accounts.[52] Here, for instance, are Herbert's comments on sati and the social degradation of widows:

a iust reuenge, for their [wives'] former too much abused liberty, growne so audaciously impudent, that vpon the least distaste nothing but the harmelesse lives of their too much louing Husbands, would satiate their lustfull boldnesse, procured by poyson, till by Parliament this course was taken (to burne their Wiues with their dead bodies) to secure themselves from future dangers.[53]

Herbert's remarks are unusual in that they stress what is only implicit in most accounts: that sati is no more than womankind's just deserts. They act as a particularly potent counter to the heroic image of the sati: rather than stand as an emblem of the faithful wife, she merely becomes a reminder of female licentiousness. The belief in sati as a penalty for husband-murdering is a satisfying interpretation for the European mind: it explains a disturbing rite in familiar terms of crime and punishment and coincides with the Christian sense of the sinfulness of woman. Rajeswari Sunder Rajan draws an instructive analogy between this 'mythical "original" cause' of sati and the logic of tyranny which constructs 'imagined scenarios . . . of subaltern insurrection to justify measures of social control.'[54] More specifically, the explanation provides a parallel with the position of women under English law. On the accession of James I in 1603, women had no legal rights; they were considered the property of either their father or their husband. A husband's rule over his wife was like that of a feudal lord. If a wife plotted to kill her husband (or a servant to kill a master) this was treated as treason, and punished by the harshest form of the death penalty available: being burnt alive.[55]

Many of the writers stress the social pressures that force the widow to become a sati. Abraham Roger, a Dutch missionary, explains that the sati's decision is greatly influenced by the horrors of widowhood:

les femmes, qui demeurent, & qui ne sont pas brusler, sont mesprisées, et obligées de porter comme une marque d'infamie devant tout le monde: on leur coupe les cheveux; elles ne peuvent point manger de *Betel*; elles ne peuvent point porter de joyaux, ny se remarier; en un mot on leur fait tous les affronts, & tous les desplaisirs, dont on peut s'imaginer.[56]

(the women who remain and are not burnt are despised, and made as it were to bear the mark of their infamy publicly: their hair is cut off, they can never chew *betel*; they can neither wear any jewelry, nor remarry; in short they are subjected to all the affronts and annoyances imaginable.)

This emphasis on the deprivations of life as a widow strikingly anticipates the arguments of late nineteenth-century British and Hindu women writers. Jenny Sharpe has claimed these as specifically feminist interventions in the discourse on sati.[57] According to Rajeswari Sunder Rajan, such arguments continue to inform the anti-sati compaign today. The ill-treatment of widows is considered one of the central factors determining the widow's compliance in the rite. Ideological indoctrination is another.[58] Bernier's notion of the power of tradition to condition behaviour, which is far less typical of seventeenth-century views, seems to approach this idea:

> Many persons, whom I then consulted about this custome of Women burning themselves with the Bodies of their Husbands, would perswade me, that what they did was from an excess of affection they had for them: But I understood afterwards, that it was only an effect of Opinion, prepossession and custome; and that the Mothers, from their youth besotted with this superstition, as of a most vertuous and most laudable action, such as was unvoidable to a Woman of honour, did also infatuate the spirit of their Daughters from their very infancy: Although, at the bottom, it was nothing else but an Art of the Men, the more to enslave their Wives, thereby to make them have the more care of their health, and to prevent poisoning of them.[59]

Bernier deflates the heroic image of the sati by stages: contrary to general opinion, sati is not the action of a devoted wife, but the result of female conditioning, and this, in turn, is simply a means of ensuring male control. Bernier presents his findings as if he were digging through layers of accumulated misconception to reveal the truth. The urge to deny the heroism of sati results in a search for the custom's origins within society.

Social pressure on the widow to burn herself can be reinforced by actual compulsion. This forms the second main European argument against the heroic status of the sati: the view that the woman is being forced to die against her wishes (another element shared with the contemporary campaign against sati).[60] In seventeenth-century accounts, the agents of this coercion are generally perceived as the brahmans. Bernier describes their methods of intimidation: 'I have seen some of them [widows], which at the sight of the Pile and Fire, appear'd to have some apprehension, and that perhaps would have gone back, but 'tis often too late: Those Demons, the *Brahmans*, that are there with their great Sticks, astonish them, and hearten them up, or even thrust them in.'[61] The sati is a frightened victim of devil-priests, not the self-sacrificing heroine. In some versions, such as this by Tavernier, the brahmans drug her, greedy for the jewellery which, vulture-like, they pick from her ashes:

> many of our *Europeans* are of opinion, that to take away the fears of death, which terrifies humanity, the Priests do give her a certain Beverage to stupify and disorder the senses, which takes from her all apprehension of her preparations for death. 'Tis for the *Bramins* interest that the poor miserable creatures should

continue in their resolutions; for all their Bracelets as well about their legs as their arms, the Pendents in their ears; their Rings sometimes of Gold, sometimes of Silver . . . all these belong to the the *Bramins*; who rake for them among the ashes when the party is burn'd.[62]

By depicting the brahmans as the self-interested instigators of sati, attention is deflected away from the sati towards the priests; they become the main protagonists. Brahmans are presented as the crafty agents of a religion that deludes widows into suicide: the third main argument against the heroic status of the sati. Roger describes the persuasive techniques and fake religious incentives employed by the priests to convince the widows to burn themselves:

cela se fait par l'addresse, & les langues cauteleuses des *Bramines*, qui ne se contentent pas de leur apporter les exemples de celles, qui l'ont fait; mais disent de plus, que leur mary . . . peut recevoir beaucoup de bien par là; car si elle se laisse brusler avec son mary par pur amour, & par pure & simple affection, qu'elle a euë pour luy, que cela ne luy tournera pas seulement à bien en la vie future; mais qu'elle delivera son mary des peines de l'Enfer, quoy qu'il aye esté impie: ils sont aussi accroire aux femmes, que si elles font cela par pur amour, qu'elles ne sentiront pas si vivement les peines du feu: & qui est-ce, qui leur en peut dire le contraire, n'ayant parlé à personne, qui leur ait rapporté, comme elle s'y est trouvée?[63]

(this is achieved by the skill, and the wily tongues of the brahmans, who are not content with supplying examples of those who have done it, but say moreover that their husband . . . could gain greatly by it, for if she allows herself to burn with her husband through pure love, and through the pure and simple affection that she had for him, it will not only be to her advantage in the future life, but she will deliver her husband from the punishments of hell, however impious he had been: they also make the women believe that if they do this through pure love, they will not feel the torments of the fire so acutely: and who is there who can tell them the contrary, since they never have spoken to anyone who reported how she found it there?)

This is a sort of blasphemous parody of Christian sacrifice: Christ, out of his love for humanity, died to redeem mankind from its sinful state and open the way to eternal life; the sati, out of love for her sinful husband, is to die to save him from hell to enjoy a better future life. The analogy is reinforced by the use of Christian terms, 'l'Enfer' (hell) and 'la vie future' (the future life); while the final ironic comment about the widow not being able to find anyone to tell her if self-immolation is painful highlights the essential difference between the two sacrificial deaths: Christ came back to tell the disciples about his resurrection, but no sati has ever returned. The teachings of the brahmans pervert biblical truth, and the brahmans themselves are often depicted as devils, as in Bernier's stick-brandishing demons. Athanasius Kircher, in his *China . . . Illustrata* of 1667, represents them as 'la troupe infernale des sacrificateurs' (the infernal troop of sacrificers), and the sati as a victim of hell who delivers her soul into the hands of demons 'qui au lieu de la conduire dans les champs Elisiens, comme ils se persuadent, la menent dans les flammes eternelles pour y continuer un supplice qui n'aura jamais de fin' (who rather than conducting her to the Elysian Fields, as they believe, lead her into eternal flames to continue a never-ending torture there).[64]

The idea that the widow's funeral pyre is a foretaste of hell fire is carried into the iconography of sati. There are two main methods of sati which the travel accounts record: one where the widow sits or lies down next to her husband's corpse on the unlit funeral pyre, and a second where she leaps into an already blazing pit. Many of the illustrations of sati show the widow jumping into the funeral pyre rather than lying next to her husband. This is of course partly because the leaping version creates a more dramatic visual image—the woman is captured at the very moment before she is burnt—but the choice must also be influenced by its associations with hell. Like a damned soul, the widow jumps down into a fiery pit (Figs 4 and 5). The demon (Fig. 4) announcing the title of Roger's work reinforces these hellish associations.

The European reputation of the sati seems to have reached its nadir: a hell-bound victim of custom, coercion and pagan delusion, how could she possibly be redeemed? It is a sign of the deep ambivalence of some European writers that, despite the apparent obstacles, they do indeed attempt to reclaim her. One way is to view the sati not from a Christian perspective, but treat her rather as a literary figure, a tragic heroine. Suicide, as represented in classical texts and on the contemporary stage, seems to have been acceptable. In *The English Debate on Suicide from Donne to Hume*, S. E. Sprott argues that 'Brutus on his own sword and Cleopatra holding the asps to her breast appear to have been granted an existence in art that was not read at the time as a direct humanist thesis on the ethics of suicide. Outside literature, the pagan morality was unacceptable, though paraded on the stages and in novels.'[65] Travel literature, a capacious genre, could easily span the boundaries between 'ethics' and 'art'; writing about sati ranges from Christian diatribe and anthropological enquiry to high tragedy.

To qualify as a tragic heroine, the sati must defy all suggestion of coercion by her composure. The idea that sati is merely customary must

Indian Women / 57

FIG. 4: Title page of *La Porte Ouverte*
by Abraham Roger (1670), Bodleian Library, Oxford.

58 / *India Inscribed*

Fig. 5: Engraving of sati from *Itinerario Voyage ofte Schipvaert* by Jan Hughen Van Linschoten (1596), British Library.

be eclipsed by her individual stature. Pietro della Valle, an Italian traveller, who deals at unusual length with an instance of noble sati, distinguishes between the cruel custom and the heroism of individual widows: 'a Custom, indeed cruel and barbarous, but, withall, of great generosity and virtue in such Women and therefore worthy of no small praise.'[66] The praise that della Valle offers the sati takes the form of literary immortality. Greatly impressed by 'Giaccamà', a widow resolved to burn herself, he promises to spread her fame: 'so far as my weak pen could contribute, her Name should remain immortal in the World. . . . My Muse could not forbear from chanting her in a Sonnet which I made upon her death, and reserve among my Poetical Papers.'[67]

While we can only speculate on the nature of della Valle's poem, the sonnet form, conventionally addressed to a distant mistress, seems particularly well suited to the inaccessible sati. Giaccamà is turned into a literary figure: the subject of a sonnet and the heroine of the promised account. This literary transformation is exactly the type of fame that the sailor, William Hawkins, imagines motivates the widows to kill themselves: 'because they will be registered in their books, for famous and most modest and loving Wives, who leaving all worldly affaires, content themselves to live no longer than their Husbands.'[68]

The literary tribute is the European equivalent of Hindu reverence. A story about a sati can even be turned into a moral example: Manucci's editor, Catrou, comments that a description of a sati is *'as useful a Lesson of conjugal Fidelity, as the Constancy of the Heroes of Toxaris was among the Athenians of the Highest Friendship'*.[69] The literary account of sati takes on mythic status to become an exemplum. Significantly, Catrou compares the sati with a Greek story about Scythians, situating her in a non-Christian context.

The literary representation of noble sati also draws on the theatrical associations of the ceremony. The structural similarities of sati to dramatic spectacle are evident: the widow is the centre of intense attention, surrounded by a crowd of onlookers, and the Westerner is usually powerless to intervene. The European observer is simultaneously drawn in admiration towards the widow and repelled by the horror of the act. Pulled emotionally in two directions, the onlooker is like a spectator at a tragedy, attracted by pity and repelled by terror, to use Aristotelian terms. François Bernier is well aware of the dramatic quality of sati; he terms it a 'direful Tragedy'.[70] In fact, a similar scene had been represented on the Greek stage in Euripides' play, *Suppliants*. Evadne, the widow of Capaneus, one of the seven chiefs of Argos killed in battle against Thebes, determines to prove her courage and love through self-sacrifice. In a dramatic climax, she refuses to listen to her father's pleas and leaps from a cliff to her death in Capaneus' funeral pyre.[71]

It comes as no surprise then to find that Dryden, in his tragedy based on Bernier's account, *Aureng-Zebe*, should include a sati; what is unexpected is that it is a *Muslim* princess, Melesinda, who burns herself after the death of her husband, Morat. Dryden is prepared to create an entirely anomalous situation—Bernier makes it clear that sati was exclusive to Hindus—to exploit the theatrical potential of the practice. Of course, Dryden is too concerned with dramatic propriety to stage the burning itself; Melesinda enters, dressed in white, at the back of a procession of priests. She is referred to as 'Sad Melesinda', but rejects this assumption of sorrow:

> You wrong my love; what grief do I betray?
> This is the triumph of my nuptual day.
> My better nuptuals, which in spite of fate
> Forever join me to my dear Morat . . .
> In vain you would bereave me of my lord,
> For I will die. Die is too base a word;
> I'll seek his breast, and kindling by his side,
> Adorned with flames, I'll mount a glorious bride.[72]

As Derek Hughes has pointed out, 'the flames of love and death are indivisible' for Melesinda.[73] Such an association is interestingly prefigured by Evadne in *Suppliants*. Contemplating her imminent suicide, Evadne imagines death as another wedding in Hades:

> Flames reddening o'er me,-
> To nestle to his side,
> In Cora's bowers a bride![74]

It seems that Dryden may have known *Suppliants* only from a summary supplied by Corneille;[75] however, the identification of sati with marriage was a recurrent trope in travel literature on India, a metaphor which carried a half-hidden reference to the familiar *double entendre* of death as orgasm. Thomas Herbert, for example, provides an overtly erotic description of a sati: 'she roabs her tender body with a transparent Lawne, her armes, leggs, and thighes, are fettered with wanton chaines of love . . .'[76] The voyeuristic male gaze is fixed unwaveringly on the sati; even in the destruction of her physical self, the Hindu woman is liable to be depicted in sexual terms.

For Dryden, however, sati presents an occasion for high tragedy and the celebration of stoic virtue. Earlier in the play, Melesinda patiently endures imprisonment and is described as surpassing even Roman fortitude:

> Her chains with Roman constancy she bore,
> But that, perhaps, an Indian wife's is more.[77]

Yet this noble rhetoric is undermined both by the action of the play and by the comments of bystanders. The audience has witnessed Morat's repeated rejection of Melesinda; one character reasons that she has 'no right to die; he was not kind', another urges her not to be deluded by any 'false show of fame'.[78] The problem of representing sati as heroic is addressed in the preface to the first printed edition of *Aureng-Zebe* (1676). Attempting to answer the criticism of 'some of the fair ladies' in his audience, Dryden offers an account of his female character's actions. While he 'dare[s] not vindicate' sati, 'so neither can ... [he] wholly condemn' it:

> I have made my Melesinda ... a woman passionately loving of her husband, patient of injuries and contempt, and constant in her kindness to the last; and in that, perhaps, I may have erred, because it is not a virtue much in use. Those Indian wives are loving fools, and may do well to keep themselves in their own country, or at least to keep company with the Arrias and Portias of old Rome; some of our ladies know better things.[79]

Dryden's serious-sounding praise is undercut by glancing irony. Melisinda is classed with two types of feminine courage, Arria and Portia, both of whom committed suicide: the first as an example to her husband, the second on hearing that she had become a widow. Dryden's approbation of Indian and classical wifely submission entails ironic attacks on current English feminine mores: constancy 'is not a virtue much in use', and the ladies in his audience 'know better things' than the heroines of antiquity. Once again, the representation of Indian women reveals the preoccupation with domestic discussions of feminine morality.

If Dryden finds it hard to seal the sati in a distant exemplary role, travel writers cannot always contain her within the conventions of stage tragedy. This is because of the crucial difference between sati and drama: the heroine *really* dies. Consider, for example, this anecdote from Tavernier which highlights the grotesque disparity between theatrical display and the horror of being burnt alive:

> An Idolater dying, and the Fire being ready prepar'd for the burning of the Body, his Wife who had no Children, by the permission of the Governour, came to the

Fire, and stood among the Priests and her Kindred, to be burnt with the Body of her deceas'd Husband. As they were taking three turns, according to the custom, about the place where the Fire was kindl'd, there fell of a sudden so violent a Shower, that the Priests willing to get out of the rain, thrust the Woman all along into the Fire. But the Shower was so vehement, and endur'd so long a while, that the Fire was quench'd, and the Woman was not burn'd. About midnight she rose, and went and knock'd at the door of one of her kinsmens Houses, where Father *Zenon* and many Hollanders saw her, looking so ghastly and grimly, that it was enough to have scar'd them; however the pain that she endur'd did not so far terrifie her, but that three days after accompany'd by her Kindred, she went and was burn'd according to her first intention.[80]

The shower of rain spoils the tragic dignity of the ceremony; the sati 'misfires' and so reveals the terrible physical suffering involved. The tragedy is in danger of degenerating into black farce with the ultimate *coup de théâtre*: the return of one thought dead. But after the horrible humour of the parodic ressurection, the widow's undaunted resolution to burn herself again restores her tragic stature.

This central problem in the representation of the sati as tragic heroine—the fact that she really suffers and dies—may in part account for a common reaction among European observers of sati: that of incredulity. The shift from drama to reality is disorientating. Bernier writes of his difficulty in comprehending the noble stoicism of a sati:

To represent unto you the undaunted cheerfulness that appear'd in her countenance, the resolution with which she marched, wash'd her self, spoke to the people; the confidence with which she look'd upon us, view'd her little Cabin, made up of very dry Millet-straw and small Wood, went into this Cabin, and sate down upon the Pile, and took her Husband's Head into her Lap, and a Torch into her own Hand, and kindled the Cabin, whilst I know not how many *Brahmans* were busie in kindling the fire round about: To represent unto you I say, all this, as it ought, is not possible for me; I can at present scarce believe it my self, though it be but a few days since I saw it.[81]

Bernier asserts that he cannot describe the scene to his readers because he can hardly believe it. While this assertion is in part a rhetorical ploy to heighten the sense of the extraordinariness of sati, it has important implications. Here, as elsewhere, Bernier seems to be questioning the assumption that it is always possible for the West to comprehend the East. This admission of the inadequacy of language endows the sati with an unknowable, independent otherness.

The sense of the sati's heroic autonomy was not to persist into colonial representations. In a Foucauldian essay, Lata Mani argues that colonial discourse invariably represents satis as victims, either of religion, or of Hindu male coercion.[82] She says that, in accounts of sati written by colonial officials, widows are denied any subjectivity or individual will. I would suggest that this change of emphasis is related to the new British role; Gayatri Spivak sees a similar connection when she writes that the 'leap of *suttee* from private to public has a clear and complex relationship with the changeover from a mercantile and commercial to a territorial and administrative British presence'.[83] In the early nineteenth century, sati moved into the public sphere, it became a matter of administrative concern; widows had to apply to British officials for permission to perform the rite in accordance with guidelines supposedly derived from Hindu scripture. Unlike earlier European observers, colonial administrators were in a position of authority, assigned a supervisory role which hinged on the question of whether a sati was 'voluntary' or not. Mani argues that even 'voluntary' sati was 'interpreted not as evidence of the will of the widow, but testimony of her subjection to religion'. She continues: 'the widow thus nowhere appears as a full subject. If she resisted, she was considered a victim of Hindu male barbarity. If she conceded, she was seen as a victim of religion'.[84] What Mani overlooks is the break that this denial of agency marks with earlier European representations. As I have already argued, earlier accounts solve the problem of how to depict a determined, courageous sati by adopting a classical literary framework. This option is simply not available to the later writers: the colonial regime cannot undermine its own authority by elevating its subjects to the status of classical heroines.

These seventeenth-century Indian/classical heroines are not always the composed picture of conjugal fidelity. In the revised second edition of Thomas Herbert's *Travels*, the sati is more a Dido-like image of desperate love. This is the state which Le Moyne in *La Gallerie des Femmes Fortes* describes as that tumultuous and precipitate despair of the Greeks and Romans which, together with sati, contravened Christian law. Herbert seems to envisage sati as a kind of a literalized metaphor: 'when Death has cut in two their Union; shee [the widow] conceits her selfe a loathed carkasse to live after him.'[85] To escape the metaphorical 'loathed carkasse' of widowhood, the sati actually turns herself into ashes. The choice of the verb 'conceit' is interesting; there may be a pun on its literary usage; the poetic conceit of dying for love certainly seems to underlie the whole description:

upon sight of the flame [the widow] seemes transported beyond measure; she sees the carcasse of her Husband layd upon a pyle of pretious wood, and when the fire begins to embrace him, like a mad Lover she bids Farewell to her Parents, children, and friends, and willingly incorporates her selfe with fire; which quickly makes them one, and nothing; nothing extant save fame, flame, and ashes. Of which the Poët, thus of old.

> Et certamen habent lethi, quae viva sequatur
> conjugium; pudor est non licuisse mori.
> Ardent victrices, et præbent pectora flammæ;
> imponuntque suis ora perusta viris.
>
> (*They strive to die, and who best speed can make;*
> *They blush, grim Death so slowly to o'ertake.*
> *The Conquerors burn, their brests yeeld to the fire,*
> *And to their husbands, their burnt lips aspire.*[86])

The quotation comes from Propertius III xiii 19–22, and forms part of a complaint on the faithlessness of women in which sati is held up as an exeception: a remote, shining example of loyalty. By citing it, Herbert firmly situates sati in a non-Christian, literary context, and enhances the stature of the sati with classical textual authority.[87]

Edward Terry, chaplain to the East India Company, seems to be parodying this literary adulation of the sati in the second, expanded edition of his *Voyage*. In his description of a sati, the widow goes to her death voluntarily, if drugged:

and though she have no bonds but her own strong affections to tie her unto those flames, yet she never offers to stir out of them. But

> *Her breathlesse Husband then she takes*
> *In foulded arms; this done she makes*
> *Her humble sute to th' flames to give*
> *Her quick dispatch, she cannot live*
> *Her honour dead. Her friends there come*
> *Look on, as if 't were Martrydom;*
> *And with content are hither led,*
> *As once to view her marriage bed.*

And thus, she being joyfuly accompanied unto the place of her dying by her Parents and other friends, and when all is fitted for this hellish Sacrifice, and the fire begins to burn; all which are there present shout, and make a continual noise so long as they observe her to stir, that the screeches of that poor tortured Creature may not be heard.[88]

The passage begins much like a heroic account apart from the fact that the sati has drugged herself. She settles calmly on the pyre, and we are presented with what seems to be a laudatory verse, except that halfway through there is a reference to the horrors of widowhood: 'she cannot live / Her honour dead'. The sense of heroism is completely deflated by the following prose description of the 'hellish Sacrifice' where the noise of the crowd drowns the widow's screams. Terry seems to insert the verse to maximize the shock of the 'hellish Sacrifice'; the reader is jolted from the literary idiom into a Christian diatribe which continues for over a page. Terry's use of the heroic mode makes for a highly ambivalent description, and indeed some writers display seemingly contradictory reactions to sati; Herbert, for instance, deems it lascivious womankind's just deserts, but represents it as dying for love, Bernier writes of sati as alternately heroic, sacrificial or socially conditioned. Ambivalence is of course inherent in the European male response to the act.[89] There is the patriarchal appeal of sati as the ultimate demonstration of wifely submission and chastity. The figure of the sati functions as a potent emblem of patient female suffering, an Indian sister to those two literary heroines, Griselda and Lucretia, identified by Lisa Jardine as central symbols for the Renaissance: Griselda who endures her husband's innumerable cruelties without complaint, and Lucretia who, rather than live with the dishonour of rape, takes her own life.[90] But then suicide is a far from glorious action in a Christian context, and the writers must also negotiate the conflict between the contemporary ethical framework and the classical literary tradition. Additional complications arise with the radically different reactions to voluntary and compelled suicide.

If we return to Terry's account of sati we see that he focuses these contradictions on a double image of the sati: the 'Martyrdom' that the widow's friends come to watch and the 'hellish Sacrifice' that he himself perceives. Terry is pointing out the impossibility of a non-Christian martyrdom: the sati dies for her husband, not Christ. He may be referring to the practice of representing the noble sati like a saintly martyr. Compare, for instance, the description of a widow's death from Nicholas Withington's account of his travels of 1612–16 with John Foxe's narrative of Mistress Lewis' martyrdom from *Acts and Monuments*, the standard Protestant martyrolgy, first published in 1563:

[the *sati*] taking her husbands head in her lap, and bids them put fire, which done, her friends throw oile and other sweete perfumes on her, she enduring the fire with admirable patience, loose and not bound.

[Mistress Lewis] shewed such cheerfulness, that it passed man's reason, being so devoid of any fear, and so patient. . . . When the fire was set upon her, she neither struggled nor stirred, but only lifted up her hands towards heaven, being dead very speedily . . .[91]

The similarity in the representation of the deaths of sati and martyr is evident, although the comparison is of course sacrilegious and never made explicit.[92] In both accounts, attention is concentrated on the conduct of the dying woman and what it reveals of her mental state. The role of the eyewitness is thus central to both; the observer personally verifies the women's fortitude, authenticating the unbelievable act.

The observer is often foregrounded in accounts of sati, as in this description by a French traveller, Charles Dellon:

> The first time that I was an Eye-witness of this Tragical Ceremony, I took most particular notice of all Passages and Circumstances that attend it; she that sacrificed her self did not appear to be above twenty Years of Age; she look'd upon her Funeral Pile with a very settled Countenance, shewing not the least marks of sorrow at her approaching fate; she with her own hands set fire to the combustible matter that surrounded her; I was very near the Pile, so that I could exactly see her lift up her deceased Husband's Head, and press her Cheeks to his, which done, she pulled her Veil over her Face, and died without the least appearance of regret.[93]

Dellon's precise description of the sati's demeanour, with the final telling detail of her last gesture of modesty, veiling her face, highlights some important elements in the representation of sati. Unlike much of the writing about Indian women, sati claims a basis in observed fact. The ultimate expression of chastity, it is the only manifestation of Hindu female conduct that is substantiated by personal observation. The intimate display of conjugal devotion—a wife caressing her husband's cheek—which would normally be conducted in private, far from the travel writer's gaze, is here played out in the public arena. Sati thus functions as a powerful counter to stories of Hindu female promiscuity and occult sexual practices.

The foregrounding of the observer also enhances the writer's own status; he has witnessed a notable act and basks, as it were, in the reflected glory of the sati. Mandelslo treasures a bracelet belonging to a sati as a keepsake, tangible proof that he was actually present at her death:

> Having look'd upon it [the pyre] with a certain contempt, she took leave of her kindred and friends, and distributed among them the rings and bracelets she had about her ... I think she perceiv'd in my countenance that I pitied her, whence it came that she cast me one of her bracelets, which I had the good hap to catch, and still keep, in remembrance of so extraordinary an Action.[94]

The emphasis on the presence of the eyewitness provides the author with an opportunity to write himself into the narrative. Pietro della Valle devotes a long section to his meeting with Giaccamà, the widow resolved to die.[95] He asks her about her family, her motives and the customs of sati, trying, unsuccessfully, to convince her to desist. In Bernier's encounter with a would-be sati, he manages to dissuade her from burning with a terrible image of her children's orphaned destitution: Bernier steals the widow's glory to become the hero himself.[96]

The most famous story of a disrupted widow-burning, dating from a slighty later period, is that associated with Job Charnock, English 'founder' of Calcutta. The narrative originates in Alexander Hamilton's *New Account of the East Indies* of 1727. Hamilton was one of the private traders operating unofficially in India in an attempt to break the monopoly of the East India Company. As the Company's Chief Agent in Bengal from 1685 to 1692, Charnock was Hamilton's main adversary.[97] Hamilton characterizes him as a harsh autocrat who 'reigned more absolute than a Rajah', and then recounts how Charnock

> went one Time with his ordinary Guard of Soldiers, to see a young Widow act that tragical Catastrophe, but he was so smitten with the Widow's Beauty, that he sent his Guards to take her by Force from the Executioners, and conducted her to his own Lodgings. They lived lovingly many Years, and had several Children, at length she died, after he had settled in *Calcutta,* but instead of converting her to *Christianity,* she made him a Proselyte to *Paganism,* and the only Part of *Christianity* that was remarkable in him, was burying her decently, and he built a Tomb over her, where all his Life after her Death, he kept the anniversary Day of her Death by sacrificing a Cock on her Tomb, after the *Pagan* Mannner; this was and is the common Report, and I have been credibly informed, both by *Christians* and *Pagans,* who lived at *Calcutta* under his Agency, that the Story was really True Matter of Fact.[98]

It is tempting to read this account as an early version of the rescued sati romance—a popular topos in later novels. But we should note that Charnock kidnaps, rather than rescues, the widow who has caught his eye. Should we regard the abduction as an abuse of power? Certainly the outcome of the tale is far from conventional. The two live lovingly together but Charnock, neglecting his duty to convert the widow, succumbs to paganism himself. This narrative does not conform to that paradigmatic 'sentence' which Gayatri Spivak has identified as central to later constructions of sati—'White men are saving brown women from brown men'.[99] In this early version of the apparently familiar story, the brown woman is leading the white man to damnation. The unexpected turn of events is signalled by the repeated, overemphatic assertions of the account's veracity. The hybridized figure of Charnock turns the story of redemption into a cautionary tale about the dangers of inter-racial sexual contact. Hamilton's narrative plays on the European fear of Indianization—a recurrent anxiety which, we will see, haunts many later accounts. The idea of the Englishman reduced to paganism by an Indian woman both breaches the boundary between Self and Other, and implies a renunciation of masculine authority.

The threat of female sexuality, evident in so much of the writing discussed in this chapter, is nowhere more apparent than in a characteristically obscene outburst from Richard Head's *The English Rogue*. Like Hamilton, Head offers a disturbing image of the English adoption of Indian ritual, but the shock is intensified because Head imagines the transplantation of Indian rites to England. Recording the standard explanation for the introduction of sati—the female lechery and husband-murdering deterrent—Head mock-seriously suggests that the promiscuity of English women merits similar legislation:

For my part, I could wish for the like custom enjoyn'd on all married English females (for the love I bear to my own Country) which I am confident would prevent the destruction of thousands of well-meaning-Christians, which receive a full stop in the full career of their lives, either by corrupting their bodies by venemous medicaments administered by some pretended Doctors hand (it may be her Stallion) unto which he is easily perswaded, by the good opinion he hath of his wifes great care and affection for him: or else his body is poysoned by sucking or drawing in the contagious fumes which proceed from her contaminated body, occasion'd by using pluralities for her venereal satisfaction, and so dies of the new consumption.[100]

Widow burning figures here as the means to regulate and punish female sexuality. The shifting, ambivalent reactions to sati found in travel literature—Head's source material—are completely ignored. Sati is deprived of any association with chastity, and instead combined with the menacing sexuality which acts as its foil in the travel accounts.

In breaching the dividing line between Christian and pagan, this misogynist proposal conflates 'our' women with 'theirs'. These death-dealing, lascivious women are located in England, rather too close for comfort. It would of course be more reassuring if they were situated in a foreign land. In the travel accounts, the barriers of distance and difference protect the sanctity of the home and the marriage bed. For the Indian woman becomes the focus of male European desires and fears: a body to be veiled, revealed or consumed in flames. An ambivalent compound of chastity, sexual appetite, and the death wish, she is a fantasy woman in an imaginary land.

Indian Women / 69

NOTES

1. John Sprint, *Bride-Woman Conseller*, quoted in Antonia Fraser, *The Weaker Vessel: Woman's Lot in Seventeenth-Century England* (1984; rpt London, 1989) 526–7.
2. Lisa Jardine, *Still Harping on Daughters: Women and Drama in the Age of Shakespeare* (Hemel Hempstead, 1983) 161, 168n 66.
3. John Fryer, *A New Account of East India and Persia*, ed. William Crooke, 2 vols (London, 1909–15) i. 88–9.
4. Jean de Thévenot, *Indian Travels of Thevenot and Careri*, ed. Surendranath Sen (New Delhi, 1949), 66. See also Pietro della Valle, *The Travels of Pietro della Valle in India*, ed. Edward Grey (London, 1892) 45–6.
5. François de la Boullaye le Gouz, *Les Voyages et Observations dv Sievr de la Bovllaye Le-Gouz* (1653; rpt Paris, 1657) 148.
6. Suzanne Rodin Pucci, 'The Discrete Charms of the Exotic: Fictions of the Harem in Eighteenth-Century France', in *Exoticism in the Enlightenment*, eds G. S. Rousseau and Roy Porter (Manchester, 1990) 150.
7. La Boullaye le Gouz, 154.
8. Rana Kabbani, *Europe's Myths of Orient* (1986; rpt London, 1988) 18.
9. La Boullaye le Gouz, 146.
10. I am grateful to Dr Andrew Topsfield of the Ashmolean Museum, Oxford, for this point.
11. Samuel Purchas, *Hakluytus Posthumus or Purchas his Pilgrimes*, 20 vols (Glasgow, 1905–7) iv. 375–6.
12. François Bernier, *The History of the Late Revolution of the Empire of the Great Mogol*, 6 parts (London, 1671) 'A Letter to Mr de la Mothe le Vayer', 49–50.
13. Bernier, 'A Letter to Mr. de la Mothe le Vayer', 50.
14. Fryer, i. 353; F. F. Catrou, *The General History of the Mogol Empire* (London, 1709) title page; Catrou, 318.
15. Fryer, i. 327.
16. Ibid., 327–8.
17. Homer, *The Odyssey* xi. 427; Fryer, i. 328.
18. Fryer, i. 328.
19. Jean Baptiste Tavernier, *The Six Voyages of Jean Baptista Tavernier*, 2 vols (London, 1678) ii. 121; Thomas Coryat in *Early Travels in India, 1583–1619*, ed. William Foster (London, 1921) 278–9.
20. Jardine, 127–30.
21. Catrou, 330.
22. Ibid., 331.
23. Ibid., 326.
24. Ibid., 328.
25. Fryer, i. 328.
26. Catrou, 331–2.
27. Ibid., 334.
28. Tavernier, ii. 37.

29. John Huighen Van Linschoten, *Discours of Voyages into the Easte and West Indies*, 4 vols (London, 1598) i. 64; Philip Baldaeus, 'A true and Exact Description of the Most Celebrated *East-India* Coasts of Malabar and Coromandel', in *A Collection of Voyages and Travels*, ed. A. and J. Churchill, 6 vols (London, 1732) iii. 754.
30. Thomas Herbert, *A Relation of Some Yeares Travaile* (London, 1634) 41.
31. See Fryer, ii. 77; Herbert, 187, 192; della Valle, 39.
32. Fryer, ii. 77; Della Valle, 224.
33. Marco Polo, *The Most noble and famous travels of Marcus Paulus* (London, 1579) 34–5, 79, 80–1.
34. John Ovington, *A Voyage to Suratt* (London 1696) 212–13.
35. I am using the 1863 English translation of the original Italian edition of 1510.
36. Ludovico di Varthema, *The Travels of Ludovico di Varthema*, trans. George Percy Badger (London, 1863) 203.
37. François Pyrard de Laval, *Voyage de François Pyrard de Laual*, 2 vols (1611; rpt Paris, 1619) ii. 66–7.
38. Pyrard de Laval, ii. 135. See also Herbert, 40–1.
39. Pyrard de Laval, ii. 135. This drug, dutrea, mentioned in Linschoten, i. 60 and by many subsequent authors, figured in the list of enquiries for travellers published in the *Philosophical Transactions* by the Royal Society in 1667, in an attempt to demystify the drug and find out if it actually existed.
40. John Albert de Mandelslo, 'The Voyages & Travels of J. Albert de Mandelslo' in *The Voyages & Travels of the Ambassadors sent by Frederick Duke of Holstein, to the Great Duke of Muscovy, and the King of Persia*, trans. John Davis (London, 1662) 27.
41. Mandelslo, 29.
42. Fryer, i. 148.
43. C. W. R. D. Moseley, 'Richard Head's "English Rogue": A Modern Mandeville?' *Yearbook of English Studies* i (1971) 105; H. F. Watson, *The Sailor in English Fiction and Drama* (New York, 1931) 102–5.
Head follows Herbert's account of religious orgies very closely:

> Againe (O griefe to speak it) in these parts, the people are so extreamely Idolatrous, and ouerswayed by the insatiable gulph of perdition the Deuill, that they adore a great massie Copper gilded Idol, whose Statue is glouriously mounted vpon a Chariot which mooues with eight mighty wheeles, ouerlaid with Gold, the ascent vp to the Idoll vpon the Chariot is spacious and easie by many and enlarging steps, on which sit with sober visage, the Priests and other little Girles who in way of deuotion (impure sanctitie) prostitute themselues to the libininous heat of wicked men, the better thereby to enrich their *Pagode*, or adored Deuill; and for which their dutifulnesse, they are entitled, *the Pagodes children*: these *Nemeses* with their Priests giue Sacrifices to the Deuill (fond zeale of their besotted Parents to destinate their prettie children, from their infancie, to such an abominable libertie.)

Herbert, 192.

Indian Women / 71

> They are in these parts so extreamly idolatrous, and so over-swayed by the Devil, that they adore a great Idol made of Copper gilded, whose statue is carried up and down, mounted on a glorious charriot, with eight very large wheels overlayed with gold, the ascent or steps to the Charriot are very large & capacious, on which sit the Priests, attended by little young girles, who for devotion sake prostitute themselves freely to the heat of any libidinous spectator; for so doing, they are intitled the *Pagodes* children: A very strange zeal in their bewitched or besotted Parents, to destinate the off-spring of their bodies, from their non-age, to such an abominable liberty. . . .

Richard Head, *The English Rogue*, 3 parts (London, 1666) iii. 98.

44. Head, iii. 90; iii. 116–19; iii. 91. After Latroon's borrowed wedding night, he finds out that the bride was only seven years old, but this is normal, he is assured, girls of seven 'being extreamly salacious and leacherous and as fit, nay, as prone to enjoy man at that age as *Europeans* at fourteen', Head, iii. 90. This is an exaggerated version of the travel writing tradition of Indian women's early puberty, often set at ten or twelve years old. See Mandelslo, 73.
45. Fraser, 89.
46. Fryer, i. 281; Catrou, 164. See also Herbert, 36, 42; Mandelslo, 77.
47. Purchas, ix. 35–6. See also Ovington, 230, Tavernier, ii. 124.
48. Ian Maclean, *Woman Triumphant: Feminism in French Literature 1610–52* (Oxford, 1977) 19, 82–3.
49. Pierre le Moyne, *La Gallerie des Femmes Fortes* (Lyon, 1667) 350.
50. John Sym, *Lifes preservative against self-killing* (London, 1637) 193.
51. Sym, 192–3.
52. The earliest version of the story may be by the Greek writer, Diodorus Siculus, see R. C. Majumdar, ed., *Classical Accounts of India* (Calcutta, 1960) 240–1. For other seventeenth-century versions, see Ovington, 343–4; Linschoten, 71; Charles Dellon, *A Voyage to the East-Indies* (London, 1698) 47.
53. Herbert, 191–2.
54. Rajeswari Sunder Rajan, *Real and Imagined Women: Gender, Culture and Post-Colonialism* (London, 1993) 94.
55. Fraser, 5.
56. Abraham Roger, *La Porte Ouverte Pour Parvenir à la Connoissance du Paganisme Caché* (Amsterdam, 1670) 133–4.
57. Jenny Sharpe, *Allegories of Empire: The Figure of Women in the Colonial Text* (Minneapolis, 1993).
58. Rajan, 19.
59. Bernier, 'A Letter to M. de la Mothe le Vayer', 122–3.
60. Rajan, 19.
61. Bernier, 'A Letter to M. de la Mothe le Vayer', 126. See also Henry Lord, *A discouerie of the Sect of the Banians* (London, 1630) 13.
62. Tavernier, ii. 169–70. See also Thévenot, 120; Ovington, 344.
63. Roger, 133.
64. Athanasius Kircher, *La Chine d'Athanase Kircher* (Amsterdam, 1670) 206. See also Purchas, ix. 44–5.

72 / India Inscribed

65. S. E. Sprott, *The English Debate on Suicide from Donne to Hume* (La Salle, Illinois, 1961) 13.
66. della Valle, 267.
67. Ibid., 276–7.
68. Purchas, iii. 49.
69. Catrou, Preface, unsigned 4th page.
70. Bernier, 'A Letter to M. de la Mothe le Vayer', 119.
71. *Euripides*, trans. Arthur S. Way, 4 vols (1912, London, 1962) iii. *Suppliants* l. 980–1071.
72. John Dryden, *Aureng-Zebe*, ed. Frederick M. Link (London, 1972) v. 617–20, 631–4.
73. Derek Hughes, *Dryden's Heroic Plays* (London, 1981) 123.
74. *Suppliants* l. 1020–2.
75. This is indicated by Dryden's reproduction of Corneille's comments on Euripides' play in Dryden's *Essay of Dramatick Poesie* which was published in 1668, seven years before the first production of *Aureng-Zebe*. See *The Works of John Dryden*, eds E. N. Hooker and H. T. Swedenberg et al., 19 vols (Berkeley, 1956-) xvii. 26 and note.
76. Herbert, 309.
77. *Aureng-Zebe* III. 68–9.
78. Ibid., v. 623–4.
79. Ibid., 'Dedicatory Epistle' l. 242; l. 261–9.
80. Tavernier, ii. 84.
81. Bernier, 'A Letter to M. de la Mothe le Vayer', 125–6.
82. Lata Mani, 'The Production of an official Discourse on *Sati* in early nineteenth-century Bengal', in *Europe and its Others*, ed. Francis Barker et al., 2 vols (Colchester, 1985) i. 107–27.
83. Gayatri C. Spivak, 'Can the Subaltern Speak?' in *Colonial Discourse and Post-Colonial Theory: A Reader*, eds Patrick Williams and Laura Chrisman (Hemel Hempstead, 1993) 94.
84. Mani, 117.
85. Thomas Herbert, *Some yeares Travels*, 2nd edn (London, 1638) 309.
86. Ibid., 309–10.
87. The same quotation from Propertius is cited in a discussion of sati in Fryer, ii. 18, where it is followed by a reference to Dido's death.
88. Edward Terry, *A Voyage to East India*, 2nd edn (London, 1655) 324–5. Punctuation as in original.
89. Herbert, 191–2, 309–10; Bernier, 'A Letter to M. de la Mothe le Vayer' 122–3, 125–8. See also Dellon, 49–50. Compare Rajan, 47–8, on later colonial representations of sati: 'in the colonial encounter, the Hindu "good wife" is constructed as patriarchy's feminine ideal: she is offered simultaneously as a model and as a signifier of absolute cultural otherness, both exemplary and inimitable'.
90. Jardine 182–6.
91. Purchas iv. 172; John Foxe, *Foxe's Book of Martyrs*, ed. A. Clarke (London, 1888) 840.

92. Compare Rajan, 45.
93. Dellon, 49–50.
94. Mandelslo, 41.
95. della Valle, 273–7.
96. Bernier, 'A Letter to M. de la Mothe le Vayer', 116–19.
97. J. P. Losty, *Calcutta: City of Palaces* (London, 1990) 16.
98. Alexander Hamilton, *A New Account of the East Indies*, 2 vols (Edinburgh, 1727) ii. 8–9
99. Spivak, 92.
100. Head, iii. 92.

CHAPTER THREE

India on Europe's Conscience: Eighteenth-Century Missionary Accounts

For the first three-quarters of the eighteenth-century, European attention was focused on India largely through the medium of missionary accounts. In 1702, the French Jesuits published a collection of letters from missions around the world, the *Lettres édifiantes et curieuses*, the first of a thirty-four volume series which was to continue until 1776. These widely popular texts were countered by the letters of the small Danish Lutheran mission based at Tranquebar on the south-east Indian coast. Unlike the travel literature considered earlier, these missionary letters show few signs of anxiety or self-contradiction in their representation of India. Certainty and consistency are the defining characteristics of missionary rhetoric; inevitably so, since both publishing ventures were intended to justify and finance their respective missions' activities.

As Sylvia Murr has shown, the *Lettres édifiantes* were published at a time of increasing opposition in Europe to the Jesuit Order.[1] Jesuit practice in India, established in the seventeenth century by Roberto de Nobili, had long been controversial.[2] Nobili taught that missionaries would gain the respect of high-caste Hindus only if they completely dissociated themselves from the Portuguese, whose behaviour, especially their neglect of caste distinctions and consumption of meat and alcohol, caused Hindus such offence. The Jesuits therefore distinguished themselves from the other Catholic missions operating in India—the Franciscans, Dominicans, Augustinians, Theatines and Capuchins— and from the large secular clergy based in the archdiocese of Goa, by their accommodation to Hindu customs. They projected an image similar to that of the Hindu samnyasin; they aimed to live austere, unpolluted, scholarly lives and study Sanskrit texts to equip themselves for religious debate. Jesuit converts could continue to observe most of their caste rules and the brahmans among them retain their distinctive hair style and sacred thread. Other Catholic orders were suspicious of Jesuit methods and resented their privileges and independence. In 1703 the Pondicherry-based Capuchins complained to Rome about the Jesuits. The papal authorities, already worried about Jesuit methods in China, dispatched a papal legate to investigate. The following year, certain elements of 'Indianized' Jesuit practice were prohibited, and a papal bull of 1744 confirmed the ruling. Hostility to the Society increased throughout Europe; Jesuits were accused of political ambition and intrigue. In Portugal, a decree of 1759 banned Jesuits from the kingdom, and in 1764 Jesuits were outlawed in France. Finally, in 1773, Rome ordered the suppression of the Society. In India, French Jesuit property was confiscated and the missionaries absorbed into another order.

Throughout this troubled period, the Jesuits used the *Lettres édifiantes* as part of their attempt to meet their detractors' accusations and to win public support. In these texts, the Society's missionary endeavours are represented as successful, the members as virtuous and untainted by contact with idolatrous practice. The letters' self-justificatory function becomes increasingly transparent in the later volumes. The final collection, published three years after the suppression of the Society, contains the only letter from India written by a non-Jesuit. The writer claims to be impartial, to be speaking 'en homme disintéressé'. Playing devil's advocate, he questions a brahman on Jesuit conduct, suggesting that the Jesuits are more concerned with trade than conversion, and that they discriminate against the lower castes.[3] The brahman denies the charges indignantly: Jesuits lead self-denying, exemplary lives; educating the young, caring for the low-caste poor, spreading peace and good will. He defends the Jesuits despite his Hindu allegiances:

Vous vous trompez grossiérement . . . quoique mon état & ma Religion exigent de moi de vous laisser dans l'erreur, les obligations que je vous ai m'engagent à vous tirer de celle òu vous êtes, non que je croie votre Religion meilleure que la mienne, mais je veux qu'il soit dit parmi votre nation qu'un prêtre Gentil n'est pas homme à en imposer . . .[4]

(You are making a gross mistake . . . although my position and religion demand that I should leave you in error, my obligations to you compel me to disabuse you, not that I believe that your religion is better than mine, but I want it to be said among your nation that a pagan priest is not a man to be imposed on . . .)

The voice of the pagan other, articulated through a layman, is offered as conclusive proof of Jesuit good conduct. This double device of distancing serves to authenticate the evidence. By including such a letter, the editor demonstrates his eagerness to vindicate the Society's cause, albeit retrospectively.

The Lutheran missionary writers did not anticipate such a hostile public reaction. Their letters appear to have been written in response to the *Lettres édifiantes*, justifying Lutheran practice through implicit and explicit contrast to Jesuit methods. Tranquebar, the base of the first Protestant mission in India, was established in 1706 by two German missionaries sent by the Danish King. Unlike the Jesuits, the Lutherans retained their European dress and liturgy, and concentrated on the study of Tamil to translate the Bible and other religious texts. The Germans, contemptuous of Jesuit conversion tactics, accused them of being more interested in the quantity than the quality of their converts, and stressed the need for thorough religious instruction in evangelical work. The newly arrived Lutherans at least in part defined their missionary role in opposition to that of the long-established Jesuits.

Translations of the Tranquebar letters appeared in England through the intervention of the chaplain to Prince George, Danish-born husband of Queen Anne. The English, despite their growing commercial involvement in India, had no mission of their own: the East India Company generally discouraged evangelism as potentially unpopular with the local inhabitants and detrimental to trade. The cause of the Danish mission was however promptly taken up by the Society for Promoting Christian Knowledge, which arranged for direct financial aid, religious literature, and later a printing press to be sent to Tranquebar. The SPCK's adoption of the Danish mission was formalized in 1726; when one of the missionaries moved from Danish-ruled Tranquebar to British-controlled Madras, the SPCK undertook to pay his salary, as it later did for other missionaries operating in British territories. The Tranquebar mission therefore consisted of Germans financed by both Denmark and England: a recently established, small enterprise with broad European support—a marked contrast to the large Jesuit mission, forced to defend itself against increasingly hostile European attacks.

Given the contrast between the state of the Lutheran and Jesuit missions and the evident antagonism between the two, it is inevitable that the two denominations should play out their doctrinal differences in the setting of India. But as Stephen Greenblatt has noted of Renaissance accounts of the New World, this goes beyond religious polemic: 'Catholics and Protestants tended to ask different questions, notice different things, fashion different images'.[5] I examine below the contrasting representations of evangelical activity offered by the two missions, focusing particularly on power relations between missionaries, Hindus, and Indian Christians. We can, however, identify a distinctive discourse created by both missions which differs notably from the secular discourses already discussed. The Hindu figures in these letters as reformable, susceptible to European persuasion and direction. The rhetoric of evangelism seeks to create a sense of European obligation towards benighted Hindus and Indian congregations, and to encourage financial support with the promise of a heavenly reward. The representation of European authority, responsibility and profit in missionary accounts feeds back into secular discourses by providing an important model for the later literature of colonial rule.

'Seasonable Supplies of Money'

The publication of missionary letters was dictated by financial need. In the process of generating funds, the missionary writers turn Indians into objects of European charity. The Jesuits make appeals on behalf of their destitute congregations, arguing that their poverty is a direct result of conversion. Although converts were permitted to observe their caste rules, they were rejected by the Hindu community, deprived of both caste status and a means of earning a living. The converts, suffering for their faith, are represented as deserving objects of European pity:

Nous esperons que les personnes pleines de zéle & de charité auront pitié de cette Chrestienté désolée; c'est dans ces occasions plus que jamais qu'il seroit necessaire que nous eussions de quoy tirer nos pauvres Néophytes de l'extréme misere où les a réduits leur constance à pratiquer L'Evangile que nous leur enseignons.[6]

(We hope that zealous and charitable people will take pity on this distressed Christianity; it is in these circumstances more than ever that we need to have the wherewithal to extricate our poor converts from the extreme poverty to which they have been reduced by their constancy in practising the Gospel that we teach them.)

The cause of the converts' poverty lies in their adherence to the Gospel 'that we teach them'. That 'we', although actually designating only the missionaries, seems to expand to embrace the 'zealous and charitable' readership. These letters work to establish a sense of communal European identity and responsibility. Subsequent appeals reinforce this concept of European duty:

A la vûë de ce que souffroient ces généreux Néophytes, helas! nous disions-nous, qu'il y a de personnes riches & charitables en Europe qui se feroient un devoir de soulager ces pauvres gens leurs freres en Jesus-Christ, s'ils estoient témoins comme nous de ce qu'ils endurent pour la défense de leur foy.[7]

(At the sight of the sufferings of these generous converts, 'Alas', we said to each other, 'there are rich and charitable Europeans who would make it their duty to help these poor people, their brothers in Jesus Christ, if they were witnesses like us to what they endure for the sake of their faith'.)

The idea of the Christian community, represented by the figure of brotherhood in Christ, reformulates the relationship between East and West. A similar sense of communal obligation and moral responsibility is exploited in a request for funds to rebuild a charitable home for widows and orphans destroyed by a fire in Delhi:

Que deviendront tant de jeunes veuves, & tant de jeunes enfans Chrétiens? A quoi ne sont-ils pas exposés? & qu'il est triste que notre pauvreté nous mettre hors d'état de leur procurer des secours, que je serois à portée de leur faire tenir?[8]

(What will become of so many young Christian widows and children? What will they not be exposed to? And is it not sad that our poverty makes it impossible for us to give them the help that I would like to extend to them?)

The answer to these rhetorical questions clearly lies in the purses of European readers. The homeless young widows and orphans—pathetic, vulnerable and susceptible to vice—flatter Europe's sense of financial and moral strength by their need for support. Both this and the previous brothers-in-Christ appeal operate indirectly: the first writer reports on missionary conversations, and the second simply throws out a volley of rhetorical questions. That such appeals can be indirect suggests that the exercise of charity has become part of the routine structure of relations between India and Europe.

The main incentive offered to a charitable contributor is a heavenly reward, but a secondary attraction could best be termed spiritual control: the benefactor directs the religious welfare of the Indian. Charity, often conceived of as a particularly feminine virtue, offers this form of power to female benefactors. A letter addressed to the Comtesse de Soudé maps out the extent of this charitable authority:

vostre pieté va chercher jusqu'aux extremitez du monde des Nations que la malheur de leur naissance a plongées dans l'Idolâtrie, & par le secours que vostre zele me procure, vous contribuez autant qu'il dépend de vous, à leur conversion & à leur salut. Vos largesses ne se bornent pas même à la vie présente, vous les portez au delà du tombeau, par les mesures que vous avez prises, afin que les effets de vostre charité subsistent encore, lorsqu'il aura plû à Dieu de vous retirer de ce monde.[9]

(your piety will seek out nations at the very ends of the world plunged into idolatry by the misfortune of their birth, and through the aid provided by your zeal, you contribute so much that their conversion and salvation depend on you.

have taken will carry on beyond the grave, so that the effects of your charity will
remain after it has pleased God to take you from this world.)

The lines of spiritual control radiate out from the European centre to the
Indian periphery. The missionary stresses the gratifying extent of the
countess's personal power over the Indians whose conversions she has
financed. But her influence stretches beyond the ends of this world, into
the next; as she buys Indian souls, she ensures a place in heaven for her
own.

Another benefactor, Madame de S. Hyacinthe, a nun from Toulouse,
is told that a number of Indian babies have been named in her honour:

> Il y en a même plusieurs qui m'ont prié de donner à leurs Enfans, lorsque je leur
> confére le Baptême, le nom du Saint, & de la Sainte que vous portez: ainsi on en
> voit qui s'appellent *Mouttou*, ce qui signifie Hyacinthe; d'autres se nomment
> *Mouttamel*, qui veut dire Marguerite. Par ce moyen-là, votre nom est connu &
> révéré jusques dans ces terres Barbares, & vos Saints Protecteurs y sont spécialement
> invoqués.[10]

(Some of them have even asked me to christen their children with your saints'
names; so there are those who are called *Mouttou*, which means Hyacinthe; and
others called *Mouttamel*, which is to say Margaret. By this means, your name is
known and revered as far afield as these barbarous lands and your patron saints
are specially invoked here.)

This naming process draws on the concept of the church as Christ's
family, with the perpetuation of names through the generations. It also
suggests a quasi-maternal role for the French nun. But the sign of affiliation has a proprietorial edge too: to give a name is a form of ownership.
These christenings, as Stephen Greenblatt would say, demonstrate 'the
appropriative power of naming'.[11] The long reach of the benefactor's
power is signalled by the translations of her names into barbarous tongues.
In her absence, the Indians pay the nun a kind of homage, remembering
her in their prayers:

> ils sont tous couverts de vos dons, car je partage avec eux les pieuses marques de
> votre libéralité, & il ne s'en trouve aucun parmi eux, qui portant au col les Croix,
> les Agnus, & les Médailles, dont vous m'avez envoyé une si grande quantité, ne
> se souvienne dans leurs prieres des largesses de leur généreuse Bienfaictrice.[12]

(They are all covered with your gifts because I share the pious signs of your
generosity with them, and among those who wear the many crosses, holy lambs
and medals which you sent me around their necks, there is not one who does not
remember in their prayers the liberality of their generous benefactress.)

The crosses and religious medals sent by Madame de S. Hyacinthe also mark the converts out as God's and her own. She has bought herself a mention in their prayers, a spiritual return on her investment in the mission.

Benefactors were also repaid with worldly recognition: the *Lettres édifiantes* reached a wide public. Most of the letters in the collections are addressed to other Jesuits, either in Europe or in different missions in India. Non-Jesuit correspondents, singled out for their generosity, would be placed among those distinguished by missionary endeavour. Of course, their inclusion might also help the Jesuit cause: powerful benefactors would be identified as the Society's allies. Besides receiving publicity, contributors could also buy the right to information about India. The missionaries answer queries about Indian life, directly addressing the concerns of individual benefactors. Thus the judge, Monsieur Cochet de Saint Vallier, learns about Indian law, and the Comtesse de Soudé is informed about Indian women.[13]

Benefactors—female as well as male—are thus offered the chance to exercise a degree of textual control. The letter to the Comtesse de Soudé concerns the position of Hindu women within marriage and signals an important shift in the representation of Indian women; away from the sensational, towards the domestic. The unusual subject matter suggests that the recipient—evidently a woman of status and financial power— exerts some influence over the nature of the representation. The writer, Père de Bourzes, criticizes the treatment of Indian women:

elles sont moins les compagnes que les esclaves de leurs maris. Le stile ordinaire est que le mari tutoye sa femme, & que la femme ne parle jamais à son mari ny de son mari qu'en termes les plus respectueux. Je ne sçay si c'est par respect ou par quelque autre raison que la femme ne peut jamais prononcer le nom de mari. Il faut qu'elle se serve en ces occasions de periphrases & de circonlocutions tout à fait risibles. On n'est point surpris que le mari batte sa femme & l'accable d'injures: si elle fait des fautes, ne faut-il pas la corriger, disent-ils? La femme n'est jamais admise à la table du mari; nous n'osons presque dire qu'en Europe les usages sont tout differens. . . . D'ailleurs la belle-mere est une rude maistresse: elle se décharge toujours sur sa belle-fille de tout le travail domestique, & quand elle donna ses ordres, c'est toujours d'une maniere dure & imperieuse.[14]

(They are less the companions than the slaves of their husbands. It is common practice for the husband to address his wife familiarly, and for the wife never to speak to or of her husband except in the most respectful terms. I do not know whether it is through respect or for some other reason that the wife can never pronounce the name of her husband. On these occasions she must use quite laughable round-about phrases and circumlocutions. No-one is surprised if the husband beats and swears at his wife: they say, if she makes mistakes, shouldn't she be corrected? The wife is never allowed to eat with her husband; we almost dare not say that European customs are quite different..... Moreover the mother-in-law is a hard mistress: she hands over all the domestic work to her daughter-in-law, and when she gives her orders, it is always in a harsh and imperious manner.)

Père de Bourzes displays an awareness of household politics which suggests the influence of the ongoing debate about the status of women in eighteenth-century Europe. The domestic focus and the writer's linguistic facility imply a familiarity with Hindu society that could best be termed proto-ethnographic, while the tone might be described as proto-feminist. The writer is cast in the role of participant-observer and writes with all the authority of cultural knowledge, producing one of the earliest descriptions of the Hindu wife's domestic subservience.

The variations in the tone and subject matter of the letters are not only determined by the individual recipients, but also by the sheer number of Jesuit writers. Letters from one missionary are occasionally grouped together, but more often they are scattered through the volumes, which are printed over the years, forming haphazard collections from Jesuits throughout the world. The multiplicity of authorial voices manages to convey a sense of work in progress, of a vital corporate enterprise ranging all over the world. The looseness of the structure seems to carry the implication that other contributors can join in, that new benefactors can have their questions answered and themselves contribute to the text. That the form of the *Lettres édifiantes* encourages financial participation from the readership is highlighted by the different format adopted for the second edition of 1780, which was to become a standard repository of knowledge about all the Jesuit missions in distant lands. The preface to the new edition, published seven years after the suppression of the Jesuits, explains that the letters have been rearranged into four parts dealing with separate geographical regions. With no further need to generate funds, and no prospect of future additions, the *Lettres édifiantes* have been transformed into a fixed reference work.

While the well-established Jesuit missions span the world, the newly arrived Danish mission, as yet without a congregation, has to generate a sense of European commitment to the conversion of the Hindus. Rather than convince Europeans of their obligation towards an already existing Christian community, the Lutherans must preach the duty of enlightening pagans. At the start of the mission's activities, the Lutherans create their own rhetoric of evangelism:

Truly, any one that is himself a true Member of Christ, must needs be melted into most tender Inclinations towards the poor deluded Pagans, by such endearing Marks of God's overflowing Goodness as he has had confer'd on him: And will feel a yearning of his Bowels for so many Millions of Souls remaining still under the Power of Satan, unto whom the Light of the Gracious Gospel hath not yet appear'd. Verily, whosoever brings a *Willing* Offering, towards the Release of these Captives, be it either by hearty *Prayer*, or by good *Advice*, or by outward *Supplies*, or by any other Means, tending to the Enlargement of the Church, will not lose his Reward in that Day, wherein even a Cup of *Cold Water* shall not be forgotten. Every Gift (whether Temporal or Spiritual) that is bestow'd on each Member, is given to *PROFIT* withal: that so the whole Body may be edify'd in Christ Jesus. 'Tis LOVE makes the Circulation.[15]

The muddled and excessive figurative language of this preface from the English translation of the first Tranquebar letters, the *Propagation of the Gospel in the East*, attempts to communicate a kind of compulsive charitable urge towards the conversion of the heathen. The reader is first enjoined to consider God's benevolence towards himself through a contrast with the plight of the pagans: their 'poor deluded' state helps to define his own happy condition. The resulting sense of indebtedness to God is supposed to provoke a strong desire—represented as physical compulsion by the biblical term 'yearning in his bowels'—to contribute to the pagans' conversion. In a sense, the heathen are to be internalized by the reader: they are to feature in the reader's prayers, thoughts and expenditure. Indians and Europeans are united in the figure of the all-encompassing body of Christ, where the life blood is made up of prayer, funds and love. But the circulation is also conceived in economic terms, where donations work as profitable investments. The rhetoric of fund-raising easily slips from the biblical to the financial.

The German missionaries set out the obligations of Europeans towards the Indians with pragmatic directness:

we find by experience, that for propagating the Gospel among the Heathens, next to the *GRACE* of *GOD* nothing is more expedient of any outward Help, than a *blameless Life, and seasonable supplies of Money, for establishing all manner of good Foundations*. We design to draw up a certain *Scheme of Proposals* about carrying on this Work, and to lay it before his Majesty the King of *Denmark*. It were to be wish'd, that all Protestant Princes in *Europe*, would join hand in hand together, for pushing on a Work tending to the Conversion of so many Millions of ignorant Souls . . .[16]

The task of supporting the mission is envisaged as a union of 'all Protestant Princes in Europe'; a powerful force to counter the unspoken opposition of Catholicism. The internationally backed project of evangelism is described in suitably impressive terms: 'a Work tending to the Conversion of so many Millions of ignorant Souls'; the mission is promoted as a

India on Europe's Conscience / 83

glorious endeavour that would add to the prestige of the monarchs involved. India is represented as a challenge to Protestantism, a thrilling test of religious strength.

Much of this excitement is generated because the mission is new. The letters trace the missionaries' progress, describe initial conversions in detail, and so draw the reader into the developing narrative. Correspondence is part of the missionary contract:

> Tis to Day just a Twelve Month, since you, dear Fathers and Brethren, first offered me that Pastoral Function, which I am now actually entred upon for the Service of the *Malabar*-Heathens; and having conversed with 'em these Three Months, and together with my Fellow-Labourer pretty near viewed the Condition they live in; I thought my self in Duty bound, to acquaint you as well as I can, with the *present State of this* Eastern *Nation*.[17]

The immediacy of this writing seeks to involve the reader and cultivate a sense of commitment to the mission. The reader is given an actual chance to participate financially with the inclusion at the back of the text of 'A Proposal for Printing the New-Testament in Portuguese; In order to be dispers'd among the Natives at Malabar, and other Parts of the East-Indies, and also for furnishing some other Helps to the Missionaries sent thither to Propagate the Gospel'. The SPCK in fact adopted this proposal and arranged for the printing of the Portuguese New Testament, as a later instalment of the *Propagation of the Gospel* reports. The readers' contributions form part of the developing narrative.

As the Tranquebar mission became more established, it supplemented the regular volumes of letters by publishing abridgements to reach a wider public. The preface to the 1745 French translation of the abridged letters clearly states its aim of reaching the popular European market. Towards the end of this shortened version, there is a description of the contributing readers. The public which the book was intended to reach is in a sense created by the text itself with a long roll-call of the countries in which benefactors live, an extract from a contributor's letter and a touching story of a poor man's donation. Presented as tangible proof of the public interest already aroused by the mission, the passage is designed to spur readers into emulation:

> On ne peut qu'être saisi d'admiration lorsqu'on lit la liste du grande nombre des bonnes ames d'Allemagne, d'Angleterre, de Dannemarck, de Suéde, de Livonie, de Russie, de Silésie, d'Italie, & du Levant, qui contribuoient pour les Payens nouvellement convertis au Christianisme. *La nudité & la faim des Néophites Malabares me perce le cœur,* disoit une Dame de distinction, en écrivant aux

Missionaires; *& je vous envoye un colier de perles de deux rangs, afin que l'argent que vous en retirerez soit appliqué à acheter les vêtemens pour les Indiens indigens & à soulager leur misére.* . . . Il y en avoit même, qui, touchés du triste état de quelques membres de l'établissement Evangélique, se privoient d'une partie de leur nécessaire pour les soulager dans leur indigence. Un garcon de métier, qui n'avoit que trente sols qu'il avoit épargnés du fruit de son travail & qu'il destinoit à s'acheter un habit, les donna avec plaisir, en apprenant par la relation des faits de la Mission Evangélique, qu'il y avoit dans les Indes des personnes plus pauvres que lui.[18]

(One cannot but be struck with admiration when one reads the list of the great number of good souls in Germany, England, Denmark, Sweden, Livonia, Russia, Silesia, Italy, and the Levant, who gave money to the Pagans who have been recently converted to Christianity. *The nudity and the hunger of the Malabar converts pierced my heart,* said one, a lady of distinction, writing to the missionaries; *and I am sending you a two-string pearl necklace, so that the money which you get for it can be used to buy clothes for destitute Indians and relieve their misery.* . . . There were even those who, touched by the sad state of some members of the Evangelical establishment, went without a part of their basic necessities to relieve them in their indigence. A young workman who only had thirty shillings saved from the fruits of his labour which he intended to spend on a suit of clothes for himself, gave them with pleasure on learning through the account of the works of the Evangelical Mission that there were people in India poorer than he was.)

Pity for the converts' state overrules the distinctions of nation, class and gender. For Protestants in all the countries listed, the object of charity is located in India. The narratives of the lady's string of pearls and the workman's renounced suit of clothes represent the same charitable impulse at opposed ends of the social scale. However it is significant that the workman's self-denying contribution is valued more highly than that of the wealthy woman. This is a reiteration—albeit with a change of gender—of Christ's teaching that the widow's mite is worth more than the largesse of the rich. As is often the case, the mission's fund-raising propaganda acquires biblical resonances. This appropriation of biblical authority strengthens the mission's aim of placing European support for the conversion of Indians within the framework of accepted Christian duty.

The charity of both contributors is aroused by the destitution of the converts. The strength of the emotive appeal is evident and the concept of the Indian as an object of pity is central to the mission's fund-raising strategies. This is equally true of the *Lettres édifiantes,* as we have already seen. Between them, the two missons create an image of the Indian as a figure of pathos: an antecedent of the contemporary Western reaction to the so-called Third World. Indeed, the *Lettres édifiantes* contain some of the earliest and most extensive accounts of the suffering caused by an Indian drought and in particular, two graphic and painful descriptions of famine.

One of these accounts is contained in Père Saignes' letter to Madame de S. Hyacinthe which also reports the naming of babies in her honour. At times of famine, the missionaries write, desperate Hindu parents are prepared to sell their children to the missionaries, who first baptise and then try to raise them; all this requires money, as a letter written in 1753 explains:

> Quand leurs parens ne peuvent plus les nourrir, ou que ces enfans se trouvent dans un danger de mort, les mères, pour s'en débarrasser, viennent nous les vendre. Aussi-tôt nous les baptisons & nous leur donnons une nourrice. . . . Il seroit à souhaiter que les aumônes qu'on nous fait ici & celles qui nous viennent de France fussent plus abondantes; nous pourrions acheter un plus grand nombre d'enfans. . . .[19]

> (When their parents can no longer feed them, or when these children are in danger of dying, the mothers, to dispose of them, come to sell them to us. We immediately baptise them and give them a nurse. . . . is to be hoped that the alms given to us here and those which come to us from France will be more plentiful; we will then be able to buy a larger number of babies . . .)

The fund-raising rhetoric, which turns Indian babies into commodities, has as much to do with saving souls as saving lives. Père Saignes concludes his account of the drought with a reflection on the spiritual benefits of such baptisms *in extremis*:

> Au milieu de tant de malheurs, nous n'avons eu qu'une seule consolation, c'est de donner le saint Baptême à une infinité d'enfans de parens Infidéles. Le jour de Saint Hyacinthe qui étoit votre Fête, je donnai votre nom à un enfant qui s'envola au Ciel le même jour, & qui prie maintenant pour vous.[20]

> (In the midst of so much adversity, we have only one consolation, that is to give the holy rite of baptism to an infinite number of children of heathen parents. On Saint Hyacinthe's day which was your feast day, I gave your name to a child who flew up to heaven the same day, and who prays for you now.)

Here we can see that the practice of proprietorial naming is connected with the pathetic image of the suffering Indian. Funding and pathos go hand in hand: all the main descriptions of famine in the *Lettres édifiantes* are contained in letters written to benefactors.[21]

Père Saignes' account of the drought explores these relations between affliction and charity:

Pendant ces deux anneés-là il n'est pas tombé une seule goutte de pluye; les Puits, les Etangs, plusieurs Rivieres même ont été à sec: le ris, & tous les autres grains ont été brûlés dans les campagnes, & rien n'étoit plus commun parmi ce pauvre Peuple, que de passer un & deux jours sans rien manger. Des Familles entieres abandonnant leur demeure ordinaire, alloient dans les bois pour se nourrir, comme les animaux, de fruits sauvages, de feuilles d'arbres, d'herbes, & de racines. Ceux qui avoient des enfans, les vendoient pour une mesure de ris; d'autres qui ne trouvoient point à les vendre, les voyant mourir cruellement de faim, les empoisonnoient pour abréger leurs souffrances. Un Pere de Famille vint me trouver un jour, 'nous mourons de faim', me dit-il; 'ou donnez-nous dequoi manger, ou je vais empoisonner ma femme, mes cinq enfans, & ensuite je m'empoisonnerai moi-même'. Vous jugez bien que dans une occasion pareille, on sacrifie jusqu'à ses propres besoins.[22]

(During these two years, not a single drop of rain fell; the wells, the ponds, even several rivers ran dry; rice, and all the other cereals were scorched in the fields, and nothing was more common among this poor people than to pass one or two days without eating anything. Whole families left their normal homes, and went into the woods to feed themselves like animals on wild fruit, the leaves of trees, grasses and roots. Those who had children sold them for a measure of rice, others who could not manage to sell them, watching them cruelly starve to death, poisoned them to cut short their suffering. A father of a family came to find me one day, 'we are starving to death', he said to me; 'give us something to eat, or I will poison my family, my five children, and then I'll poison myself'. You appreciate that in such a situation, one gives away even the basic necessities of life.)

The report begins with a general description of how the drought upends the normal structures of life: rivers run dry, people behave like animals and parents kill their children. The account then focuses on a specific encounter, the father's desperate attempt to gain alms. The famine victim is the ultimate suppliant: he makes the missionary directly responsible for his own life and that of his family, compelling the Jesuit to help him. In this most extreme of examples, where the European has the power of life and death over the Indian, we can clearly see how the act of charity involves the exercise of authority.

Europe's domination of India through charity does not, however, imply Western moral superiority. Rather, Indian conduct is proposed as an example to the West: in a year of famine, a convert donates all his money to the poor, trusting in God for his own survival.[23] This selfless action offers a complete contrast to those begging techniques that we have just considered: the starving man threatens suicide to help himself, whereas the convert chances death to help others. The Indian in this case is less the dependent object of Western pity, more the dazzling embodiment of Christian virtue. The charitable impulse, relocated in the East, surpasses the Western specimen. Père Bouchet comments that such an example is unlikely to find many imitators in Europe.[24] The Indian church takes the moral lead, providing examples for the European church to copy. The European 'mother' church is relegated to pupil status. This sense of the two churches' role reversal is reinforced by a number of comparisons which liken Indian converts to saints and members of the early church. Père Martin compares a convert's ascetic, penitential life to that of St Jerome, one of the four Latin fathers of the church.[25] The convert's imitation of St Jerome is quite unknowing; with divine guidance, he fixes on the same penance. The Indian example is appropriated to the model of European church history.

Early-church comparisons can be found throughout the *Lettres édifiantes*. Imprisoned by a Muslim governor, Père Bouchet and a group of converts are visited by a female catechumen who, despite difficulties and insults, regularly brings them alms. She reminds Père Bouchet of earlier supporters of the church:

Toutes les fois qu'elle entroit dans la prison, sa presence me rappelloit le souvenir de ces saintes Dames Romaines, qui dans les premiers Siecles de l'Eglise, prenoient soin des Chrestiens prisonniers pour JESUS-CHRIST.[26]

(Every time that she entered the prison, her presence reminded me of those holy Roman lades who in the first centuries of the Church cared for the Christians imprisoned for JESUS CHRIST.)

If the hardship suffered by Christians in India recalls the situation of the early church, then the opposition of Muslim authority parallels Roman persecution. The Jesuits themselves are special targets for oppression. We note that Père Bouchet is included among the 'prisoners for JESUS CHRIST', implying that the missionary shares the early-church piety of the Indian converts.

Jesuits are often associated with concepts of saintly virtue. Writing to a would-be missionary, Père Bouchet likens the Jesuits' suffering to that experienced by St Paul.[27] He refers to a passage in Corinthians II, in which St Paul enumerates the dangers faced by missionaries:

in journeyings often, in perils of waters, in perils of robbers, in perils by mine own countrymen, in perils by the heathen, in perils in the city, in perils in the wilderness, in perils in the sea, in perils among false brethren; in weariness and painfulness, in watchings often, in hunger and thirst, in fastings often, in cold and nakedness.[28]

By citing Pauline authority, Père Bouchet claims a quasi-biblical status for the narratives of dangerous Jesuit exploits in the *Lettres édifiantes*.[29]

88 / India Inscribed

The missionaries become heroic saints, striving against the odds to convert the pagans. India is turned into an arena for religious adventure, the setting for displays of virtue and heroism. By situating the Indian church in the Christian past, the writers imply that the future of the church in India will match the historic progress of the church in Europe: the eventual triumph of Christianity is anticipated.

Protestant writers also employ the figure of the early church, but more often in relation to the Indian Christians of St Thomas. The community of St Thomas Christians in South India claims to have been converted by the apostle Thomas, at the very start of the Christian era. Some modern scholars concede this as a possibility, others suggest that they were converted by East Syrian traders from the area around the Persian Gulf, at some time between the fourth and sixth centuries.[30] The church was in any case well established by the time that the Portuguese arrived in India. The Catholics, disapproving of the St Thomas Christians' allegiance to the Patriarch of Babylon, brought them under the rule of Rome at the Synod of Diamper in 1599. This act is regarded by eighteenth-century Protestant writers as a terrible violation of the purity of St Thomas Christianity. For Protestants, the St Thomas Christians represent the survival of the original, uncorrupted faith of the early church.[31] The antiquity of the St Thomas Christians, their independence from Rome, and certain doctrinal similarities perceived by Protestants between the Indian faith and their own, are paraded as a kind of vindication of Protestantism:

lorsque les Portugais arrivèrent dans les Indes Orientales environ l'an 1500. pour y faire un établissement, il y avoit une Eglise très ancienne de Chrétiens, dont presque tous les dogmes conviennent avec ceux de la Religion Reformée. Ces Chrétiens Orientaux, séparés depuis le cinquiéme siécle de toutes les autres Communions, étant sous l'obéissance d'un Patriarche indépendant de l'Empire Romain, & n'ayant aucun commerce avec l'Eglise Romaine, admettent les mêmes Sacremens que nous, nient formellement la Transsubstantiation & la Présence réelle, ont en horreur le culte des Images, & presque toutes les Traditions Romaines qui sont rejettées par les Protestans.[32]

(when the Portuguese arrived in the East Indies around the year 1500 to establish a colony there, they found a very ancient Christian church, and most of its dogmas agreed with those of the Reformed Religion. These Eastern Christians, separated since the fifth century from all the other communions, owing obedience to a Patriarch independent from the Roman Empire, without contact with the Roman church, recognize the same sacraments as us, formally deny transubstantiation and the actual presence, detest the cult of images, and almost all the Roman traditions which are rejected by the Protestants.)

The St Thomas Christians provide Protestantism with a type of doctrinal pedigree.

In Mathurin Veyssière de la Croze's *Histoire du Christianisme des Indes*, Protestantism's Indian cousins shine with every possible virtue and talent. De la Croze praises the St Thomas Christians for their industriousness, intelligence, eloquence, courtesy, honesty, chastity, sobriety, military prowess, agility and good health.[33] The subjection of these paragons to the rule of the Portuguese, the most corrupt and degenerate race in the world, outrages de la Croze:

N'étoit-ce pas choquer directement les Notions les plus communes de la Raison, que de vouloir, sous prétexte de Religion, soumettre des Gens tels que les Chrêtiens Malabares, à des hommes aussi pervers & corrompus, qui l'étoient ces Conquérans des Indes, qui auroient eu besoin que les Chrêtiens des Indes allassent chez eux prêcher par leur exemple les bonnes mœurs & la pratique de l'Evangile?[34]

(Does it not directly offend the most common notions of reason to subordinate such a people as the Malabar Christians, in the name of Religion, to men as depraved and corrupt as these conquerors of the Indies who themselves would have needed the Indian Christians to go among them to preach good morals and the practice of the gospel through their example?)

The vehemence of this condemnation of Portuguese Catholic rule derives from the identification of St Thomas Christians with Protestants. But this attack is also among the earliest critiques of colonial rule in India. De la Croze questions the logic of corrupt Portuguese authority over good Indians; religion is merely a pretext for European domination, it would be more appropriate for the Indian subjects to give religious instruction to their European rulers. De la Croze is suggesting a role reversal similar to Père Bouchet's proposal that the conduct of Indian converts should set a moral example for the European church. But there is an important difference: while the Jesuit champions a flourishing, transplanted version of European doctrine, de la Croze claims the supremacy of a long-established Indian faith, albeit one that he perceives entirely in European terms. This Indian Christianity, de la Croze argues, should be the focus of European interest and research.[35] The St Thomas Christians, too long subjected to Catholic interference, deserve Protestant support. De la Croix fosters a sense of European obligation towards the Indian Christians by playing on anti-Catholic sentiment and the concept of the brotherhood of Christ. The St Thomas Christians are to be the object of serious study, perhaps even incorporated in the Protestant tradition.

As for the Jesuits, they regard St Thomas Christians as Nestorian heretics, renegades easily converted to Islam.[36] Claude Marie Guyon, Jesuit author of *A New History of the East-Indies, Ancient and Modern*, launches a bitter counter-attack against de la Croze's arguments and person:

> At the Hague in 1724, there appeared a book entitled, *The Christianity of the Indies*, the errors and partiality have disgusted all reasonable men. The author is an apostate monk, by the name Viessiere la Broze [sic], formerly benedictine of Corbia, who has merited by his zeal and learning to be made library-keeper and antiquarian to the King of Prussia. From the title of his work, one should imagine to find therein the rise, progress, and establishment of the christian religion in the Indies: but nothing was more remote from the author's intention. His sole design . . . has been to revenge the cause of Nestorius, to canonize his followers, to justify his blasphemies, to write against the third general council of Ephesus, to undertake the defence of mahometanism, to let loose against the Roman church that fury which the protestants now blush for in the first reformed . . . to decry the synod of Diamper . . . and lastly to pour out all the bitterness and acrimony of his zeal against a society which he hated, for other reasons, best known to himself.[37]

While much of Guyon's anger is directed at his apostate rival, this passage of invective demonstrates the pitch of intensity that religious polemic on India can reach. As Jesuits and Lutherans fight for public support, one representation is pitted against another. India has become a battleground for religious controversy.

Missionary Methods

Much of the conflict is centred on the Jesuits. If Jesuit missionary techniques aroused uneasiness among other Catholics, they embodied all the worst excesses of the Roman Church for Protestants. Yet the Jesuit letters, as the main source of information on distant lands, were read by non-Catholics, albeit with caution and considerable suspicion. Lockman, the Protestant translator of an English edition, *Travels of the Jesuits* of 1743, prefaces the text with two opposed images of the Jesuits: the Jesuits' own angelic self-projection, and their detractors' diabolic representation:

> Our Jesuits may be considered in two very different Lights. In the one they appear as celestial Ministers, in the other as infernal Spirits. Can we possibly figure to ourselves a more amiable Being, than a Man, who, after enriching his Mind with the noblest Treasures of Knowledge, voluntarily quits his Friends, his Relations, and his native Country; hazards himself to all the Perils of the Sea; and afterwards goes ashore, tho' scarce provided with any Necessaries, among a barbarous

People, with whose Language he is utterly unaquainted; there roves, in their wildest Solitudes, in danger, every Moment, of falling down Precipices, or into deep Chasms of the Earth; of being murthered by wild Beasts or by the Natives; and all this solely from a Desire of polishing their Minds, of assisting their corporeal Part, and of saving their Souls? Now such they are represented by themselves and their Adherents.

On the other Hand, if we reflect on a Man whose only Design, in acquiring Learning, is to impose upon his Fellow-creatures; who, under the Cloak of Religion, and to serve a Sett of detestable Politicians, undertakes long Voyages; visits foreign Regions, and there ingratiates himself with the several Natives of them, in order to seize upon their Riches; and make them Slaves in their own Country, where, amid their virtuous Ignorance, they enjoyed undisturbed Felicity: Can Imagination frame a more horrid Creature than this? Such is the Character their Antagonists give of them. This double view puts me in mind of a Picture I have seen representing an Angel, when, turning up the Bottom of it, a cloven Foot appears.[38]

The Jesuit as heroic, self-denying saint confronts the manipulative agent of European exploitation. Both images belong to the realm of the imaginary: 'Can we possibly figure to ourselves a more amiable Being . . . ?' and 'Can Imagination frame a more horrid Creature than this?'. The hyperbolic style and ever-extended syntax of each catalogue suggest that the editor is aware of both parties' consciously opposed techniques of representation. In response, he offers a 'double view', an ambiguous picture of an Angel with a cloven foot.

The editor's own view is a modified version of the diabolic image: a translation scattered with 'cloven' footnotes. Consider, for example, an annotated letter about the Jesuit reclamation of a church that had been abandoned and used as a temple:

'T was a Spectacle very glorious to our Religion, and the same Time worthy of Compassion, to see the needless Pains, which the poor Idol-Priest in question took, whilst he was removing his Gods. The *Christians* were urgent with him to quit the Place; and, to make the greater Dispatch, they themselves took the Idols, and set them upon the Ground with no great Ceremony. By this Means several were broke, on which Occasion he himself would gather up the scatter'd Fragments; weeping at the same Time bitterly, but not daring to complain, since he only was forc'd out of a Place which did not belong to, and had been usurp'd by him.*

*Some Persons would say, what Business had the Jesuit to leave his Native Country, and sail to another so many thousand Miles distant from it, there to disturb the Natives in their Possessions? 'Tis whimsical enough to hear our Traveller describing the Anxiety of this *Heathen*-Priest, whilst he was carrying away his Idols; and his Vexation at seeing them broke to Pieces; and by whom?

By a Sett of People who were going to put other Idols in their Place. The Jesuit was no less an idolatrous Priest than the *Heathen*; and therefore his Behaviour on this Occasion was altogether barbarous and *Anti-Christian*; so far was this from being *a Spectacle so very glorious to the Christian Religion*, as he is pleased to term it.[39]

Lockman entirely rejects the Jesuit representation of the incident. He shows no regard for the authority of his original, and quite abandons the customarily self-effacing tone of the translator. His own voice predominates: the footnote subverts the text and undermines the whole concept of Jesuit evangelism.

Lockman likens Catholicism to pagan idolatry to discredit the mission. This is a common Protestant strategy, as Wilhelm Halbfass has pointed out; similar analogies can be found throughout the literature on India.[40] Lutheran writers represent the activities of their mission in terms of religious conflict as much with the Catholics as the Hindus. In the prefatory verse to the 1745 abridgement of the Tranquebar letters, the translator describes the joint battle against Papist and heathen waged by Ziegenbalg, one of the pioneer missionaries:

> ... animé du zéle qui l'entraine,
> Il combat les erreurs de l'Eglise Romaine;
> Il déclare la guerre au Culte des faux Dieux,
> Et montre au naturel ce qu'il a d'odieux.[41]

> (... animated by the zeal which carries him along,
> He fights the errors of the Roman Church;
> He declares war on the cult of false gods,
> And reveals all that is hateful in its true light.)

Rattled along by the doggerel rhythm, the reader barely pauses for breath between Ziegenbalg's fight with the Roman church and his war against the cult of false gods. The Catholic and heathen Other are almost conflated; both are in need of evangelical enlightenment, as we read a few pages on:

les *Missionaires* Catholiques Romaines, qui eux-mêmes avoient besoin d'être éclairés par la lumiére de la foi Evangélique, & purifiés d'une infinité d'erreurs aussi grossières, que celles qu'on voit régner dans la Religion Payenne. Néanmoins, leur exemple a fait naître l'émulation.[42]

(the Roman Catholic missionaries, who themselves needed to be enlightened by the evangelical faith, and purified of an infinite number of errors as gross as those which prevail in the pagan religion. Nevertheless, their example gave rise to emulation.)

The last sentence turns Lutheran contempt for the Jesuits into ambivalence. This fine balance perhaps best accounts for the Lutheran preoccupation with their Jesuit rivals. The Lutherans consolidate their own role by defining it against that of the Jesuit mission; it is necessary for them to condemn Jesuit practice in order to justify their own.

The Jesuits vindicate their project only with reference to God. Their accounts are full of reported miracles. Direct evidence of God's sanction is furnished by missionary immunity from attack by snakes and wild beasts:

Il faut dire pour la gloire de Dieu, que, par rapport aux serpens, il semble qu'il y ait sur les Missionaires une Providence particuliere. En effet il est inoui qu'aucun d'eux eu ait jamais été mordu . . . Je ne puis omettre encore un trait favorable de la Protection céleste. Nous voyagions sur les dix heures du soir, & nous étions occupés . . . à reciter le chapelet; lorsqu'un tigre de la grande espece parut au milieu du chemin, & si près de moi qu'avec mon bâton j'aurois pu l'atteindre. Quatre Chrétiens qui m'accompagnoient, éffrayés à la vue du danger, s'écrierent, *sancta, Maria*. Alors le terrible animal s'écarta un peu du chemin, & marqua pour ainsi dire, par sa posture & par ses grincemens de dents le regret qu'il avoit de laisser échapper une si belle proie.[43]

(It should be said for the glory of God, that it seems that a special providence operated over the missionaries with regard to snakes. Indeed it is incredible that none of them was ever bitten. . . . I cannot omit another favourable sign of heavenly protection. We were travelling at about ten at night and we were busy telling our beads; when a large tiger appeared in the middle of the path, and so close to me that I could have touched it with my staff. The four Christians who were accompanying me, alarmed at the sight of danger, cried out *sancta Maria*. Then the frightful animal moved back a little from the path, and by its attitude and gnashing of its teeth showed, so to speak, the regret it felt at letting such prime prey escape.)

In the first chapter we saw Europeans regard dangerous animals as embodiments of the threatening strangeness of India; now those wild beasts are rendered impotent: God will not allow the terrors of an alien land to disrupt the work of his mission. The description of the raging tiger's paralysis vividly testifies to the Virgin's power. Accounts of such miracles both vindicate the Jesuits and demonstrate the reality of divine and saintly intervention. As Sylvia Murr points out, the missionary writers intend their letters to reinvigorate their readers' faith at a time when Catholicism was coming increasingly under attack from libertines, atheists, sceptics and, above all, from the Philosophes.[44]

Some of the Jesuit letters prose direct challenges to their critics' lack of faith. Such is the case with Père Bouchet, who writes with great conviction, and at considerable length, to prove the existence of demons in India. These devils possess pagan priests when they deliver oracles; the accuracy of the predictions and the terrible contortions of the priests' bodies indicate genuine diabolic possession. The oracles fall silent when a Christian appears, and Hindus themselves acknowledge that only conversion to Christianity will exorcize the demons.[45] Père Bouchet argues that even European freethinkers would be incapable of explaining such phenomena.[46] Such tangible proof of satanic power may no longer exist in Europe—its absence spawns disbelief—but India renews the intensity of religious experience. Bouchet, in his discussion of exorcism, employs the familiar early-church comparison to convey this revitalization of faith:

> N'est-il pas bien consolant... de voir renouveller sous nos yeux non-seulement la ferveur, mais encore les miracles de la primitive Eglise?[47]

(Is it not truly consoling to see renewed before our eyes not only the fervour, but also the miracles of the primitive Church?)

India restores a sense of the miraculous to European faith. Hinduism, as a manifest work of Satan, provides Christianity with devils to destroy: an element lacking in eighteenth-century Europe with the decline in witchcraft prosecution. The devil is defeated through conversion. Proof of God's victory is provided by the accounts of multiple baptisms that regularly appear in the *Lettres édifiantes*. In one day, Père Bouchet baptises five hundred converts and has to have his exhausted arms supported to complete the task.[48] Such scenes, where a single missionary saves huge numbers of pagan souls from damnation, emphasize the thrilling drama of conversion. They present the reader with an exciting image of heroic enterprise and a flattering representation of Western influence over Indians.

The *Lettres édifiantes* invariably portray Jesuits in positions of authority over Indians. Accounts of religious debates with brahmans generally show the missionary in perfect control, manipulating and outwitting the gurus; the end—the Hindus' ignominious defeat—is never in doubt. On one occasion Père Bouchet reports that an argument based on Cartesian principles failed to make any impression but, he reassures his correspondent, he knows many arguments that brahmans find unanswerable.[49] Père Calmette identifies this as an invaluable missionary tactic:

> une des parties les plus essentielles au progrez de la Foi, est la gentilité décreditée, réduite au silence dans la dispute, forcée en mille occasions de convenir de son erreur...[50]

(One of the most essential elements for the progress of the Faith is the discrediting of paganism, reduced to silence in debate, forced on a thousand occasions to admit its error . . .)

The Jesuit demands that the Hindu acknowledge the supremacy of Christian logic. Refusing to distinguish between individuals, Père Bouchet assumes that all brahmans are equally vulnerable: in a letter, he outlines a number of tried and tested arguments guaranteed to reduce any Hindu to silence.[51] Most of these examples begin with premises drawn from Hinduism, then step by step the opponent is drawn into self-contradiction or a logical dead end. One such argument runs as follows: the missionary asks if mankind was created by Brahma, the Hindus say yes. Were all the first men created equal? No, say the unsuspecting Hindus, they were of varying rank and condition. But, rejoins the missionary, these new men had neither sinned nor been virtuous in a previous life, so how can their inequality be explained? If the sin or virtue of an earlier existence cannot account for mankind's original condition, why should it do so now? The Hindus are lost for an answer, they want to deny everything and claim instead, in direct contradiction to Hindu doctrine, that the world had no beginning. Thus, Père Bouchet confidently predicts, will all Hindus be routed.[52] Once the Hindu is reduced to silence, it becomes the missionary's duty to supply him with the correct answers. After humiliation comes enlightenment. This, according to Père Bouchet, is the set course for all such encounters. With a pre-scripted dialogue to guide them, the Jesuits remain in command.

On one occasion, Père Bouchet behaves like a more imaginative teacher. Staying in a Buddhist monastery in Siam, he tries to convince the head monk of the errors of the doctrine of transmigration:

je lui dis que toutes les fois qu'il buvoit de l'eau du *Menan*, il commettoit plusieurs meutres: il se mit à rire de ma proposition; mais il fut tout-à-fait déconcerté, lorsqu'ayant mis un peu d'eau dans un de ces beaux microscopes que nous avions apportez d'Europe, je lui fis voir plusieurs animaux, qui estoient dans l'eau même dont il venoit de boire.[53]

(I told him that every time that he drank the water of the *Menan*, he committed several murders; he began to laugh at my assertion; but he was utterly disconcerted when, having placed a little water in one of those beautiful microscopes which we had brought from Europe, I made him see several animals which were in the very water that he was about to drink.)

Père Bouchet is revealing the truth about the natural as well as the spiritual world; the Jesuits harness science in the service of conversion. One missionary writes that a globe and world map were presented to an Indian prince to gain permission to build a church; and Père Calmette, recording the occasion that Raja Jai Singh invited Jesuits into his kingdom to teach Western astronomy, remarks that the sciences could be God's principal instrument to enlighten the heathen.[54] The missionaries act as the disseminators of Western techniques of viewing and comprehending nature, the earth and the heavens, working towards the imposition of a standardized, modernized world picture.

The Jesuit image of the missionary as a powerful figure of authority is modified by the representations of the Lutherans at Tranquebar. The Lutheran accounts do not feature marathon baptisms; indeed, this is one of the Jesuit practices that the Germans attack. The Lutheran attitude to conversion of course derives from Protestant belief in the importance of individual rationality, whereas the mass baptisms of the Jesuits reflect Catholic emphasis on the ceremonial aspect of conversion. The Germans dismiss the claims of multiple conversion made in the *Lettres édifiantes*: Catholic 'converts' lack instruction even in the fundamentals of Christianity, and numbers are the Jesuits' only concern.[55] The Lutherans, by contrast, lay the emphasis on thorough religious instruction:

> [Catholic] Proselytes are ignorant of Christianity; knowing little more than *Ave Maria, Pater-noster*, and how to cross themselves on all Occasions. But our Protestant Missionaries know of no other Method of Converting the Heathens, but that of the Apostles themselves, *viz* Persuasions and convincing Reasons, setting forth the Corruptions of Human Nature, and the Necessity of a Mediator . . .[56]

This assertion of evangelical integrity comes from the preface of a work produced by the Tranquebar mission called *Thirty four Conferences between the Danish Missionaries and the Malabarian Bramans (or Heathen Priests) in the East Indies, Concerning the Truth of the Christian Religion: Together with some Letters written by the Heathens to the said Missionaries*. The title itself indicates the change in the rhetoric of conversion. The Lutherans represent themselves as talking with, rather than at, the Hindus. As Tzvetan Todorov has observed

> c'est en parlant à l'autre (non en lui donnant des ordres mais en engageant un dialogue avec lui) que je lui reconnais, seulement, une qualité de *sujet*, comparable à celui que je suis moi-même.[57]

(It is only in talking to the Other (not in giving him orders but in engaging him in dialogue) that I recognize in him a subjectivity comparable to my own.)

The Lutherans concede the Hindus' individuality, state their objections to Christianity, and even allow them space in print to express their own religious convictions. Instead of presenting standard arguments to humiliate the Hindu, the Lutherans record particular discussions, conducted with a certain decorum, which do not necessarily end with the missionary's triumph. The first Conference, for instance, opens:

Upon the Sixth of March, 1707, I *Batholomew Ziegenbalgen* was visited by a Grave and Learned *Braman:* And asking him, what he propos'd to himself by his Friendly Visit, he reply'd, That he desir'd to confer with me amicably about the great Things and Matters of Religion.

As the conversation finishes, the brahman concludes:

I cannot blame any Part of all that you have said; but still I am of the same Opinion, that if we lead Lives morally inoffensive, and strictly vertuous, we have no need of the Christian Religion, to make our Persons or Actions more acceptable to God. I don't comprehend how Baptism and Faith can influence my Actions, or procure me the Forgiveness of Sins.[58]

Ziegenbalg presents his account as an authentic historical record: he dates the encounter and names himself, as though asserting the truth of his evidence. He produces a text which draws attention to the seriousness of its intent. Ziegenbalg represents himself as treating the brahman with considerable respect: he welcomes him politely and the 'Grave and Learned' Indian responds in kind. When he leaves, the brahman articulates his reservations clearly and with a certain dignity. His intentions are good, he simply lacks faith. Ziegenbalg's parting advice is that this want can be supplied through prayer. Thus the enlightenment of the heathen is the result of their direct communion with God, not, as in the Jesuit account, the only possible response to the missionary's overwhelming argument.

The *Thirty four Conferences* include a section entitled 'Letters from the Heathens to the Missionaries'. For the first time, European readers are presented with apparently unmediated Indian testimony. The letters offer a Hindu response to Christian doctrine. One correspondent praises the 'Law of the Christians' as 'holy, just and good', but objects to 'your eating of Cow's Flesh, spitting in your Houses, and some other daily Nastinesses committed by you'. Annexed to these acts of uncleanliness is the sacrament of the eucharist, an insurmountable obstacle to Hindu conversion: 'your giving out that you eat the Body of Christ, and drink his Blood in the Sacrament; which I humbly conceive, none of us will ever be able to comprehend'.[59] This Hindu version of the eucharist renders it distastefully literal, evidence of Christian defilement stronger even than 'daily Nastinesses'. The familiar symbol, refracted through the Indian account, becomes alarmingly Catholic (actual transubstantiation), not to say cannibalistic. While the letter provides evidence of Hindu misconception, it also offers an unsettling moment of self-estrangement.

The *Thirty four Conferences* provide a number of glimpses of this Other perspective. In one debate, the brahmans turn the missionaries' arguments back on themselves. They counter the Lutheran claim that Hindu faith is unreasonable and cannot be demonstrated, with the assertion that there are many elements in Christianity 'that are not capable of a Demonstration; but are to be received by Faith', which itself echoes the Lutheran doctrine of Justification by Faith Alone. However, the illustration which the Brahmans provide is less familiar: 'For does it not seem the Height of Unreasonableness to suppose him to be the Saviour of the World, who was of a mean Parentage, had but as mean an Education, persecuted by his Country-men, and at last was hang'd by publick Authority upon an infamous Cross?'[60] While this version of Christ's life may furnish proof of brahmanical preoccupation with caste, there is an understandable worldly logic at work in the rejection of the authority of a social outcast. There is nothing unreasonable about the brahmans themselves; their religion is another matter.

'IDOLATROUS WORSHIP'

Jesuits and Lutherans share the same basic assumptions about Hinduism: that an early belief in a supreme God was obscured by a mass of deceptive, idolatrous fictions. Interestingly, both Jesuits and Protestants identify the source of this idolatry as poetry. The readers of the *Lettres édifiantes* learn that

> les Poëtes du Païs ont par leurs fictions effacé peu à peu de l'esprit de ces Peuples les traits de la Divinité. La pluspart des livres Indiens sont des ouvrages de pöesie, pour lesquels ils sont fort passionnez, & c'est de là sans doute que leur Idolâtrie tire son origine.[61]

(the poets of the country have through their fictions effaced little by little the traces of divinity from the spirit of these peoples. Most Indian books are poetic works, for which they have a great passion, and it is from these without doubt that their idolatry originates.)

While Ziegenbalg, in his discussion with the brahman, attributes the Hindus' delusions to the compelling power of verse:

I am all Amazement, when I see your Blindness in not discerning Spiritual Things; as if you had sworn Eternal Allegiance to the Dictates and Poetical Fictions of Lying Bards; who riding upon the Ridges of Metaphors and Allegories, have rhimed you into the Belief of lying incomprehensible Perplexities.[62]

The sense of the purely literary nature of Hindu belief is reinforced by the heightened style employed by Jenkin Philipps, Ziegenbalg's translator. He makes use of assonance and alliteration—'riding', 'Ridges', 'rhimed'—and chooses a metaphor to enact as well as describe the poets' figurative practice: 'riding upon the Ridges of Metaphors'. Once Hinduism has been represented as a poetic construct, the missionaries can treat the religion like a piece of literature. The Jesuits regard Hindu teaching as a confused allegory of Judeo-Christian belief, while the Lutherans accord it the status of classical mythology.

The Jesuits follow the long-established European interpretation of Hinduism which emphasized supposed correspondences between Hindu and Judeo-Christian belief. These similarities were regarded as evidence that Judaism was the world's oldest religion. They proved the biblical account of the original unity of mankind: before Babel, everyone worshipped the same God; after Babel, with the scattering of the human race, only the Jews retained the perfect faith, other nations' religions were debased, half-forgotten versions. Thus Hindu belief in a supreme God, although obscured by later corruptions, originally derived from Judaism.[63] Père Bouchet argues for more extensive correspondences between the religions, claiming that Jewish trading contact and the Indian voyage of St Thomas had influenced Hinduism. For Père Bouchet, Hindu teaching is a complex, confused allegory in which Jewish and Christian elements appear under different names and guises. Among others, he deciphers Hindu stories of the creation, Eden and the Flood; Brahma is Abraham, Krishna is Moses, Rama is Samson; there are Hindu versions of the Trinity, and the sacraments of baptism, the eucharist and confession.[64] This intricate explication of Hinduism in Judeo-Christian terms is specifically designed to further the work of the mission; the Jesuits find no other use for research into Hindu belief. Père Calmette writes that his mission had been entrusted with the collection of Indian books for Louis XV's newly founded oriental library, and comments:

> Nous en retirons déjà de grands fruits pour l'avancement de la Religion: car ayant acquis par ce moyen là des Livres essentiels, qui sont comme l'arcenal du Paganisme, nous en tirons des armes pour combattre les Docteurs de l'Idolatrie, & ce sont celles qui les blessent le plus profondément.[65]

(We already derive from them great fruits for the advancement of religion, for having thus acquired the essential books which are like the arsenal of paganism, we draw from them arms to fight against the doctors of idolatry, and they are the weapons which wound most deeply.)

The military metaphor expresses the Jesuit attitude particularly well: Hinduism is perceived merely as an enemy to be conquered by Jesuit forces. The writer anticipates the eventual triumph of Jesuit power. Although the Jesuits were in charge of the acquisition of Hindu texts for the French king, Père Calmette seems unaware of any interest that they might hold for non-missionary Europeans. The Lutherans, on the other hand, consider that 'in searching their [Hindu] Notions, one might discover things very fit to entertain the Curiosity of many a learned Head in *Europe*'.[66] But the Lutherans also stress the importance of Hinduism to their missionary work: 'a competent Insight into the Grounds their idolatrous Worship is raised on . . . may in time prove a Means to strike at the very Fundamentals of their Religion, and convince 'em of the Groundlesness the whole Structure of their Idolatry rests on.'[67] The image of undermining the building of idolatry, although less violent than Père Calmette's comparable military metaphor, is still a vivid figure of destruction.

Later Protestant texts, however, emphasize the scholarly value of Hinduism. De la Croze equates Hinduism with classical mythology, according it the status of a subject worthy of scholarly research.[68] The books and customs of the Hindus should be treated like classical texts: scholars could plunder them for evidence in their pursuit of religious and historical truths. Research into contemporary Hinduism would reveal facts about antiquity. This invitation to scholars is based on the assumption that non-European societies were not subject to European laws of progress, that they were essentially static, arrested in their primitive state. This 'denial of co-evalness' (to use Johannes Fabian's phrase) means that the study of Hinduism could illuminate the origins of religious error. Here the missionaries were following paradigms established for the study of savage societies. In her discussion of early European concepts of savagery, Margaret Hodgen comments that

it became axiomatic that contemporary savage cultures, possessed of the properties of oldness and persistence, also possessed historical intimations. They could be used as a form of documentation. With classical or other dated manifestations of high antiquity, their analogues, they possessed the latent power of disclosing an early, aboriginal, or 'primitive' condition of mankind.[69]

Interestingly, Hodgen characterizes the European use of alien cultures as a 'form of documentation'. This is the practice of both Lutherans and Jesuits with regard to Hinduism. The religion is represented in textual terms—as poetry, fiction or mythology; in this form, it can be 'read', and then subjected to scholarly interpretation. De la Croze presents Hinduism as a challenge to intellectuals, made all the more attractive by stressing Hindu belief in a supreme God. This not only endorses the biblical account of Babel, but gives Hinduism a distinct advantage over Greek and Roman religion. Considering the centrality of classical texts to European education, de la Croze is proposing a substantial advance in Hinduism's reputation.

Although De la Croze's proposal that the West should regard Hinduism as a subject of scholarly research appeared in 1724, such a study had in fact already been completed by Ziegenbalg in 1713. But it was not published until his nineteenth-century biographer unearthed the manuscript from the Lutheran mission archives at Halle in Germany. Ziegenbalg's work was suppressed by the mission authorities who reasoned, as the preface of the English translation of 1869 relates, that 'the printing of the "Genealogy of the South-Indian Gods" was not to be thought of, inasmuch as the Missionaries were sent out to extirpate heathenism, and not to spread heathenish non-sense in Europe.'[70] The church authorities may have been unable to accept its validity, but the study is important as an indication of the quality of Lutheran scolarship. When resurrected, the book was to become a standard work on Hinduism for the nineteenth century.

THE WORD OF GOD

In their attempt to 'extirpate heathenism', the Lutherans' prime tool was the Tamil translation of the Bible. The printing press at Tranquebar, source of the Tamil Bible, was shown off to Indian visitors who were 'astonish'd at this rare Invention, never known before in these Countries'.[71] The Tamil Bible becomes a potent emblem for the mission. The Lutherans allege that the Jesuits burn all the copies of the Tamil Bible that they find.[72] Inevitably such acts invoke the memory of other book burnings for the Lutherans:

Les Missionaires espéroient que la version de la Bible produiroit dans les Indes le même fruit qu'elle avoit operé en Europe depuis la Reformation.[73]

(The missionaries were hoping that the version of the Bible would produce the same fruit in the Indies that it brought about in Europe after the Reformation.)

The associations of religious energy conveyed by the reference to the

102 / *India Inscribed*

Reformation are similar to those carried by the early-church comparisons already considered. But this updating of the age of religious excitement works to affiliate Indian converts to Europeans, to bring them closer to home.

The new intimacy in the representation of Indians is well illustrated by an unusually detailed account of the conversion of a religious mendicant. This is an absorbing story which affords the reader a close-up view of the life and enlightenment of a Hindu. It is obviously intended to prove the evangelical efficacy of Christian literature in the vernacular, to demonstrate that the printed word of God leads to redemption. The Hindu holy man, a potter by trade, invites Schultze, one of the Lutheran missionaries, to his father's house:

> Lorsqu'ils y furent arrivés, le Potier fit voir au Missionaire les livres de la Religion Chrêtienne qui lui étoit tombés entre les mains, & qui sortoient de l'Imprimerie de Tranquebar. Ensuite il manifesta à Mr. Schultze, en présence de son Pére & de toute sa famille, le désir qu'il avoit de s'instruire d'une Religion qui seule pouvoit le rendre heureux; & témoignant au Missionaire une grande confiance, il lui fit l'aveu de plusieurs circonstances de sa vie.[74]

(When they arrived, the potter showed the missionary the Christian books from the printing press at Tranquebar which had fallen into his hands. Then he signified to Mr. Schultze, in the presence of his father and all his family, the desire he had to be instructed in a religion which alone could make him happy, and showing great confidence in the missionary, he confided in him the circumstances of his life.)

The Hindu takes the missionary into his home, introduces him to his family, and tells him his life story. The European is drawn into a new kind of relationship with an Indian; and this intimacy is extended to the reader who shares in the Indian's confidences.

For ten years, the potter had led the life of a religious mendicant, but had scarcely been able to raise enough money to pay his dues to the brahman. Accustomed to a lazy, wandering life, he had acquired the reputation of a holy man capable of banishing snakes so that he could impress people, win their respect and alms. He also used supernatural arts:

> pour en imposer davantage, il se servoit de secrets de Magie qui le rendoient hors de lui-même & dans un état peu naturel par des contorsions affreuses, & qui lui procuroient même des mouvemens convulsifs: de façon qu'étant après cela fort affoibli, il tomboit sans connoissance; Qu'enfin il alloit souvent mendier de village en village, marchant avec des *sandales* hérissées de pointes de fer & le dos chargé d'une caisse de *secrets magiques*. Telle étoit la situation de ce Pénitent du

Paganisme, lorsque les livres des Chrétiens qu'il avoit lûs, firent tomber les écailles de ses yeux pour voir la vérité.⁷⁵

(to make more of an impression, he made use of the secrets of magic which put him in a trance and through terrible contortions into a barely natural state, which even made him go into convulsions, so that afterwards he would be greatly weakened and fall down unconscious. Then he often went begging from village to village, walking in sandals spiked with iron nails, and on his back a box of magic secrets. This was the state of this pagan penitent when the Christian books which he read made the scales fall from his eyes to see the truth.)

The picture of the Indian's pre-enlightenment life is one of assorted acts of depravity. His penitential practices are like the extravagances of the Catholics, while his arcane magical knowledge suggests communion with the devil. His contortions are as much of the spirit as the body. A prime candidate for damnation, he is evidently in grave need of conversion. This need is met by the Lutheran literature—a textbook case of conversion.

The potter's narrative presents an exemplary conversion as a real life story. The account, framed as the Indian's confidence, is designed to convince the reader of its veracity. Just as the potter shows Schultze the actual books that converted him, so the author assures the reader that visible proof of the Hindu's enlightenment can be found in Europe: the penitential sandals are now on display at Halle, the training centre for Lutheran missionaries.⁷⁶ The sandals are discarded as the potter's gesture of renunciation of his former existence, and turn into emblems of the mission's power to reform the lives of Indians.

The Jesuits are equally eager to prove their ability to transform India. How better to convey this than by focusing on that scene of horror central to the European representation of India—the sati? Père Martin gives a long and dramatic account of a mass sati at a local prince's funeral, where one of the widows herself perceives the act in Christian terms. The Prince's principal wife, after a dignified farewell speech instructing the heir to govern with paternal care, exclaims

'Helas! . . . à quoi aboutit la felicité humaine? Je sens bien que je vais me precipiter toute vive dans les Enfers'; & aussi-tost tournant fierement la teste vers le bûcher, & invoquent le nom de ses Dieux, elle se lance au milieu des flammes.⁷⁷

('Alas! . . . what does human happiness lead to? I am well aware that I am about to throw myself alive into hell'; and immediately turning her head proudly towards the pyre, invoking the name of her gods, she threw herself in the middle of the flames.)

This outburst on damnation implies her Christian frame of reference. It also draws on a characteristic Western trope: the funeral pyre as a foretaste of hell fire. The incident is explained later:

> Elle avoit eu à son service une femme Chrestienne, qui l'entretenoit souvent des grandes véritez de la Religion, & qui l'exhortoit à embrasser le Christianisme: elle goûtoit ces véritez, mais elle n'eut pas le courage de renoncer à ses Idoles: elle eu conçut pourtant de l'estime pour les Chrestiens, & elle se déclaroit leur protectrice en toute occasion; la vûë des flammes prestes à la consumer, lui rappella sans doute le souvenir de ce que cette bonne Chrestienne lui avoit dit sur les supplices de l'Enfer.[78]

(She had in her service a Christian woman, who spoke to her often of the great religious truths, and urged her to embrace Christianity: she tasted these truths, but did not have the courage to renounce her idols: she had however conceived a respect for the Christians, and she stepped forward as their protector on all occasions; the sight of the flames ready to consume her, reminded her without doubt of all that this good Christian had told her of the torments of hell.)

The sati, convinced of Christian truths but as yet unconverted, demonstrates the progressive power of Catholicism to infiltrate Hindu culture. But her Christian convictions are too feeble to remove her from the Hindu context. Her weakness is matched by that of a Christian onlooker who rejects the appeal of another sati:

> Il y en eut une qui plus timide que ses Compagnes, courut embrasser un Soldat Chrestien & le pria de la sauver. Ce Neophyte ... fut si effrayé, qu'il repoussa rudement sans y penser cette malheureuse, & qu'il la fit culbuter dans le bûcher. Il se retira aussi-tost avec un fremissement par tout le corps, qui fut suivi d'une fiévre ardente, accompagnée de transport au cerveau, dont il mourut la nuit suivante sans pouvoir revenir à son bon sens.[79]

(There was one who was more timid than her companions, who threw herself at a Christian soldier and begged him to save her. This convert was so scared that without thinking he roughly pushed this unfortunate woman away, and made her fall into the pyre. He left immediately, shaking all over; a burning fever followed, accompanied by a seizure of which he died the following night, without regaining consciousness.)

Non-intervention leads directly to the Christian's own demise. The moral is obvious: a Christian's duty is to free the sati, to alter the Hindu course of events. The writer here anticipates the nineteenth-century British campaign for the abolition of sati by implying that Christianity must function as an agent of change in India.

A subsequent letter narrates the story of a successful escapee sati. A high caste widow is forced by her family to consent to be burnt:

Après les cérémonies ordinaires elle monta donc sur le bûcher, ou six hommes vigoureux & robustes eurent ordre de la lier; mais soit que les cordes dont ils se servirent ne fussent point assez fortes, soit qu'ils l'eussent mal attachée, aussi-tôt qu'elle sentit les premières atteintes de la flamme, elle fit un si grand effort qu'elle rompit ses liens & se sauva chez nos Néophites, qui la cachèrent pendant quelques jours: ensuite on lui administra le Baptême. Elle est aux yeux des Gentils un objet d'exécration & l'opprobre de sa caste; mais nous la regardons comme le modèle & l'exemple des personnes du sexe qui embrassent la Loi de l'Evangile; & cette femme justifie parfaitement la haute idée que nous avons conçue de sa vertu.[80]

(After the customary ceremonies she then climbed on the pyre, where six healthy, well-built men were ordered to tie her, but whether the ropes which they used were not strong enough or whether they were badly tied, as soon as she felt the first touches of the fire, she made such an immense effort that she broke her bonds and ran away to our converts who hid her for several days: then she was baptised. She is in the eyes of the pagans an object of abomination and a disgrace to her caste; but we regard her as a model and example of members of the female sex who embrace the law of the Gospels; and this woman perfectly justifies the high opinion that we formed of her virtue.)

In a dramatic enactment of the Christian doctrine of salvation, the sati triumphs over the repressive death-dealing forces of Hinduism. For the Jesuits, she is an exemplary convert because she embodies the missionary principle of change: the abhorred sati is resurrected as the virtuous convert. Appropriately enough, she becomes a catechist herself: a contributor to the European project to transform India.

Although, as we have seen, the two denominations endlessly contest each other's accounts, they share the desire to change and domesticate India: to turn strange, menacing pagans into safe, familiar Christians. India is incorporated into the European redemptive economy of circulating prayers and funds. Members of the one family of Christ, Indians and Europeans are linked by bonds of gratitude and obligation, pity and faith. Missionary writing demonstrates how the alien other can be controlled, suggesting how India itself can be tamed and re-formed in the European image.

Notes

1. Sylvia Murr, 'Les conditions d'émergence du discours sur l'Inde au siècle des Lumières', *Collection purusartha* vii (1983) 233–84.
2. See Ines G. Županov, 'Aristocratic Analogies and Demotic Descriptions in the Seventeenth-Century Madurai Mission', *Representations* 41 (1993) 123–48,

for an account of the controversy between the two early Jesuit missionaries, Roberto Nobili and Gonçalo Fernandes.
3. *Lettres Edifiantes et Curieuses Ecrites des Missions Etrangers par quelques Missionnaires de la Compagnie de Jesus*, 34 vols (Paris, 1707–76) xxxiv (1776) 309 [misnumbered 409]–318.
4. *Lettres édifiantes*, xxxiv (1776) 310–11.
5. Stephen Greenblatt, *Marvelous Possessions: The Wonder of the New World* (Oxford, 1991) 8.
6. *Lettres édifiantes*, iii (1713) 214–15.
7. Ibid., xiv (1720) 307.
8. Ibid., xxv (1741) 448.
9. Ibid., xii (1717) 57.
10. Ibid., xxiv (1739) 186.
11. Greenblatt, 83.
12. *Lettres édifiantes*, xxiv (1739) 186.
13. Ibid., xiv (1720) 322–410; xii (1717) 74–7.
14. Ibid., xii (1717) 74–6.
15. *Propagation of the Gospel in the East: being an Account of the Success of two Danish Missionaries, Lately sent to the East-Indies, for the Conversion of the Heathens in Malabar* (London, 1709) xxx.
16. *Propagation of the Gospel*, 50.
17. Ibid., 32.
18. Jean Lucas Niecamp, *Histoire de la Mission Danoise dans les Indes Orientales*, 3 vols (Geneva, 1745), iii. 149–50.
19. *Lettres édifiantes*, xxxii (1774) 109–10.
20. Ibid., xxiv (1739) 228.
21. The first important description of famine occurs in the 'Lettre du Pere de Bourzes.... A Madame la Comtesse de Soudé', *Lettres édifiantes*, xii (1717) 59–60; the second appears in the 'Lettre du P. Saignes.... A Madame S. Hyacinthe, Religieuse Ursuline à Toulouse', *Lettres édifiantes*, xxiv (1739) 226–8; the third is found in the 'Lettre du P. Trembloy.... A Monsieur ***' *Lettres édifiantes*, xxxiv (1776) 187–94.
22. *Lettres édifiantes*, xxiv (1739) 226–8.
23. Ibid., xv (1722) 313–14; see also xv (1772) 293.
24. Ibid., (1722) 314.
25. Ibid., ix (1711) 268.
26. Ibid., xi (1715) 34.
27. Ibid., xv (1722) 272.
28. Corinthians II, 11. 26–7.
29. See for instance *Lettres édifiantes*, ii (1707) 1–56 for imprisonment and execution; *Lettres édifiantes*, xi (1715) 1–74 for imprisonment and torture.
30. See Stephen Neill, *A History of Christian Missions* 2nd edn (Harmondsworth, 1986) 45–6; Leslie Brown, *The Indian Christians of St. Thomas: An Account of the Ancient Syrian Church of Malabar* (Cambridge, 1956) 2.
31. Niecamp, i. ix.

32. Ibid., x.
33. Mathurin Veyssière de la Croze, *Histoire du Christianisme des Indes* (La Haye, 1724) 88–94.
34. de la Croze, 99.
35. Ibid., 423.
36. Claude Marie Guyon, *A New History of the East-Indies, Ancient and Modern*, 2 vols (London, 1757) i. 476–8.
37. Guyon, i. 469–70.
38. J. Lockman, *Travels of the Jesuits*, 2 vols (London, 1743) i. xii.
39. Ibid., i. 477.
40. Wilhelm Halbfass, *India and Europe: An Essay in Understanding* (New York, 1988) 48. See for example Niecamp, i. 106 (note), 238; de la Croze, 310; *Thirty-four Conferences between the Danish Missionaries and the Malabarian Bramans*, trans. Jenkin Philipps (London, 1719) ii, iv, 304 [misnumbered 364], 349.
41. Niecamp, i. xxxv.
42. Ibid., 2.
43. *Lettres édifiantes*, xxxiv (1776) 247–9.
44. Murr, 239.
45. *Lettres édifiantes*, ix (1711) 66–9; 103–4; 112.
46. Ibid., (1711) 83–4.
47. Ibid., 122.
48. Ibid., xv (1722) 297–8.
49. Ibid., xiii (1718) 218–20.
50. Ibid., xxi (1734) 459.
51. Ibid., xiii (1718) 200–21.
52. Ibid., 200–3.
53. Ibid., 217–18.
54. Ibid., xvi (1725) 212; ibid., xxi (1734) 454.
55. Niecamp, i. iv, 228.
56. *Thirty four Conferences*, xxi.
57. Tzvetan Todorov, *La Conquête de L'Amerique* (Paris, 1982) 138.
58. *Thirty four Conferences*, 1; 16.
59. Ibid., 324.
60. Ibid., 251.
61. *Lettres édifiantes*, x (1713) 15–16.
62. *Thirty four Conferences*, 3.
63. See P. J. Marshall, *The British Discovery of Hinduism in the Eighteenth Century* (Cambridge, 1970) 20–3; Margaret T. Hodgen, *Early Anthropology in the Sixteenth and Seventeenth Centuries* (Philadelphia, 1964) 222–326.
64. *Lettres édifiantes*, ix (1711) 1–60.
65. Ibid., xxi (1734) 455–6.
66. *Propagation of the Gospel*, 30.
67. Ibid., 30.
68. de la Croze, 424–5.
69. Hodgen, 332.

108 / India Inscribed

70. Bartholemew Ziegenbalg, *Genealogy of the Malabarian Gods* (Madras, 1869) xv, quoted in Stephen Neill, *A History of Christianity in India*, 2 vols (Cambridge, 1984) ii. 33.
71. *Thirty four Conferences*, 202.
72. Niecamp, i. 213.
73. Ibid., ii. 62.
74. Ibid., 144.
75. Ibid., 145.
76. Ibid., 145–6.
77. *Lettres édifiantes*, xiii (1718) 25.
78. Ibid., 27–8.
79. Ibid., 26–7.
80. Ibid., xxxii (1774) 111–12.

CHAPTER FOUR

'Foreign Conquerors' and 'Harmless Indians': British Representations of Company Rule

In his journal of the years 1615 to 1619 Sir Thomas Roe, the first English ambassador to the Mughal court, describes an interesting faux pas in his dealings with Emperor Jahangir. Roe intends the anecdote as a warning to diplomats against possible future embarrassment. On being presented with a painting of Venus and a satyr, the emperor wanted to know the 'interpretation or morall' of the scene:

This I repeate for instruction to warne the company and him that shall suceed me to be very wary what they send, may be subject to ill Interpretation: for in that point this King and people are very pregnant and scrupulous, full of jealousie and trickes, for that notwithstanding the King conceited himselfe, yet by the passages I will deliver my opinion of this conceit, which ... hee would not presse hard upon me. But, I suppose, he understood the Morall to be a scorne of Asiatiques whom the naked Satyre represented, and was of the same complexion and not unlike; who being held by Venus a white woman by the Nose, it seemed that shee led him Captive.[1]

Roe's point is not that Western art will be misunderstood outside the cultural context of Europe; rather he considers the emperor's 'morall'—European derision of Asians—to be wilful misinterpretation, an example of Mughal 'jealousie and trickes'. And yet the emperor does not express his opinion directly. It is the English ambassador who contrasts the beauty and power of the white European Venus with the bestiality and helplessness of the dark-skinned Asian satyr. Roe himself reads racial dominance into the painting: Venus holds the satyr by the nose, a contemptible, even ludicrous, emblem of Asian subservience. This double act of interpretation—of both the picture and the signs of imperial displeasure—evinces that curious mixture of insecurity and arrogance which characterizes Roe's response to the Mughal court. Roe, ever aware of his sense of national dignity, is nevertheless in a position of anxious dependency, as a foreign ambassador suing for trade concessions from Jahangir.

There is a reference to this episode in a text published over a century later in 1761, Richard Owen Cambridge's *Account of the War in India, between the English and French, on the Coast of Coromandel, From the Year 1750 to the Year 1760*. The introduction includes excerpts from Roe's account intended, according to Cambridge, to convey something of the contemporary workings of the Mughal court; for although the splendour of the imperial household may be diminished, Cambridge argues, Mughal practices remain largely the same over centuries.[2] Yet despite this assertion of unchanging continuity—a typical European characterization of Indian society—Roe's anecdote is significantly revised in Cambridge's paraphrased version:

It happened there was among the presents, a picture of Venus leading a Satyr by the nose. The Mogul when he saw this, shewed it to his courtiers, and bid them remark the action of the woman, the blackness of the Satyr's skin, and other particulars, giving them to understand, he considered it as a reflection on the people of Asia, whom he supposed to be represented by the Satyr, as being of their complexion; and that the Venus leading him by the nose, denoted the great power the women in that country have over the men.[3]

Cambridge cuts out Roe's mediating role; the emperor expresses his opinion about the painting directly. More importantly, the painting now symbolizes the subordination of Asian men to women, omitting all mention of European dominance.

The difference may seem slight, but I want to argue that this story and its retelling embody crucial developments in the nature of British involvement in India during the seventeenth and eighteenth centuries. At the time that Cambridge is writing, East India Company forces controlled Bengal. Roe's words of diplomatic caution, that the emperor might be offended by the image of an Asian satyr 'led . . . Captive' by a European Venus are, by 1761, politically irrelevant: Clive had already thwarted an attempt by the Mughal heir-apparent to reassert his rights. Cambridge has, consciously or otherwise, revised the narrative in the light of contemporary military and political events. During this period British dominion is becoming a reality and, I would argue, writers such as Cambridge are involved in the project to explain and justify that role.

Here I shall first examine the way that a wide range of texts produced in the latter half of the eighteenth century promote the idea of British rule; then how they articulate its attendant anxieties. The question of whether Britain intended (or even wanted) to become a colonial power in India continues to be an issue of debate among historians.[4] I want to argue that much of this writing seeks to persuade readers that British dominion in India is possible, and that it is beneficial to Indians. These texts appeared at a time when Company rule was still vulnerable: newly established, threatened militarily by Mysore, under attack in parliament over the administrations of Clive and Warren Hastings. Subsequent chapters will discuss these challenges to the Company, but I will first consider the confidence-boosting images of British rule constructed in the face of such threats. Many accounts attempt to prove that India is susceptible to British conquest and control, often by demonstrating the inadequacies of Mughal rule. Others celebrate the blessings of Company government, and even texts which attack British conduct in India endorse, at the same time, the Company's right to rule. The anxious assertion of power also manifests itself in what Suleri has termed 'the colonial will to cultural description'.[5] I analyse the strategies employed by authors to claim an intimate and all-pervasive knowledge of India, but I also ask if the discourse of authority is limited or contested, if there are signs of Indian defiance and resistance. Just how safe are the Indian subjects constructed? How do texts, particularly novels, articulate and attempt to resolve anxiety over the security of Company rule?

'THE PROGRESS OF BRITISH ARMS'

If we return to Cambridge's revision of Roe's narrative, we find that it is the emperor himself who suggests that the picture represents the domination of Mughal men by women. Far from being the kind of perverse misinterpretation that Roe attributes to Jahangir, Cambridge deems this image particularly appropriate:

It was indeed too apposite an emblem; and this, together with the annexed picture, taken from real life in the country, will give a just representation of the luxurious indolence in which they pass the greatest part of their lives. . . . As they sit for the most part (when they are not with their women) upon their sofas, smoking, and amusing themselves with their jewels, taking coffee or sweetmeats, seeing their quails fight, or some such like pastimes; nothing surprises them so much as to see a European walk about a room; and none but their very young people ever ride for amusement or exercise only.[6]

The emperor condemns his own society unwittingly: his interpretation of the painting epitomizes the effeminate degeneracy of Mughal men who loll luxuriously on sofas, watching quail-fights (a kind of eastern parody of cock-fights, particularly because of the cowardly associations of the birds' name). The immobile Mughals are contrasted with the active European, who walks around when he could just as well sit down. This caricature of Mughal indolence is a version of a widespread stereotype, one which affirms the easy superiority of Europeans over a corrupt race.

Mughal degeneracy is often depicted as a decline: when transported to India, the Mughals lose the 'bold, hardy, martial' characteristics of the Tartar people. Luke Scrafton attributes this, in his *Reflections on the Government of Indostan* of 1763, to the debilitating effects of contact with Indians:

At first they abhor the sensuality and effeminacy of their masters; but by degrees their native manners wear off, they adopt the luxury they despised, they marry the women of the country, and their children or at the utmost their grandchildren, have nothing remaining of their Tartar origin; like our English hounds, when sent abroad, the first breed of which retains some little of the qualities of a hound, but the next are no better than curs.[7]

Scrafton's choice of simile is significant: to compare a race of men to dogs at once dehumanizes them and implies that they can be mastered. The mongrel Mughals are to be regarded with the contempt that their hybrid state deserves.

Like hounds no longer capable of hunting, the Mughals, according to the British, preserve the external appearance of power long after its reality has vanished. Robert Orme, historiographer to the East India Company from 1769, published his monumental *History of the Military Transactions of the British Nation in Indostan* in 1763. He characterizes Mughal government as an elaborate sham:

Amongst other instances of the contempt with which the majesty of the emperor is treated, the governors of provinces have counterfeited, without hesitation, letters, orders and patents, from the court, but have even hired men to act the part of officers invested by the Great Mogul with the power of conferring with them on the affairs of their government. The mock delegates are received with great pomp in the capital: the vice-roy or Nabob humbles himself before the pretended representative, who delivers in public his credentials, and the fictitious orders he has been instructed to enforce. These measures are practised to appease the minds of the people, who still retain so much reverence to the blood of Tamerlane, that a viceroy always thinks it necessary to create an opinion amongst them that he is a favourite with the emperor, even when he is in arms against his authority.[8]

The empty signs of Mughal power—forged imperial letters, orders and patents—are stage props in a theatrical spectacle designed to dupe the masses. It is interesting to compare this representation of Mughal rule with the depiction of Jahangir's court by Sir Thomas Roe, discussed in the first chapter.[9] Roe employed dramatic imagery to undermine Mughal court etiquette, comparing displays of imperial favour and extravagant obeisances to the overblown gestures of actors. In Roe's account the theatre always remained a metaphor for the court; but Orme, writing in 1763, turns government into actual theatre to demonstrate the illusory nature of Mughal power.

Orme depicts a fragmented empire where provincial governors assume, or rebel against, imperial authority. This concept of imperial decline, which forms the basis of British historical discourse about eighteenth-century India, was to persist well into the twentieth century. In the introduction to his 1988 volume of *The New Cambridge History of India*, Christopher Bayly outlines the changes in historical thought since the original publication of *The Cambridge History of India* in 1929:

> The *Cambridge History* starts from the assumption that the centralized Mughal empire was in purely degenerative decline, along with the Indian economy and society. Consequently, the English East India Company was forced to intervene in order to protect its own trade and the political stability of its clients. Now, however, the Mughal empire seems a much less substantial hegemony, its decline a much more complex and ambiguous process, and the society of eighteenth-century India much more varied than the stereotype of decline and anarchy which is the unwritten emblem of the authors of 1929.[10]

It is clear from this that colonial historiography demonstrates a remarkable continuity. In 1763, a Mughal empire in chaos implies the possibility of British intervention; in 1929, a Mughal empire in decline legitimizes that involvement.

The eighteenth-century idea of imperial decline owes much to an earlier theory of eastern misgovernment: the concept of 'oriental despotism', which emerges in its fullest form with Montesquieu in his *Esprit des lois* of 1748. Much has been written about the prevalence and history of this idea, notably by Franco Venturi.[11] The ease with which the Mughals gained despotic sway over the Indians and deprived them of their rights is typically explained in terms of climatic influence. Alexander Dow, who published the first two volumes of his *History of Indostan* in 1768, added a third in 1772 which included 'A Dissertation concerning the origin and nature of Despotism in Hindostan', clearly based on the framework provided by Montesquieu. This volume of Dow's work, although deeply critical of Company policy in Bengal, also suggests that Indians are a race designed for subordination. In the essay's opening paragraph, Dow discusses Indian susceptibility to despotism:

> GOVERNMENT derives its form from accident; its spirit and genius from the inherent manners of the people. The languor occasioned by the hot climate of India, inclines the native to indolence and ease; and he thinks the evils of despotism less severe than the labour of being free. Tranquillity is the chief object of his desires. His happiness consists in a mere absence of misery...[12]

Dow's assertion that Indians regard freedom as too great an effort and his negative definition of Indian happiness as 'mere absence of misery' reduce Indians to passive ciphers, a people ripe for oppression. A more emphatic expression of a related idea can be found in John-Henry Grose's *Voyage to the East-Indies*, published in 1757. In his description of the Mughal administration of Surat, Grose observes that the Muslims employ Hindus to collect taxes from the Hindu population. Here the Hindu is not the indolent victim, but a willing collaborator: 'it has been observed, that none are more rigorous exacters over the Gentoos, nor readier to abet, or even set on foot any vexation or extortion from them than these Gentoos themselves. One would imagine oppression was their element, and that they could not breathe out of it.'[13] Grose represents the Hindus as if they were a separate species; as if their very existence were dependent on oppression.

As the East India Company began to replace Mughal rule in Bengal, writers increasingly stress the inherent submissiveness of Indians. Dow, for example, reasons that the 'mild, humane, obedient, and industrious' Hindus 'are of all nations on earth the most easily conquered and governed' and that Hinduism 'from its principles, of the greatest degree of subordination to authority . . . prepares mankind for the government of foreign lords'.[14] In Dow's version of Indian history, colonialism seems to fit neatly into the structure of Hindu society and religion: he creates a sense of 'natural' inevitability about British dominion. It should be noted that in an earlier volume of his *History*, Dow proposed the British military conquest of all of India.[15]

If Hinduism itself suggests 'the government of foreign lords', then military conquest can be represented less as an act of aggression, more as a kind of logical progression. It is as if the impetus for British action derived from India rather than Britain; as if Indians themselves were responsible for their state of subjection. Robert Orme modifies this idea by implying that it is the Indians' excessive love of commerce which incites other nations to invade them:

NOTHING seems to have been wanting to the happiness of this nation, but that others should have looked on them with the same indifference with which they regard the rest of the world. But not content with the presents which nature has showered on their climate, they have made improvements when they felt no necessity. They have cultivated the various and valuable productions of their soil, not to the measure of their own but to that of the wants of all other nations; they have carried their manufactures of linnen to a perfection which surpasses the most exquisite productions of Europe, and have encouraged with avidity the annual tributes of gold and silver which the rest of the world contest for the privilege of sending to them. They have from time immemorial been as addicted to commerce, as they are averse to war. They have therefore always been immensely rich, and have always remained incapable of defending their wealth.[16]

Indian exploitation of natural resources, production of luxury goods, greed and military ineptitude combine to lay the country open to invasion. This lack of foresight is a failing which British writers frequently attribute to Indians: Grose defines it as 'preferring, like most of the Orientals, a momentary present profit, either to a lasting one, or to a much greater one, if at any distance of Time'.[17] To criticize another race for short-sightedness is of course to imply the prescience of one's own. The British writer and his readers share the privileged vantage point and longer perspective of the historical narrative.

To the European advantage of forethought can be added military superiority.[18] Orme writes his history with the express intention of giving 'a just idea of the superiority of European arms, when opposed to those of Indostan'.[19] British military supremacy, a favourite theme of many writers, finds an emphatic advocate in Jemima Kindersley, the wife of a lieutenant-colonel in the Bengal Artillery; her *Letters from the Island of Teneriffe, Brazil, The Cape of Good Hope, and the East Indies* were published in 1777. Kindersley writes that 'Nothing can more justly show their [the Mughals'] present military and political force than the progress of the British arms, since the English, in comparison of the black people, are but as a handful of men.'[20] The image of a tiny number of Company troops defeating vast Mughal forces is a striking representation of British military power. The numerical disparity unequivocally expresses the two races' supposed strength. While the use of the casual approximation, 'a handful of men', conveys the ease of British victory and seems to carry, through a figurative slippage, the sense that power is within the British grasp. Indeed, Dow employs a similar phrase in his outline of the proposed British conquest of the whole of India: 'It is apparent ... that the immense regions of Hindostan might be all reduced by a handful of regular troops.'[21]

Some writers project this sense of British military superiority onto Indians themselves: Luke Scrafton attributes to Indian troops belief in the superhuman power of the British. Stressing the disparity in the size of the two armies, Scrafton describes the fear and capitulation of the Indian forces at Patna when faced by Clive:

> such was the reputation of our arms, that though they had repeated and certain intelligence of the small number of our forces, they thought it folly to offer to contend with us: Nor is this astonishing to those who know what strong fatalists these eastern people are, who look on fighting against a fortunate man, as contending with GOD HIMSELF. When you tell them of any successful commander, they never ascribe his successes to any human virtue, but lift up their eyes, and say, '*A happy fate attends him*;' and when once a man has gained the reputation of being fortunate, nothing seems desperate in their eyes.[22]

Adopting the privileged position of an expert, one who knows 'what strong fatalists these eastern people are', Scrafton demonstrates that Indians are incapable of opposing an ascendant British army: the tendency to surrender and deify the British is written into their superstitious system of belief.

Orme relates a similar instance in his description of Clive's capture of Arcot:

> On the 31st [August 1751] he halted within 10 miles of Arcot, where the enemy's spies reported, that they had discovered the English marching with unconcern through a violent storm of thunder, lighting, and rain; and this circumstance, from their notions of omens, gave the garrison so high an opinion of the fortitude of the approaching enemy, that they instantly abandoned the fort, and a few hours after the English entered the city, which had no walls or defences, and marching through 100,000 spectators, who gazed on them with admiration and respect . . .[23]

Superstition enfeebles the Indians; it transforms aggression into awe and soldiers into spectators: the citizens invite the British into Arcot. With its instant transformations and happy ending, this episode reads like a fairy tale. The narrative seems to suggest that it is this nursery genre that best suits the ignorant Indians and their foolish beliefs.

Indian armies, hampered by childish fears of thunder storms and fatalistic resignation, are further incapacitated by the disloyalty of their troops. Orme observes that

> The armies of the Mahomedan princes of Indostan are composed of distinct bodies of troops inlisted by different leaders; who, with their bands, enter into, and quit the service of different princes, according to the advantages which they

expect to receive. Hence the degree of reliance which a prince can have on his army is proportioned to the treasures of which he is possessed, joined to his inclination to disburse them; and it is common in the wars of Indostan to see large bodies of troops going over to the enemy on the very field of battle.[24]

The obvious implication of this picture of unreliable, defecting mercenaries is that British troops need fear little serious opposition.

The image of Indian soldiers violates every European concept of warfare; the troops are ill disciplined, disloyal and fearful. British writers are then faced with a problem: how to justify the use of sepoys in the Company army? The solution generally offered is that, under the influence of British leadership and drill, Indian soldiers can be turned into a respectable fighting force. As Cambridge writes:

SUCH of the natives as have been disciplined and encouraged by Europeans, and formed into a regular infantry, under officers of their own, and generally known by the name of Sepoys, have familiarized themselves to fire arms, and behaved well behind walls; and when we give them serjeants to lead them on, they made no contemptible figure in the field.[25]

But this rewriting of the Indian stereotype of military incapacity itself throws up new problems: for, if Indians can be taught to fight effectively, can they not also learn to defeat their teachers? By communicating the secrets of their military superiority, have not the British undermined the very basis of their power? British writers typically reject this idea, but the frequent confusion or complexity of their refutations reveals the difficulties and anxieties involved in their position.

Luke Scrafton's arguments illustrate this ambivalence well:

Military discipline is so contradictory to the genius and constitution of the people, that neither example nor experience can ever make them capable of it; and the common apprehension of our teaching the Indians to beat us, is without the least foundation. It is not that they want natural courage, but they have no motive to spur them on to danger, except the example of their leader, who is always mounted on an elephant, equally conspicuous to his own men and our field pieces, and his death is sure to be followed by the flight of his troops. Colonel Clive has indeed made use of this principle to great advantage, in disciplining our seapoys, by forming them into battalions, under the command of the best of our officers; since which they have, on several occasions, proved little inferior to Europeans.[26]

Scrafton's initial statement that the Indians are inherently incapable of military discipline is contradicted by his subsequent assertion that Clive successfully disciplined sepoys; while his claim that the Indians could never defeat the British is undermined by his final assessment of Clive's Indian troops as 'little inferior to Europeans'. Scrafton's faulty reasoning reveals the very anxiety which he is trying to assuage—a sense of insecurity about sepoys, a fear of the consequences of entrusting the weapons of power to a subject people.

The contradictions in Scrafton's position, Homi Bhabha would argue, are characteristic of the racist stereotype which is 'curiously mixed and split, polymorphous and perverse, an articulation of multiple belief . . . what is being dramatized is a separation—*between* races, cultures, histories, *within* histories—a separation between *before* and *after* that repeats obsessively the mythical moment of disjunction.'[27] The native is incapable of discipline, until he is subject to British control; as a sepoy he can be trained but he is still a native, so still undisciplined; therefore he must remain under British control, for he requires further training. Nearly forty years later, readers continue to be assured that sepoys pose no threat. In 1802, the Reverend William Tennant published a collection of letters, written in the 1790s, under the splendid title, *Indian Recreations; consisting chiefly of Strictures on the Domestic and Rural Economy of the Mahomedans & Hindoos*. Tennant attempts to substantiate his claim that 'there is little to be apprehended from their [the sepoys] engaging in the army of any hostile power', by representing Indian soldiers as mindless components of a fighting machine:

Deprive them of the [European] officer, who may be regarded as the acting spring, and they are unable to execute any movement however simple: discontinue their exercise for a short time, and they will resume it with a consciousness of their own incapacity; every trial is ineffectual till again they are wound up anew by the labour of fresh instruction.[28]

The idea of discipline transforming a man into a mechanical part originated, according to Foucault, in the late eighteenth century. But Tennant is not here giving voice to the Foucauldian concept that 'the soldier has become something that can be made; out of formless clay, an inapt body, the machine required can be constructed'.[29] For in India, Tennant asserts, discipline has little to do with the automation of the sepoys: 'The reduction of a body of men to mere mechanical motions, in which the excellence of discipline has been supposed to consist, is the work of nature herself upon the natives of India.'[30] Tennant deprives the sepoys of any agency whatsoever; constitutionally inert, they remain 'ineffectual till again they are wound up' by their British commanders.

British writers also attempt to banish the fear that Indian princes, learning from the success of the Company's forces, might in time defeat them with European-style armies. Jemima Kindersley presents this as a hypothetical scenario which she then refutes at some length:

it may be urged, that all the black princes will see the good consequences of a well-conducted army: they will follow the example of the Europeans, will consider their own numbers; and, after being often beat, at last conquer their conquerors. The Romans, without the advantage of numbers, by copying from all their enemies, became their masters.

And Charles the twelfth of Sweden, for some time invincible, taught his enemies the art of war. But experience alone will never effect this; there were other causes. Every Roman fought for himself, for his lands and his liberty: the love of their country was their predominant principle, even to enthusiasm.

And the enemies of Charles the twelfth, with all their experience, would never have been able to oppose him, had they not been governed by a prince who had wisdom and fortitude enough to conquer first the superstition, and ignorant barbarism of his country: he led his subjects to a love of virtue, of the sciences, of their country, and their king.

A despotical government absolutely prevents the growth of these virtues in Hindostán; which occasions mighty and insurmountable obstacles to their ever conquering the Europeans.[31]

Kindersley cites historical examples with the sole intention of dismissing them. The thesis of British defeat is set up only to be demolished: the passage functions as a kind of rhetorical enactment of the invincibility of British power. Discipline and imitation are insufficient for victory, the troops must be motivated by higher principles—by patriotism, the pursuit of knowledge or virtue—abstractions of which Indians can have no conception. Kindersley bases her argument on the concept of 'oriental despotism': European historical precedents become irrelevant when confronted with this symbol of alien government, this absolute barrier between East and West.

Yet British fears of the threat posed by local princes and sepoy disloyalty were not without foundation. Peter Marshall, in *Bengal: The British Bridgehead*, observes that the loyalty of the Bengal army could never be taken for granted, noting that in 1764 'many of the sepoys had shown little inclination to fight' on behalf of the British.[32] Challenges to British power were real: in 1756 Siraj-ud Daula briefly gained control of Calcutta, while the sultanate of Mysore, during its period of expansion under Haidar Ali and Tipu Sultan, seriously shook British authority in the south. Placed in this context, emphatic assertions of British invulnerability sound more like attempts to bolster national confidence.

One account, more than any other, reveals the horror with which the British regarded native power. J. Z. Holwell's *Genuine Narrative of the Deplorable Deaths of the English Gentlemen, and Others, who were suffocated in the Black-Hole in Fort-william, at Calcutta*, was published in book form in 1758, and reprinted the same year in *The Annual Register*. This is the account of the deaths of 123 captives taken by Siraj-ud Daula, the nawab of Bengal, at the capture of Calcutta in 1756. After a night spent in the Black Hole, only twenty-three of the prisoners remained alive. At least that is Holwell's version of events. The accuracy of the *Genuine Narrative* has long been questioned: Holwell has been accused of self-justificatory exaggeration and fabrication. But Lord Curzon, viceroy from 1898 to 1906, elevated the story into one of the enduring myths of empire, and cast Holwell as a founding father of British India.[33] Holwell certainly writes a heroic part for himself, emphasizing his selfless devotion to duty as he details the stages of his battle for survival among the delirious, the dying and the dead: fighting for air and pleading for water, drinking the sweat from his shirt but finding his urine too bitter, succumbing to despair but resisting the impulse to kill himself. It is not surprising that his story should have caused a great stir when published; references to the event abound in contemporary texts, and the name of the prison soon became proverbial.[34]

One of the most interesting elements of Holwell's account is its reversal of the respective roles for Westerners and Indians established by centuries of European writing about India. In the *Genuine Narrative*, the Indian guards are the observers of a scene of British distress; throughout the earlier literature, European travellers have usually been the onlookers at displays of Indian suffering, such as sati and the penances of Hindu and Muslim holy men and devotees. The habitual observers now find the subjects of their gaze staring back at them. This exchange of visual dominance encapsulates the larger shift in power relations, and also serves to highlight central differences in the representation of the two nationalities: Europeans characteristically regard the self-imposed sufferings of Indians with horror, while most of the soldiers of Siraj-ud Daula are said to delight in the sight of their captives' distress. Holwell asks 'Can it gain belief, that this scene of misery proved entertainment to the brutal wretches without? But so it was; and they took care to keep us supplied with water, that they might have the satisfaction of seeing us fight for it, as they phrased it, and held up lights to the bars, that they might lose no part of the inhuman diversion.'[35] The guards' 'inhuman diversion', breaks all bounds of human behaviour, relegating them, so to speak, from the species.

Siraj-ud Daula's reputation for cruelty is shared by Haidar Ali and Tipu Sultan of Mysore, as we shall see. The ruthlessness of these regimes serves to enhance the Company's own favourite image of benign paternalism. In 1765 the Mughal emperor granted the Company the diwani of Bengal, which empowered the British to collect revenues on payment of an annual tribute; by 1772, the governor and council had direct responsibility for civil justice and the financial management of the province. These duties required a new self-image: that of a responsible, caring ruling power. This was all the more important as charges of British profiteering and extortion in Bengal became widespread following the parliamentary enquiry of 1772-3 into Clive's activities, and again after 1786-7, the well-publicized start of the nine-year-long impeachment of Warren Hastings.

This theme of benevolent British rule found convenient narrative expression in the pacification of the hill tribes on the Bengal/Bihar border, the Santhals of Chota Nagpur.[36] The British collector of the districts of Rajmahal and Bhagalpur was the hero of the piece. Appointed collector in 1779, Augustus Cleveland was supposed to have stopped the hill peoples from raiding the surrounding country and induced them to form a batallion of sepoys: all through his powers of persuasion alone, or, in some accounts, with additional help from a small financial inducement.

William Hodges describes Cleveland's methods in the illustrated account of his *Travels in India*, published in 1793.[37] Hodges was a professional artist who had participated in Captain Cook's second voyage to the Pacific in 1772-5. In India, Hodges was patronized both by Warren Hastings and by Cleveland himself, with whom he toured forested regions of Bihar. Hodges would no doubt have had a particular interest in representing the government of both his patrons (Hastings then being impeached) in glowing terms:

By a variety of attentions, by little presents, and acts of personal kindness, he [Cleveland] so subdued their [the hill chiefs'] ferocious spirits, that they promised to desist entirely from their usual depredations; and returning to their families and their people, the whole body became earnest to be personally introduced to this humane and benevolent stranger. Mr Cleveland had by this time digested his plan, which he brought forwards by degrees, and whatever he proposed they instantly agreed to. He sent presents to their wives, and wherever he saw he caressed their children, decorating them with beads; and to their Chiefs he presented medals, as a mark of his friendship, and as a reward for their improving civilization. At length, when he found them prepared for the accomplishment of his plan, he ordered cloaths to be made, like those of the Seapoys in the Company's service for a few, he furnished them with firelocks, and they became regularly drill'd. Vain of their newly acquired knowledge, these new soldiers soon imparted the enthusiasm to the rest of the nation, who earnestly petitioned for the same distinction. Thus, at their own request, a battalion was formed for the preservation of good order, and in less than two years, he had a fine corps of these people embodied, for the express purpose of preserving from injury the very country that had for centuries before been the scene of their depredations.[38]

Hodges' depiction of Cleveland's tactics of ingratiation—distributing presents and kissing babies—seem a cross between those of an explorer hoping to win the natives' favour and a modern politician's electioneering tactics. But the democratic analogy is misleading; for although Cleveland wants to give the impression that the hill tribes choose to submit to the British, the people actually have no choice at all. It is this peculiar balance between free-will and coercion that is interesting. Hodges praises Cleveland for his expert manipulation of the Indians, for the skill with which he makes them happily accept his plan: 'whatever he proposed they instantly agreed to'. The hill people are represented as naive children who are won over with trifles and do not perceive that they are being manipulated. Like pupils at school, they receive 'medals . . . as a reward for their improving civilization' and, childishly boasting of their new soldiering skills, make their peers jealous and eager to join in the game as well. Under Cleveland's direction, the wayward marauders willingly submit to education and discipline. Felix Padel has recently pointed out that Cleveland's tactics included mass trials and a number of executions, but these are entirely absent from the popular accounts of his activities.[39] Cleveland occupies a position at the head of a long line of British officials who kindly control natives throughout the world in the literature of colonial rule. The type originates just at the moment that British authority is subject to domestic attack. One might say that Hastings's impeachment calls the type into being. Cleveland represents the ability of the British to reconcile Indians to their state of subjection, and simultaneously look after Company interests. Hodges explains Cleveland's motivation as that of 'humanity . . . added to the desire of improving the revenue of this part of his district for the Company's benefit': the epitome of disinterested, benevolent, profitable British rule.[40]

Hodges's representation of Cleveland has much in common with the portrait provided by John Shore to mark the collector's untimely death, the 'Monody on the Death of Augustus Cleveland' of 1786. Shore (who later was to become governor-general) was Cleveland's cousin, and sees him as the hill tribe's 'tutor, lord and parent':

> As some fond sire instructs his darling son,
> With fost'ring care he led wild nature on;
> And now, where rapine mark'd the blood stain'd field,
> The well-till'd glebes a smiling harvest yield;[41]

The civilizing touch of British rule refashions both the people and the region; the second couplet, with its tight 'before' and 'after' structure conveys the sense of this complete transformation.

Further reference to Cleveland's activities can be found in a volume of the *Asiatick Researches*, the widely read journal of the learned Asiatic Society of Bengal, founded in 1784 by Sir William Jones with the encouragement of Warren Hastings. The fourth volume, published in 1795, contains an article by Lieutenant Thomas Shaw, entitled *On the Inhabitants of the Hills near Rajamahall*. Shaw provides a version of the hill people's creation story in which the different races of mankind are represented as seven brothers, each with their own particular attributes, who are sent down from heaven to earth. The seventh brother, ancestor of the hill people themselves, is the most miserable; old and sick, he is condemned to a life of hardship:

considered an outcast, and ordered to inhabit these hills, where finding neither clothes, nor subsistence, he and his descendents necessarily became thieves, in which practice they continued, till such time as MR CLEVLAND wisely conciliated their attachment to the *English* government, by a liberal generosity and munificence, while he entered their hills unattended, putting the utmost confidence in their faith, and made engagements to settle on their chiefs an inconsiderable monthly sum, in consideration of their good and peaceful behaviour and obedience, to which they have rigidly adhered; and this, it is related, put an end to their predatory incursions and marauding.[42]

In an extraordinarily smooth transition from myth to actuality, the British are thus written into the tribal creation story. This incorporation of Company rule into local mythology implies the unequivocal acceptance of the British by the hill people, and British rule, represented by wise, generous Mr Cleveland, becomes as inevitable as the story's conclusion.

Shaw provides concrete proof of Indian affection for the British. He notes that after Cleveland's death, the hill tribes spoke of him 'with reverential sorrow', and that the local Indian officials 'erected a monument to the memory of MR CLEVELAND, nearly in the form of a Pagoda'.[43]

124 / *India Inscribed*

The grateful Indians come close to deifying the collector with their temple-like memorial, while the Company raises its own monument, projecting a sense of the durability and solidity of its rule by inscribing Britain firmly on the face of India. Shaw reproduces the whole of the lengthy Company epitaph which details Cleveland's humanitarian exploits, even transcribing the lapidary lineation. And because Shaw has already recounted the achievements which the epitaph summarizes, he is also repeating his own narrative, as though to establish beyond doubt the fact of British benevolence. With the authoritative tone of public monumental inscription to endorse his description, Shaw produces a self-confirming narrative.

In fact this inscription did enjoy a kind of immortality. It is reproduced, in part at least, in Kipling's short story, 'The Tomb of His Ancestors', published in the 1898 collection *The Day's Work*. The inscription is discovered, half-effaced and somewhat abbreviated, by John Chinn, third in the line of Chinns to serve in India among the Bhils, a tribal people. On the reverse side of the monument, Chinn finds an equally illegible and shortened version of Shore's 'Monody'. In the story, the tomb belongs to Chinn's grandfather, who pacified and settled the Bhils—'who had made the Bhil a man'—and whom the grateful Bhils have deified.[44] The tomb has become a shrine to 'Jan Chinn' the first, and John Chinn the third is himself regarded as a 'demi-god twice born, tutelary deity of their land and people'.[45] Although the gap between John Chinn's mortal and god-like identities is exploited to considerable comic effect, Kipling's story reconfirms the Cleveland narrative, asserting once more British dominion over Indian hearts and minds. This fusion of the characters of Cleveland and Chinn clearly appealed to Philip Mason in his 1954 study, *The Men who ruled India*. Mason almost conflates Cleveland with his fictional counterpart, remarking that Cleveland's monument 'is no longer "hung about with wild flowers and nuts, packets of wax and honey, bottles of native spirit and infamous cigars" as Jan Chinn's was'.[46] Mason is so attracted to this figure that he indulges in a ruminative aside: Cleveland, 'one feels, had not expected thanks and had been loved'.[47] Although these passages were omitted in the 1987 abridged version of his study, Mason's 1954 rendition of the Cleveland narrative testifies to its enduring appeal.

The British image of benign rule seems to be largely constructed around the exploits of individuals. A second hero is Rear-Admiral Watson, commander-in-chief in the East Indies from 1754 to 1757, who assisted Clive in the recapture of Calcutta from Siraj-ud Daula in 1757. The main author of Watson's reputation is Edward Ives, '[f]ormerly

Surgeon of Admiral Watson's Ship', whose *Voyage from England to India* was published in 1773.[48] Watson, like Cleveland, is remembered with affection by Indians at his death. Ives writes that: 'His *integrity, humanity, generosity*, and *disinterestedness* of heart were such, as to become almost proverbial among the natives, as well as the *Europeans* residing in the East Indies.'[49] Watson's near-proverbial status is a kind of linguistic memorial to his benevolence. He is incorporated in the language of the Indians much as Cleveland enters tribal mythology; the British are leaving their mark on Indian culture.

The narrative which constructs Watson as the epitome of benevolence was first published anonymously in the November issue of *The London Magazine* of 1757. It appears again in Ives' *Voyage* with a footnote identifying Ives as the author of the earlier account in 'one of the monthly magazines'.[50] It seems significant that this story should reappear in 1773, just when the Company's image required sprucing-up: the year after the British assumed responsibility for the administration of justice in Bengal and the start of the parliamentary inquiry into the allegations against Clive. The episode with which we are concerned occurs at the end of the siege of Gheria, when the victorious Watson visits his captives, the family of the fort's commander, Tulaji Angria, who had himself already fled. Tulaji Angria, a Maratha chief who disrupted Company trade by attacking British shipping, is described as 'an arbitrary, cruel tyrant', in marked contrast to Watson, who displays every possible virtue in his dealings with the prisoners.[51] This is from Ives' second version of the story in the *Voyage*:

> Admiral Watson, soon after the reduction of the place, took an opportunity of visiting these unfortunate captives; and the interview between them was beyond measure affecting. Upon his entering their house, the whole family made a grand *salaam*, or reverential bending of their bodies, touching the very ground with their faces, and shedding floods of tears. The admiral desired them to be comforted; adding, 'that they were now under his protection; and that no kind of injury should be done them.' They then again made the *salaam*. The mother of *Angria*, though strongly affected with these testimonies of goodness and humanity, yet could not help crying out, 'that the people had no king, she no son, her daughters no husband, the children no father!' The admiral replied, 'that from henceforward they must look on him as their father and their friend.' Upon which the youngest child, a boy of about six years old, sobbing said, '*Then you shall be my father*,' and immediately took the admiral by the hand, and called him '*father*.' This action of the child's was so very affecting, it quite overpowered that brave, that good man's heart, and he found himself under a necessity of turning from the innocent youth for a while, to prevent the falling of those tears, which stood ready to gush from his eyes.[52]

This tableau incorporates many of the characteristic elements of the literature of sensibility: the feeling man moved to tears with benevolent concern at the plight of the vulnerable female victim and children. It is difficult to imagine a more explicit or popular expression of benign paternalism: the infant prince calls the admiral father, and takes him by the hand. The scene is so 'affecting' not only because of the thick layers of pathos and sentiment, but also because it enacts the British ideal of colonial relations: the childlike Indian spontaneously entrusts his fate to the kindly British adult.[53]

This scene finds an interesting parallel in an episode recorded in Orme's *History* concerning the capture of the fort of Bobbili by the French under the Marquis de Bussy.[54] The Indian defenders, led by Ranga Rao, fight with great ferocity, refusing all French offers of mercy, until defeat appears inevitable. Then the soldiers turn on their own families whom they massacre to save from European defilement, before returning to the city walls to die in combat themselves. Orme depicts the slaughter in emotive terms:

they proceeded, every man with a torch, his lance, and poinard, to the habitations in the middle of the fort, to which they set fire indiscriminately ... and every man stabbed without remorse, the woman or child, whichsoever attempted to escape the flames and suffocation. Not the helpless infant clinging to the bosom of its mother saved the life of either from the hand of the husband or the father.[55]

The pathos and the horror are intended to excite the reader's indignation at the 'atrocious prejudices' which provoke the massacre.[56] But the representation has further implications for a British readership: it demonstrates the complete failure of the French, Britain's rivals in India, to reconcile Indians to their dominion. The scene functions as the antithesis to those images of happy Indian acceptance of British rule which we have already considered, and implies that French rule is not viable in India. We should note that Orme's *History* was published three years after the decisive British victory over the French at Wandiwash, the battle in which de Bussy was taken prisoner.

When the French enter the fortress of Bobbili, the sight of the devastation horrifies them:

Whilst contemplating it, an old man, leading a boy, was perceived advancing from a distant recess: he was welcomed with much attention and respect, and conducted by the crowd to Mr Law, to whom he presented the child with these words; 'This the son of Rangarao, whom I have preserved against his father's will.' Another emotion now succeeded, and the preservation of this infant was felt by all as some alleviation to the horrible catastrophe, of which they had been the unfortunate authors. The tutor and the child were immediately sent to Mr Bussy, who, having heard of the condition of the fort, would not go into it, but remained in his tent, where he received the sacred captives with the humanity of a guardian appointed by the strongest claims of nature . . .[57]

This narrative can be read as a variation on Ives' story about Watson; it is worth considering the differences between the two accounts. Watson visits his captives to exercise active benevolence, whereas de Bussy's generosity is the reflex action of relief intended to bring about 'some alleviation to the horrible catastrophe'. Tulaji Angria's son spontaneously entrusts himself to Watson's care, while Ranga Rao's heir is presented by his tutor; Watson behaves like a father, de Bussy like a guardian. Both representations possess a theatrical quality: if the first most resembles the conclusion of a comedy, with its satisfying restoration of a family unit, then the second is like the end of a tragedy, with Ranga Rao's heir the sole sign that life might continue amidst the general carnage. Only Britain can furnish India with a happy ending.

The idea that British rule guarantees Indian happiness is articulated by Sir William Jones who, as I shall show, still quite inappropriately enjoys the reputation of a disinterested scholar. In his 'Tenth Anniversary Discourse', delivered to the Asiatic Society of Bengal in 1793, Jones describes British possessions in India as 'these *Indian* territories, which providence has thrown into the arms of *Britain* for their protection and welfare'. But the relationship is not one-sided, for Britain too 'derives essential benefit from the diligence of a placid and submissive people'.[58]

This perception of the mutual and related advantages of colonial rule is central to the construction of the British self-image: Indian well-being is necessary for the productivity which makes Britain rich. The more prosperous the country, the larger the revenues collected by the Company; the greater the output, the better for Company trade. This line of reasoning produces many a rosy representation of the state of agriculture and industry in British-ruled Bengal. These images of prosperity are also intended to counter charges made against the Company of exploitation, particularly accusations of cruel negligence in the years of 1769 to 1770, a period of terrible famine, when a quarter of the population of Bengal starved to death, and many of the survivors turned vagrant. Consider for example this description of Bengal a decade after the famine from Hodges' *Travels*:

FROM the apparent state of the country, a just estimate may generally be formed of the happiness or the misery of a people. Where there is neatness in the cultivation of the land, and that land is tilled to the utmost of its boundaries, it may reasonably be supposed that the government is the protector and not the oppressor of the people. Throughout the kingdom of Bengal it appears highly flourishing in tillage of every kind, and abounding in cattle. The villages are neat and clean and filled with swarms of people.[59]

There is an implicit reference here to the debate in Britain about the propriety of Company rule (Warren Hastings, we should remember, was Hodges' patron). Hodges depicts a settled, repopulated and thriving Bengal which, the reader is to infer, has completely recovered from the effects of the famine. In Bhagalpur, one of the districts administered by Cleveland, Hodges finds an absolute idyll:

The care that was taken in the government, and the minute attention to the happiness of the old people, rendered this district, at this time, (1781) a perfect paradise. It was not uncommon to see the manufacturer at his loom, in the cool shade, attended by his friend softening his labour by the tender strains of music. There are to be met in India many old pictures representing similar subjects, in the happy times of the Mogul government.[60]

The choice of a weaver to represent the blessings of good government is significant. Textiles formed one of the Company's major exports, and the image of a contented, industrious artisan at his loom carries pleasing overtones of profitable trade. The analogy with Mughal painting is also important. Hodges suggests that his image of beneficent British rule is similar to Mughal pictures of comparable scenes; by linking the Bengal administration to the heyday of the Mughal empire, Hodges seems to imply that the Company, rather than the emperor in Delhi, is the rightful successor to Mughal rule. Past Mughal regimes are invoked as a source of legitimacy for British rule, but the present Mughal government is represented as corrupt and incompetent. A later passage in the *Travels* describes the district of Agra, ruled by the Mughals, but harassed by the violent and frequent incursions of the Marathas:

This fine country exhibits, in its present state, a melancholy proof of the consequences of a bad government, of wild ambition, and the horrors attending civil dissentions; for when the governors of this country were in plenitude of power, and exercised their rights with wisdom, from the excellence of its climate, with some degree of industry, it must have been a perfect garden; but now all is desolation and silence.[61]

The misgovernment of the Mughals and resulting devastation of their provinces justifies British intervention. The Company alone can restore India to its former prosperity; the idyll of Bhagalpur proves that the garden of India can flourish once more.

The 'Spirit of Observation'

A thorough knowledge of the subject people was considered essential for efficient colonial rule. While many authors either announce or imply the depth of their knowledge of the Indian character, Baltazard Solvyns was the first European to attempt systematically to chart the population of Bengal. Solvyns, a Belgian artist, was resident in India from 1790 to 1804. Initially encouraged by Sir William Jones, Solvyns declared his intention to produce '250 coloured etchings descriptive of the manners, customs, character, dress, and religious customs of the Hindoos' in 1794.[62] The etchings were finally published in book form as *Les Hindous, ou Description de leurs moeurs, coutumes et cérémonies* in Paris from 1808 to 1812 with a bilingual text in French and somewhat shaky English. Solvyns's work is notable as the first major attempt to order and represent the various Hindu castes and occupations pictorially; he could be considered a pioneer anthropological illustrator. Solvyns himself announces the seriousness of his intentions when he situates his work among that of a long roll-call of scholars and authors including Jones, Dow, Orme, Holwell, Hodges, and the members of the Asiatic Society, claiming that such writers have left only his own area of research uninvestigated.[63] Indeed the ambitious breadth of Solvyns's work parallels the comprehensive scope of the first volumes of the *Asiatick Researches* and his painstaking project to chart the Hindu people perfectly exemplifies that Linnaen 'impulse to classify nature and man into types' which Said, following Foucault, regards as central to late-eighteenth-century discourse.[64] In fact, Solvyns describes his careful working methods almost as if he were a botanist examining a specimen:

> The drawings from which are engraved the numerous plates with which this work is enriched, were taken by myself upon the spot. Instead of trusting to the works of others, or remaining satisfied with the knowledge contained in preceding authors, I have spared neither time, nor pains, nor expence, to see and examine with my own eyes, and to delineate every object with the most minute accuracy...[65]

Solvyn's emphasis on the scientific rigour of his techniques of observation appears a manifestation of the 'anxious impulse to insist that colonized peoples can indeed be rendered interpretable within the language of the colonizer' which for Suleri reveals the absence of colonial authority.[66] Suleri notes that domination 'could comprehend the parameters of its cultural invasion only by looking all too attentively at Indian races', and indeed Solvyns promises to reveal the Indian people to Europe as they had

130 / *India Inscribed*

never been seen before.[67] His illustrations cover an extraordinary range of aspects of Indian life: varieties of occupation and dress, Hindu ascetics and religious festivals, musical instruments, vehicles and boats, even methods of smoking. The scale of his project is echoed by the physical size and expense of the four folio volumes: the set, partly printed in colour, was sold at 1728 francs, and with additional hand-tinting, at 2600 francs.[68]

Solvyns's aim is to render all of Bengali society visible and intelligible to his European readership. He even brings back illicit records of forbidden sights: picturing a wealthy 'kept mistress or concubine', he comments that she is '[a]ccesible only to the person who keeps her, no other visitor is admitted; which makes it very difficult for Europeans to penetrate to the interior of her apartments.'[69] The *double entendre* is surely significant: Solvyns is entering that hidden domestic region of Hindu female sexuality, mythologized by generations of travel writers, in order to reveal its secrets. Few aspects of Indian life escape our voyeuristic gaze. Religious rules prohibiting the presence of strangers are flouted without compunction: 'many Hindoos pretend, that the matrimonial ceremony is null if it can be proved that a stranger was present at it. I could not therefore have represented it, if I had not found means of seeing it unperceived, and taking an exact sketch of this mysterious solemnity.'[70] The scientfic pursuit of authentic knowledge automatically takes precedence over any consideration of local customs, indeed it justifies their violation.

Perhaps the clearest indication of Solvyns's anxious desire to establish an easily comprehensible system to classify Hindu society is his inclusion, at the end of the work, of several studies of heads of representatives of different castes in the manner of later anthropometric studies. Solvyns asserts that each caste has 'its appropriate physiognomy, its characteristic features' by which its members can be identified:

The *Brahmun* has a mild and pious air; the *Kuttery* is haughty and bold in appearance: cunning and mercantile caution is marked on the countenance of the *Byce*. If none of these characteristics are perceived in the physionomy of an *Hindoo*, we may safely pronounce that he is of the *sooder* cast, and if we are to carry our spirit of observation a little farther we shall soon be able to ascertain with tollerable [*sic*] accuracy what is the nature of his occupation in that cast.[71]

Solvyns fantasizes that one day Hindu society will display itself like a perfectly ordered and coherent reference work, allowing the informed European to read the status and occupation of Hindus from the index of their faces. The system is simple and possesses its own self-evident logic: of course brahmans look mild and pious, while it is only to be expected that the warrior caste, 'Kutterrys' (ksatriyas), should appear haughty and bold. Appearance here discloses identity in an entirely unproblematic fashion, and so Solvyns promises his readers an easy-to-use key to the complexities of the Hindus.

This desire to proclaim mastery over a mass of people and a new appreciation of the picturesque qualities of Indian appearance combine in the first texts to celebrate the diversity of Indian life. Consider this description by the painter, William Hodges, from his illustrated *Travels in India* of 1793:

> It is extremely pleasant to observe the variety of travellers that are to be met with on the road; either passing along in groups, under the shade of some spreading tree, by the side of the wells or tanks. In one part may be seen the native soldiers, their half pikes sticking by their side, and their shields lying by them, with their sabres and matchlocks; in another part is, perhaps, a company of merchants, engaged in calculation, or of devotees in the act of social worship; and in another, the common Hindoo pallankeen bearers baking their bread.... On the whole, I must say, that the simplicity and primitive appearance of these groups delighted me.[72]

This passage is accompanied by two plates of Indian types: 'A Peasant Woman of Hindostan', and 'A Sepoy Matchlock Man'. The sense of pleasurable wonder at the heterogeneity of Indian society originates in the period that India is first being charted, mapped and named. During these decades Indian artists also began to produce Company school paintings of Indian types to supply the demand for picturesque Indian souvenirs. Hodges's description notably prefigures Kipling's celebration of the travelling masses in *Kim*. In the third chapter, the old soldier details the huge variety of Indians to be seen on the Grand Trunk Road: 'All castes and kinds of men move here. Look! Brahmins and chumars, bankers and tinkers, barbers and bunnias, pilgrims and potters—all the world going and coming.'[73] For Kipling, the Grand Trunk Road is a 'wonderful spectacle ... such a river of life as nowhere else exists in the world'; and a similar appreciation of the diversity of Indian life underlies Hodges's description.[74] But we must remember that, in *Kim*, undercover knowledge of the native population is gathered to serve governmental ends, and Hodges's text is in part a record of an official tour by his patron, Warren Hastings, through British-controlled Bengal and Bihar. In both cases the delight in variety is also pleasure in the assertion of colonial knowledge and authority.

The relation of knowledge to power and deception exemplified by *Kim* is characteristic of an identifiable colonial genre: that of the disguised

European moving incognito through society. The European protagonist may be a spy, as in *Kim*, or an anthropological investigator, as in Edward William Lane's *Manners and Customs of the Modern Egyptians*, a text skilfully analysed by Said.[75] A less well-known example is furnished by George Forster's epistolary travel account, *A Journey from Bengal to England*, published posthumously in 1798. A Company servant, returning overland from his posting in Madras, Forster disguises himself as a Mughal merchant in an attempt to visit an English officer in Lucknow without attracting attention:

> I approached the door of an officer's quarter, and desired the servants to acquaint their master, that a Moghul merchant, of whom there are many at Lucknow, requested permission to see him. Though the entreaty was urged in the softest and most pursuasive tone within the compass of my speech, they flatly and roughly rejected it, saying that their master was eating his breakfast. Anxious to obtain the wanted information, I tried another door that seemed less closely guarded, but there also my prayer was prefered in vain; and having nothing in my pocket to strengthen the argument, I was obliged to retire; though the day was extremely hot, and the distance to my lodging was at least four miles. This occurrence, however productive of temporary inconvenience, gave me satisfactory proof of the efficacy of my disguise, and the fluency of my Mahometan language. Many, I dare say, are the unfortunate plaintiffs in our Indian world, who unable to purchase a passage through the gates of the great, are thrust away by their rude and rapacious domestics.[76]

For Forster, the experience of being treated with contempt confirms his assumed identity: to be considered inferior is an inevitable aspect of membership of the subject race. Of course the frustration that Forster experiences is merely local; it is more than offset by the satisfaction of being able to trick Indians. Forster's impersonation of a Mughal merchant is based on linguistic and anthropological expertise. His disguise proves the success of the British project, demonstrated by such publications as the *Asiatick Researches*, to acquire a detailed and complete knowledge of India and its people. Thus while appparently being humiliated, Forster is in fact demonstrating the extent of British understanding and control. This sense of superiority is heightened by the reader's complicity: forewarned of Forster's scheme, we necessarily share in the deception. Forster's impersonation skills grant him the authority to speak for those he is mimicking: he generalizes from his experience to lament the fate of 'unfortunate plaintiffs'. At the same time that Forster appropriates the native voice to speak for the mass of Indian petitioners, he places the Indian domestic servant class under surveillance, condemning their greed and brutality. Thus positioned both inside and outside Indian society, both participant and observer, Forster embodies the colonial aspiration for omniscience and omnipresence.

Forster's disguise admits him to a new intimacy with the people, an increased familiarity which is signalled by a shift in narrative tone, from the formal to the anecdotal. Forster enters a kind of Hogarthian underworld peopled by comic grotesques: he wrangles with an ugly hostess who takes offence, as at an indecent proposal, at his request to stay the night in her inn; while a drunken Pathan and his tone-deaf musician divert him for a few hours:

I passed this evening in the company of a Patan, who was returning to his home from Lucknow, where he had expended the greatest part of his estate in the society of the ladies, and in the pleasures of arrack; but in the last he very copiously indulged. In the course of two hours and a half, I beheld him with amazement empty two bottles of a spirit so harsh and fiery, that the like dose must have turned the head of an elephant. The Patan made an apology for this excessive potation, by observing, that it removed from his mind every sensation of sorrow and melancholy—passions, which, he said greatly annoyed him in his cooler moments. This jovial Mahometan was attended by an old musician, marvellously ill apparelled, and deficient in the larger portion of his teeth, who during the interludes of his master's amusement, strummed on a miserable guitar, which he accompanied with some of Hafez's odes; but uttered in a voice that would have struck dismay into the fiercest beast that ranges the forest.[77]

By shedding his British identity, Forster has gained admission to a world where Muslims display their vices and indulge in ludicrous behaviour. Muslim luxurious indolence is here rewritten as degeneracy: the Pathan's alcohol consumption suggests that he is equipped with a constitution of animal robustness, and the raucous singing implies an equally degraded taste. Much of the condescending humour of the passage derives from the fact that the Pathan and his toothless serenader are unaware that they are being observed by the critical eye of 'a civil servant on the Madras establishment'.[78]

Because he can claim to have witnessed how natives *really* behave, Forster's disguise confers additional authority on his text. Later in his narrative, he relates a story intended to demonstrate the depth of his knowledge of the Muslim character. Spending a night in a mosque on the Afghan/Indian border, Forster finds himself reprimanded by a mullah for omitting to perform his evening prayers, even though Forster pleads ill health. When Forster appears to be asleep, the same priest attempts to rob him. This elicits an outraged aside, addressed to the recipient of the letter, concerning the duplicity of Muslims in general:

> What think you, my friend, of these Mahometans, who, if they wash and pray at the five stated times, abstain from wine and the flesh of hogs, and utter a string of Arabic ejaculations which they do not understand, believe that they have procured the divine licence to violate the laws of justice. This opinion is not formed on the moment, but has arisen from long experience and the intimate intercourse, which my various occupations in India have produced; and is now so firmly substantiated by undeviating testimony, that it shapes my general sentiments of the Mahometan character. When they daringly commit these acts on each other, even amidst the rites of their religion, what is it to withold their attacks on those of a different faith?[79]

Although Forster has learnt Muslim ways so well that he can impersonate one convincingly—indeed, for the purposes of this argument, he classes himself among them—his 'intimate intercourse' with Muslims has bred only distrust, contempt and condescension. Forster fortifies himself against the transgressive potential of cultural cross-dressing by asserting his original identity in the ringing tones of moral and intellectual supremacy.

But not all texts sound such notes of cultural confidence. Forster's denigration of Muslim integrity implies the continuing need for British supervision and government, but other narratives challenge that authority. The anonymous novel, *Hartly House, Calcutta*, published in London in 1789, focuses on an English woman's relationship with a brahman engaged to instruct her in the tenets of Hinduism. The novel relates in epistolary form the Indian experiences of a young woman, Sophia Goldborne, who undertakes the passage to Calcutta to stay with the Hartly family. Sophia's letters to her friend Arabella in England tell of her enthusiastic participation in the busy social round—receptions, expeditions, trips to the theatre, a military review and the races. As one of the few unmarried English women of her class in Calcutta, she is beseiged by admirers and suitors. But Sophia is also a lady of sensibility, and she demonstrates many of the characteristics of that fictional type. Of a feeling disposition, she is prone to fits of grief occasioned by her mother's death. She is liable to fall to her knees in moments of emotional intensity, to swoon when agitated, and to melt into tears at affecting scenes in the theatre.

Sophia's letters home reveal her increasing admiration for Hindu belief. Her enquiries into Hinduism are represented as a kind of feminized version of orientalist scholarship. At the time of the novel's publication, William Jones, having learnt Sanskrit under the tuition of pandits, was delivering his anniversary discourses on Indian culture to the Asiatic Society of Bengal, and convening a committee of pandits to act as legal advisers to the Company. Jones's activities were of course motivated by the desire to assert British authority in the courts, but Sophia's interest in Hinduism is closely related to the mutual attraction which develops between her and her brahman informant. The pursuit of knowledge in the service of power is translated in the novel into the feminized discourse of sentimentality. The novel is, I think, the earliest depiction of an European woman's romantic involvement with an Indian; but the interpretation of the novel offered by A. L. Basham as an uncomplicated flowering of humanistic tolerance and racial harmony is unconvincing, for the events are related through the less than reliable letter-writing persona of Sophia, a heroine of considerable inexperience and immaturity.[80]

Throughout the novel, the reader is aware that Sophia is in the process of growing up: like so many heroines of late-eighteenth-century novels, she is at that formative age between the end of schooling and the onset of marriage. The frivolous tone of her letters and her obvious lack of self-knowledge clearly indicate her immaturity. If we briefly trace the course of Sophia's love for the brahman and his religion, we will realize that the situation is more complex and ambiguous than Basham allows. Sophia first decides to find out about Hinduism when she learns about the young brahman; she confides in Arabella:

(shall I own to you a most extravagant piece of vanity, which has recently sprung up in my mind?) an admirer, Arabella, of his [the brahman's] character would be proof of my attractions I should be proud of.

I will tell Mrs. Hartly my whim, and engage his relation to introduce him. The compliments which I at present receive, are all of the common-place kind, and may with equal propriety be addressed to any sister female; but to please a Bramin I must have perfections of the mental sort, little inferior to the purity and benignity of angels;—in a word, my good dispositions would be cultivated and brought forward by such an acquaintance, and my bad ones corrected; and, as celibacy is their engagement, the soul would be the only object of attachment and admiration.[81]

The first thing to notice is that Sophia initiates the relationship. This inverts the gender relations of her own social circle, for Sophia spends much of her time waiting for her English suitors to make advances. She summons the brahman and determines to make him her admirer, her virtue protected by his vow of celibacy. This vow seems to ward off the possibility of inter-racial sex, but the vain and frivolous tone alerts the reader to the danger implicit in Sophia's confident assertion of the purely platonic nature of the relationship. And indeed this proceeds along lines which are flattering to Sophia and often verge on flirtation, although it never oversteps the boundaries into full-blown romance. After a period of dangerous sickness, Sophia asks the brahman in what form he thinks she would have been reborn, had she died while she was ill: 'He smiled—blushed, I think—and gave me to understand, that I should never have lost the power of pleasing, because I have not exercised that power unworthily in my human shape.'[82] The brahman's definition of Sophia's attractiveness as 'the power of pleasing' is singularly appropriate: she exercises this power over the brahman to make him her admirer.

It is notable that while the brahman was accompanied by an interpreter at their first meeting, by this stage in their relationship, the intermediary seems to have disappeared, and the brahman and Sophia appear to communicate directly. Indeed there is no need for a translator because the brahman has by now been admitted into the discourse of civility, mixing his theology with drawing room compliments. Here, for example is his explanation of Hindu fatalism:

'We resolve every event,' said the aimiable Bramin, 'into the divine appointment, and dare not repine.'

'This is a very delightful doctrine in theory, Sir,' returned I.

—'And salutary in practice Madam,' replied he, 'as the man before you is a living testimony;—for that he was born a Bramin, he submits to, as the will of Heaven—and that you are the loveliest of women, he acknowledges with pious resignation.'

I was astonished—Mrs Hartly was silent—and the Bramin retired, with more emotion than quite accorded with his corrected temper, as if he felt he had said too much.

Wretch that I am, Arabella! this confession, which I shall ever remember with pain, did I, in the idle gaiety of my heart, ardently aspire after.[83]

It is only after Sophia has achieved her aim, after she has elicited a near declaration of love from the brahman, that she admits the foolishness of her scheme, going on to express her regret at the impossibility of platonic friendships between the sexes. Sophia has severely tried the strength of the brahman's vow of celibacy, pushed him to the limits of propriety, made him say 'too much' and show 'more emotion than quite accorded with his corrected temper'. She has proved her 'power of pleasing' at the expense of his religious integrity. A few pages later, however, Sophia has lost all awareness of the ambiguities of the relationship, assuring Arabella that 'love ... is not so spontaneous an effect (in general) of a friendship between the sexes, in India as in England; the object of admiration being mental charms'.[84] This observation immediately follows a description of the brahman's exquisite good looks which is itself preceded by Sophia's announcement of her 'conversion' to Hinduism: 'Ashamed of the manners of modern Christianity (amongst the professors of which acts of devotion are subjects of ridicule, and charity, in all its amiable branches, a polite jest) I am become a convert to the Gentoo faith, and have my Bramin to instruct me *per diem*.'[85] This declaration is perhaps the most arresting passage of the novel. It seems to open up a whole new realm of cultural possibilities, and has indeed been interpreted as such by Basham, among others. But we should look more carefully at the Hinduism which Sophia embraces. We need go no further than the next sentence to find Sophia exclaiming: 'What a sweet picture would the pen of Sterne have drawn of this young man's person'. Sophia chooses Laurence Sterne, a founding father of the genre of the sentimental novel, as the ideal author to depict the brahman.[86] Sophia's version of Hinduism is closely allied to sentimental belief in the natural goodness of humanity, demonstrated through humanitarian concern for others. She describes 'this doctrine of metempsychosis' as 'the religion of humanity' for Hindu 'hearts are softened into a tender concern for the kind treatment of every creature living'. In her account, Hindu teaching is reformulated as an education of the sensibility, one of the aims of the sentimental novel itself: 'For love, this young priest affirms, refines the sentiment, softens the sensibility, expands our natural virtues, extinguishes every idea of jealousy or competitorship, and unites all created beings in one great chain of affection and friendship.'[87] Hinduism is thus annexed to sentimentalism, and India subjected (somewhat belatedly) to the cult of sensibility that had swept across Europe in the preceding decades.

Throughout the novel the brahman is never referred to by name and so is never properly individualized; he simply represents Hindu piety and virtue in an appealingly sentimental form. His lack of a name means that Sophia can, in a sense, possess him: she terms him 'my Bramin'. More importantly, his namelessness renders his role in the narrative dispensable: a little later in the novel the brahman is struck down with sickness and dies unexpectedly in the night. Sophia laments his loss, but immediately after she classes herself among 'we Christians'; and there is no further mention of her 'conversion' to the 'Gentoo faith'. The rest of Sophia's letters primarily concern her courtship by an eligible young Englishman, and the novel ends with her marriage and passage home. The novel thus conforms to the pattern which Mary Louise Pratt has identified as characteristic of the colonial love stories set in Africa and elsewhere which enjoyed a vogue in the late-eighteenth-century; stories 'in whose dénouements the "cultural harmony through romance" always breaks down. Whether love turns out to be requited or not, whether the colonized lover is female or male, outcomes seem to be roughly the same: the lovers are separated, the European is reabsorbed by Europe, and the non-European dies an early death'.[88]

Sophia emerges unscathed from her contact with Hinduism and resumes her former cultural identity. By the end of the novel Hinduism has dwindled in significance for Sophia. She writes that on their return her father will come laden with 'large assortments of Eastern manufactures' for Arabella, but Sophia will not flaunt herself inappropriately; she will rather 'affect the Gentoo air, which is an assemblage of all the soft and winning graces priests or poets have yet devised a name for'.[89] The 'Gentoo air' is here no more than a fashionable pose, as much a commodity as those 'Eastern manufactures' destined for home consumption. Indeed, Sophia's interest in the brahman only briefly compromises her position of colonial dominance, for although he is entertained in the drawing room and flirted with, Sophia remains in charge of her dealings with the brahman. The author has explored two extremely sensitive issues—that of a romantic liaison between an English woman and an Indian man and of the attraction of Hinduism for a Christian—both of which could seriously challenge cultural identities and shake the balance of colonial power (and would be unimaginable later, in the aftermath of 1857). It is striking that contemporary notices and reviews of the novel do not comment on the romance or Sophia's Hindu leanings, noting only its instructive and elegant delineation of Eastern and European manners.[90] I would argue that this silence suggests, not so much that the reviewers find these issues too threatening to address, as that the author has managed to limit the sense of danger. The novel works to elide cultural difference, turning the brahman into a drawing room suitor and Hinduism into sentimentalism. The point is not that humanistic tolerance and racial harmony are allowed to flower, but that a potentially subversive situation is contained; the narrative functions as a kind of enactment and resolution of anxiety, or, we might say, an exercise in constructing a safe colonial subject.

The Anglo-Indian encounter and the process of cross-cultural education provide the themes for a second epistolary novel, published some years after *Hartly House*, which explores relations between the Indians and British, this time from a Hindu perspective. Elizabeth Hamilton's *Trans-*

lation of the *Letters of a Hindoo Rajah* addresses, like *Hartly House*, a complex area of colonial interaction. Issued initially in 1796 and running to five editions by 1811, the novel was Elizabeth Hamilton's first major work; she went on to write a number of conservative and evangelical texts, including an antiquarian novel on classical life and a very popular didactic tale of Scottish peasant life. Elizabeth Hamilton was the sister of Charles Hamilton, a founder member of the Asiatic Society of Bengal, who produced a history of the Rohilla Afghans and translated the *Hedaya*; and in her first novel Hamilton draws heavily both on her brother's work and that of his fellow Asiatic Society members. The *Letters* are dedicated to Warren Hastings, her brother's patron and friend, and presented as if they were a work of oriental scholarship, with a 'Preliminary Dissertation' on Hindu society and learned footnotes to authenticate and elucidate the text. As Gary Kelly and Nigel Leask have pointed out, the *Letters* number among the 'Anti-Jacobin' novels of the 1790s.[91] For Hamilton, Britain's role is the same in India and Europe: to protect traditional cultures against the dangerous innovations of both Islam and the French Revolution. The 'translation' is supposedly based on the private correspondence of Zaarmilla, a Hindu raja, with letters written before and during his travels to England. For all its scholarly apparatus, the novel has a clear place in the literary tradition of the oriental traveller's letters home from Europe, a genre established by Montesquieu's *Lettres Persanes* (1721), the Marquis d'Argens's *Lettres Chinoises* (1739) and Oliver Goldsmith's *Citizen of the World* (1762). The novel's main satirical targets are the moral failings of the British upper classes, but it also offers an interesting commentary on the role of the Indian as observer and interpreter of the British. Zaarmilla's view—that of a naïvely ardent anglophile—is balanced by the critical gaze of Sheermaal, a brahman traveller whose observations on English life are intended to discourage the raja from his voyage.

Zaarmilla's love for the British dates from a chance encounter with a wounded English officer during a skirmish between the Hindu inhabitants of Rohilkhand and their Afghan conquerors. The English soldier was a prisoner of the Rohilla Afghans, but his captors abandoned him in their flight from the Hindus. As he convalesces, the officer teaches Zaarmilla about life in Britain—about Christianity, liberty, representative government and a non-caste society—lessons which leave the Indian marvelling at English wisdom and virtue (much as the Indophile Sophia Goldbourne wonders at Hindu goodness and piety). But the officer's sudden death cuts short the course of instruction, and the raja decides to seek further enlightenment amongst the British himself.

Zaarmilla's friend and correspondent Maandara attempts to dissuade the raja from embarking on his travels by forwarding reports written by Sheermaal, a brahman recently returned from Britain. These accounts depict a morally depraved, irreligious land, with virtue surviving only in the cottages of the poor and the remote regions of Scotland. Among other injustices and moral lapses, Sheermaal describes the horrors and misery of the slave trade, represents the hypocrisy of men who exclaim against the cruelty of sati in India but tolerate prostitution and female destitution on the streets of London, and notes the small and inattentive congregations at church services. Indeed, Sheermaal is inclined to think the British entirely incapable of serious religious devotion, until he observes the profound concentration exercised during the 'Poojah of idols, termed CARDS . . . [to which] the major part of the people devote their time; sacrificing every enjoyment of life, as well as every domestic duty to the performance of this singular devotion'.[92] The brahman significantly misinterprets British culture: to characterize gambling as worship is to suggest the spiritual bankruptcy of the nation—Sheermaal speaks truer than he knows.

This kind of cross-cultural misrepresentation is characteristic of the 'oriental letters home' genre; the foreigner's mistake is transformed into the telling insight. The form is common in the non-fictional writing of the period too. Edward Moor, in his account of the Third Mysore War, ridicules allied Maratha soldiers for their inability to comprehend the British habit of taking exercise by walking to and fro; the Marathas first think such needless exertion a sign of insanity, then conclude that since the British are never observed in acts of worship, it must be the Christian form of prayer.[93] The Marathas' unwitting deprecation of British piety exploits the satirical potential of cross-cultural misinterpretation, but Hamilton's joke is more sophisticated. Sheermaal's initial premise—that playing-cards represent deities—builds into a parody of British oriental scholarship. The brahman embarks on a William Jones-like study of the genealogy of 'the painted idols of the Europeans':

That the origin of the rites of these divinities may be traced to the favoured country of Brahma, will not admit of a doubt. The flower, which one of the Goddesses carries in her hand, bears such a striking resemblance to the Lotus, that, at first sight, any impartial person must recognise the adored figure of the bounteous Ganga. . . . In the course of a few years investigation, I do not despair to prove the real family of every one of these painted idols; and in the prosecution of this laborious work, I shall not disdain to imitate the method pursued by the antiquarians of England, for 'wise men will not disdain to learn, even from the counsel of fools'.[94]

But who, the reader is bound to ask, are the wise men, who the fools? Sheermaal's hopelessly skewed diffusionist theories result from the misapplication of British scholarly techniques. Britain does not offer itself up to Indian scrutiny in the way that the subcontinent reveals itself to the members of the Asiatic Society.

The learned endeavours of just such Company scholars attract the attention of Zaarmilla who, Sheermaal's warnings notwithstanding, embarks on his search for British knowledge. The raja encounters a group of English officers engaged in the study of Sanskrit and Indian astronomy—characters no doubt based on Hamilton's brother and his Orientalist circle. Awed by their expertise, Zaarmilla sings their praises in strains which, as we shall see later, are familiar from descriptions of William Jones: the British scholars are reclaiming Indian history from oblivion, restoring ancient knowledge previously lost to the natives. The raja continues to boost the colonial self-image with a description, clearly indebted to William Hodges's *Travels in India*, of the thriving state of lands under British control and the dereliction of Muslim-ruled provinces.[95] Travelling with the officers in Bengal, through intensely picturesque countryside, thronged with peacocks and parrots, Zaarmilla stops at a small settlement where the happy villagers seem to have stepped straight from the pages of Hodges's *Travels*: '[the] peaceful inhabitants we found busied at their looms, beneath the friendly shade of a far spreading banyan. In one of the hundred arbours formed by the descending branches, sat a musician, who softly touched the chords of a zena: to the sweet sound of which, the women, and children, were listening with mute attention.'[96] Hamilton reproduces Hodges's image of the industrious weaver, bathed in shade and music, examined earlier in this chapter. But now the scene is witnessed by an Indian, this time a member of the subject race celebrates the blessings of Company rule. The sense of willing Indian co-operation in the colonial project is reinforced by the anecdote itself: the villagers respond to the English officers' request for provisions with eager acquiescence: 'Is not this your country?—command in it what you please!'[97]

But the raja is not simply a colonial apologist; many of his observations are as mistaken as Sheermaal's playing-card hypotheses, but in Zaarmilla's case they stem from his naïve good faith. To give one example: although the raja is at first shocked by the frequency and ease with which English soldiers introduce the name of God into conversation, he realizes subsequently that this derives from 'a consciousness of their own superior piety, which they, doubtless, imagine entitles them to this degree of familiarity with their Maker'.[98] Equipped with a childlike confidence in

British virtue, a faith that can transform blasphemy into piety, Zaarmilla embarks on his travels to England. The distorted perceptions of this innocent abroad offer Hamilton considerable satirical scope and countless opportunities for cross-cultural mistakes. But by the end of his stay even Zaarmilla has gained sufficient insight to endorse Sheermaal's view that true virtue is found only in country retreats, far from the corruption of London.

Cross-cultural misinterpretation, Hamilton's favourite satirical device, is notable in that it hits two targets at once: the corrupt society, and the blundering oriental. The joke's double butt leaves the reader feeling chastened, but still able to condescend to the ignorant foreigner, with the sense of superiority cushioning the blow. It is the reader who recognises the implied censure and, as an *unwitting* critic, the Indian cannot lay claim to any substantial moral authority over the society criticised. By deploying this essentially safe form of satire so frequently, the novel limits the subversive power of the Indian critique of British society.

Articulating Anxieties

Many of the writers in this period are engaged in the attempt to produce non-threatening images of the colonial subject. The figure of the anglicized Indian is in some ways a reassuring one, implying a flattering identification with the colonizer. But as Homi Bhabha has argued, colonial mimicry is also menacing, for the resemblance is never complete—*'almost the same, but not quite'*. The colonial subject appears as a distorted, displaced version of the colonizer, as an imitation which troubles the colonizer's own sense of identity.[99] One of the earliest accounts of an anglicized Indian ruler appears in an article by William Hunter, the 'Narrative of a Journey from Agra to Oujein', which was published in the sixth volume of *Asiatick Researches* of 1799. Hunter was a member of the British party that met Raghunath Hari, the Subadar of Jhansi, whom he describes in some detail:

he appeared to be about sixty years of age, rather below the middle stature, his countenance bespoke intelligence, and his manners were pleasing. Having had occasion, on account of some bodily infirmity, to repair to the *English* station of *Kanhpoor*, for medical assistance, he had contracted a relish for *European* manners and customs. He had discernment enough to perceive our superiority in arts and science, over his countrymen; and possessing a spirit of liberal enquiry, and an exemption from national prejudices, which is very uncommon among the natives of *Hindustan*, he was very desirous of gaining a knowledge of our improvements. Next morning, when we returned his visit, he received us in an upper room of the castle, which, instead of *Hindustany muslum*, was furnished with chairs and tables, in the *European* manner. He showed us several *English* books, among which was the second edition of the *Encyclopædia Britannica*. Of this he had got all the plates neatly copied by artists of his own. To get at the stores of science which these volumes contain, he had, even at that advanced period of life, formed the project of studying the *English* language. He expressed great anxiety to procure a teacher, or any book that could facilitate his pursuit; and was highly gratified by Lieutenant McPHERSON'S presenting him a copy of GILCHRIST'S Dictionary. He entertained us with several tunes on a hand-organ, which he had got at *Kanhpoor*, and exhibited an electrical machine, constructed by a man in his own service. The cylinder was a common table shade; with this he charged a vial, and gave pretty smart shocks, to the no small astonishment of those who were the subjects of his experiments, and of the spectators. . . . He even proposed sensible queries, on the nature of the electric fluid, and the parts of the phial in which the accumulation took place . . . which showed that he did not look on the experiments with an eye of mere childish curiosity, which is amused with novelty; but had a desire to investigate the cause of the phænomena. I am sorry to add, that this man, being, about two years ago, seized with some complaint, which he considered as incurable, repaired to *Benares*, and there drowned himself in the *Ganges*.[100]

Raghunath Hari admires the customs that he is imitating: his anglophilia provides pleasing proof to his British visitors of their 'superiority in arts and science, over his countrymen'; hence their approbation of his intellectual powers and manners. The subadar's reliance on the *Encyclopedia Britannica* and 'GILCHRIST'S Dictionary' for his cultural, scientific and linguistic information pays tribute to the British ability to present and classify knowledge. His use of these reference works to learn about England seems to echo the British project to master India through textual accounts, particularly when we remember that this description appeared in the *Asiatick Researches*, the journal of the Asiatic Society of Bengal. But the subadar's version of British learning is best suited to his European-style drawing room: a barrel-organ's repertoire comprises his stock of western musical knowledge and a machine that dispenses electric shocks represents his understanding of science. This trivialized image of British science and culture undermines the serious aspirations of the learned journal in which it is published. While Hunter acquits Raghunath Hari of 'mere childish curiosity', his concluding comments imply that, in the end, the subadar's scientific promise amounts to nothing: he reverts to the superstitious type by drowning himself in the Ganges. The subadar's adoption of the customs and interests of an English gentleman is represented as partial and ultimately unsuccessful: '*almost the same but not white*', to quote Bhabha's aphorism.[101] The description of Raghunath Hari's proud display of his English artefacts and limited scientific knowledge can be read as a kind of parody of the researches of the Asiatic Society.

But it is not only as imperfect resemblance that the anglicized Indian unsettles British authority. The wealthy Parsi community of Bombay is represented by Edward Moor as a merchant elite that replicates the elegance of European aristocratic life in the colony:

Some of them also have poor Europeans on their pension list, to whom are given a weekly allowance, and food and cloathing. To their private charity and benevolence, they add all the public show and expense necessary to give dignity to their riches. Some of them have two or three country houses, furnished in all the extravagance of European taste; with elegant and extensive gardens, where European gentlemen are frequently invited, and where they are always welcome to entertain their own private parties. . . . We have seen Parsee merchants give balls, suppers, and entertainments to the whole settlement; and some of them ride in English chariots, such as a nobleman in England need not be ashamed to own, drawn by beautiful animals that every nobleman cannot equal in his stud. The Parsees have been often known to behave to English gentlemen, respecting pecuniary concerns, in a manner highly liberal; and although instances might be given to the contrary, and instances might also be given, where individuals, elated by their riches, have forgotten the respect due to English gentlemen, still they are but instances, and are not more reprobated by any than themselves.[102]

Moor defines the Parsis' social status entirely in financial terms—emphasizing their lavish charity and hospitality, sumptuous lifestyle and generosity in extending credit—continually reminding the reader that the community's prestigious position is sustained by trading fortunes. But this display of wealth is compared to that of the English *nobility*. The status of the aristocracy, eroded in Britain by the growing economic power of the middle classes, is challenged in India by Parsi merchants. The instabilities and class confusions of domestic society are reproduced and further complicated by racial difference in the colony. The Parsis occupy a position of economic dominance, maintaining European pensioners and lending money to European gentlemen; and this financial power is at times translated into acts of social rebellion 'where individuals, elated by their riches, have forgotten the respect due to English gentlemen'. But almost as soon as these moments of subversion are mentioned, they are dismissed. The community as a whole knows its place, is aware that Parsi wealth cannot equal English dignity, and that members who presume to challenge British primacy deserve rebuke. Moor attempts to still the anxiety generated by Parsi riches with the suggestion that the rules of colonial hierarchy are policed by the Parsis themselves.

If wealthy Parsis can be relied on to regulate themselves, Indian traders at the opposite end of the social scale most definitely cannot. On 30 August 1787 the *Calcutta Gazette* announced that the garrison's bazaar had been reorganised in an attempt to stamp out Indian corruption:

> The plan of a new pucka Bazar in Fort William, as intended by Sir John Macpherson, and laid out by the Chief Engineer, is now completed, with many extensive improvements. . . . The new shops in this Bazar are all registered, and the Tarif of rates so precisely fixed, and under such nice checks, as to prevent every imposition of the natives; none are retained in it without a special licence of the Commandant, and previously subscribing to all the rules and restrictions within which he has thought proper to confine their conduct.
>
> The old Bazar, composed of an irregular and confused heap of straw huts, not only collected filth and threatened contagion, but proved in fact an asylum for every thief that escaped the hands of justice in Calcutta: robberies were of course daily committed, without the possibility of detection, and the servants of Officers corrupted and seduced either by example, or the easy opportunities offered them of disposing of the property of their masters; while a dark arcanum of roguery was to be met with in every corner of the Bazar, and an Alchymist ready, who could, without any decomposition of its parts, convert, by a few strokes of the hammer, a silver spoon into a pair of Bracelets in a trice.[103]

The untrustworthiness of the Indian lower classes is here expressed in terms of the physical environment: crooked natures inhabiting crooked lanes. Hidden from the British gaze, the bazaar-dwellers spread disease and deceit, elude justice and practice secret arts that transform British property into Indian finery. Nothing is stable; people and objects vanish without trace. Plans and regulations are drawn up to 'confine' native conduct: shops, prices, and individuals are registered, everyone and everything becomes subject to surveillance. British order and control are established through legislative and architectural means. Foucault would term this 'disciplinary space', that is a design which aims to 'eliminate the effects of imprecise distributions, the uncontrolled disappearance of individuals, their diffuse circulation, their unusable and dangerous coagulation' and to establish instead 'presences and absences, to know where and how to locate individuals, to set up useful communications, to interrupt others'.[104]

While British authority confidently announces its ability to eradicate the 'dark arcanum of roguery' within a military garrison, the intimate space of the home proves less susceptible to colonial discipline. Writers generally suspect their Indian servants of systematic fraud. Bhabha argues that it is paradoxically in the home that the 'unhomeliness' of life in the colony is most apparent: 'The recesses of the domestic space become sites for history's most intricate invasions. In that displacement, the borders between home and the world become confused; and, uncannily, the private and the public become part of each other, forcing upon us a vision that is as divided as it is disorientating.'[105] The anxieties of colonial rule manifest themselves most clearly in the home. Many writers complain of the caste restrictions which necessitate the employment of a different servant for each domestic task. The British are hugely outnumbered by their servants at home, just as they are more generally in the colony. The recalcitrance and untrustworthiness of servants (another familiar complaint) is also read as a sign of Indian resistance.

Why should servants be such unreliable colonial subjects? In part, at least, because all servants, Indian or British, were considered suspect by their employers. As Bruce Robbins has shown, in eighteenth-century Britain, 'there was a sudden and well-documented new anxiety on the part of masters and mistresses about the damage that servant spies and informants could do'. Edmund Burke, for instance, believed that 'the very servant who waits behind your chair' could gather enough information to become the 'arbiter of [his master's] life and fortune'.[106] The servant sees too much, knows too much, does too much. For the employment of servants in itself involves a potentially threatening renunciation of control. Servants—be they barbers, with a razor to the master's throat, or cooks who could reach for arsenic instead of salt—hold their employer's life in their hands.[107]

There is also of course a long European literary tradition of witty servants who answer back, trick and deceive their masters. Originating in Roman comedy, the theme continues through Elizabethan and Restoration drama, reaching its fullest flowering in the works of Molière. This dramatic precedent, according to Robbins, forms the basis for the representation of servants in the novel.[108] One text that is characteristic of this tradition is Jonathan Swift's comic *Directions to Servants* of 1745 which lays down the rules that govern servant conduct, enumerating the various ways to mislead, manipulate and disobey masters. But in India, according to works such as Innes Munro's *Narrative of the Military Operations on the Coromandel Coast* of 1789, Hindu servants lack even the most basic sense of subservience. Munro, Lieutenant and Captain in the campaign of 1780–84 against Mysore, blames notions of caste purity:

As Europeans eat any kind of meat, the Indians have been induced to rank them in the *pariar*, or lowest cast of people; and the Gentoos, or Malabars, tell you that, although they are obliged through necessity to serve us, they consider themselves of a much more dignified and gentlemanly rank in life than any European. If you should ask a common *cooly*, or porter, what cast he is of, he will answer 'the same as master, *pariar-cast*.'[109]

Indian servants do not know their 'proper' station. Replacing European social hierarchies with their own caste rules, they represent the Indian potential for insubordination. In fact Munro locates the site of resistance to foreign dominance in the servant/master relationship: 'It seems to be an invariable maxim with all of them to prey as much as possible upon Europeans, being contented with that mode of retaliation for the conquest of their country.'[110] Although many writers comment on the untrustworthiness of Indian servants, Munro complains at length of organized embezzlement, and even suspects the washermen and tailors of Madras of a pact whereby European-made clothes are subjected to overvigorous pounding during washing to bring the tailors more business.[111] Munro's theory of servant sharp practice as a form of anti-British protest deserves some analysis. He establishes a parallel between the servant/master and colonized/colonizer relationships. This correspondence highlights the disparity in scale between the original act of conquest and the Indian reprisal of petty fraud, revealing an awareness of the imbalance of power, but also conveying a sense of the ineffectualness of Indian resistance. The Indian servants' revenge does little to unsettle larger structures of power. Of course, it could be argued that the British were not mistaken in identifying such acts as signs of protest. For James Scott, activites like embezzlement and lying on the part of subordinates are a disguised form of resistance. Scott argues that by paying close attention to political acts that are disguised or off-stage, we can map a realm of possible dissent.[112] This is true, but I would argue that British writers largely situate Indian resistance among the servant classes in an attempt to keep it within familiar bounds. The threat is domesticated and containable when it issues from a subordinate source—as Munro writes, 'they are obliged through necessity to serve us'.

For Munro, instances of servant insubordination can be turned to the master's advantage. He includes an anecdote, told to him by a 'gentleman of rank, who has been in this country for some time, and thoroughly understands the language and customs of the natives':

One evening, as he [the gentleman] passed along a narrow street in the Black Town, he was suddenly surprised by an extraordinary noise proceeding from a neighbouring house, and yet in a greater degree when he heard his own name called out aloud. Having had the curiosity upon this to peep into the window from whence the sound came, he was not a little astonished, though at the same time greatly diverted, to perceive a gang of dubashes [household stewards] amusing themselves round a table and each assuming the name and character of his European master in the most ridiculous manner imaginable. There was not a foible that their masters possessed that had not been exhibited in the most ludicrous style; and so strongly were this same gentleman's failings represented by his own servant, particularly his austerity to those under his command, that he declared it ever afterwards made a sensible difference for the better in his conduct towards them.[113]

This passage seems to enact that 'dialectic of disguise and surveillance' which Scott argues 'pervades power relations between the weak and the strong'. The Indians have been observing their masters closely as they serve them, offering as Scott says 'a performance of deference and consent while attempting to discern, to read, the real intentions and mood of the potentially threatening power holder'. At the same time the master is 'producing a performance of mastery and command, while attempting to peer behind the mask of subordinates to read their real intentions'.[114] In this scene, the master catches the servants with their masks off, but realizes that they too have seen behind the masks of their masters. The Indians challenge established power relations through their carnavalesque impersonation of their masters. But this liberating deflation of authority is itself acted out under British surveillance. Their parodic mimicry functions as a reprimand, turning the gaze of power back on itself, and the incident is interpreted as a salutary lesson in dubash management: the gentleman moderates his behaviour in the interest of good master/servant relations; his modified conduct in turn guarding against future disruption of the status quo.

The subject of servant insurrection had been addressed some years before Munro in an anonymous novel entitled *The Memoirs of a gentleman, who served several years in the East Indies.* Published in London in 1774, with a dedication signed C. W., the novel purports to be the autobiography of a German surgeon who, after numerous adventures and misadventures across Europe, sets out on a voyage to India. There his picaresque career continues with varied romances (including liaisons with a sati whom he rescues and a close-guarded Muslim wife) a tiger attack and a period spent sharing a friendly hermit's cave. At one point, falling under the influence of a debauched Danish surgeon, he abducts village women to fill his own seraglio. Such is our hero's character; but even he disapproves of the activities of the Danish surgeon who, along with the village women, kidnaps brahmans and forces them to consume meat and alcohol, steals and christens Indian children and treats his servants with extreme harshness. The last offence is the greatest:

> the worst of all was, he was too cruel to the black people, especially to his own servants, which induced me to remonstrate to him on the impropriety of his conduct, because these people might one day take up arms against him. One afternoon, when he went to sleep, we got six stout black fellows with drawn swords, to stand round his bed, intimating, that they would cut him to pieces, which awaked him in a terrible fright. This appearance was too frightful to be expressed, but the reader may easily conceive some notion of it, when he considers that he was reduced from the condition of a petty tyrant to that of a prisoner.[115]

Reasoning that cruelty to Indians is inadvisable because of the possibility of violent reprisal, the hero pre-empts such an outburst by means of a bloodless mock uprising. Through a cautionary masquerade, stage-managed by a European, the Indians are deprived of their own ability to defy their master. This enactment of rebellion—the tableau of one vulnerable European surrounded by several strongly armed Indians—serves as a kind of exorcism of the fear of native insurgency. As for the servants themselves, they show no inclination to revolt; long accustomed to the surgeon's manner, 'they paid no regard to it'.[116]

Denied the possibility of open defiance, Indian servants are allowed the option of passive resistance, a mode of dissent which grants Indian servants considerable manipulative ability. Edward Ives's *Voyage from England to India* of 1773 tells the story of one such cunning servant:

> It happened, that an *English* officer being with his *Indian* servant in a public house at *Cuddalore*, was in a very violent passion, in consequence of something that had passed between them in conversation: In the midst of the master's fury, his philosophical servant calmly placed himself at his full length on the floor, with his face towards the ground, at the same time stopping his ears with both his hands. In this posture he continued, until his master's passion had somewhat subsided; when getting upon his feet, and respectfully approaching him, he dryly said, '*Indeed, master makes poor servant's head sick: master is very strong man, but servant is very weak man: if master speak honey words, then servant can do anything for master, but when master frightens poor servant, then he makes poor servant sick, master's business no can be done*'. The officer replied with a hearty d-mn; but on recollection felt the justness of the rebuke, and saw very plainly that before they could again proceed on business, it would be necessary for him to conform to the rules which the *Indian* had so sagaciously and artfully suggested for his conduct.[117]

The servant certainly comes off best from this encounter: clever, self-possessed and coolly rational. He turns his body into a symbol of resistance, refusing to hear or carry out orders. His moment of protest and defiance is liberating but short-lived; the servant refuses to co-operate only so long as the officer remains enraged, he then sets out the terms of the master/servant relationship along uncontentious lines: 'master is very strong man, but servant is very weak man'. Although he dictates the rules to his master, the servant presents his criticism as if it were advice on how to get the best service from him. What is particularly interesting about Ives's treatment of the servant is the extended use of Indian English dialogue. We have heard snatches of this pidgin before from Munro's coolie. Emerging in the last decades of the eighteenth century, this is the language of colonial servant classes, generally characterized in these texts as comically mangled, cheeky and reproachful; a distinctive, hybrid, servant voice that can use the rulers' language to answer them back. It is a rare means of dissent allowed to Indians by British authors.

If Indian mastery of English is comical, British knowledge of *Indian* languages is altogether a more serious matter, which is often presented as a means of preventing insubordination. Early linguists repeatedly announce their success in breaking the obstructive power of Indians. William Jones, as we shall later see, claims that his mastery of Sanskrit and Arabic enables him to shed light on the obfuscations of the Indian lawyers, the court pandits and maulavis.[118] And George Hadley, compiler of the first Urdu grammar, observes in a footnote to a dialogue about the cross-examination of a spy who is caught fabricating military intelligence that: 'Was there no inducement of convenience to learn the language of the country we reside in, this dialogue sufficiently enforces the absolute necessity of it, particularly for those of the military establishment, as being necessary to the preservation of our lives.'[119] This is an unusually overt expression of anxiety over the power of Indians to subvert British authority. In fact grammars, which Bernard Cohn has argued are very important tools in the colonial 'language of command', frequently refer to the difficulties posed by disruptive Indian subjects.[120] At the heart of the discourse of mastery lurks this fear of resistance. Hadley's dialogues, which are bilingual exercises in practical language use, rehearse such situations as an exchange between a British master and his household steward about the fraudulent extortions of the steward's deputy. Hadley observes that 'Persons in authority must be very careful how they place confidence in their servants, as it is almost incredible to say what villainy is perpetrated under the sanction of their names'.[121] He comments on the Urdu phrase given to the steward translated as 'the world is master's': 'This miserable stile was adopted by even the better sort, who would use it at the very time they were endeavouring to procure your removal, and privately complaining and soliciting your ruin in the council.'[122] Even as they express deference, Indians may be undermining an Englishman's position.

The fear of Indian insincerity and untrustworthiness which surfaces in Hadley's grammar points to a more general anxiety over the security of British rule in India; an anxiety which was manifested in the removal of Indians and people of mixed race from important posts in the Company administration under Cornwallis in 1793. It is this anxiety which, I would suggest, underlies the construction of many of the images of safe Indian subjects discussed in this chapter. Of course, the British are writing themselves into the role of benign and confident rulers to counter opposition at home. But they also share the common predicament of all colonial regimes: a fundamental sense of insecurity which can rarely be allowed direct expression, but which keeps surfacing to be repeatedly allayed. Let's leave the last word to John Gilchrist, author of the Urdu dictionary (a copy of which was presented to the anglicized subadar of Jhansi) and Urdu grammar which superseded Hadley's work. Gilchrist gives voice to fears about the security of British rule in an unusually explicit manner. Writing in *The Oriental Linguist* of 1798, he recognizes the Indian potential for political organization and resistance; he warns the British never to trust Indians too far, always to recollect 'that We are foreign Conquerors, and not one to some thousands', that Indians will 'always consider [us] as Aliens in this country. . . . And if an opportunity fatal to us do offer, these very harmless Indians will embrace it and expel us accordingly'.[123]

NOTES

1. Samuel Purchas, *Hakluytus Postumus or Purchas His Pilgrimes*, 20 vols (Glasgow, 1905–7) iv. 393.
2. Richard Owen Cambridge, *An Account of the War in India* (London, 1761) xvi–xvii.
3. Cambridge, xxvii–xxviii.
4. P. J. Marshall, 'British Expansion in India in the Eighteenth Century: A Historical Revision' *History* lx (1975); and P. J. Marshall, 'A Free though Conquering People: Britain and Asia in the Eighteenth Century', transcript of Inaugural Lecture, delivered at King's College, 5 March 1981.

5. Sara Suleri, *The Rhetoric of English India* (Chicago, 1992) 7.
6. Cambridge, xxviii.
7. Luke Scrafton, *Reflections on the Government of Indostan* (London, 1763) 22–3.
8. Robert Orme, *A History of the Military Transactions of the British Nation in Indostan*, 2 vols (London, 1763) i. 128.
9. See Purchas, iv. 325, 328, 370, 381.
10. C. A. Bayly, *Indian Society and the Making of the British Empire: The New Cambridge History of India*, ii. 1 (Cambridge, 1988) 3.
11. Franco Venturi, 'Oriental Despotism', *Journal of the History of Ideas* xxiv (1963) 133–42. See also Bernard S. Cohn, *An Anthropologist among the Historians and Other Essays* (Delhi, 1987) 211–12.
12. Alexander Dow, *A History of Indostan*, 2 vols (London, 1768); 3rd vol. (London, 1772) iii. 'A Dissertation concerning the Origin and Nature of Despotism in Indostan', vii.
13. John-Henry Grose, *A Voyage to the East Indies* (London, 1757) 171–2 (misnumbered as 161–2).
14. Dow, iii. 'A Dissertation concerning the Origin and Nature of Despotism in Indostan', xxxv; 'Plan for Restoring Bengal to its Former Prosperity', cxxviii.
15. Dow, ii. 'History of the Mogul Empire', 94–6.
16. Orme, i. 7–8.
17. Grose, 108.
18. See Gayl D. Ness and William Stahl, 'Western Imperialist Armies in Asia', *Comparative Studies in Society and History* ixx (1977) 2–79, for a historical assessment of how 'relatively small European forces gained ascendance over masses of native troops'. Unfortunately the authors address their British sources very uncritically.
19. Orme, i. 223.
20. Jemima Kindersley, *Letters from the Island of Teneriffe, Brazil, The Cape of Good Hope, and the East Indies* (London, 1777) 165.
21. Dow, ii. 'History of the Mogul Empire', 94.
22. Scrafton, 121.
23. Orme, i. 187.
24. Ibid., 49.
25. Cambridge, viii–ix.
26. Scrafton, 108.
27. Homi Bhabha, *The Location of Culture* (London, 1993) 82.
28. William Tennant, *Indian Recreations; consisting chiefly of Strictures on the Domestic and Rural Economy of the Mahometans & Hindoos*, 3 vols (1802, London, 1804) i. 393.
29. Michel Foucault, *Discipline and Punish*, trans. Alan Sheridan (Harmondsworth, 1979) 135.
30. Tennant, i. 393.
31. Kindersley, 204–6.
32. P. J. Marshall, *Bengal: The British Bridgehead: Eastern India 1740–1828: The New Cambridge History of India* ii. 2 (Cambridge, 1987) 95.

33. See Brijen K. Gupta, *Sirajuddaullah and the East India Company 1756–7* (Leiden, 1962) 71–2, for an outline of the debate about the authenticity of the Black Hole story.
34. For a full account of the Black Hole story and its numerous versions and retellings, see my essay, '"The Fearful Name of the Black Hole": the Fashioning of an Imperial Myth', in Bart Moore-Gilbert, ed., *Writing India, 1757–1990* (Manchester, 1996).
35. J. Z. Holwell, *A Genuine Narrative of the Deplorable Deaths of the English Gentlemen and Others, who were suffocated in the Black-Hole in Fort-William, at Calcutta* (London, 1758) 19.
36. The *Short Review of the British Government in India* (London, 1790), an anonymous pamphlet intended to justify Company rule, cites the pacification of the Rajmahal hill tribes as one of the major achievements of the British government of Bengal (p. 98).
37. Hodges' description of Cleveland was printed as an extract in the *Annual Register* (1793) 43–7.
38. William Hodges, *Travels in India, during the Years 1780, 1781, 1782, & 1783* (London, 1793) 89–90.
39. Felix Padel, 'British Rule and the Konds of Orissa: A Study of Tribal Administration and its Legitimating Discourse', unpublished D.Phil. thesis (Oxford, 1987) 145, note 19.
40. Hodges, 89.
41. John Shore, 'Monody on the Death of Augustus Cleveland', *Asiatic Annual Register* i (1798–9) 'Poetry': 202.
42. Thomas Shaw, 'On the Inhabitants of the Hills near Rajamahall', *Asiatick Researches* iv (1795) 47.
43. *Asiatick Researches* iv (1795) 105. Compare with a similar account of the deification of a collector, Tilman Henckel, by grateful Indians, dated 24 April 1788 from W. S. Seton-Karr, ed., *Selections from Calcutta Gazettes of the years 1784, 1785, 1786, 1787, and 1788* (London, 1864) 253: 'It is a fact that the conduct of Mr H—in the Sunderbands has been so exemplary and mild towards the poor Molungees or Salt manufacturers, that to express their gratitude they have made a representation of his figure or image, which they worship amongst themselves. A strong proof that the natives of this country are sensible of kind treatment, and easily governed without coercive measures.'
44. Rudyard Kipling, *The Day's Work* (London, 1898) 114.
45. Ibid., 114.
46. Philip Mason, *The Men who Ruled India*, 2 vols (London, 1954) i. 149.
47. Ibid., 149.
48. Edward Ives, *A Voyage from England to India* (London, 1773), title page.
49. Ibid., 179–80.
50. Ibid., 87.
51. Ibid.
52. Ibid.
53. In fact, other publishers also tried to cash in on the story. In 1754 a book entitled *A New History of the East-Indies* by one Captain Cope was first

published. The parts of this book dealing with India were actually an unacknowledged but complete plagiarism of an earlier work, published in 1727, by Alexander Hamilton called *A New Account of the East Indies*. This fact is not noted by H. K. Kaul in his *Travels in South Asia: A selected and annotated Bibliography of Guide-books and Travel books on South Asia* (Delhi, 1979) in his entry (no. 380) for Cope. There is mention of a Captain Cope in Cambridge's *Account of the War in India*, 9, in the record of military activities for 1750, but we cannot be sure if this is the supposed author of the plagiarism. A second edition of Cope's disreputable *New History* appeared in 1758, the year after Ives' account of Captain Watson's exploits was published in *The London Magazine*. This second edition of Cope, although just a reprint of the first, boasted a new title page which promised among other things 'a Full Account of the Taking and Destruction of *Tulagee Angria* the Pirate, by the ENGLISH'; a promise which the book does not deliver. The use of this false claim to catch the book-buying public's attention testifies to the popularity of the story.

54. For a very different version of events at Bobbili, see Quintin Craufurd, *Sketches relating to the History, Learning, and Manners, of the Hindoos* (London, 1790) 306–15.
55. Orme, ii. 258.
56. Ibid.
57. Ibid., 258–9.
58. William Jones, 'Tenth Anniversary Discourse', *Asiatick Researches* iv (1795) 8, 9.
59. Hodges, 17.
60. Ibid., 27.
61. Ibid., 123.
62. Mildred Archer, 'Baltazard Solvyns and the Indian Picturesque', *The Connoisseur* clxx (Jan.-April 1969) 12–14. See also Christopher Pinney, 'Colonial Anthropology in the "Laboratory of Mankind" ' in *The Raj: India and the British, 1600–1947*, ed. C. A. Bayly (London, 1990) 252.
63. F. Baltazard Solvyns, *Les Hindous, ou Description de leurs moeurs, coutumes et cérémonies*, 4 vols (Paris, 1808–12) i. 20.
64. Edward W. Said, *Orientalism* (1978; rpt Harmondsworth, 1985) 119; Michel Foucault, *The Order of Things An Archeology of the Human Sciences* (London, 1970) 125–65.
65. Solvyns, i. 21.
66. Suleri, 7.
67. Ibid., 18.
68. Archer, 14.
69. Solvyns, ii. 2nd no., 2.
70. Ibid., 6th no., 1.
71. Ibid., iv. 9–10.
72. Hodges, 30–1.
73. Rudyard Kipling, *Kim* (Harmondsworth, 1987) 105.
74. Ibid.

75. Said, 158–64.
76. George Forster, *A Journey from Bengal to England*, 2 vols (London, 1798) i. 82–3.
77. Forster, i. 90.
78. Ibid., n1.
79. Ibid., ii. 48–9.
80. A. L. Basham, 'Sophia and the Bramin', *East India Company Studies: Papers presented to Professor Sir Cyril Philips*, eds Kenneth Ballhatchet and John Harrison (Hong Kong, 1986) 28.
81. *Hartly House, Calcutta* (Dublin, 1789) 92–3.
82. Ibid., 184.
83. Ibid., 191–2.
84. Ibid., 199.
85. Ibid.
86. The choice of Sterne is perhaps suggested by an analogy in *A Sentimental Journey* where a monk of other-worldly appearance is compared to a brahman. See Laurence Sterne *A Sentimental Journey* (Oxford, 1984) 6. It is also worth noting that in *The Journal to Eliza* (discovered only in 1851) Sterne adopts the persona of the Bramin and addresses Eliza as the Bramine.
87. Ibid., 136–7, 191.
88. Mary Louise Pratt, *Imperial Eyes: Travel Writing and Transculturation* (London, 1992) 97.
89. *Hartly House* 276.
90. *Monthly Review* (1790) Jan-April N.S. I: 332; *Critical Review* 68 (1789) 164; *Analytical Review* (1789) May–Aug, 147.
91. Gary Kelly, *Women, Writing, and Revolution 1790–1827* (Oxford, 1993) 131–43; Nigel Leask, *British Romantic Writers and the East: Anxieties of Empire* (Cambridge, 1992) 101.
92. Elizabeth Hamilton, *Translation of the Letters of a Hindoo Rajah*, 2 vols (London, 1796) i. 96–7.
93. Edward Moor, *A Narrative of the Operations of Captain Little's Detachment* (London, 1794) 92.
94. Hamilton, i. 150–1.
95. Ibid., 202–3.
96. Ibid., 212.
97. Ibid., 213.
98. Ibid., 217–18.
99. Bhabha, 86.
100. William Hunter, 'Narrative of a Journey from Agra to Oujein', *Asiatick Researches* vi (1799) 24–5.
101. Bhabha, 89.
102. Moor, 382–3.
103. Walter Scott Seton-Karr, ed., *Selections from Calcutta Gazettes* (5 vols) (London, 1864–9) i. 205.
104. Foucault, *Discipline and Punish*, 143.

156 / *India Inscribed*

105. Bhabha, 9.
106. Bruce Robbins, *The Servant's Hand: English Fiction from Below* (New York, 1986) 108.
107. Ibid., 139–42.
108. Ibid., xi.
109. Innes Munro, *A Narrative of the Military Operations, on the Coromandel Coast, against the combined forces of the French, Dutch, and Hyder Ally Lawn* (London, 1789).
110. Ibid., 26–7.
111. Ibid., 41. For other examples of warnings against untrustworthy servants see Solvyns, iv. 1st no., 1; Ives, 51–2; Eliza Fay, *Original Letters from India (1779–1815)*, eds E. M. Forster and M. M. Kaye (London, 1986) 179–81, 182.
112. James Scott, *Domination and the Arts of Resistance: Hidden Transcripts* (New Haven, 1990) 20.
113. Munro, 29–30.
114. Scott, 3–4.
115. *Memoirs of a Gentleman, who resided several years in the East Indies* (London, 1774) 145.
116. *Memoirs of a Gentleman*, 146.
117. Ives, 49.
118. John Shore (Lord Teignmouth), *Memoirs of the Life, Writings, and Correspondence of Sir William Jones* (London, 1804) 264; Garland Cannon, ed., *The Letters of Sir William Jones*, 2 vols (Oxford, 1970) ii. 742.
119. George Hadley, *A Compendious Grammar of the Corrupt Dialect of the Jargon of Hindostan*, 4th ed. (London, 1796) 197.
120. Bernard S. Cohn, 'The Command of Language and the Language of Command', *Subaltern Studies IV* (1985) 276–329.
121. Hadley, 208.
122. Hadley, 211.
123. John Gilchrist, *The Oriental Linguist* (Calcutta, 1798) 299–300.

CHAPTER FIVE

'Geographical Morality': The Trial of Warren Hastings and the Debate on British Conduct in India

SINCE the commencement of this memorable Trial, Westminster Hall has not seen so numerous or so brilliant an assemblage of persons as crouded every part of it this day. By eight o'clock in the morning the avenues leading to the Hall, through New and Old Palace Yards, were filled with ladies and gentlemen of the most respectable appearance, many of them Peeresses in full dress, who stood in the street for upwards of an hour before the gates were opened. The exertions made to push forward, with a view to get convenient seats, had like to have proved fatal to many.[1]

The glittering crowds that thronged to hear Richard Sheridan's opening speech in the impeachment of Warren Hastings may well have been drawn by the playwright's reputation for dramatic oratory, as much as by the charges themselves. Certainly India had never before been displayed on such a prominent stage: the formal start of Hastings's trial in 1788, with virtuoso performances by the opposition managers of the prosecution—Edmund Burke, Charles James Fox, Charles Grey and Sheridan—marks the high point of public interest in Company affairs. But while the sight of peeresses queuing in the street to hear speeches about India was unprecedented, the impeachment was, in a sense, only the most visible enactment of concerns that had been repeatedly expressed in a number of texts published during the 1770s and '80s. These decades, marked by the loss of the American colonies, saw the first public show of uneasiness at British conduct in India: what was the precise role of the East India Company? What constraints, if any, did Company servants operate under? The textual debate between supporters and opponents of the Company reveals what Homi Bhabha has called the 'agonistic uncertainty contained in the incompatibility of empire and nation', and the impeachment of Hastings plays out that ambivalence by putting 'on trial the very discourse of civility within which representative government claims its liberty and empire its ethics'.[2] How did the textual debate over India inform the rhetoric of both the managers and the counsel for the defence during this nine-year-long impeachment?

INDIAN CONTROVERSIES

Trials are of course adversarial by nature: the prosecution and the defence offer competing accounts of the same events. In the Hastings impeachment these contesting representations both draw on and contribute to a well-established tradition of polemic about Company rule. In the decades following the assumption of diwani, a succession of scandals turned the question of the government of India into a particularly sensitive political issue. Allegations of greed and brutality had formed the basis of a parliamentary enquiry in 1772 into Clive's activities. The Council of Madras came in for severe censure: first for involvement with the nawab of the Carnatic's invasion of Tanjore in 1773; and then for the deposition and death in captivity of the governor, George Pigot, who had attempted to reinstate the raja of Tanjore. From 1774 the Calcutta Council was split into two warring factions by the intense rivalry between Philip Francis and Warren Hastings; a confrontation which directly contributed to the proceedings against the governor-general.

This series of controversies generated a stream of partisan texts. London agents were appointed to put the cases of Indian contestants: Edmund Burke learnt his Indian campaigning skills as pamphleteer on behalf of his distant cousin William Burke, an agent for the raja of Tanjore. These decades also saw a great increase in the size and circulation of the daily press, and newspapers avidly promoted the Indian interests of their political backers. As David Musselwhite has pointed out, in effect the trial of Hastings took place not in the House of Lords but in the pages of the press—in letters, articles, commentaries and cartoons.[3]

One clear indication of how contested the issue of the government of India had become is the number of texts which were printed expressly to answer allegations made in earlier publications. William Bolts, a Dutch merchant based in Calcutta, who had been involved in a number of long wrangles with the Bengal Council, travelled to London to press his case with the directors. There, in 1772, he published his *Considerations on India Affairs*, a vehement attack on Clive and his successor, Verelst, which alleged that the Company government was corrupt, oppressive, exploitative and despotic. This widely read diatribe was considered so detrimental to the Company's reputation that the directors invited Verelst to respond. The same year, the ex-governor duly published *A View of the Rise, Progress, and Present state of the English Government in Bengal: including a reply to the misrepresentations of Mr. Bolts, and other Writers.* Not to be outdone, Bolts retorted with an extended edition answering Verelst in 1775. This tit-for-tat publishing history exemplifies something of the combativeness of writing about India during the period.

The opening paragraphs of Verelst's first chapter address the issue of such textual debate. Following a lengthy introduction refuting Bolts, Verelst likens writing about India to pictorial representation:

WHEN a portrait is presented to our view, those acquainted with the original readily pronounce upon the degree of similitude in the copy. They easily perceive the whole to be unlike, and can even discover where the smaller traits of truth, in particular parts, are made subservient to the purposes of fals[e]hood; yet would it be difficult to make a by-stander comprehend the manner in which each feature was perverted. I have nevertheless endeavoured to prove, in the introductory discourse prefixed, that the picture which Mr Bolts has exhibited of Bengal manners bears no resemblance to the real state of affairs, or to the conduct of those concerned. After all, perhaps, the best means of detecting misrepresentation, is to contrast it with a faithful likeness. To delineate justly the subject, shall therefore be my next attempt.

The reader must not, however, expect a laborious detail. It is more consistent with the design of this work, to give a general map of the country, leaving to others the task of tracing the more minute divisions.[4]

What is striking about this passage is the way that Verelst's analogies slide one into another. Likening Bolts's work to a portrait that distorts its subject, Verelst first asserts that his own account will avoid such failures of mimesis, will form a more accurate portrait ('a faithful likeness') or rather 'a general map of the country'. One mode of representation is substituted for another: portraiture gives way to cartography. A concern with detail ('the manner in which each feature was perverted') disappears in favour of the broad outline ('a general map'). The subject of these varying forms of representation also shifts: from the individual whose portrait is being painted, to the more generalized theme of 'Bengal manners', and finally to the country itself.

The movement of these analogies—away from an artistic mode of representation towards a scientific one, away from the individual subject to the geo-political—suggests a desire for an authoritative, unassailable method of representation. Yet in his attempt to escape those charges of prejudiced misrepresentation which he has levelled at Bolts, Verelst employs a range of shifting, unstable analogies which tend to foreground the very problem of representation itself. These analogies make it even clearer that Verelst and Bolts are locked in a contest of competing representations.

There are several other examples of texts in direct dispute with one other. William Mackintosh published his *Travels in Europe, Asia, and Africa* in 1782, and Joseph Price responded the same year with his pamphlet, *Some Observations & Remarks on a late Publication intitled Travels in Europe Asia and Africa*. Mackintosh's narrative, published under his initials alone, supports Francis in his campaign against Hastings. But the text does not dwell on grave allegations of misconduct; rather it focuses on the apparently trivial issue of the indolence and extravagence of the British in Calcutta. One of its most notable passages is an extended description of a typical day in the life of an Englishman. The Company servant spends his hours in ease and dissipation, working for perhaps four of them, devoting the rest to socializing and dining. The account of his morning routine sets the tone for the whole section:

ABOUT the hour of seven in the morning, his durvan (porter or door-keeper) opens the gate, and the viranda (gallery) is free to his circars, peons (footmen) harcarrahs (messengers or spies) chubdars (a kind of constables) huccabadars and consumas (or steward and butler) writers and solicitors. The head-bearer and jemmadar enter the hall, and his bed-room at eight o'clock. A lady quits his side, and is conducted by a private stair-case, either to her own apartment, or out of the yard. The moment the master throws his legs out of bed, the whole possé in waiting rush into his room, each making three salams, by bending the body and head very low, and touching the forehead with the inside of the fingers, and the floor with the back part. He condescends, perhaps, to nod or cast an eye towards the solicitors of his favour and protection. In about half an hour after undoing and taking off his long drawers, a clean shirt, breeches, stockings, and slippers, are put upon his body, thighs, legs, and feet, without any greater exertion on his own part, than if he was a statue, The barber enters, shaves him, cuts his nails, and cleans his ears. The chillumjee and ewer are brought by a servant, whose duty it is, who pours water upon his hands, to wash his hands and face, and presents a towel. . . . The superior then walks in state to his breakfasting parlour in his waistcoat; is seated; the consummah makes and pours out his tea, and presents him with a plate of bread or toast. The hair-dresser comes behind, and begins his operation, while the huccabadar softly slips the upper end of the snake or tube of the houcca into his hand. While the hair-dresser is doing his duty, the gentleman is eating, sipping, and smoking by turns.[5]

This passage defies easy classification, hovering somewhere between reportage and satire. The opening string of Indian names argues for the account's authenticity, but at the same time carries a sense of comic excess, while the description of the Englishman's pompous bearing is more obviously humorous. The emphasis on detail could either imply a parody of a ceremonial court levee or suggest a faithful reconstruction of the minutiae of daily life. This passage has in fact been quoted by Suresh Chandra Ghosh in his study, *The Social Condition of the British Community in Bengal 1757-1800* to provide evidence for his account of the life of 'the well-to-do senior but bachelor officials of the Company'.[6] Yet the uncertainty of tone troubled contemporaries, who raised questions, familiar from Verelst's discussion of Bolts, about the relation of the given representation to an Indian reality. One contemporary reviewer, bemused by the intricacies of 'Oriental politics', wondered how seriously the account should be taken:

If such are the silken things from which the Hindostans are to form their ideas of Britons, we are disgraced there in every sense of the word. But as the writer certainly intended to hold them out to contempt, it may be no more than justice to suppose, that the picture is as strongly coloured as particular instances of extreme Eastern British foppery could justify. We wish to extend our charity to the utmost limits.[7]

According to the reviewer, if Mackintosh's account is a composite portrait of a small number of individuals (rather than the generic image which Mackintosh claims) then the damage suffered by the national reputation is limited.

A more thorough exoneration of the Company is offered by Joseph Price's pamphlet. Although Price ended his life a bankrupt, at the height of his career he was a wealthy Free Merchant and one of the most prominent Bengal shipowners. A staunch and vociferous supporter of Hastings, and the author of several pamphlets in his defence, Price had himself complained of ill treatment from Francis. In his reply to the *Travels*, he first identifies the author from his initials, then accuses Mackintosh 'of entering so deeply into the spirit of party' that he neglected to take 'truth as his guide'.[8] He considers the picture of Company servants an affront to British honour, asking the reader to consider 'what a situation Englishmen will be in all over Asia, if these volumes are suffered to pass into currency with impunity'.[9]

In his attempt to undermine Mackintosh's representation of the dissolute Englishman, Price employs a similar strategy to the reviewer. He does not defend the wealthy Englishman's right to a life of luxury, but rather accepts the terms of the attack. Indolence is to be deplored: the account is a 'strong but highly caricature likeness of the manners of the Europeans in general who serve in Asia'; only the most high-ranking East India Company officials live in such 'pomp and state', and the 'lazy and indelicate custom of being dressed and undressed in the manner he describes, never is practised by any but such as grow very corpulent, and not always by them'.[10] He proceeds to restrict the application of the description even further, suggesting that it might be an individual portrait of Mackintosh's host in Calcutta.[11] The majority of Company servants, Price asserts, lead active, blameless lives, riding before daybreak, working diligently, studying Indian languages in their own time, with only such vices as 'even Mr. *Mackintosh's* fair cousins would not condemn'.[12] In his study of British life in Bengal, Ghosh quotes Price's objections to Mackintosh's account, but significantly elides Price's reference to the wholesome pleasures of British life in India—'sitting in an armed chair, smoking a hooker, drinking cold water ... and wearing clean linnen'. This omission leads Ghosh to assert, incorrectly, that Price concedes that Company servants indulge themselves.[13] Rather, invoking the stable values of hearth and home, and claiming the ultimate endorsement of divine authority, Price presents his rival account of Bengal life as an absolute refutation of Mackintosh's representation: 'For let this mouth piece of party, and vile scandalizer of private character, say what he will, as many Englishmen go from Bengal to Heaven, in proportion to their number, as do from Great Britain.'[14]

This confident assertion of the consistency of British conduct, regardless of geographical location, counters the idea expressed in Mackintosh's text (and, we shall see, later elaborated by Burke) that Company servants were transformed by India—a process described by the reviewer of the *Travels* as 'the alterations that a plain old English acquaintance may undergo by removal to the banks of the Ganges'.[15] Mackintosh's account of the morning routine in Calcutta can be read as a kind of enactment of this process of Indianization. Returning to the passage, we notice that it opens with a description of servants massing outside the Englishman's house, the long list of their Indian names figuring a kind of oriental excess. As soon as the master wakes 'the whole possé in waiting rush into his room'; the Indians enter the Englishman's most private chamber and set about attending to his physical needs. His female companion of the night (who must be Indian since she is treated with tellingly little ceremony) has already been dispatched, and the servants proceed to wash and clothe him. The passive master, compared to an inanimate 'statue', seems sapped of all manly vigour; a feminized figure who recalls Belinda in Pope's *Rape of the Lock*, pampered by maids at her toilet. The description of the servants' intimate ministrations and the itemization of his garments and the parts of his body carry a small but significant sensual charge: 'after undoing and taking off his long drawers, a clean shirt, breeches, stockings, and slippers are put upon his body, thighs, legs and feet'. It is interesting to note that at this point, Mackintosh's grammar begins to break down: there is no subject and the verb is unexpectedly passive; a construction which serves to highlight the sense of an unmanly loss of agency. Contemporary readers were fully aware of the implications of Mackintosh's description: Price, we remember, termed this 'the lazy and *indelicate* custom of being dressed' (my emphasis), and the reviewer of the *Travels* referred to the Company servants as effeminate 'silken things'.[16]

This portrait of the effete, immobile Englishman recalls images of Mughal 'luxurious indolence' in the work of Richard Owen Cambridge and Luke Scrafton, discussed in Chapter 4.[17] Scrafton writes of the loss of the Mughals' martial character through debilitating contact with 'the sensuality and effeminacy' of India. These representations are intended to suggest Mughal incapacity for the task of government. By evoking such images of Mughal languor, Mackintosh implies that India has similarly enfeebled the once active British, and loads his representation of Company servants with multiple associations of Eastern degeneracy. That is to say, Mackintosh, and other critics of Company rule, borrow from an established repertoire of Indian images. Anti-Company writing is notable for the appropriation and inversion of many of those pro-Company representations already discussed. Such opposed representations fracture the idea of a stable colonial identity: is the Company servant active and upright, or languid and orientalized? The dividing line between Self and Other becomes increasingly blurred; the colonizer, as Bhabha observes, is troubled by the recognition of similarities with the native: 'not Self and Other but the otherness of the Self inscribed in the perverse palimpsest of colonial identity'.[18]

Oriental Despotisms

In the textual contest over India, certain shared terms and images circulate freely across the partisan divide. The most important of these migrating terms is 'despotism'. Together with its attendant vocabularly—cruelty, tyranny, oppression—this was widely supposed to be the defining characteristic of oriental government. William Bolts's *Considerations on Indian Affairs* of 1772 was one of the first texts to transpose the language of oriental despotism to Company rule. In a near oxymoron, Bolts describes Company servants as 'European Bashaws', and designates the British monarch 'an Asiatic Potentate'. Such terms demonstrate the arresting effects achieved by such a transplantation.[19] Bolts angrily protests (as Adam Smith would subsequently argue) that the Company's monopolies are oppressive and its rule, based on an unholy alliance of commercial and ruling power, is despotic. Instances of corruption and exploitation fill his pages: Company agents imprison and flog those who break the terms of their monopolies, and silk winders choose to cut off their thumbs rather than work for their British task masters.[20]

Following Bolts's example, Alexander Dow published the third volume of his *History of Indostan* the same year. Dow's opposition to Clive's government, conceived during service in the Company army, is also expressed in the language of Eastern despotism. He condemns the corruption of the North Indian and Persian officials employed by the Company in comprehensive terms:

Every petty officer in the state, every clerk of the revenues, assumed the tyrant in his own department. Justice was totally suspended; and the fear of being plundered by a superior, was the only check that remained against the commission of the most atrocious crimes. Every instance of abstaining from the most cruel oppressions, proceeded from indolence: every act of tyranny from the love of money.[21]

These loanwords from the vocabulary of Eastern rule induce in the reader an unsettling sense of self-estrangement: terms hitherto associated with an alien system of government are here applied to the familiar Company. The disruptive power of such rhetorical strategies is implicitly acknowledged by Lucy Sutherland when she cites Bolts and Dow as responsible for turning public opinion against Clive and preparing the ground for the parliamentary inquiry into his activities.[22]

The most significant addition to the body of anti-Company writing was the publication in 1776 of the English translation of the massive *Histoire philosophique et politique des deux Indes*. A monumental attack on colonial practice throughout the world, the *Histoire* was published under the name of the Abbé Raynal but was written in association with a number of collaborators, including Diderot. The work plagiarizes a great many authors, including Dow and Holwell.[23] Marshall observes that the widely read English translation, which went through twelve editions between 1776 and 1794, was highly influential at the time of the trial of Warren Hastings.[24]

In the *Histoire,* the Company is condemned as oppressive, exploitative and corrupt; its government, concerned solely with profit, behaves with criminal negligence during the devastating Bengal famine of 1770. According to the *Histoire,* Company rule is simply a harsher version of the Mughal dominion; an administration which makes

> the people of Bengal regret the despotism of their ancient masters. . . . A settled plan of tyranny has taken the place of authority occasionally exerted. The exactions are become general and fixed, the oppression continual and absolute. The destructive arts of monopolies are carried to perfection, and new ones have been invented. In a word, the company have tainted and corrupted the public sources of confidence and happiness.[25]

Here the association between British and Mughal despotism is made explicit: the British have not merely taken on the qualities of their predecessors, they have out-tyrannized them.

During the course of the 1770s, then, it became something of a commonplace for critics of Company rule to declare it a despotism. But the issue was complicated by the trial of Warren Hastings, when those arguments used against the Company were, in a final twist, modified to support the Hastings administration. One of the most contentious points in Hastings's defence (both at the time and in subsequent discussions of the impeachment) was the assertion, which Marshall suggests was written by Nathaniel Halhed, that the 'whole history of Asia is nothing more than precedents to prove the invariable exercise of arbitrary power'. This claim implied that Hastings's actions were permissible precisely because they took place in an Indian context.[26] Although Hastings later redefined arbitrary power as 'discretionary power',[27] his counsel attempted to substantiate the arbitrary power claim with textual authority by reading 'extracts from Bernier, Catrou, Gibbon, Montesquieu, Dow, Major Rennel, and many other unexceptionable writers, in order to prove, that previous to our establishment in India, its history is a history of the treasons, murders, poisonings, cruelties, and despotism of the rankest kind; each author stating, that the lands, lives, and properties of every man in India depended solely upon the will of the Sovereign.'[28]

Heading the prosecution, Burke countered the conventional representation of the despotic Indian past with his own interpretation of Islamic government, arguing at length that the defence's position was untenable and that it failed to justify the oppressions committed by Hastings's government. Marshall has commented that the 'arbitrary power' section of Hastings's defence, written by Halhed, did not accurately reflect

Hastings's views on Indian government. Marshall adds that in 'demolishing Hastings's claims to arbitrary power, Burke was probably destroying a target of his own construction'.[29] Burke no doubt seized upon the target with such enthusiasm because of the associations which had accumulated around the idea of despotism in the years of debate preceding the trial.

Although earlier in his career Burke had condemned Muslim government in conventional despotic terms, his ideas on oriental despotism had changed radically by the time of the impeachment. Burke explained his position on the second day of his opening speech. He asserted that the idea of arbitrary power was a perversion, a contradiction in terms, because all men were inevitably subject to divine law. He further argued that Islamic government could not be termed despotic since Islam taught the rule of law.[30] With the whole construct of oriental despotism apparently dismantled, Burke hoped to undermine the arguments of Hastings's defence completely and portray Hastings as a misguided pretender to a non-existent tradition of oriental despotism.

But at the same time as he accused Hastings of using the fictitious pretext of despotism to justify his actions, Burke described Hastings presenting himself to the House of Lords 'not as a British Governor, answering to a British Tribunal, but as a Soubahdar, as a Bashaw of three tails'.[31] Burke is here exploiting the same disturbing sense of cultural dissonance as that produced by Bolts's phrase 'European Bashaws'. While denying the existence of oriental despotism in order to undermine Hastings's position, Burke borrows rhetorical effects from the arsenal of critics who attacked Company rule as a despotic regime. Burke, who was extremely widely read in the European literature of India, appears to be drawing on the tradition of anti-Company writing to imply that Hastings had adopted the role of a despotic pasha and had therefore incriminated himself. In this instance, and at other points in the trial, Burke is having it both ways: repudiating the idea of oriental despotism, while opportunistically making use of its negative associations.

In a stimulating discussion of the Hastings trial, Sara Suleri examines the rhetorical manoeuvre whereby Burke represents Hastings as the epitome of arbitrary power and, at the same time, empties the notion of arbitrary power of all meaning. According to Suleri, the figure of Hastings personifies the operation of colonial power. For Burke is uncannily aware that colonialism is based on the illegitimate exercise of arbitrary power. But as he cannot admit the illegitimacy of the whole colonial enterprise, Burke displaces the charge of arbitrary power onto one individual. Hastings is made responsible for all the iniquities of colonialism in the

'Geographical Morality' / 167

hope that the larger project will be purged by his prosecution. However the extravagance of Burke's rhetoric suggests that, at a subterranean level, he realizes that these crimes far exceed the scope of any one man.[32]

Suleri's argument is ingenious, but a closer examination of the specific textual context of the trial suggests that Burke's 'understanding ... of the nature of colonialism's relation to arbitrary power' need not belong to the realm of the uncanny.[33] Freud defines the uncanny as 'the frightening element [which] can be shown to be something repressed which *recurs*'.[34] It is surely unnecessary to invoke Burke's unconscious when texts like Raynal's *Histoire* would have supplied him with abundant examples of the despotic nature of colonial rule.

For Burke's rhetoric, although extraordinary in its intensity, is deeply indebted to the contemporary discourse on India. As we have seen, there were plenty of texts shot through with the sense of colonial guilt. It is a recognition of the 'shared intimacy of guilt' which, Suleri persuasively argues, is at the root of Burke's rage against Hastings.[35] The courtroom audience is implicated in this guilt largely through Burke's technique of staging scenes of extreme horror. The audience is forced to witness atrocities carried out in the name of British rule. The tradition of Eastern cruelty (the governing principle of oriental despotism) informs the most notorious section of Burke's opening speech, the graphically lurid account of the outrages supposed to have been committed in the district of Rangpur under Devi Singh, the extortionate revenue farmer appointed by Hastings. The diatribe unleashed by Burke at this point deploys the full force of Ciceronian invective, as Geoffrey Carnall has observed.[36] Burke spoke at length and with great passion of the varied and inventive methods of torture employed to extract the last rupee from the inhabitants: hands and feet beaten and crushed, children scourged in front of their parents, virgins being raped in public, nipples ripped from breasts, torches applied to genitals.[37] (Mrs Sheridan fainted at this point, a footnote in *The History of the Trial* observes.[38]) Peter Marshall says Burke must have been aware that the reports which furnished the basis of his account were unreliable, and that since the allegations concerned Devi Singh, they were immaterial in the specific charge against Hastings.[39] When the Lords did in fact decide that the account of Devi Singh's cruelty was inadmissible as evidence, Burke objected to the ruling, 'for if ever there was a case in which the honour, the justice, and the character of a country were concerned, it was in that which related to the horrid cruelties and savage barbarities exercised by Deby Sing, under an authority derived from the British Government, upon the poor forlorn inhabitants of Dirachpore.'[40]

This protest indicates why Burke chose to include such tendentious matter in the charge. Apart from its obvious value as a horrifying showstopper, the Devi Singh description yokes together two concepts generally considered incompatible: the 'authority derived from the British government' and 'savage barbarities'; a coupling which invokes the idea of British despotism.

Burke repeatedly attempts to strengthen his case by reference to concepts familiar from the textual debate about Company rule. Towards the end of the trial, in a speech on Oude, Burke represents the Hastings administration as a 'Masquerade' that 'invested Slaves with authority, and turned Governors into Slaves'. Hastings is 'the great Master of the Machinery' who 'had so long dazzled the eyes of the world with the splendour of his pantomimical deceptions'.[41] These theatrical images recall Robert Orme's 1763 depiction of Mughal government discussed in Chapter 4. Orme characterizes the Mughal provincial administration as an elaborate sham spectacle, an empty show of power. By associating Hastings's government with the Mughal regime which it displaced, Burke's description suggests the instability of British authority and hints at an Asian source for its ills.

The East's corrupting influence was a common theme in the literature attacking Company rule. Marshall has traced the history of the idea that Eastern imperial possessions 'infected' the British state. Eighteenth-century historians generally attributed the collapse of Rome to its Asian conquests: the large standing army required to sustain the empire diverted political power from the citizens, and the riches which flooded in from the East enervated and corrupted the people. It was widely feared that Indian wealth and luxury would similarly debilitate Britain.[42]

The idea that the Company and the nation had been infected by the ills of Indian government received its most famous exposition in Samuel Foote's comedy, *The Nabob*, first performed in 1772. It has been suggested that this play was written in direct response to a parliamentary speech by Clive in which he claimed that the notoriety of returned 'nabobs' was unmerited since 'there has not yet been one character found amongst them sufficiently flagitious for Mr Foote to exhibit on the theatre in the Haymarket'.[43] In a neat demonstration of the interrelation of public debate and literary representation, Foote answered this challenge with a script that plotted the Machiavellian manoeuvres of Sir Matthew Mite, a recently returned Company servant, who 'owes his rise to the ruin of thousands' and his great fortune to the 'spoils of ruined provinces'.[44] Mite's victims, Sir and Lady Oldham, whose name points to their status as established members of the upper classes—old money as opposed to Mite's new—have fallen on hard times. Mite's proposal of marriage to the Oldham daughter offers a chance to revive the family fortunes and provide the upstart Mite with social status. Responding to her brother-in-law's observation that 'Sir Matthew is a profound politician, and will not stick at trifles to carry his point', Lady Oldham concludes that 'With the wealth of the East, we have too imported the worst of its vices'.[45]

Burke dwelt on such anxieties in his May 1789 speech on the bribery charge against Hastings. He spoke of the impeachment not merely as the trial of an individual but 'as a great *censorial* prosecution, instituted for the purpose of guarding Great Britain from the vices of Asia'.[46] For the '*open, honest, candid* and *ingenuous*' character of the British was under threat from Asian perfidy:

> should the subjects of Great Britain who serve in India be suffered to pursue any longer the maxims of Asia, they will bring home her *vices* as well as her *wealth*, and *both* will over-run the land. Those vices, if they are suffered to spread, will destroy the genius and character of the people, who will become like the Asiatics, reserved, dissembling, plotting, treacherous and perfidious. . . . From the wealth of Asia our *liberty* may apprehend its ruin—a deluge of Asiatic spoilers and delinquents may pour into the Senate, and corrupt the sources of our Constitution. To-day the Commons are prosecuting the Asiatic delinquents—tomorrow those delinquents may be the Commons.[47]

Burke's warning that Britain was in imminent danger of turning into India reads like an inversion of the narrative of colonial conquest: Indian vices 'will over-run the land'. The passage enacts a process of Indianization similar to that rehearsed in Mackintosh's description of the Company servant. The flood of the orient will invade the very heart of the body politic, utterly changing the nature of the British character. The alarming idea of the transformation of the Self into the Other has been discussed by John Barrell in relation to Thomas de Quincey. Barrell argues that 'De Quincey's life was terrorized by the fear of an unending and interlinked chain of infections from the East, which threatened to enter his system and to overthrow it, leaving him visibly and permanently "compromised" and orientalized.'[48] While in his nightmarish fantasies, the East threatens to invade de Quincey himself, in the anti-Company rhetoric, Indianization is always perceived *externally*, as something infecting one's fellow countrymen. But both De Quincey and Burke share a similar sense of unstoppable, pernicious influence of the East.

The term 'nabob', in its evolving usages, embodies this process of

Indianization. Following the Clive controversy and Samuel Foote's play, the Anglicized form of nawab/nabab, the Indian title of rank, became a general term of abuse directed against the British who returned enriched from India.[49] The term was fraught with class jealousy and envy of new money. It implied recently acquired social and political status—the very spectre of a disrupted hierarchy which haunted Burke so powerfully. In a splendidly entitled tract of 1783, *The Saddle put on the Right Horse; or, an Enquiry into the Reason Why certain Persons have been denominated Nabobs; With an Arrangement of those Gentlemen into their proper Classes, of Real, Spurious, Reputed, or Mushroom, Nabobs,* Joseph Price again attempted to clear Company servants from the charge of immorality and exploitation, focussing in this pamphlet on the term 'nabob' itself. Price counters the trope of contagious Asian vices with an account of the communicable virtues of the East:

The manners of the Hindoos are, perhaps, the most inoffensively mild and engaging, of any people on earth.... A young man, in a continual habit of intercourse with such a people, must imbibe some of their patient and placid ideas. Universal charity, and general hospitality, are natives of Asia, and are practised by the Hindoos towards all strangers, as far as their customs and religious prejudices will admit. Young minds are attracted by example; and it is the general opinion, that if in any part of the world, Englishmen are pre-eminently famous for the social and domestic virtues, the Company's servants in the East Indies are they.[50]

Price attempts to redefine the nature of the influence exerted by India over the British: the idea suggested by the term 'nabob'—cruel Muslim avarice—is replaced by a contrasting image of gentle Hindu generosity. In Price's account, the process of Indianization involves no radical change of identity; it simply serves to reinforce the morals of young men who are already 'well instructed in the principles of the Christian religion'.[51] Such a sense informs his use of the word 'Indians' to designate both the British in India and the Indian people:

Our enemies say, that we Indians are a proud, insolent, and rapacious people; that we have, by our avarice, driven to distress, ruin, and death itself, millions of unhappy Indians. To such daring, vague, and indefinite charges and assertions, I oppose the general tenor of conduct of the India gentlemen, who have returned to this kingdom within the last twenty years...[52]

Price undercuts the charges of 'nabobism' by identifying the British ('we Indians') with their alleged victims ('unhappy Indians'). He goes on to argue that 'India gentlemen'—a more dignified version of the same term—return to become upright members of British society, and thus are scarcely likely to have been guilty of 'cruelties, so infamous and diabolical' whilst in India.[53]

Such appeals to common sense notions of the stability of character are rejected by Burke in his opening speech on Hastings's claim to arbitrary power. Burke asserts that in India Hastings had undergone a complete transformation. His conduct

> had been distinguished for an adherence, not to the general principles which actuate mankind, but to a kind of GEOGRAPHICAL MORALITY—a set of principles suited only to a particular climate, so that what was peculation and tyranny in Europe, lost both its essence and its name in India. The nature of things changed, in the opinion of Mr Hastings; and as the seamen have a custom of dipping persons crossing the EQUINOCTAL, so by that operation every one who went to INDIA was to be UNBAPTIZED, and to lose every idea of religion and morality which had been impressed on him in EUROPE.[54]

Burke is describing not so much a process of Indianization here, but rather a renunciation of a European identity. The self is not turning into the other, but rather turning against itself. The equatorial un-baptism comes close to the 'diabolical' activity dismissed by Price: a blasphemous parody that marks the birth of a non-Christian.

Burke's geographical metaphor highlights the sense of distance and difference that underlies many of the contesting representations of India which we have discussed. It marks an absolute distinction between behaviour in Britain and in India, where the 'nature of things changed, in the opinion of Mr Hastings'. The distorted perceptions of East India Company servants form a recurrent theme in Burke's oratory. Already in his 1785 speech on the Nawab of Arcot's Debts, Burke spoke of the perverted emotions of the officials in the Carnatic. Though the province was ravaged by the sultans of Mysore, the British still imposed exorbitant tax demands: 'they felt nothing for a land desolated by fire, sword and famine; their sympathies took another direction; they were touched with pity for bribery, so long tormented with a fruitless itching of its palms ... they were melted into compassion for rapine and oppression, licking their dry, parched, unbloody jaws.'[55] Such a rhetorical manoeuvre recalls Holwell's representation of the delight of Siraj-ud Daula's guards as they watched the 'inhuman diversion' of the sufferings of the British in the Black Hole. The British have again taken on an Indian identity, but it is not just a human one. The metonym of 'unbloody jaws' develops into a whole animal in Burke's later attack on Hastings: he is 'like the tyger of that country', withdrawing 'into a cavern, to indulge with unobserved enjoyment in all the wanton caprices of his appetite'.[56] Hastings has adopted the characteristics of the beast that had come to symbolize the savageness of India, and through its association with Tipu Sultan, was also becoming the emblem of cruel tyranny.

This menacing Asian identity is ignored in Frans de Bruyn's study of Burke's portrayal of Hastings.[57] For de Bruyn, Burke's depiction of Hastings is structured solely around the paradigm of the gothic novel, a pattern reassuringly familiar to his audience. De Bruyn sees in Burke's depiction of Hastings the typical characteristics of the gothic villain: his unrestrained greed often represented as sexual aggression, and his victim—India's wealth—personified as a helpless woman. Such an analysis, although locally illuminating, ignores Burke's extensive and more significant debt to images generated by the debate on India.

The Nabob and the Creole

Both de Bruyn's and Suleri's reading of Burke's rhetoric neglect the significance of another contemporary debate, that on slavery. Peter Marshall has pointed out that at the start of the impeachment India and the slave trade were linked, both in parliament and outside, as issues which raised questions about the morality of British policy overseas.[58] In 1788, for instance, a volume of poetry dedicated to William Wilberforce, entitled *Poems Chiefly on Slavery and Oppression*, was published by one Hugh Mulligan. The collection included American and African Eclogues featuring nobly suffering slaves, and an Asiatic Eclogue concerned with the fate of a princely house of Indostan attacked by the greedy, tyrannical British. Interestingly the same volume contained a European Eclogue that addressed the issue of oppression in Ireland. Such concerns were also linked in the parliamentary activities of Burke, who championed Irish causes throughout his career, and was involved in drafting legislation against slavery: in 1780 he produced a plan for its reform, in 1789 he supported the first of Wilberforce's many anti-slavery motions, and in 1792 he submitted to the Home Secretary a 'Sketch of a Negro Code'— his plan for the emancipation of Britain's slaves.[59]

The campaigning tactics of the anti-slavery movement and Burke's rhetoric have certain general features in common: pathos, righteous indignation, occasional sensationalism. More specifically, both aim to establish an awareness of the implications of Britain's trade. Burke wanted to suggest a direct link between Indian suffering and his British audience. In his opening speech, after the catalogue of Devi Singh's cruelties, Burke paused dramatically, head in hands, then resumed. The inhabitants of

Rangpur, he said, 'gave almost the whole produce of their labour to the East-India Company: those hands which had been broken by persons under the Company's authority, produced to all England the comforts of their morning and evening tea. For it was with the rent produced by their industry, that the investments were made for the trade to China, where the tea which we use was bought.'[60] Burke reduces the intercontinental movement of Company trade—Indian opium to China, Chinese tea to Britain—to a human scale. The homely image of a cup of tea becomes a sign of British exploitation.

Burke was not alone in his use of tea as an emblem for Asian suffering. In 1792 *Tea and Sugar, or the Nabob and the Creole; A Poem, in two Cantos*, was published under the pseudonym, Timothy Touchstone. As the title suggests, this satiric poem linked British cruelty in the East and West Indies, allotting a canto each to a ruthless exploiter of Indians and a torturer of enslaved Africans. The Nabob, Bob Snare, finds his match in the malignity of the Creole slave owner. The opening canto traces Snare's bloody rise from a lowly lawyer's son, via preferment from his father's friend, Sir Rupee, to military fame and titled nabobhood. But worldly success does not bring contentment, and remorseful visions—'fancied sprites, / Of murder'd Indians'—prompt him 'To the keen Razor, and by that, he dies'.[61] This may allude to Clive's career, which ended in suicide in 1774, but more explicit reference is made to the charges facing Hastings and the ongoing trial: 'Fair Freedom . . . Order'd the Culprits to her fav'rite isle, / T'answer for their actions, greatly vile'.[62] The first canto closes with an address to the reader which makes the connection between East Indian trading practice and West Indian slave-labour quite explicit:

> Thus, Briton's, are procur'd the Eastern wares,
> Your Iv'ry Cabinets, and your Iv'ry Chairs;
> Your Silks, your costly Gems, and baneful TEA,
> Pernicious DRUG!—to health an enemy!
> Which for to gain, thousands of Indian's bleed,
> And base Corruption's ready-growing seed
> Is largely strewn, o'er *Britain's* famous land,
> By an unprincipled, a savage band.
>
> Having shewn how Eastern Luxury is gain'd
> I'll further shew, how SUGAR is obtain'd.[63]

The image of pain-laden tea which Burke had earlier used, is here expanded into a patriotic attack on the wider corrupting influence of foreign luxury products.

The desire to foster a sense of British responsibility towards suffering

174 / India Inscribed

Indians informs Richard Clarke's 1773 poem, *The Nabob: or, Asiatic Plunderers*. Based on the allegations of Dow and Bolts against the Company, the poem takes the form of a dialogue about the appropriate response to oppression in India. Framed as an argument between the engaged, campaigning author and his uncommitted friend, the poem's structure expresses the contested nature of responses to the government of India. The friend opens the debate:

> CONCERNS it you who plunders in the East,
> In blood a tyrant, and in lust a beast?
> When ills are distant, are they then your own?
> Saw'st thou their tears, or heard'st thou th'oppressed groan?[64]

The author retorts that a sense of Christian brotherhood extends across geographical boundaries:

> Where'er oppression lifts its iron hand,
> It strikes my brother in a distant land.
> Clime, colour, feature, in my bosom find
> The friend to all; their stamp is still mankind,
> And mankind too to noblest blood ally'd,
> For he who bled for me, for them too dy'd.[65]

Such an argument resurfaces later in the slogan of the anti-slavery movement: 'Am I not a Man and a Brother?'[66] The author here claims kinship with Indians rather than with his fellow countrymen, asserting a sense of community which overrides racial and national affiliations. This appeal to brotherhood in Christ of course draws on the structure of East/West relations established by missionary rhetoric.

UNSTABLE IDENTITIES

Reversals of customary affinities underlie much anti-Company rhetoric. I have, above, traced the ways in which Company servants assumed threatening Asian identities, how the familiar turned into the exotic. But the exotic also turned into the familiar: Indian governments were at times endowed with qualities more often associated with the British. Such is the case in Burke's construct of India. As Peter Marshall has pointed out, Burke argued that before the destructive intervention of the Company, the kingdoms of Tanjore and Rohilkhand were flourishing, well-governed polities.[67] The high level of cultivation in both spoke of the subjects' security of property and freedom from oppression. This is of course reminiscent of the picture of British paternalistic care analysed in the preceding chapter.

The prosecution often depicted Hastings's abuse of authority by contrasting the state of kingdoms languishing under his control with their previous health. In his introductory speech on the Benares charge, Charles Grey read from a letter which, he claimed, was written by Chait Singh, the former raja of Benares. The charge against Hastings concerned his alleged incitement of Chait Singh to rebel, a revolt which, when crushed, facilitated the extension of British power in Benares. Grey extracts a passage that celebrates the former prosperity of the country:

'My fields', says the Rajah, 'are cultivated, my towns and villages full of inhabitants, my country is a garden, and my RYOTS (husbandmen) are happy. The principal merchants of India, from the security of my government, resort to my capital, and make it their residence . . .'—When Mr Hastings on the contrary, went through those districts, Famine and Misery stalked hand in hand through the uncultivated fields and deserted villages. There were found only the aged and the infirm, who were unable to fly; robbers, prepared to kill; and tygers, whose ferocity marked the desolation of the scene.[68]

Certain elements of this description, including the passage from Chait Singh's letter, recall an earlier attack on Clive, published in the *Gentleman's Magazine* by 'an officer who lately served in Bengal' in 1772. The *Gentleman's Magazine* was the most influential of eighteenth-century periodicals; aimed at a wide middle-class readership, it tended to champion humanitarian causes. This first account represented Bengal before the intervention of 'the *Prince and Father of Nabobs*', as a garden-like country, well-populated and farmed, full of contented labourers; during Clive's administration, it became a waste land inhabited by wild beasts and the destitute. In fact, attacks on Clive were often couched in such terms, but the officer's account is particularly interesting for its literary resonances. He writes:

I have travelled over that country, when it was in reality *the garden of the world*; when the villages were large, populous and flourishing; when the extensive plains were cover'd with lowing herds and laughing herdsmen; and when the manufacturer sung unmolested under every shady tree.

I have since travelled over that country, when the villages were become habitations of foxes, when the once fertile plains were become immeasurable wastes, inhabited only by the growling tyger and the howling jackal; and when the few half-starved manufacturers, whom rapine and avarice had left, beheld me with jealousy and fear.[69]

In its thriving state, Bengal is depicted as an English country idyll. The writer quotes Marvell's description of pre-Civil War England, the edenic 'Garden of the World ere while' from 'Upon Appleton House' to suggest that the British have again lost a paradise through violence.[70] The italicization here draws attention to the allusion, but a little further on, the writer slips in the phrase 'lowing herds', which quotes, slightly inaccurately, from Gray's 'Elegy Written in a Country Churchyard'. Gray's well-known opening lines, 'The Curfew tolls the knell of parting day / The lowing herd wind slowly o'er the lea', set what was to become, through the work's great influence, an almost quintessentially English pastoral scene. By using much-cherished images of home to represent pre-British Bengal, the writer suggests that the British have inflicted the damage on themselves, that they have harmed both their national interests and own self-image. The correspondence between the officer's account and Grey's later description of Benares demonstrates how the rhetoric of the Clive controversy fed into the debate on Hastings. Both passages in turn generated two more: the description of Bengal in Hodges's 1793 *Travels in India*, which was itself reworked in Hamilton's *Letters of a Hindoo Raja* (discussed in the preceding chapter). Writing in defence of his patron, Hastings, Hodges inverted the earlier descriptions: Bengal under Hastings's rule is 'highly flourishing in tillage of every kind, and abounding in cattle. The villages are neat and clean and filled with swarms of people'.[71]

Again we find that the debate on India is structured around pairs of opposed representations. This rhetorical strategy is often combined with an abrupt temporal dichotomy that splits the history of India into two periods: before the imposition of British rule and after. Hastings's leading Counsel, Edward Law, announces his intention to present his case along such lines. He opens the defence with a narrative of the blood-soaked history of Asian tyranny 'to shew what a happy change had been effected by the prevalence of British power', and to prove 'that Mr Burke was wrong in his description of India "enjoying all the happiness of the golden age, the wolf drinking with lamb . . . before we planted the dagger of aminosity there." The fact was the direct contrary—nay, was more than the direct, it was the contrary in aggravation—for the sylvan wolf not only ate up the sylvan lamb, but the human wolves preyed upon each other.'[72] The telling phrase '[t]he fact was the direct contrary—nay, was more than the direct, it was the contrary in aggravation' epitomizes much of the debate over India: all the attempts to refute and outdo opponents, all the rhetorical overreaching. The contested versions of the transformation effected by British rule help to fix 1765, the date that marks British accession to diwani, as 'the sharp historic chasm' which Ranajit Guha sees as the 'gift of the Age of Enlightenment which continues to influence historical judgment down to the present day'.[73] The debates between nationalist historians and colonial apologists over the harmful or beneficial consequences of British rule are prefigured in the exchanges of the 1770s and '80s.

Edward Law may draw a distinction between Burke's fanciful 'golden age' and his own factual account, but because he elaborates on Burke's figures of the wolf and the lamb, his own version of the Indian past partakes of the same language of myth. Just as it became apparent in the course of Verelst's attempt to discredit Bolts that both authors were engaged in a battle of competing representations, so too Law, in dismissing Burke's account as a fiction, inadvertently implicates his own.

INDIAN TESTIMONIALS

Both the prosecution and defence attempted to avoid the charge of misrepresentation by grounding their cases in an Indian reality. Indian witnesses were summoned to the House of Lords; but not, of course, in person. Burke asserted that religious prohibitions against travel prevented Hindus from representing their own grievances in Britain, for fear of a loss of caste. Arguing against a Lords ruling that the minutes of a Calcutta Council meeting were inadmissible as evidence, a decision which excluded the testimony of Hastings's banyan, Burke contended that such transcripts furnished the only channel of communication between Hindus and their rulers. For 'if any *Gentoo* were to be prevailed upon to come to England, he was to be considered as a person *disregarding all* OBLIGATIONS of RELIGION, and *consequently* NOT *entitled to* CREDIT *as a* WITNESS'.[74] Doubly muted—first by caste rules, then by the British interpretation of those rules—the Hindus had no voice of their own.

This institutionalized silencing had a further cause. According to Burke, the death sentence meted out in 1775 to Raja Nandakumar effectively stifled Indian complaints. Nandakumar, who was associated with Francis's campaign against Hastings, had alleged that the governor-general had accepted bribes in exchange for government appointments. He was quickly arrested and charged first with conspiracy, then with forgery. Tried by Hastings's old friend, Sir Elijah Impey, Nandakumar was condemned to death for forgery by the retrospective implementation of a British law. British public opinion endorsed the opposition claim that this constituted a grave miscarriage of justice.[75] For Burke, in his 1783 speech on Fox's East India Bill, the sentence amounted to 'a murder not of Nundakumar only, but of all living testimony, and even of evidence yet unborn. From that time not a complaint has been heard from the natives against their governors'.[76]

If Nandakumar's execution muted Indian protest, an account of the raja's fortitude before death represented a powerful, if indirect, charge against British justice. Written by the sheriff who had reluctantly overseen the hanging, Alexander Macrabie (who, significantly enough, was Philip Francis's brother-in-law), the account depicts the raja's noble stoicism in minute detail, observing his conduct the day before and his expression on mounting the scaffold, praising 'his steadiness, composure, and resolution, throughout the whole of this melancholy transaction'. It also recounts, by way of contrast, Macrabie's own emotional distress; on visiting Nandakumar in jail, the sheriff comments, 'I found myself so much second to him in firmness, that I could stay no longer'.[77] Various elements of the description—Nandakumar's fortitude, the intense, troubled gaze of the onlooker—recall European accounts of sati. Indeed this narrative conveys a similar sense of moral outrage as many of the representations of sati. But in this case the disapproval is directed inwards, against the Company administration which Macrabie himself served. The resulting sense of self-alienation, of revulsion at the activities of the British government and of sympathy for an Indian victim fed directly into the tradition of anti-Company writing.

When Macrabie's account was published in the *Gentleman's Magazine* in 1780, its editorial introduction compared Nandakumar's conduct to that of Major John André, a British hero of the War of American Independence: '[t]his Asiatic knew, like André, how to remove infamy even from the gallows'.[78] To liken Nandakumar to André, who nobly suffered execution in the service of his country, was to highlight this sense of confused national identity. It comes as no surprise then, to learn that the account was harnessed by the opposition in its attempted prosecution of Sir Elijah Impey in 1788. Sir Gilbert Elliot, heading the case against Impey, read the whole narrative to the Commons as part of his reply to Impey's defence. The speech was recorded by the *Annual Register*, the periodical with which Burke was closely connected, and the narrative was considered significant enough to be reprinted in an extensive footnote.[79]

The sufferings of Indian princes also formed one of the favourite themes in the prosecution of Hastings. The managers found much rhetorical mileage in championing the causes of the noble oppressed. Gagged by terror (caused by Nandakumar's execution) and by religious prohibitions against travel, the Indians, so Burke's speeches imply, had to rely on the prosecution managers as their mouthpiece. The Indian voice was recreated in British accents. We have already seen how statements attributed to Indians, such as Chait Singh's letter, were worked into the existing framework of anti-Company rhetoric; at times, the managers even took on Indian roles. Just before Grey quoted from Chait Singh's letter, Charles James Fox acted out a dramatic dialogue between the deposed raja and an Englishman: 'In an apostrophe the most beautiful that can be imagined, Mr Fox made the injured Cheyt Sing the utterer of his own complaint to the House'.[80] The raja laments his fall from 'felicity': 'I was', said he, 'the Sovereign of a fertile country, happy and beloved. . . . This was the situation of which I boasted; but what is now the reverse? I am a wretched exile, dependent on the bounty of those who were my enemies, but whose enormities are now buried in their sympathy for my distress.'[81] As David Musselwhite comments, Chait Singh here 'becomes the hero of romantic pastoral with gothic overtones'.[82] In the dialogue, the Englishman takes on the unsympathetic role of the defender of the Company's actions. According to the official British position, Chait Singh had breached his agreement with the Company by failing to pay his tribute at Benares: 'You forget,' replied an Englishman, 'that though a Sovereign Prince at Patna, at Benares you were but a Zemindar; in the latter character you were guilty of disobedience, and are therefore sentenced to a judicial exile.'[83] The roles of Indian and Englishman are defined by their respective languages: the pathetic appeal of the victim, and the legalistic judgement of the ruler. The audience responds to the emotive power of the Indian lament rather than the cold precision of the English ruling, the voice that represents the national interest. As in the account of Nandakumar's execution, the rhetoric induces a sense of self-estrangement.

Hastings's defence also attempted to create an Indian presence in court. In 1787 Hastings's friends in Bengal were asked to gather Indian testimonials in support of the former governor-general; although, Marshall comments, '[t]hose acquainted with Indian conditions might well doubt their value as spontaneous expressions of opinion', they were useful adjuncts to the defence case.[84] At the end of his opening speech in 1791, Hastings introduced them as essential evidence that cut through the confusion of opposed representations:

It has been the fashion in the course of this Trial, sometimes to represent the natives of India as the most virtuous, and sometimes as the most profligate of mankind. I attest to their virtue, and offer this unanswerable proof of it:

When I was arraigned before your Lordships in the names of the Commons of Great-Britiain, for sacrificing their honour by acts of injustice, oppression, cruelty, and rapacity, committed upon the Princes, Nobles, and Commonalty, of Hindostan, the natives of India of all ranks came forward unsolicited to clear my reputation from the obliquy with which it was loaded. They manifested a generosity, of which we have no example in the European world: their conduct was the effect of their sense of gratitude for the benefits they had received during my administration.

My Lords, I wish I had received the same justice from my country.[85]

Hastings here appropriates the claim of the prosecution to speak for the Indian people, by having the natives speak for him. He also adapts the prosecution tactic of disrupting national affiliations: the Indians identify themselves with the cause of a British governor-general, and he in turn feels an affinity with them, rather than the unjust British. His view of Indian virtue is solipsistically defined only with reference to himself. The spontaneity of their gratitude is represented as a specifically Indian form of generosity, an uncalculated outpouring of affection, far removed from all suspicion of political constraint.

Hastings obviously hoped that the testimonials would furnish 'unanswerable proof' for his case in the debate on India. The testimonials themselves, issued in book form in 1789, claimed to be definitive and irrefutable. A translation of a Persian address, sent with the seals of 278 of the most prominent Hindu and Muslim residents of Benares, aimed 'by representing Facts' to 'remove the Doubts that have possessed the Minds of the Gentlemen in England'.[86] Burke, of course, was not so easily convinced. He claimed that the testimonials all expressed suspiciously similar sentiments, and 'remarked humorously upon the stile of these attestations, which, he said, all bore evident marks of *European* birth', arguing that they had first been written in English, then translated into Persian 'and adorned with all the lofty metaphors of the *East*; and then turned once more into *English* for the benefit of their Lordships'.[87] Scripted by Hastings' friends, Burke argues, the testimonials are simply another form of representation, one that gains an Indian veneer through linguistic artifice. The process of translation—the very means that should facilitate communication between governors and governed—here obscures the authentic expression of Indian opinion.

Burke's contention that the defence had appropriated the voice of the Indians of course applies equally to his own case. But some of the testimonials do indeed sound remarkably like the pro-Company narratives that justify British rule. In 1792 Edward Law, referring to the great range of Indians who issued testimonials, quoted one sent by the hill people of Rajmahal and Bhagalpur:

we formerly lived on the Hills, like the beasts of the forests, and during the government of Mr. Hastings became like other men, and the qualities and honour of men were instilled into us. Formerly our means of subsistence were no other than those of plunder and rapine, and we existed with the greatest difficulty; but now, by the wise conduct of that Gentleman, we live at ease, and, like others, are happy and *satisfied with the Company.* As this ease and civilization, which has produced respect to us *among mankind, has been the effect of Mr. Hastings's conduct and management,* we never experienced other than kindness, nor have any one of us heard any oppression from him.[88]

This passage evokes those narratives of civilizing rule constructed around the figure of Augustus Cleveland, collector of Rajmahal and Bhagalpur under Hastings, described in the preceding chapter. The contrast which the hill people draw between their former savage condition and their present enlightened state echoes John Shore's description of Cleveland's activities in his monody of 1786. In Shore's elegy, the collector educated the people in the ways of settled life: 'With fost'ring care he led wild nature on', turning the 'blood stain'd field' into 'well-till'd glebes'.[89] The transformations effected by Company rule are also celebrated in Thomas Shaw's 1795 account of the same community's creation story, discussed in the same chapter. According to Shaw, the advent of British government was incorporated into tribal mythology to symbolize the end of their miserable outcaste status. This myth functions much as the testimonial, for in both the hill people themselves confirm the beneficence of Hastings's rule. Both aim, to borrow a phrase from Thomas Plumer, one of Hastings's counsel, to prove that '[t]he voice of India was undoubtedly on the side of Mr Hastings'.[90]

But the defence case was not always helped by the testimony of Indians. In December 1790 a debate was held in the House of Commons on the question of whether or not the impeachment should be pursued to its conclusion. Colonel Macleod, formerly commander of the king's regiments during the second Mysore war, spoke for the ending of the trial. In a speech which played straight into Burke's hands, he recalled the many conversations he had held with Tipu Sultan:

he had often sat up with him all night in his tent, and been treated by him with the greatest familiarity; that this Prince, whose abilities and penetration no man could dispute, had invariably spoken of Mr Hastings in the warmest terms of respect, though he described him as the greatest enemy he had in the world, having by the assistance he afforded to the Carnatic and Bombay during the war enabled those Presidencies to stop the progress of his arms. . . .[91]

Macleod's remarks place him among the minority of British commentators who depict Tipu as an able ruler rather than a tyrannical despot (the final chapter details this ambivalence in the British response to Tipu). While Tipu is defined as deeply antagonistic to the British, he is credited with shrewd perspicacity. Hastings's qualities must indeed be great, Macleod implies, if they are acknowledged by such a rival as Tipu. The colonel attempts to shield Hastings from the damaging implications of association with Tipu by stressing the enmity between the two. But the mere fact that Tipu, then at war with the British, and whose name was generally understood as synonymous with despotism, should be cited as a character referee provided Burke with ample opportunity for ridicule. Burke dismissed the account as yet another representation, this time of a fantastic Eastern variety, 'a kind of *Arabian Night's Entertainment*', and wondered whether the colonel addressed the sultan as '*Marcus Aurelius*, or any other great hero of antiquity, renowned for the mildness and liberality of his character'. Macleod's oriental fictions, Burke implies, are a travesty of European cultural and moral values, and have no place in serious parliamentary debate. A testimonial from Tipu was entirely irrelevant, it being 'but bad logick' to argue 'that because Tippoo Saib said, in a midnight conversation, that Mr Hastings was a good man, therefore the Impeachment brought in the name of all the Commons of England ought to be put an end to'.[92]

The assumption that Burke attacked—namely that the proceedings of the British parliament should be linked to personal encounters in India— in fact formed the basis of much pro-Company writing. After Hastings's acquittal, for instance, an anonymous letter (dated 26 October 1795, and signed 'A RAMBLER') was published in the *Gentleman's Magazine* to vindicate the outcome of the impeachment. The writer recalls a boat trip to remote villages along the Hooghly, 'purposely to sound the natives relative to Mr Hastings'. Having 'left white faces for some days', he instructed the boatmen to stop at markets, where he 'threw as much good-nature into . . . [his] countenance' as he could, and casually questioned the men he met. Starting with general observations on the plentiful produce for sale, the conversation was directed towards political matters: 'I then remarked what security and happiness they enjoyed under Lord Cornwallis, which was agreed to by a respectable Salam to his name. Turning the thought suddenly—*But how did you like Mr. Hastings?* My memory must never forget the joy that beamed on their faces; and many of them salamed to the ground, saying, *he was good above all*—What can I say more?'[93] The writer employs a number of devices to guarantee the authenticity of this testimony to Hastings's benevolence. The journey up country, away from Calcutta where many Indians were directly dependent on the British for their livelihood, is supposed to ensure a disinterested response. The informal, non-coercive appearance of the encounter effectively obscures the imbalance of power in the exchange. And the studiedly good-natured expression assumed by the questioner contrasts with the genuine joy on the Indian faces. The Hastings impeachment, because of its emphasis on Indian testimony, has introduced a degree of self-consciousness into the government of India, a sense that British rule is itself appraised by its Indian subjects. But such an awareness is generated by the need to endorse a polemical position. Indian opinion is of little intrinsic interest to the British.

Anecdotes of Indian approbation were intended to counter the many narratives produced by critics of Company rule which featured Indian recrimination. One of the earliest and most influential of these was the account by a Calcutta Company servant of the 1770 drought and famine in Bengal. Appearing in the September 1771 issues of the *Gentleman's Magazine* and the *London Magazine*, it was reprinted in the *Annual Register* for 1771, prefaced by an editorial reference to its initial publication '*a considerable Time ago*', with a comment to endorse its authenticity: '*we are sorry (for the Honour of the Country and the Interests of Humanity) to observe, [that it] has not yet been contradicted*'.[94] The narrative alleges that as the drought advanced, Company servants stockpiled rice, planning to profit from rising prices. When supplies failed, Calcutta was flooded with famine victims hopelessly seeking relief. Thousands died in the streets, their corpses 'mangled by dogs, jackalls, and vultures'.[95] Dwelling on such lurid details—specifying which parts of the body were consumed by which birds and beasts of prey—the account, like Burke's later speech on the atrocities at Rangpur, was clearly designed to shock. But other sections were evidently pathetic in intent:

I have counted from my bed chamber window in the morning when I got up forty dead bodies laying within twenty yards of the wall, besides many hundreds laying in the agonies of death for want, bending double, with their stomachs quite close contracted to their back bones. I have sent my servant to desire those who had strength, to remove further off, whilst the poor creatures, looking up with arms extended, have cried out, Baba! Baba! my Father! my Father! This affliction comes from the hands of your countrymen, and I am come here to die, if it pleases God, in your presence. I cannot move; do what you will with me.[96]

This passage combines the pathos of the death scene with the chilling authority of the famine victims' accusation. The dying Indians' cry is at once pitiful and heavy with foreboding. While the writer is distressed at the famine victims' plight, he is also implicated in the actions of the administration that reduced them to such misery. The resulting sense of guilt and self-alienation is, as we have seen from the accounts of Nandakumar's execution and Chait Singh's deposition, a characteristic element of anti-Company rhetoric. The term of address used by the starving Indians—'Baba! my Father!'—points up the failure in paternalistic care; and the direct appeal to the writer (and, by implication, to the readers, his fellow countrymen) sharpens their dying accusation. The deaths are laid, both literally and metaphorically, at the British door.

The unspoken implication of the account—that such crimes will be judged by God—is made explicit during Hastings's trial, in Burke's excursus on Devi Singh's outrages at Rangpur: 'He then called upon their Lordships to prevent the effects of the Divine indignation upon the British empire, by bringing to justice the man who could employ so infernal an agent. Those wretched husbandmen would, with those shattered hands lifted up to Heaven, call down its vengeance upon their undoers.'[97] Burke's suffering Indians, like the famine victims of the preceding decade, appeal for justice with outstretched arms. Such invocations appear related to the rhetoric of the anti-slavery movement, which often threatened slave-traders and slaving nations with the wrath of God. John Wesley, for instance, in his widely disseminated pamphlet, *Thoughts upon Slavery*, warned slavers that on Judgment Day 'will the Great GOD deal with You, as you have dealt with *them* [the slaves], and require all their blood at your hands. And, at that day it shall be more tolerable for Sodom and Gomorrah than for you!'[98]

Such apocalyptic language enters the vocabulary of Indians themselves in an extraordinary anonymous text, *A Short History of English Transactions in the East Indies*, published in 1776. The main body of the work attacks the Company in terms familiar from Bolts and Dow, but the final chapter offers a striking prefiguration of the trial of Hastings. The author imagines the proceedings of an international court, empowered to adjudicate on a case brought against the British by the Indian people. The tribunal, a kind of United Nations, composed along lines suggested by the 'Great Design' of the Duc de Sully, unites 'the heads of civilised states . . . for the purposes of preserving peace upon earth, promoting justice, and repressing the wrong done to one country by another, at the expence of the whole'.[99]

Alighting from their camels, the dejected deputies from Bengal, Bihar and Orissa enter the senate. 'Who', the author asks, 'is that whose pale but wise and manly face reddens with a blush? I think it is one of the deputies from England. Why should he change colour? What has he known of the people of the country these ambassadors are from? Silence—they begin to speak—'.[100] And the Indian case commences. Their fathers, the ambassadors say, welcomed the first English traders to their land, particularly when they learnt that they adhered to the Bible, which contained 'such maxims of piety, justice, virtue, and goodness, as rendered all the learning of the East but as a glimmering taper in the presence of the midday sun'.[101] But the visitors violated every one of these tenets, stealing the wealth of India and trampling justice underfoot. Their faith in Biblical truths undiminished, the Indians launch into a lengthy complaint, calling for divine vengeance on the British nation, using the words of Ezekiel and Samuel. Endowed with Biblical authority, verses and verses of Old Testament retribution thunder portentously from their mouths.

In the first quotation (Ezekiel 35, although the author omits specific references) it is the Indians who are in the position of the injured Israelites, and the British who are classed as the heathen Edomites, whose nation God will lay waste.[102] In the second passage, from 2 Samuel 21, the British are cast as the Israelites, to whom God sends a famine for their unjust slaughter of the pagan Gibeonites or Indians.[103] Such inconsistent identification is as disruptive as the confused sense of national affiliation produced by much anti-Company rhetoric. Who, the reader is left wondering, should qualify as God's chosen people—the Indians or the British?

The oppressed Indians might be allowed to call down God's wrath, but in *this* world, they are kept firmly in their place. In his 1786 speech on the Rohilla War in the Commons, Burke characterized the abused Indians as impotent supplicants: 'he addressed the House with much earnestness and pathos. He placed before them the millions of their fellow-creatures who had no other prospect of relief than what they derived from Parliament. This was the only door of mercy that was open to them. He did not threaten the House with the effects of their disappointment. They were not likely soon to avenge their wrongs.'[104] Such a pathetic appeal (a form familiar from the Jesuit missionary letters analysed previously) places Burke's Indian masses in a position of complete dependence on their rulers. For Indians to be championed, they must be represented as victims, as abused subjects incapable of disrupting the colonial *status quo*.

Colonial power is in fact implied everywhere in the representation of Indians and Company servants. Conditions in the colony were inevitably subordinate to the concerns of British authority; the texts and speeches were less focused on their supposed subject—India—than on Westminster or Calcutta politics. The terms of the political debate

186 / *India Inscribed*

effectively circumscribed what could be said. Images answered each other across the partisan divide: they were appropriated, inverted, recirculated in a self-enclosed discursive economy. By the 1770s and '80s, India had become such deeply contested rhetorical territory that the mechanics of representation were on show as never before.

Notes

1. *The History of the Trial of Warren Hastings*, 5 parts (London, 1796) i. 74. I have decided to use *The History of the Trial of Warren Hastings* as the primary source for the impeachment speeches in this chapter. Although its editorial notes are clearly biased in favour of Hastings, it is one of the fullest contemporary accounts of the whole course of the trial. In *The Impeachment of Warren Hastings* (Oxford, 1965) Peter Marshall describes *The History of the Trial of Warren Hastings* as a compilation based on newspaper reports (p. 195). Accounts of the speeches vary however, and whenever possible I provide references to variant texts in later editions based on transcripts of court shorthand writers' notes. The later editions are Edward Bond's *The Speeches of the Managers and Counsel in the Trial of Warren Hastings*, 4 vols (London, 1861) and P. J. Marshall's *India: The Launching of the Hastings Impeachment 1786–1788: The Writings and Speeches of Edmund Burke* vi (Oxford, 1991), which is preferred for its accuracy.
2. Homi Bhabha, *The Location of Culture* (London, 1994) 96.
3. David Musselwhite, 'The Trial of Warren Hastings', in *Literature, Politics and Theory, Papers from the Essex Conference 1976–84*, ed. Francis Barker *et al.* (London, 1986) 92.
4. Henry Verelst, *A View of the Rise, Progress, and Present State of the English Government in Bengal: Including a reply to the Misrepresentations of Mr. Bolts and other Writers* (London, 1772) 43.
5. William Mackintosh, *Travels in Europe, Asia, and Africa*, 2 vols (London, 1782) ii. 214–16.
6. Suresh Chandra Ghosh, *The Social Condition of the British Community in Bengal, 1757–1800* (Leiden, 1970) 187.
7. *Monthly Review* lxvii (1782) 250, 254.
8. Joseph Price, *Some Observations and Remarks on a late Publication, intitled, Travels in Europe, Asia, and Africa*, 2nd edn (London, 1782) 42.
9. Price, *Some Observations*, 107.
10. Ibid., 92–3.
11. Ibid., 93.
12. Ibid., 94, 96.
13. Ibid., 96; Ghosh, 187.
14. Price, *Some Observations*, 96.
15. *Monthly Review* lxvii (1782) 252.

'Geographical Morality' / 187

16. Price, *Some Observations*, 93; *Monthly Review* lxvii (1782) 254.
17. Richard Owen Cambridge, *An Account of the War in India* (London, 1761) xxviii.
18. Bhabha, 44.
19. William Bolts, *Considerations on Indian Affairs* (London, 1772) xi, 221.
20. Ibid., 194–5.
21. Alexander Dow, *A History of Indostan*, 2 vols (London, 1768), vol. 3 (London, 1772) iii. 'State of Bengal under the East-India Company', xciv–v.
22. Lucy S. Sutherland, *The East India Company in Eighteenth-Century Politics* (Oxford, 1952) 221.
23. Compare for instance Abbé Guillaume Raynal *A Philosophical and Political History of the Settlements and Trade of the Europeans in the East and West Indies*, trans. J. Justamond, 3rd edn, 5 vols (London, 1777) i. 39–40 with Dow, i. xxv–xxvii; Raynal, i. 404–7 with J. Z. Holwell, *Interesting Historical Events, Relative to the Province of Bengal, and the Empire of Indostan*, 2nd edn (London, 1766) i. 199–200.
24. P. J. Marshall, *Impeachment* xvi.
25. Raynal, i. 453.
26. P. J. Marshall, *Impeachment*, 183; *Journals of the House of Commons* xli. 696.
27. Bond, ii. 494.
28. *The History of the Trial* v. 3; cf. Bond, ii. 537–40. Bond quotes the authorities at length.
29. P. J. Marshall, *Impeachment*, 183; *The Writings and Speeches of Edmund Burke* vi. 267.
30. *The Writings and Speeches of Edmund Burke* vi. 350–2.
31. Ibid., 346; cf. Bond i. 76. No such phrase is recorded in the summary of the speech in the *The History of the Trial*. See footnote 1.
32. Sara Suleri, *The Rhetoric of English India* (Chicago, 1992) 47–52.
33. Ibid., 47.
34. Sigmund Freud, *Art and Literature; The Pelican Freud Library*, vol. XIV, ed. Albert Dickson, 363.
35. Suleri, 46.
36. Geoffrey Carnall, 'Burke as Modern Cicero', *The Impeachment of Warren Hastings*, ed. Geoffrey Carnall and Colin Nicholson (Edinburgh, 1989) 81–2.
37. *The Writings and Speeches of Edmund Burke* vi. 413–22; *The History of the Trial* i. 6–8.
38. *The History of the Trial* i. 7.
39. *The Writings and Speeches of Edmund Burke* vi. 413.
40. *The History of the Trial* iii. 54. This forms part of the debate about the admissibility of evidence which is not included in Bond.
41. *The History of the Trial* v. 131, 132. Cf. Bond iv. 486:
    I think it is necessary that your Lordships know the ground upon which Mr. Hastings stood; that you should know the fairy land in which you are to act, which is perpetual masquerade, where no one thing appears to you as it is, where the person who seems to have the authority is a slave, where the person who seems to be the slave has the authority, where no one thing

appears in its true and natural shape; and therefore in that ambiguous government everything favours fraud, everything favours peculation, everything favours violence, everything favours concealment.

Cf. Bond iv. 507:

You have, by the master of the mechanism of the great opera of India—an opera of fraud, deception, tricks and harlequin proceedings—you have it all laid open before you.

42. P. J. Marshall, ' "A Free though Conquering People": Britain and Asia in the Eighteenth Century', inaugural lecture in the Rhodes Chair of Imperial History, Kings College, London, 5 March 1981, 6–7.
43. Mark Bence Jones, *Clive of India* (London, 1974) 272–3.
44. Samuel Foote, *The Nabob* (London, 1778) 4, 5.
45. Ibid., 13.
46. *The History of the Trial* ii. 38. Cf. Bond ii. 208: 'a great censorial prosecution, for the purpose of preserving the manners, characters and virtues, that characterise the people of England.'
47. Ibid., 38–9. Cf. Bond ii. 208–9:

Those people pour in upon us every day. They not only bring with them the wealth which they have, but they bring with them into our country the vices by which it was acquired. . . . But if you once teach the people of England, by the sucesses of those who practise this fraud, a concealing, narrow, suspicious, guarded, conduct—if you teach them qualities directly the contrary to those by which they have hitherto been distinguished—if you make them a nation of concealers, a nation of dissemblers, a nation of liars, a nation of forgers—my Lords, if you in one word turn them into a people of banyas—the character of England, that character which, more than our arms and more than our [commerce], has made us a great nation—the character of England will be gone and lost. Our liberty is as much in danger as our honour and national character. . . . And do we not know that there are many men, full of wealth, who wait . . . the event of this prosecution to let loose all the corrupt wealth of India, acquired by the oppression of that country, to the corruptions of all the liberties of this, and to fill the Parliament with men who are now the objects of its indignation? To-day the Commons of Great Britain prosecute the delinquents of India; to-morrow the delinquents of India may be the Commons of Great Britain.

48. John Barrell, *The Infection of Thomas De Quincey: A Psychopathology of Imperialism* (New Haven, 1991) 15.
49. Henry Yule and A. C. Burnell, eds *Hobson Jobson* (1886; Calcutta, 1986) 610.
50. Joseph Price, *The Saddle put on the Right Horse* (London, 1783) 20.
51. Ibid., 65–6.
52. Ibid., 66.
53. Ibid.
54. *The History of the Trial* i. 4. Cf. *The Writings and Speeches of Edmund Burke* vi. 346:

we are to let your Lordships know that these Gentlemen have formed a plan of Geographical morality, by which the duties of men in public and in private situations are not to be governed by their relations to the Great Governor of the Universe, or by their relations to men, but by climates, degrees of longitude and latitude, parallels not of life but of latitudes. As if, when you have crossed the equinoctal line all the virtues die, as they say some animals die when they cross the line, as if there were a kind of baptism, like that practised by seamen, by which they unbaptise themselves of all that they learned in Europe, and commence a new order and system of things.

55. Ibid., v. 523.
56. *The History of the Trial* v. 153. This is included in an editorial round-up of Burke's most striking invective.
57. Frans De Bruyn, 'Edmund Burke's Gothic Romance: The Portrayal of Warren Hastings in Burke's Writings and Speeches on India', *Criticism* xxix, no. 4 (1987) 415–38.
58. *The Writings and Speeches of Edmund Burke* vi. 5.
59. James Walvin, *England, Slaves and Freedom, 1776–1838* (Basingstoke, 1986) 98.
60. *The History of the Trial* i. 8. Cf. *The Writings and Speeches of Edmund Burke* vi. 419:

> These are the hands which are so treated, which have for fifteen years furnished the investment for China from which your Lordships and all this auditory and all this Country have every day for these fifteen years made that luxurious meal with which we all commence the day. And what was the return of Britain? Cords, hammers, wedges, tortures and maimings were the return that the British Government made to those laborious hands.

61. Timothy Touchstone (pseud.), *Tea and Sugar, or the Nabob and the Creole; A Poem in two Cantos* (London, 1792) 7, 8.
62. Ibid., 8.
63. Ibid., 9–10. Punctuation as in original.
64. Richard Clarke, *The Nabob: or, Asiatic Pluderers* (London, 1773) 3.
65. Ibid., 4–5.
66. Walvin, 104.
67. *The Writings and Speeches of Edmund Burke* vi. 81.
68. *The History of the Trial* i. 20. Cf. Bond i. 304:

> My fields are cultivated; my villages are full of inhabitants; my country is a garden; and my ryots are happy. My capital is the resort of the principal merchants of India, from the security I have given to property.... But what a different picture do the Company's province's present! There famine and misery stalk hand in hand through uncultivated fields and deserted villages. There you meet with nothing but aged men, who are not able to transport themselves away, or robbers and tigers in the fields, now overgrown with woods.

69. *Gentleman's Magazine* xlii (1772) 69.

190 / *India Inscribed*

70. Andrew Marvell, 'Upon Appleton House', l. 322.
71. Hodges, 17; Hamilton, i. 212.
72. *The History of the Trial* v.3. Cf. Bond ii. 533. In this version, Law does not elaborate on Burke's mythological figures:

   > there is one circumstance which does not square quite with the hypothesis of the honourable Manager—that there was a sort of golden age in which the lamb and tiger laid down together, all peace and harmony, and that war and tumult were not known. Read the first page of that same history [Dow's *History*], and you will find wars carried on, much more bloody than any in our times.

73. Ranajit Guha, *A Rule of Property for Bengal* (New Delhi, 1981) 31, 32.
74. *The History of the Trial* ii. 52,56. This forms part of the debate about the admissibility of evidence which is not included in Bond.
75. Marshall, *Impeachment*, 60.
76. *The Writings and Speeches of Edmund Burke* v. 436.
77. *Gentleman's Magazine* l (1780) 555, 556.
78. Ibid., 555.
79. *Annual Register* (1788), 'History of Europe': 177–80.
80. *The History of the Trial* i. 16. Editorial comment.
81. Ibid., Cf. Bond i. 256–7. In this version Chait Singh does not speak directly of his former happiness:

   > I was Raja Cheyt Sing. I was in my own opinion an independent Prince . . . I had all the symbols and appurtenances of sovereignty, and I thought to have had a free and uncontrolled sovereignty in my own dominions, subject to obedience and tribute to the Company. That was my situation: what am I now? An exile upon the earth, supported by the charity of those who were formerly envious of my power . . .

82. Musselwhite, 99.
83. *The History of the Trial* i. 16. Cf. Bond i. 257. This version records the legal arguments at much greater length:

   > you did not observe in your agreement that the tribute you were to pay was to be paid at Benares and not at Patna. You would have had the command of your country and the enjoyment of your revenue; you would have been in the most illustrious and opulent situation of any subject in all the provinces belonging to the British government in that country; but when it was stipulated that your tribute was to be paid at Benares, from that instant you were in the situation of a depraved, degraded, zamindar. Like one you are treated; you are annihilated, exterminated. But you have no right to complain. All this you ought to have known would have been the consequence of paying your tribute at Benares.

84. Marshall, *Impeachment*, 58.
85. *The History of the Trial* iv. 103. The text in Bond is substantially the same.
86. *Copies of the Several Testimonials transmitted from Bengal by the Governor General and Council, Relative to Warren Hastings Esq.* (London, 1789) 20.

87. *The History of the Trial* ii. 3. Cf. Bond ii. 7:

> It is a pleasant thing to see the mode and character of eloquence and addresses in different countries in those that are given before your Lordships. You will see the beauty of chaste European panegyric, improved by degrees into high oriental, exaggerated and inflated, metaphor. You will see how the language is first written in English, then translated into Persian, and then retranslated into English; and you will see the beauty of those styles, which will, in this heavy investigation, tend to give a little gaiety and pleasure: there is something amusing in it.

88. *The History of the Trial* v. 8. Bond does not include this quotation from the testimonial.
89. John Shore, 'Monody on the Death of Augustus Cleveland', *Asiatic Annual Register* i (1798–9) 'Poetry' 202.
90. *The History of the Trial* v. 54. Bond does not record such a phrase.
91. Ibid., iv. 6. This debate occurred in the House of Commons and is not included in Bond.
92. Ibid., iv. 9.
93. *Gentleman's Magazine* lxv (1795) 808.
94. Ibid., xli (1771) 402–4; *London Magazine* (1771) 469–71; *Annual Register* (1771) 'Appendix to the Chronicle', 205, 205–8.
95. *Gentleman's Magazine* xli (1771) 403.
96. Ibid.
97. *The History of the Trial* i. 8. Cf. *The Writings and Speeches of Edmund Burke* vi. 419:

> However, these crippled, undone hands are in a situation in which they will act with resistless power when they are lifted up to heaven against the authors of their oppression. Then what can withstand such hands? Can the power that crushed and destroyed them? Powerful in prayer, let us at least deprecate and secure ourselves from the vengeance which will follow those who mashed, crippled and disabled these hands.

98. Walvin, 100; John Wesley, *Thoughts upon Slavery*, 3rd edn (London, 1724) 25.
99. The French statesman who served under Henri IV, famous for his *Mémoirs* of 1638 which outlined the 'Great Design': a European confederation or Christian republic to be established after the defeat of Austria and Spain. *A Short History of English Transactions in the East Indies* (Cambridge, 1776) 157.
100. *Short History of English Transactions*, 158–9.
101. Ibid., 167.
102. Ibid., 177–80.
103. Ibid., 180–1.
104. *The Writings and Speeches of Edmund Burke* vi. 110–11.

CHAPTER SIX

Sir William and the Pandits: The Legal Research, Poetry and Translations of William Jones

In 1787 both the *Monthly Review* and the *European Magazine* printed the same review of the *Asiatick Miscellany*, a short-lived, unofficial precursor of the *Asiatick Researches*. The reviewer, John Parsons, began his survey of the work of the Asiatic Society of Bengal with a profile of Sir William Jones, the Supreme Court Judge who had founded the Society. Jones was then some years into his immensely productive decade-long study of Indian culture, a project which would range across Indian law, history, philosophy, mythology, linguistics, literature and music.[1] According to Parsons, Jones was 'possessed of integrity unimpeached, and of manners most attracting; in his judicial character, the glory of the British name in India'.[2] The phrase 'of integrity unimpeached' would have had a particular resonance for the readership of 1787, for this was the year which saw parliamentary preparations for the impeachment of Warren Hastings. Although Jones had been associated with Hastings, who was a patron of oriental scholarship, the former governor-general's notoriety evidently served as a foil to set off Jones's shining reputation. The figure of Jones functioned—and continues to function—as a reassuring vindication of British rule.

Jones was exempt from the accusations of exploitation and personal gain levelled against many a British nabob. One of the several elegies composed after Jones's untimely death, William Hayley's 'Elegy' of 1795, applies the metaphor of accumulated Indian wealth to Jones's cultural discoveries, at once alluding to this familiar charge and clearing Jones of involvement:

> To thee, reserved in ASIA'S richest spoil,
>   Fancy and Wisdom will their wealth impart;
> Deck with their jewels, won by letter'd toil,
>   The throne of Virtue in thy steadfast heart![3]

The phrase 'ASIA'S richest spoil' seems to refer to the plunder of conquest, but the following line transforms material riches into cultural wealth. Jones's scholarly labours, his 'letter'd toil', set him apart from the mass of Englishmen in Bengal who, as we have seen in the preceding chapter, are commonly caricatured as indolent fops amassing fortunes with the minimum of effort.[4] Earlier in the poem, Jones is represented as a conqueror whose triumphs exceed those of the lesser military breed:

> The Hero! who, in fields of highest fame,
>   Beyond his peers the dart of conquest hurl'd;
> Surpass'd ambitious AMMON'S weaker aim,
>   And nobly grasp'd the intellectual world.[5]

Again the metaphor suggests an affinity with a common British type—the Company soldier—only to modify the analogy: Jones's conquests are of a more abstract order. Yet while the 'Elegy' works to separate Jones from the economic, political and military aspects of colonialism, the metaphoric links established between these forms of conquest and Jones's scholarship inevitably suggest that Jones continues the work of colonial expansion by cultural means.

But most contemporaries, and many later historians and critics, have only seen in Jones the model of the disinterested colonial scholar; a figure which owes much to the desire to improve the image of the British administration in India. In 1797 the *Monthly Review* published an article on the third volume of *Asiatick Researches*. Edited by Jones, the *Asiatick Researches* printed much of Jones's work, including his famous Anniversary Discourses to the Asiatic Society. In an unusual gesture which reveals a sense of insecurity about British power, the reviewer anticipates the end of Company rule and predicts that the findings of the Society would constitute a 'monument more durable than brass, which will survive the existence and illustrate the memory of our Eastern dominion'.[6] The choice of a learned society's journal to commemorate British achievement in India reflects the concern to redeem the reputation of British rule:

After the contingent circumstances to which we owe our present preponderance in that country shall have ceased to operate, and the channels of Indian knowledge and Indian wealth shall have again become impervious to the western world, the Asiatic Researches will furnish proof to our posterity, that the acquisition of the latter did not absorb the attention of their countrymen to the exclusion of the former; and that the English laws and English government, in those distant regions, have sometimes been administered by men of extensive capacity, erudition, and application.[7]

The pursuit of knowledge is placed in clear opposition to the profit motive. Scholarly integrity mitigates the self-interest of colonial rule.

Posterity has generally taken its cue from the *Monthly Review* and many recent commentators have seen in Jones the ideal scholar–administrator.[8] During the nineteenth-century Jones's reputation suffered from the vigorous attack launched against him by James Mill, the utilitarian denigrator of Indian culture and oriental scholarship, whose *History of British India* of 1817 was massively influential.[9] But in more recent times Mill's criticism has only enhanced Jones's status; indeed Jones now seems to stand, for some historians, as the representative figure of a golden age of late eighteenth-century scholarship which flourished briefly before the onset of colonial insensitivity and blindness. One of the most dedicated of Jones's recent devotees is his biographer, Garland Cannon, who asserts that Jones 'always resisted any political aspects of scholarship' and that he showed 'a way toward world humanism and universal tolerance'.[10]

Cannon is here attempting to defend Jones from Said who argues that Jones's research inevitably formed part of the colonial project to gain authority over the East: 'To rule and to learn, then to compare Orient with Occident: these were Jones's goals, which, with an irresistible impulse always to codify, to subdue the infinite variety of the Orient to "a complete digest" of laws, figures, customs, and works, he is believed to have achieved.'[11] Said's assessment of Jones is, however, too cursory to be convincing. He seems unaware that legal digests, or ribandha, existed within the Indian tradition, and that Jones's work therefore is more accurately described as a re-codification. Interestingly, in the passage just cited, Said uses the Shakespearean phrase, 'infinite variety' from Enobarbus's description of Cleopatra, to suggest the manifold and mysterious attractions of the East prior to the deadening touch of British classification. This is taken from Enobarbus's description of Cleopatra, surely one of the most enduring of European myths of the Oriental Other.[12] When such 'orientalizing' rhetoric enters his own discourse, Said's arguments appear particularly vulnerable.

However, Said's basic premise that it is more fruitful to place Jones within the context of colonial rule than to treat him as some kind of scholar–saint remains well founded. In fact the tradition of Jones hagiography will form one of my avenues of investigation. For while it is undeniable that Jones was truly talented, a polymath of immense energy who pioneered new fields of scholarship and displayed a remarkable sensitivity towards Indian culture, his fame is not based on his achievements alone. I shall consider the political implications of representations of Jones, both his own self-portraits and those of his contemporaries, and concentrate particularly on the identification of Jones with Hindu pandits. This association of Jones with Hindu tradition will also be traced through Jones's literary works, the *Hymns* to Hindu deities, and his translation, *Sacontala*, which reached an extremely wide European readership. Jones's fame, intellectual stature and prolific output accord him a prominent position, unusual for any one individual, in the eighteenth-century tradition of writing about India. But although he was in some respects a great innovator, I will attempt to show how Jones's work was inevitably circumscribed by the conventions of his time.

NATIVE LAWYERS

Ranajit Guha's 1988 study, *An Indian Historiography of India*, provides a useful model with which to approach the legal researches of William Jones. Guha finds the origins of British historiography on India in the reports of early British administrators.[13] Frustrated in their attempts to gain accurate information on Indian land management techniques, Company servants accused Indians of deliberately refusing to impart the specialized knowledge necessary for the collection of land revenues. Guha argues that it was this perception of the 'collusive chicanery of native agents, in withholding official intelligence from their new masters' that caused British officials to turn to the writing of Indian history, since many of the early historians laid particular emphasis on the ownership and value of the land.[14] Guha's characterization of British research as a means to break the obstructive power of Indians, and as an expression of British exasperation at their reliance on untrustworthy informants, can be extended to Jones's scholarly pursuits.

Jones obtained his judgeship at the Supreme Court in Bengal just over a decade after Warren Hastings first recommended that Indians should be governed by their own laws. This policy decision and the parliamentary act of 1781 which recognized Hindu and Muslim customs in inheritance and contract, inevitably led to British judicial dependence on indigenous legal experts, the pandits and maulavis of the courts. From 1773 to 1775 a committee of eleven pandits had worked with Nathaniel Halhed on a digest of Hindu laws, similar to those compiled for earlier emperors and kings. It reached its final published form as *A Code of Gentoo Laws* in 1776 through a complicated process of translation—from Sanskrit, through an oral Bengali version, into Persian, and then from Persian into English. The result, according to Jones, was obscure and corrupt.[15] Jones attempted to establish a more authoritative text, as he writes to Sir John Macpherson in 1786, by having the court pandit correct a copy of Halhed's Code and then 'attest it as good law, so that he never now can give corrupt opinions, without detection'. J. D. M. Derrett observes that Jones was working on the mistaken assumption that Hindu law was no longer evolving, that it could be arrested at any point and fixed for all time.[16] Indeed, this desire to recover ancient Hindu traditions underlies much of Jones's work, but as Bernard Cohn and Javed Majeed have pointed out, Jones's pursuit of authentic law was motivated by his conviction that the Hindu and Muslim court advisors were uniformly untrustworthy.[17] For Jones, textual corruption seems inevitably to imply moral corruption.

Jones explains that his motivation to study Sanskrit derived from this distrust of court pandits in a letter written to Charles Chapman, first published in the 1804 *Memoirs of the Life, Writings and Correspondence of Sir William Jones*, compiled by Lord Teignmouth, former Governor-General of Bengal. Jones describes his sense of helpless dependence on unreliable pandits: 'I am proceeding slowly, but surely . . . in the study of Sanscrit; for I can no longer bear to be at the mercy of our pundits, who deal out Hindu law as they please, and make it at reasonable rates, when they cannot find it ready made.'[18] According to Jones, the pandits' fabrications subvert not only British authority, but also that of their own legal traditions. Jones frequently reiterates his distrust of the pandits, but they are not the only source of legal corruption.[19] In his 'Charge to the Grand Jury' of 1785 he suspects 'that affidavits of every imaginable fact may be easily procured in the streets and markets of *Calcutta*, especially from the natives, as any other article of traffick'.[20] Law becomes just another of the trading commodities for which India was famed; a product manufactured by pandits, forged by traders, and sold on the streets. Addressing the Grand Jury two years later, Jones extends the range of Indian depravity:

Having spoken of the little credit, which I gave to the oath of a low native, I cannot refrain from touching upon the frequency of perjury; which seems to be committed by the meanest and encouraged by some of the better sort, among the

Hindus and *Muselmans*, with as little remorse as if it were a proof of ingenuity, or even a merit, instead of being, by their own express laws, as grievous a crime as man is capable of committing.[21]

Moral and legal codes are in complete disarray; just as laws are severed from tradition, so are oaths from truth. One incident, recorded in a letter to John Shore (later Lord Teignmouth) and published in the *Memoirs*, seems to encapsulate this chaos by revealing forgery at the very heart of the legal process. In the course of a dispute with Hindus over the form of oath-taking in court, Jones writes that a Sanskrit treatise, produced by a brahman, prohibiting the use of Ganges water, was itself a forgery.[22]

Why this insistence on perjury? For Jones, the Indian refusal to render a faithful account, either of their traditions or of themselves, seems to constitute an act of resistance to British rule. The court becomes a site of colonial confrontation where natives attempt to outwit the British and fail to satisfy what Homi Bhabha has termed the colonizer's 'vigorous *demand for narrative*'.[23] This 'narcissistic, colonialist demand that it should be addressed directly, that the Other should authorize the self, recognize its priority, fulfil its outlines', is here frustrated, and so turns into 'the *other* side of narcissistic authority ... the paranoia of power'.[24] Indians thus become endlessly mendacious, endeavouring always to trick and confound their British rulers.

Some of the frustration experienced by Jones may have been related to structural differences between British and Indian legal systems. Bernard Cohn has commented that in late-eighteenth-century India 'there was no place for an independent [legal] profession' as the British conceived it. Indian society was hierarchically ordered and those in powerful positions had agents to act for them and their clients. To Indians, Cohn argues, the 'idea of an agent to whom one had a non-recurring, one-dimensional relationship—that of lawyer-client—must have appeared alien'.[25] Jones, nonetheless, assumed personal responsibility for imposing British-style order in the courts.

Jones's legal researches—most importantly, *Al Sirajiyyah: or, The Mohammedan Law of Inheritance* of 1792, the *Institutes of Hindu Law: or, the Ordinances of Menu* of 1794 and the *Digest of Indian Laws* completed by H. T. Colebrooke after Jones's death—constitute an attempt to break the Indian monopoly of legal knowledge, assert British judicial power and restore the integrity of the Indian legal tradition. These works manifest what Majeed has called 'the larger concern of British rule to legitimize itself in an Indian idiom'.[26] Direct access to legal texts, achieved through his mastery of Sanskrit, Arabic and Persian, freed Jones from dependence on court advisers. Writing to the second Earl Spencer, his former pupil and friend, Jones explains how he had broken the subversive power of Indians within the courts:

> I have the delight of knowing that my studies go hand in hand with my duty, since I now read both Sanscrit and Arabick with so much ease, that the native lawyers can never impose upon the courts, in which I sit. I converse fluently in *Arabick* with the Maulavi's, in *Sanscrit*, with the Pandit's, and in *Persian* with the nobles of the country; thus possessing an advantage, which neither Pythagoras nor Solon possessed, though they must ardently have wished it.[27]

Once Jones can overrule them, the legal experts take on a new character: they become types of those Indian sages supposed to have been consulted by the Greeks. The figure of the antique sage is, as Catherine Weinberger-Thomas has argued, one of the most central and long-lived of European archetypes of India.[28] Certainly Jones implies that he is in touch with men who embody the authentic essence of India. In another letter to Earl Spencer he suggests a continuity between his researches and the wisdom of the ancients by placing both himself and the pandits in a prestigious line of scholarly descent. He terms his brahman informants 'that class of men, who conversed with Pythagoras, Theles [sic] and Solon'.[29] Cohn notes that Jones also saw a connection between his work and that of Emperor Justinian or Tribonian, codifier of Roman law.[30] Jones's linguistic facility has thus admitted him to a kind of timeless learned élite. Writing to Earl Spencer, he claims to have won the brahmans' respect: 'I read and write Sanscrit with ease, and speak it fluently to the Brahmans, who consider me as a Pandit'.[31] This notion of the brahmans' acceptance of Jones is particulary potent and, recurring in the works of others, becomes almost an emblem of Jones's achievement. The image of a group of scholars seems to transcend colonial power relations, yet still suggests a gratifying degree of native respect. Jones's scholarship receives the ultimate stamp of authentication: pandit status. The 'narcissistic colonialist demand' for narrative is now gratified; the untrustworthy pandits are transformed into respected fellow scholars and celebrated as proof that the Other loves the self.

Jones's legal researches were of course motivated by the exigences of colonial power. Concluding the preface to *The Institutes of Hindu Law*, a translation of the *Manava-Dharmasastra*, Jones reminds the reader of the practical application of the work: the laws are considered sacred by 'many millions of Hindu subjects, whose well-directed industry would add largely to the wealth of *Britain*'.[32] The pragmatic considerations of Company rule are offered as the ultimate justification for the translation of a text that elicits an ambivalent response from Jones. Earlier in the preface, Jones enumerates both the deficiencies and beauties of the work:

> It is a system of despotism and priestcraft . . . filled with strange conceits . . . with idle superstitions. . . it abounds with minute and childish formalities, with ceremonies generally absurd and often ridiculous; the punishments are partial and fanciful, for some crimes dreadfully cruel, for others reprehensibly slight . . . nevertheless, a spirit of sublime devotion, of benevolence to mankind, and of amiable tenderness to all sentient creatures, pervades the whole work; the style of it has a certain austere majesty, that sounds like the language of legislation and extorts a respectful awe. . . .[33]

Jones's catalogue ends with the assertion that the author believed in one supreme God. In his initial criticism, Jones draws on the vocabulary long associated with European denigration of Hinduism: 'priestcraft', 'superstitions', 'childish', 'absurd', 'ridiculous', 'fanciful'. But turning from the detailed functioning of the law, Jones employs the terminology of sublimity, devotion, and benevolence to describe the style and faith of the work. Like the missionary writers (considered in Chapter Three) who praise the elements of Hinduism that appear to coincide with Christian teaching, Jones discovers a deistic essence in the laws of Manu. Jones's ambivalence thus falls into a familiar European pattern, and does not, as Majeed has argued of this passage, reflect 'the dilemma implicit in the attempt both to respect the uniqueness of cultures, and to define a neutral idiom in which cultures could be compared and contrasted'.[34] There is little that is neutral about Jones's idiom here; directed at his audience in Britain—'a country happily enlightened by sound philosophy and the only true revelation'—it answers the demands of colonial power.

In his pursuit of authentic Indian tradition, Jones selected a committee of 'Men of integrity and learning' to act as advisers for the compilation of the *Digest of Indian Laws*.[35] He recommended each member separately in a letter to Cornwallis of 13 April 1788, so that the scholars could be entered on the government payroll. These legal experts became directly associated with the British; one of them, Jagannatha Tarkapanchanan, Jones's 'favourite Pandit', a man 'eighty nine years old, a prodigy of learning, virtue, memory and health' was later awarded a pension by the government at Jones's request.[36] Jagannatha was such a valued collaborator because his reputation among the Bengalis ensured Hindu approval of the *Digest*; Cornwallis writes that 'his Opinion, Learning and Abilities are held in the highest Veneration, and Respect by all Rank of People and the Work will Derive infinite Credit and Authority both from the Annexation of his Name as a Compiler & from his Assistance.'[37] Although the pandits endowed the British with authority, the committee is always represented as under Jones's control. In the *Memoirs*, Teignmouth clearly defines the distribution of power in this Anglo-Indian relationship: 'In the dispensations of Providence, it may be remarked, as an occurrence of no ordinary nature, that the professors of the Braminical faith, should so far renounce their reserve and distrust, as to submit to the direction of a native of Europe, for compiling a digest of their own laws.'[38] Exclusivity and secrecy—long central to the European representation of brahmans—have been abandoned; the pandits accord Jones so much honour that they accept his guidance even in the matter of Hindu law. British expertise surpasses indigenous knowledge, the pandits have been out-pandited; an act of Providence which relocates Indian tradition under British control and justifies colonial rule. The 'direction of a native of Europe' results in a digest that diverges from standard Hindu legal opinions at certain points, according to Derrett. It is surely significant that most of the anomalies which Derrett discovers concern laws on fraud, given Jones's earlier preoccupation with Indian untrustworthiness.[39] Once he has appropriated the pandits' religious and scholarly authority, Jones directs his efforts towards 'making their [the Indians'] slavery lighter by giving them their own laws'.[40] This phrase, from a letter to Earl Spencer of 1791, succinctly transfers Indian law from indigenous possession to British control: Jones restores the Indian legal tradition to the Indians.[41]

The political implications of the pandits' esteem ensure that frequent mention is made of their association with Jones. This is particularly the case in the writings of Lord Teignmouth who was, after all, governor-general of Bengal from 1793 to 1798. In a footnote to his *Memoirs*, Teignmouth quotes evidence of the respect paid to Jones by both Hindu and Muslim scholars. He introduces the pandit's testimony:

The following is a translation of a Sanscrit note written to Sir William Jones, by a venerable pundit, whom he employed in superintending the compilation of Hindu law. From my own communications with the writer of the note, I can venture to assert, that his expressions of respect for Sir William Jones, although in the Oriental style, were most sincere.

Trivédi Servoru Sarman, who depends on you alone for support, presents his humble duty, with a hundred benedictions.

VERSES

1. To you there are many like me; yet to me there is none like you, but yourself; there are numerous groves of night flowers; yet the night flower sees nothing like the moon, but the moon.
2. A hundred chiefs rule the world, but thou art an ocean, and they are mere

wells; many luminaries are awake in the sky, but which of them can be compared to the Sun?

Many words are needless to inform those who know all things. The law tract of *Atri*, will be delivered by the hand of the footman, dispatched by your Excellency—Prosperity attend you.[42]

It is notable that Teignmouth prefaces the verses with an assertion of their sincerity. 'Oriental style' compliments are usually quoted in English accounts as amusing examples of the flattery and hyperbole of Eastern courts.[43] Teignmouth's introduction shows that he is aware of this tradition, but he nevertheless presents these verses as proof of genuine esteem. Why should an exception be made in the case of Jones? Why is his identification with the Other not threatening? Nigel Leask has suggested that 'reverse acculturation' can reveal itself as a 'hegemonic strategy. To "go native" might even be the means of reflecting "our national splendour" ' so long as the self is not threatened by absorption by the Other.[44] As we will see, Jones's original cultural identity is maintained in all his transactions with the Other.

Teignmouth is also the author of one of the most abiding images of Indian devotion to Jones. When Jones's sudden death precipitated Teignmouth (then Sir John Shore) into the presidency of the Asiatic Society, he delivered an address on his predecessor's many achievements and talents. On the subject of Jones's profound knowledge of Sanskrit and the Hindu tradition, he remarks: 'The *Pandits*, who were in the habit of attending him, when I saw them after his death, at a public *Durbar*, could neither suppress their tears for his loss, nor find terms to express their admiration, at the wonderful progress he had made in their sciences.'[45] When words fail them, the pandits' tears function much as the memorial erected by the hill peoples after the death of Augustus Cleveland: as an eloquent testimony to the affection and sense of indebtedness inspired in Indians by a British official. This is such a potent emblem that Teignmouth repeats the anecdote almost verbatim in his *Memoirs*.[46] The poet William Hayley also draws on the image in his *Elegy*:

> INDIA'S mild sages, dropping many a tear,
> With admiration into anguish turn'd,
> Mourn that enlighten'd Judge they joy'd to hear.[47]

Hayley identifies the pandits with ancient Indian sages in much the same way that Jones characterized them in his letters. Later in the elegy, Hayley returns to this concept when, as his end notes explain, he alludes to 'a monumental drawing of Mr FLAXMAN, in which he has represented Sir

WILLIAM JONES collecting information from the Pandits to settle the Digest of Hindu and Mahommedan Law'.[48] The pandits feature as the mouthpiece of an unchanging ancient tradition:

> 'So justly social, and benignly sage,
> 'He searched what INDIAN wisdom could produce
> 'So hoards of knowledge from the lips of Age
> 'He drew, and fashion'd for the public use'.[49]

Jones, 'benignly sage'—a sage among sages—appropriates the time-honoured learning of India for the good of the British administration. The venerable, hoarded wisdom of the pandits is transformed into useful, public knowledge.

The 'monumental drawing' to which Hayley refers was in fact executed as a commission from Jones's widow and the memorial itself donated to University College, Oxford. Originally intended for Calcutta, the monument was given to Jones's old college when another memorial was erected in Bengal.[50] Turning to the sculpture (Fig. 6), we can clearly see the origins of Hayley's distinction between the pandits' retention of Hindu lore and its pragmatic application by Jones. Flaxman represents Jones, pen in hand, in an eagerly attentive position, his gaze directed at the group of three Indians opposite; they, by contrast, sit bowed, with eyes cast upwards or downwards, as if lost in thought. The different postures establish the power relations between them: the figure of Jones, seated at his writing desk, occupies almost as much space as the three pandits, hunched before him on the ground.

The memorial's pediment also bears analysis. Considered individually, its three elements represent different aspects of Jones's character: the lyre signifies his poetic talent, the vina his interest in Indian music and the caduceus his eloquence and reason.[51] But collectively they seem to symbolize Jones's facility for combining, crossing and interpreting cultures: the lyre and vina could be taken as classical and Indian forms of the same instrument, and the caduceus as the symbol of Hermes who mediated between two worlds, decoded messages, and explained meanings. This sense of cultural translation and exchange—the ability to 'Adapt to ASIAN airs an ATTIC lyre', to use Hayley's phrase—is central to any understanding of Jones's role.[52]

'HINDU FICTIONS'

Jones was the first European to use Hindu mythology as a literary source. His *Hymns* to Hindu deities, six of which appeared in the *Asiatick Miscellany* of 1785, and all nine in the later collections of his poetry and complete

FIG. 6: Memorial to Sir William Jones by John Flaxman (1796–8)
University College, Oxford.

works, retell Hindu myths for a European readership. In Teignmouth's words, they attempt 'to explain and adorn the mythological fictions of the Hindus, in odes which the Bramins would have approved and admired'.[53] This phrase places the *Hymns* in much the same position of brahmanical esteem as that assigned to Jones's legal work; in this case, it is the tradition of devotional literature which Jones has appropriated.

Published initially in Calcutta, the *Hymns* were widely reviewed and reprinted in England.[54] Each Hymn is introduced by an Argument; a preface which outlines the nature and activities of the deity addressed, supplies parallels with divinities from the western classical pantheon, explains allusions and stylistic decisions, includes personal anecdotes and scholarly digressions. The urbanely erudite tone of the Arguments is common to much of Jones's writing; similar, for instance, to the manner in which he delivers his presidential Discourses to the Asiatic Society of Bengal. Indeed, as Majeed points out, the prefaces are a version of Jones's Discourse 'On the Gods of Greece, Italy and India'.[55] Several critics have observed that even before Jones's arrival in India, he championed Eastern poetry as a means of reinvigorating the European poetic tradition which had 'subsisted too long on the perpetual repetition of the same images, and incessant allusions to the same fables' and needed '*a new set of images and similitudes*' which oriental poetry could provide.[56] The literary traditions of the East are at once conflated and commodified, turning into a kind of exotic item imported to enhance European traditions. The *Hymns* appear to be an attempt to substantiate this earlier assertion, to demonstrate the literary potential of Hindu mythology.

The reader of Jones's *Hymns*, if ignorant of the Hindu pantheon, would need to refer to the prefatory Arguments throughout, to check the names and attributes of gods as they occur in the odes. Jones usually provides scholarly explications, but sometimes leaves allusions obscure, referring the reader instead to other texts such as Charles Wilkins's 1785 translation of the *Bhagvad Gita*, as though to foster interest in Hinduism and, by building a web of intertextual relations, encourage further reading.[57] This close association of the Arguments with the hymns, the continuous exchange between the didactic and poetic voices, gives the *Hymns* something of the air of poetic exercises, as if they were demonstrations of the poetic possibilities of the prose introductions. One of Jones's favourite devices contributes particularly to this effect: he supplies long lists of alternative names for the deities. Consider, for instance, this extract from the Argument to 'The Hymn to Surya':

SURYA . . . has near fifty names or epithets in the *Sanscrit* language; most of which, or at least the meanings of them, are introduced in the following Ode; and every image, that seemed capable of poetical ornament, has been selected from books of the highest authority among the *Hindus*....[58]

The assertion of authenticity (a necessary claim in the decades following the Ossianic forgeries of James Macpherson) foregrounds the painstaking process of research and composition, justifying the litany of names in the Hymn on the grounds of scholarly accuracy. The poem in part borrows the form of the Sanskrit namastotra, or 'praise of names', a series of titles, epithets, functions and qualities of a deity, which form a devotional hymn:

> 'Our bosoms, *Aryama*, inspire,
> 'Gem of heav'n, and flow'r of day,
> '*Vivaswat*, lancer of the golden ray,
> '*Divácara*, pure source of holy fire,
> 'Victorious *Ráma's* fervid sire,
> 'Dread child of *Aditi*, *Martunda* bless'd,
> 'Or *Súra* be address'd,
> '*Ravi*, or *Mihira*, or *Bhánu* bold,
> 'Or *Arca*, title old,
> 'Or *Heridaswa* drawn by green-hair'd steeds,
> 'Or *Carmasacshi* keen, attesting secret deeds.'[59]

The lists of names carry a sense of plenitude, as if Jones were trying to convey something of the wealth of Hindu mythology. Such displays of Sanskritic erudition were singled out by contemporary reviewers for criticism as intrusively alien and incomprehensible to the general reader.[60]

Critics have offered various accounts of Jones's intentions in creating a new mythical lexicon. Javed Majeed argues that the *Hymns* are concerned with the definition of a Hindu identity and reflect Jones's work as a pioneer Orientalist scholar: 'Invoking the Hindu deities, Jones calls into being a newly defined Hindu world, a cultural vision which can be compared and contrasted on equal terms with any other.'[61] According to Majeed, the odes' celebration of creative nature 'reflects Jones's own creativity in bringing into being a newly defined Hinduism'.[62] Majeed reasons further that the assertive, aggressive character of this Hinduism is indicated by the descriptions of the martial deeds of the gods which occur in some of the *Hymns*.[63] Majeed's arguments throw up certain problems. He starts from the premise that Jones was preoccupied with the definition of a Hindu identity, a view of Jones's work which is based on the idea that it was orientalist research which transformed Hinduism from a great body of myth and ritual into a coherent system of belief.[64] But to suggest that the orientalists themselves were attempting to define Hindu identity rather than simply trying to systematize the religion for their own convenience seems to confuse results with motives. Jones, writing entirely for a domestic audience, was not concerned with the creation of an Indian cultural identity or a rejuvenated Hinduism. The *Hymns* lack the cultural integrity necessary to constitute Majeed's 'cultural vision which can be compared and contrasted on equal terms with any other', for they present Hindu mythology almost wholly in European guise.

This was recognized as early as 1786 by John Courtney in his eulogy of Dr Johnson's circle, the 'Moral and Literary Character of Dr Johnson', reprinted in Boswell's *Life of Johnson*. Enumerating those writers who benefited from Johnson's literary tutelage, Courtney includes

> Harmonious JONES! who in his splendid strains
> Sings Camdeo's sports, on Agra's flowery plains:
> In Hindu fictions while we fondly trace
> Love and the Muses, deck'd with Attick grace.[65]

Indian myths, peopled by the classical muses, are depicted in accordance with classical taste. The reader's delight lies in the recognition of the familiar in the strange.

The idea that Hindu culture is in some sense validated by classical analogy runs through much of Jones's work. In a letter to the second Earl Spencer, Jones conveys the excitement of his literary discoveries with a Greek parallel:

> To what shall I compare my literary pursuits in India? Suppose Greek literature to be known in modern Greece only, and there to be in the hands of priests and philosophers; and suppose them to be still worshippers of Jupiter and Apollo: suppose Greece to have been conquered successively by Goths, Huns, Vandals, Tartars, and lastly by the English; then suppose a court of judicature to be established by the British parliament, at Athens, and an inquisitive Englishman to be one of the judges; suppose him to learn Greek there, which none of his countrymen knew, and to read Homer, Pindar, Plato, which no other Europeans had ever heard of. Such am I in this country; substituting Sanscrit for Greek, the *Brahmans*, for the priests of *Jupiter*, and *Vālmic, Vyāsa, Cālidasā*, for Homer, Plato, Pindar.[66]

Jones chooses this image of a Europe deprived of the classical discoveries of the Renaissance to convey the sense of revelation at the immense riches of Sanskrit literature, for the Greek masters endow Sanskrit writers with great cultural authority. The image is so striking because it posits the unimaginable: that Greek culture might have remained neglected and obscure. The fact that European culture is inconceivable without the classical influence points to the underlying reason for the Hindu/classical analogy. Classical civilization acted as the cultural touchstone for Europe: no other criterion for judging a non-Christian culture would suggest itself, no other comparison would seem appropriate.

The classical analogue is explored at length in Jones's Discourse, 'On the Gods of Greece, Italy and India'. Jones's most substantial text on the subject of Hindu mythology takes the form of a syncretic essay which suggests that Hindu deities are essentially the same as those of the Greek and Roman pantheons. Particularly interesting here is the way in which Indian gods are slotted into the familiar pantheon; although the Hindu deities predate their classical offspring, they are of relevance only so far as they relate to the Greek and Roman versions. It is perhaps worth noting that this classical precedence is established even in the essay's title where the Indian gods are mentioned last.

Near the beginning of the essay, Jones asserts that he does not intend to insist on strict correspondences between the gods, rejecting the notion

> that such a God of *India* was *the* JUPITER of *Greece*; such *the* APOLLO: such, *the* MERCURY: in fact, since all the causes of polytheism contributed largely to the assemblage of *Grecian* divinities . . . we find many JOVES, many APOLLOS, many MERCURIES, with distinct attributes and capacities; nor shall I presume to suggest more, than that, in one capacity or another, there exists a striking similitude between the chief objects of worship in ancient *Greece* or *Italy* and in the very interesting country in which we now inhabit.[67]

Although he claims not to be dogmatic, Jones adopts an increasingly assertive tone as he draws parallels between the pantheons. He states for instance that 'RAMA . . . was the DIONYSOS of the *Greeks*', that 'PHOEBUS . . . is adored by the *Indians* as the God SU'RYA' and that 'there can be no doubt of her [Diana's] identity with CA'LI'.[68] Hindu mythology is here incorporated into the European tradition.

Similar Hindu/classical correspondences are reiterated with like emphasis in the Arguments to many of the hymns.[69] These parallels serve to locate the god within a familiar framework; once anchored, it is possible to introduce Hindu variations on classical themes. Consider for example the opening of the Argument to 'A Hymn to Camdeo': 'THE *Hindú* God, to whom the following poem is addressed, appears evidently the same with the *Grecian* EROS and the *Roman* CUPIDO; but the *Indian* description of his person and arms, his family, attendants. and attributes, has new and peculiar beauties.[70] 'The description of Kamadeva is presented to the reader as if it were a regional variant, a touch of local colour rather than the delineation of a new deity. In fact Jones sprinkles his *Hymns* with references to events and attributes shared between the mythologies of Europe and India. In the 'Hymn to Camdeo' itself, the god is equipped, Cupid-like, with bow and arrows, though the bow is composed of flowers, the bow-string of bees, and the arrows tipped with blossoms.[71] 'A Hymn to Indra' describes the abode of the gods, lovely Mount *Suméru*, where the gods feast on nectar just as on the summit of Mount Olympus.[72] Turning to the 'Hymn to Surya', we find frequent mention of the sun god's horse-drawn chariot (although unlike Phoebus's, its horses are green).[73] While the birth of Lakshmi from the waves, retold in the Hymn addressed to her, bears a strong resemblance to Venus's nativity.[74] These examples suggest not that the *Hymns* are merely Indianized versions of classical stories, but rather that Jones fixes Hindu myths in a familiar landscape and so attempts to minimize the sense of cultural dissonance. The *Hymns* demonstrate the poetic possibilities of Hindu mythology; that is, the ease with which Indian myths can be absorbed into the English literary tradition. I would argue therefore that the *Hymns* constitute an exercise in poetic appropriation.

The assimilation of Hindu mythology is promoted by Jones's poetic diction. Jones inevitably draws on the literary conventions of his day and the *Hymns* reverberate with familiar echoes.[75] The first two couplets of the opening stanza to 'A Hymn to Camdeo' are typical:

> WHAT potent God from *Agra's* orient bow'rs
> Floats thro' the lucid air, whilst living flow'rs
> With sunny twine the vocal arbours wreathe,
> And gales enamour'd heav'nly fragrance breathe?[76]

This description of natural luxuriance plots Jones's poetic territory: 'lucid air' is borrowed from Thomson's *The Seasons* ('Summer': line 309) and 'vocal arbours' is reminiscent of Dryden's 'vocal Grove' (*Eclogues* VIII, line 31). Later in the same stanza Jones's phrase 'laughing blossom' seems to draw on Gray's 'laughing flowers' from his *Progress of Poesy* (line 5). While in the Hymn's fifth verse, we find a typical eighteenth-century periphrasis for birds—'the many-plumed warbling throng'—and a reference to Kamadeva's companion, 'In heav'n clep'd *Bessent*, and gay *Spring* on earth', which owes its form, with alternate heavenly and earthly names, to the appeal to Mirth in Milton's *L'Allegro*:

> But come thou goddess fair and free,
> In heaven yclept Euphrosyne,
> And by men, heart-easing Mirth[77]

The same god of spring is given an even more extensive poetic pedigree when described in 'The Hymn to Durga' as 'He, who decks the purple year'.[78] As A. Jonston has pointed out, the phrase 'the purple year', used by both Pope and Gray, derives from Virgil's Ninth *Eclogue* (line 40) and its translations by Thomas Parnell and Dryden.[79] The weight of these allusions provides a solid literary pedigree for the *Hymns*. Gesturing towards key works in the eighteenth-century poetic canon, they imply a shared set of cultural assumptions.

In his study, *India and the Romantic Imagination*, John Drew argues that Jones combines both the Indian and English poetic traditions in the *Hymns*, allowing himself 'the freedom of invention of an English poet' but rarely compromising the 'Indian spirit'.[80] Drew argues that Jones is less interested in Hindu myths as an alternative to classical mythology than in exploring 'the common spirit which had inspired in diverse cultures a not dissimilar pantheon'.[81] This 'common spirit' takes the form of the mystical philosophy shared between the Platonist and the Vedantin traditions.[82] It is noticeable that, to substantiate this assertion, Drew quotes almost exclusively from 'A Hymn to Narayena', the only hymn to address 'the abstract power existing beyond the world of name and form'.[83] This hymn invokes God as the creative force of the universe, the spirit which pervades nature, but which is ultimately beyond the delusive world of perception (Maya). But in his enthusiasm for mystical philosophy and finding common ground, Drew pays insufficient attention to Jones's literary technique. He fails to mention, for instance, that Jones's representation of the divine relies heavily on Milton's depiction of God in *Paradise Lost*.

In the first stanza of the hymn, the 'SPIRIT of Spirits' is described as always having existed: 'Before Heav'n was, Thou art'; this must be derived from Milton's address to the Light of God in Book III: '—Before the Sun, / Before the Heavens thou wert'.[84] Jones then follows Milton's structure with a brief description of the act of creation and an appeal for poetic inspiration to enable him to fly upwards to express the vision.[85] In the second verse, Jones depicts 'BREHM', obscured by sheer brilliance of light:

> Wrapt in eternal solitary shade,
>   Th'impenetrable gloom of light intense,
>   Impervious, inaccessible, immense[86]

The reference to Milton's description of God enthroned in glory, 'Dark with excessive bright' is made all the clearer by the similar alliteration:

> Immutable, Immortal, Infinte,
> Eternal King; thee Author of all being,
> Fountain of Light, thy self invisible
> Amidst the glorious brightness where thou sit'st
> Throned inacessible. . . .[87]

The authoritative Miltonic tone is appropriate for English readers for the depiction of an omnipotent divine power. The concept of a supreme God had long been noted by Europeans as an advantage which Hinduism enjoyed over Greek and Roman religion. These Miltonic allusions seem to imply the propriety of Hindu faith, its acceptability to the Christian reader, and its eligibility for literary treatment. Such suggestions are reinforced by another Miltonic echo, this time a reference to the creation of the world from 'The Hymn to Bhavani'. The ode opens with a description of the first creative act:

> —o'er the wild abyss, where love
> Sat like a nestling dove,
> From heav'n's dun concave shot a golden ray.[88]

This image is derived from the appeal to the divine Spirit for inspiration with which *Paradise Lost* opens:

> —Thou from the first
> Wast present, and with mighty wings outspread
> Dove-like satst brooding on the vast Abyss
> And mad'st it pregnant . . .[89]

The choice of the dove, such a familiar symbol of the divine, reinforces the Christian associations of the simile. In his essay 'On the Gods of Greece, Italy and India', Jones directly elaborates the parallels between the Judeo-Christian and Hindu versions of the creation story.[90] But Jones is less interested in Drew's philosophical 'common spirit', than in situating the *Hymns* firmly within the English literary tradition.

At times Jones is quite explicit about his borrowings from English and classical literature, acknowledging a debt to Gray and Pindar for his stanzaic form, but nowhere more so than in a footnote to 'A Hymn to Surya'.[91] In the middle of the ode to the sun god, Jones inserts a stanza describing a sunrise at sea. A footnote explains that this is based in part on a letter in an annotated edition of Gray, and in part on a note quoting Jeremy Taylor which Gray's editor adds to the letter.[92] Jones evidently does not consider it incongruous to incorporate the observations of an English poet and of a seventeenth-century divine in a hymn addressed to a Hindu deity. Indeed the anglicization of the hymn is deliberately signposted, making us aware of the act of cultural appropriation.

Sir William and the Pandits / 211

The set of prints which illustrate Jones's essay, 'On the Gods', in the first volume of *Asiatick Researches* (Figs 7 and 8) represents an iconographic parallel to this practice of literary annexation. Although the prints are fairly accurate copies of late eighteenth-century East Indian paintings, they are presented in an entirely neo-classical manner.[93] Framed with a fringe of exotic foliage, each deity is mounted on a pedestal bearing a Sanskrit quotation from the *Bhagvad-Gita*, garlanded with loops of flowers. Above, an unfurled scroll announces the transliterated English version of the god's name. The decoration contains the Hindu gods within decorous European bounds.

If we turn to Jones's most famous translation—of Kalidasa's masterpiece *Sakuntala*—we can see similar forms of cultural assimilation at work. In the preface of *Sacontala*, Jones relates the history of his discovery of the play. From the *Lettres édifiantes* (which, Jones quips, may 'bear the title of EDIFYING, though most of them swarm with ridiculous errours') he first gleaned the information that in northern India 'there are many books, called Nátac, which, as the Bráhmens assert, contain a large portion of ancient history without any mixture of fable'.[94] But this proved inaccurate:

FIG. 7: Engraving of Ganesa from *Asiatick Researches* vol. i (1789)
Bodleian Library, Oxford.

FIG. 8: Engraving of Karttikeya from *Asiatick Researches* vol. i (1789)
Bodleian Library, Oxford.

when I was able to converse with the Bráhmens, they assured me that the Nátacs were not histories, and abounded with fables; that they were extremely popular works, and consisted of conversations in prose and verse, held before ancient Rájás in their publick assemblies, on an infinite variety of subjects, and in various dialects of India: this definition gave me no very distinct idea; but I concluded that they were dialogues on moral or literary topicks; whilst other Europeans, whom I consulted, had understood from the natives that they were discourses on dancing, musick, or poetry. At length a very sensible Bráhmen, named Rádhácánt, who had long been attentive to English manners, removed all my doubts, and gave me no less delight than surprise, by telling me that our nation had compositions of the same sort, which were publickly represented at Calcutta in the cold season, and bore the name, as he had been informed, of plays.[95]

With its movement from the uncertainty of multiple, shifting definitions to the lucid simplicity of the final explanation, this passage seems to enact the process of cultural familiarization. The natakas advance from the hazy remoteness of ancient courts to the clear focus of the contemporary Calcutta stage. Jones heightens the moment of recognition by reserving the explanation to the very end, like the solution to a riddle. Considered as a narrative of scholarly discovery, the anecdote deviates significantly from the standard plot, for it is the scholar who blunders unrewardingly, while his informant takes the necessary logical leap. In this instance, the leap is across the cultural divide and it is performed by an Indian; the shock of recognition is further intensified because it is a brahman who identifies the English analogue. Jones's anecdote therefore serves to convey both the connection between the brahman and his English rulers and the affinity of their respective cultures.

Jones's translation, *Sacontala*, took Europe by storm, revealing something of the literary wealth of ancient Indian civilization to a wide public. The play, first published in 1789, was reissued five times in England in the following decades. The German translation of 1791 was received with particular enthusiasm, most importantly by Goethe and Herder.[96] Raymond Schwab observes that *Sacontala* formed the 'basis on which Herder constructed an Indic fatherland for the human race in its infancy. From this sagacious work with its time honoured traditional refinement, a blasé Europe, thirsty for a golden age, could fabricate the notion of a primitive India.'[97] Twenty years after the first publication of *Sacontala*, August Wilhelm Schlegel observed that the play 'bears in its general structure such a striking resemblance to our romantic drama, that we might be inclined to suspect we owe this resemblance to the predilection for Shakespeare entertained by Jones the English translator, if his fidelity were not confirmed by other learned orientalists.'[98] The orientalist scholars were correct in maintaining that Jones did not alter the overall structure of the play, but Schlegel is not mistaken in detecting some degree of Shakespearean influence. Jones himself was responsible for designating Kalidasa 'the Shakespeare of India', a term which has enjoyed remarkable longevity.[99] In his preface to the play, Jones explains the three-stage translation process which he employed: first he translated the play from Sanskrit to Latin, then from Latin into literal English, and finally 'without adding or suppressing any material sentence, disengaged it from the stiffness of a foreign idiom, and prepared the faithful translation of the Indian drama . . .'[100] We can test Jones's assertions of fidelity against the manuscript that traces his translation in progress, from Sanskrit to Latin to literal English, preserved at the Bodleian Library.

A contemporary reviewer draws a more specific Shakespearean analogy in a description of one of the characters: 'Madhavya is styled a buffoon, and we eagerly wished to see a specimen of his courtly charater in an early and uncorrupted age. . . . He is humorous, occasionally shrewd and sarcastic, but, in general, a lively good-humoured moralist, not unlike the Touchstone of our own Shakespeare.'[101] The reviewer then quotes a passage from the play (the beginning of the second act) in which Madhavya grumbles of being forced to endure the rigours of outdoor life on an exhausting hunting expedition with the king. Part of Madhavya's complaint reads 'Are we thirsty? We have nothing to drink but the waters of mountain torrents. . . . Are we hungry? We must greedily devour lean venison, and that commonly toasted to a stick.—Have I a moment's repose at night?—My slumber is disturbed by the din of horses and elephants.'[102] If we turn to Jones's literal translation of the same passage we find 'then we must drink the waters of the mountain torrents . . . then without observing regular meal-times, we greedily eat venison, and that commonly over-roasted: my night-slumbers are constantly disturbed with the din of horses and elephants.'[103] The interrogative form of Madhavya's complaint is Jones's own addition, and seems to be derived from Shakespeare: the aggrieved character, entering alone, throws out a volley of questions, exclaiming against the treatment that he has received in the service of his master. Consider, for instance, the servant Grumio's outburst from *The Taming of the Shrew*:

Fie, fie on all tir'd jades, on all mad masters, and all foul ways! Was ever man so beaten? Was ever man so rayed? Was ever man so weary? I am sent before to make a fire, and they are coming after to warm them.[104]

Jones employs a similar rhetorical technique to enliven the speech and to reinforce a Shakespearean model for the Indian character. Madhavya thus falls into a recognizable role, a type sanctioned by English dramatic tradition.

Other alterations made by Jones reveal a concern for propriety and a desire not to offend European convention. Kalidasa's text frequently mentions Sakuntala's heavy hips. Jones evidently did not consider these a suitable attribute for the hermit heroine described as the epitome of physical beauty, and therefore converts them into 'elegant limbs' on one occasion, and entirely relocates them as 'graceful arms' on another.[105] Further anatomical adjustments include a drooping neck rather than drooping breasts and the complete omission of a reference to tapering thighs.

Jones also censors improper suggestions, particularly those concerning Sakuntala's behaviour, when first struck with love for Dushmanta, the King. Her two female friends, Anusuya and Priyamvada, debate how she should make her love known to Dushmanta. In the manuscript, they commit themselves to serving her: 'We *must* gratify the desire of our beloved'; a frank expression of the intensity of Sakuntala's desire which Jones left out of the published version.[106] When the two are brought together and the king announces that he will love only her, the stage direction describing Sacontala's expression becomes noticeably more modest in the transition from manuscript version, she '*discovers joy on her countenance*', to published form—she '*strives in vain to conceal her joy*'.[107]

Jones is equally careful not to tarnish Dushmanta's reputation. When the lovers are left alone and the wooing begins in earnest, Sacontala attempts to resist Dushmanta's advances by breaking away from him. While the Sanskrit stage direction in the manuscript states that the king 'brings her back with force', the Latin version omits the mention of force; the English version in manuscript form reads 'He draws her back', and when published avoids all suggestion of compulsion with the line 'He gently draws her back'.[108] Jones is prepared to distort the original to preserve decorum. He also absolves Dushmanta of impropriety when the king reflects on the reluctance of women to give in to love. In Jones's published translation, Dushmanta observes that

> One would imagine that the charming sex, instead of being,
> like us, tormented with love, kept love himself within
> their hearts, to torment him with delay.[109]

The fuller manuscript version reads

> Such is the lovely sex! even when they receive with great
> joy, the addresses of a lover, they give him a refusal;
> even when they desire his gratification, they make
> difficulties in gratifying him; surely, they are not
> tormented by love, but rather keep Love himself within
> their hearts and torment him with delays.[110]

Sexual desire was evidently not an emotion which Jones considered suitable to attribute to a romantic heroine. In the event, Jones seems to have assessed his audience's standards of propriety with considerable accuracy. Among the qualities of the play which one contemporary critic singled out for praise were the 'dignified morality of sentiment' and 'delicacy in the delineation of character'; while a second pronounced that '(t)he morality is pure, and the refinement, conspicuous throughout'.[111] Jones succeeds in creating a version of *Sakuntala* which does not offend European convention; as with the *Hymns*, he muffles notes of cultural dissonance.

If we turn from *Sacontala*, Jones's most substantial literary work, to one of his early, lighter pieces, the mock heroic 'The Enchanted Fruit; or, the Hindu Wife', we can detect a similar concern for propriety. This poem is derived from an incident in the *Mahabharata*. The story on which the poem is based is briefly related by Alf Hiltebeitel in his study, *The Cult of Draupadi*. Hiltebeitel translates the episode from the fourteenth-century Tamil version of the epic by Villiputtur Alvar:

Having unwittingly cut down a nelli fruit from the ashram tree of the sage Amitra . . . the Pandavas and Draupadi find out from Krsna that they can rejoin it to its stem only by uttering a series of 'truths'. The ultimate truth, the one that completes the miracle, is Draupadi's following admission: 'Like the five senses, although I have five husbands, yet still I would like to have one other man for my great husband, my great heart longs . . .'[112]

The direct source for Jones's poem occurs in a letter written by the Jesuit Père Bouchet, printed in the *Lettres édifiantes*.[113] The missionary includes the narrative to demonstrate that Hindus, though now lapsed deep into idolatry, were once Christian, for they formerly believed in confession as a means of remission of sins. In Bouchet's version of the story, Draupadi admits to a sinful thought that she wants to keep secret.[114] This confession of secret desire is transformed by Jones into an admission that once, while reading the Vedas together, Draupadi allowed a brahman to kiss her cheek.

While the degree of self-censorship is characteristic, in other respects this poem stands out as quite distinct from the rest of Jones's literary work. Originally published in the same journal as the *Hymns*, 'The Enchanted Fruit' appears to parody Jones's odes to Indian deities. While the *Hymns* attempt to provide a careful introduction to Hindu mythology, 'The Enchanted Fruit', seems to debunk the scholarly project. Equipped though it may be with an apparatus of learned footnotes, the tone of the poem is notably flippant, recalling Pope. At times, it is even subversive, as in the description of the activities of Krishna:

>—having pip'd and danc'd enough,
>Clos'd the brisk night with *blindman's-buff*;
>(List, antiquaries, and record
>This pastime of the *Gopia's* Lord)[115]

Jones uses the playful figure of Krishna to satirize his own scholarly aspirations in a parenthetical aside.

A similar self-parodic strain runs through Jones's use of botanical terms to classify Draupadi's polyandry. In the Argument to the 'Hymn to Durga', Jones digresses at length on the genus of the Indian lotos, but in 'The Enchanted Fruit' he makes fun of such pedantry:

> —sev'ral husbands, free from strife,
> Link'd fairly to a single wife!
> Thus Botanists, with eyes acute
> To see prolifick dust minute,
> Taught by their learned northern *Brahmen*
> To class by pistil and by *stamen,*
> Produce from nature's rich domain
> Flow'rs *Polyandrian Monogynian*.[116]

The 'learned northern Brahmen' is identified in a footnote as Linnaeus; the Swedish botanist, a hero of Western science, is given an Indian title, thus inverting the *Hymns*' practice of europeanizing Hindu figures. We should note that botany figured among the many pursuits of Jones himself, and also recall Jones's own assumption of pandit status. While it is hard to determine the level of self-irony at play here, the comic effect clearly arises from a sense of incongruity or cultural mismatch. The poem demonstrates that while it is perfectly acceptable to domesticate an alien culture by drawing analogies between foreign concepts and familiar ideas, it is disruptive to borrow foreign terms to describe the home culture. Athough the effect is comic, the sense of displacement experienced by the European reader when Linnaeus is designated a brahman highlights, by reversing its normal operation, the alienating effects of the process of cultural appropriation.

Jones engages in similar games of cultural disorientation in the final stages of the poem. At the conclusion of the mythological narrative, Jones addresses his female readers:

> Could you, ye Fair, like this black wife,
> Restore us to primeval life,
> And bid that apple, pluck'd for Eve
> By him, who might all wives deceive,
> Hang from its parent bough once more
> Divine and perfect, as before,
> Would you confess your little faults?
> (Great ones were never in your thoughts) . . .
> Would you disclose your inmost mind,
> And speak plain truth to bless mankind?[117]

Hindu myth is presented as the solution to the original sin: Draupadi redeems Eve. Jones playfully fuses two religious traditions, effectively inverting his Jesuit source's Christian justification of Hindu tradition. The implied slur on English female integrity is immediately countered by the martial figure of Brittania in the following stanza. Striding straight out of *The Faerie Queene*, an eighteenth-century Britomart, she marches to the Cave of Scandal and defeats the monster that dares impugn the reputation of her female compatriots. Hindu epic gives way to Spenserian saga; but just when the reader has adjusted to the new form, Jones draws another disruptive analogy: the Spenserian fight is likened to a Hindu mythological battle.[118] Jones writes from both in and outside two traditions, slipping between them. The form of the mock epic can accommodate such a dual perspective, but similar cultural transitions prove problematic in the *Hymns*.

In the 'Hymn to Lacshmi' Jones adopts a number of stances or personae. The first occurs in the conclusion of the Argument when he justifies the study of Hindu mythology in purely pragmatic terms:

We may be inclined perhaps to think, that the wild fables of idolaters are not worth knowing, and that we may be satisfied with mispending our time in learning the Pagan Theology of old *Greece* and *Rome*; but we must consider, that the allegories contained in the Hymn to LACSHMÍ constitute at this moment the prevailing religion of a most extensive and celebrated Empire, and are devoutly believed by many millions, whose industry adds to the revenue of *Britain*, and whose manners, which are interwoven with their religious opinions, nearly affect all *Europeans*, who reside among them.[119]

This assertion reminds the reader of Hastings's famous pronouncement that the study of Indian culture 'lessens the weight of the chain by which the natives are held in subjection'.[120] Jones adopts the voice of the colonial administrator who particularly values scholarship for its contribution to the authority of the ruling power.

Jones shifts from this most distanced of perspectives to take up a position within Hindu culture itself. In the opening stanza of the hymn he invokes Lakshmi as a devotee: 'Thee, Goddess, I salute; thy gifts I sing'.[121] The juxtaposition of these two stances highlights the heightened form of poetic artifice involved in Jones's literary project. Jones continues to address Lakshmi in the second person, praising her bounty and the extent of her domain for the first two stanzas, but in the third, the direct invocatory form is exchanged for a third person narrative of the goddess's life. At the conclusion of the narrative, Jones reverts to the earlier form to address the deity directly, this time not as Hindu devotee, but in the extraordinary role of the goddess's adviser on colonial and religious affairs:

> Oh! bid the patient *Hindu* rise and live.
> His erring mind, that wizard lore beguiles
>   Clouded by priestly wiles,
> To senseless nature bows for nature's GOD.
> Now, stretch'd o'er ocean's vast from happier isles,
> He sees the wand of empire, not the rod:
> Ah, may those beams, that western skies illume,
>   Disperse th'unholy gloom!
> Meanwhile may laws, by myriads long rever'd,
> Their strife appease, their gentler claims decide[122]

The brahmans' 'wizard lore' is to be replaced by 'the wand of empire' and well administered 'laws'. Here word-play ('wizard'/'wand') and punning ('lore'/'laws') combine to suggest the neat inevitability of British rule. Enlisting Lakshmi's aid for the successful continuance of colonial authority, Jones situates himself within two cultures at once. The incongruity of his position is exposed by the poem's final lines which, though ostensibly part of the prayer to Lakshmi, in fact distance the poet from Indian culture and locate him firmly back within the colonial administration:

> So shall their victors, mild with virtuous pride,
> To many a cherish'd grateful race endear'd,
>   With temper'd love be fear'd:
> Though mists profane obscure their narrow ken,
> They err, yet feel; though pagans, they are men.[123]

The final couplet is clearly spoken by a British voice to a British audience; the Indian persona is banished by the condescending tones of assured Christian superiority. The word 'pagans' alone is sufficient to redefine the speaker and the audience. That this term should figure at all in a hymn to a Hindu deity testifies to Jones's ambivalent response to Indian culture.

Throughout the *Hymns* Jones attempts to introduce Hindu mythology to a British audience equipped with an innate sense of European cultural and religious superiority. His various strategies—drawing classical analogies, adopting familiar poetic diction, alluding to canonical Western poets, observing conventions of propriety—convey a sense that Hindu culture cannot be transmitted directly, but must be mediated or europeanized. Jones implies European cultural primacy in his very advocacy of Hindu culture. These two elements would appear quite compatible to a member of an administration which encouraged cultural tolerance as an instrument of British dominion. This would also explain

220 / *India Inscribed*

why Jones evidently did not consider it inappropriate to adopt the roles of both Hindu devotee and colonial administrator in the course of the same poem: the former's freedom to worship both guaranteed, and was guaranteed by, the existence of the latter.

'Sons of Brahma'

A more forthright expression of the benefits of Hindu submission to British rule can be found in the poetic work of Sir John Horsford, the *Collection of Poems written in the East Indies*, published in 1797. Serving with the British forces in the third Anglo-Mysore war, Horsford mainly wrote on military themes, although he also composed a laudatory 'Epistle to Sir William Jones' in which he acknowledges Jones's literary influence. His poem 'The Prospect', written in 1790, predicts the final defeat of Tipu Sultan (considerably in advance of the event) and the future happy state of India under British rule:

> The sons of BRAHMA then, with pious care,
> Their high pagodas shall securely rear;
> By her [Britain] protected and by her refin'd,
> Shall BRITAIN'S name in BRAHMA'S pray'r be join'd,
> Enlighten'd EUROPE then amaz'd shall see,
> Old ASIA'S Kings to EUROPE'S bend the knee,
> Proud of her sway dependantly allied,
> And take her delegated pow'r with pride.[124]

The prayers and obeisances of Horsford's brahmans and monarchs parallel Lakshmi's blessing of colonial rule in Jones's hymn. Such images of proud submission, particularly the priests' pro-British devotions, present an striking contrast to earlier representations of brahmans in English poetry.

In the 1770s and 1780s, the decades of intense anti-Company sentiment, Eyles Irwin and John Scott, two poets indebted to Collins for the titles of their collections, and to Gray's 'The Bard' for their subject matter, fixed on the figure of the Hindu priest as the mouthpiece of Indian opposition to British rule. Irwin, an employee of the East India Company, in charge of the Carnatic revenues, published his *Eastern Eclogues* in London in 1780. The third eclogue, 'Ramah: or, the Bramin' is supposedly based on a dramatic suicide which Irwin himself witnessed. A brahman climbs to the top of a temple; before plunging to his death, which 'leaves a lesson to the British throne!', he relates the defilements that India has suffered under successive invasions, first Muslim, then European.[125] The specific occasion of his protest is the British-backed invasion by the nawab of Arcot of the Hindu principality of Tanjore in 1773. This was one of the early scandals which shook British confidence in the government of India and provided Edmund Burke with his first Indian cause. The brahman concludes with an indictment of British-Muslim alliances and prophesies the eventual defeat of the British by Muslim powers:

> Nought but distress, commotion and disgrace
> Attend your favor to the Tartar race.
> That weight remov'd which poiz'd Indostan's scale,
> Against your Cross the Crescent shall prevail:
> 'Till late you find 'twas not in vain he bled,
> Whose curses lighted on the guilty head.[126]

A footnote to these lines brings the brahman's prophecy up to date and makes the political implications quite explicit:

The balance of power should be the principal object of every state, and the restoration of the King of Tanjore shews the Company to be attentive thereto. Policy, as well as humanity, enforced this measure; which, it is to be hoped, will obviate the prophecy of our Bramin, notwithstanding there is reason blended with his fanaticism.[127]

The political views voiced by the brahman are coated with a gloss of 'fanaticism'. Figures of Indian protest like Ramah the Brahmin serve to locate criticism of Company policy in an apparently authentic Indian context.

John Scott, who never visited India, based 'Serim; or, the artificial famine', one of his *Oriental Eclogues*, on *A Short History of English Transactions in the East Indies*, published in 1776. As we have seen in the preceding chapter, this anonymous text vigorously attacked the conduct of the East India Company in Bengal, accusing servants of corruption, cruelty and extortion during the terrible famine of the early 1770s. Scott's poem concludes with a starving brahman calling on 'Birmah' for a just revenge, praying that guilty remorse should drive the rapacious English to suicide. But his own life is abruptly terminated in an ambush by a 'British ruffian'; his end being almost identical to that of the bard in Gray's poem: 'And headlong plung'd the hapless Sage into the foaming tide'.[128]

Jones effectively rejects these models of tragic, defiant, anti-British brahmans. The noble defenders of Indian life and religion take on entirely new forms in the *Hymns*. In the prefatory Argument, Jones explains that 'A Hymn to Ganga' 'is feigned to have been the work of a BRA'HMEN, in an early age of HINDU antiquity, who, by a prophetical spirit, discerns the toleration and equity of the BRITISH government, and concludes with a prayer *for its peaceful duration under good laws well administered.*'[129] Much as Thomas Shaw, whose article I discussed in Chapter Four, incorporated Cleveland into the hill people's creation story, transforming the collector into a mythological redeemer, so Jones writes British rule into Indian tradition, casting it as the fulfilment of an ancient prophecy. It is notable that Jones situates his oracular brahman 'in an early age of HINDU antiquity', thus gaining the sanction of one of India's original, venerable inhabitants. In fact, Jones's brahman even predicts Cleveland himself:

> Exalted youth! The godless mountaineer,
> Roaming round his thickets drear,
> Whom rigour fir'd, nor legions could appall,
> I see before thy mildness fall,
> Thy wisdom love, thy justice fear:
> A race, whom rapine nurs'd, whom gory murder stains,
> Thy fair example wins to peace, to gentle virtue trains.[130]

The hill people's pacification is described in terms reminiscent of those accounts, considered earlier, which represent Cleveland as a hero of benevolent British rule. The marauding tribesmen, barbarous to the point of bestiality, are won over to civilized ways by Cleveland's gentle justice. Closely identified with British discourse, the brahman has become something of a colonial apologist. The 'Hymn' concludes with his invocation of Ganga:

> Nor frown, dread Goddess, on a peerless race
> With lib'ral heart and martial grace,
> Wafted from colder isles remote:
> As they preserve our laws, and bid our terror cease,
> So be their darling laws preserv'd in wealth, in joy, in peace![131]

The brahman acknowledges the supremacy of the 'peerless' British and identifies those qualities of beneficence and military strength which, I have argued in Chapter Four, form the basis of pro-Company representations of British rule. The inverted repetition of the final couplet, with its almost interchangeable possessive pronouns—'As they preserve our laws . . . So be their darling laws preserv'd'—emphasizes that particular concern of Jones: the close association of Hindu law with the British judicial system. As Tejaswini Niranjana has observed of these lines, 'the discourse of law seems to foreground violence, but only to place it in a *pre-*colonial time, or, in other words, to suggest that the coming of the British led to the *proper* implementation of the Indians' own laws and the end of "despotic" violence and "terror".'[132]

Prophecy of course entails the sense of inevitability; Jones implies that colonial rule was ordained by fate. This suggestion is reinforced by the description of the British arrival in India—'Wafted from colder isles remote'—as if it were the wind (possibly the wind of destiny) rather than any human agency, that was responsible for the exploits of the East India Company. Jones frequently has recourse to notions of fate, divine power or inexplicable forces to account for the British presence in India: in a letter to Earl Spencer, Bengal is termed 'this wonderful kingdom, which Fortune threw into her [Britain's] lap while she was asleep', a phrase which finds an echo in 'The Tenth Anniversary Discourse' as 'these *Indian* territories, which providence has thrown into the arms of *Britain*'; while in 'An Essay on the Law of Bailments', the Bengalis are a people 'whom a series of amazing events has subjected to a *British* power'.[133] Jones elides the military and political aspects of conquest to emphasize instead the fortuitous ease of transition to British rule.[134]

It is hardly surprising that Jones's work furthers the aims of the administration which he served, and is saturated with European tropes; it is rather more curious that scholars have resisted this conclusion so long. In some quarters, Jones has acquired the status of a secular saint of disinterested scholarship, standing somehow outside history, and shedding his blessing on the whole orientalist discipline. A. L. Basham, for instance, springs to Jones's defence by caricaturing the Saidian argument: 'When Jones translated *Sakuntala* and thus introduced the Sanskrit drama to the western world, are we to believe that he consciously thought: "I am doing this in order that my country may dominate a subject people?"'[135]

I hope, however, to have demonstrated that it is fruitful to relate Jones's literary pursuits to the context of colonial rule; that whatever his intentions, however manifold his talents, in mastering Indian traditions, Jones cleared the way for a tradition of mastery. A passage from the 'Hymn to Surya' highlights the significance of Jones's cultural appropriations. Jones calls on the sun god to describe his activities, should other deities inquire, in the following terms:

> Say: 'From the bosom of yon silver isle,
> 'Where skies more softly smile,
> 'He came; and, lisping our celestial tongue,
> 'Though not from *Brahmà* sprung,
> 'Draws orient knowledge from its fountains pure,
> 'Through caves obstructed long, and paths too long obscure'.[136]

Emphasizing both his foreignness and his mastery of Hindu tradition,

224 / *India Inscribed*

Jones straddles two cultures at once. Though 'not from Brahmà sprung', he rediscovers ancient brahmanic culture; as with his legal studies, Jones is supposed to out-pandit the pandits. His scholarly pursuits are represented as geographical exploration, as the discovery of fountains, caves and paths. Knowledge of the culture is figured as knowledge of the country. The cultural explorer opens up remote regions to both Indians and Europeans, marking his discoveries with the sign of colonial power.

Notes

1. See A. J. Arberry, *Asiatic Jones: The Life and Influence of Sir William Jones (1746–794): Pioneer of Indian Studies* (London, 1946); Garland Cannon, *The Life and Mind of Oriental Jones: Sir William Jones, the Father of Modern Linguistics* (Cambridge, 1990); S. N. Mukherjee, *Sir William Jones: A Study in Eighteenth-Century British Attitudes to India* (1968; London, 1987); John Drew, *India and the Romantic Imagination* (Delhi, 1987) 43–82.
2. *Monthly Review* lxxvii (May 1787) 415.
3. William Hayley, *An Elegy on the Death of the Honourable Sir William Jones* (London, 1795) 3.
4. See 160–1.
5. Hayley, 2.
6. *The Monthly Review*, New series xxiii (August 1797) 408.
7. Ibid.
8. See for instance Percival Spear, *The Oxford History of Modern India, 1740–1975* (Delhi, 1978) 137; O. P. Kejariwal, *The Asiatic Society of Bengal and the Discovery of India's Past, 1784–1838* (Delhi, 1988) 29–74.
9. See Javed Majeed, *Ungoverned Imaginings: James Mill's* The History of British India *and Orientalism* (Oxford, 1992) 123–50.
10. Cannon, *The Life and Mind of Oriental Jones* xv, 361.
11. Edward W. Said, *Orientalism* (1978; Harmondsworth, 1985) 78.
12. William Shakespeare, *Antony and Cleopatra* II. ii. 236.
13. Ranajit Guha, *An Indian Historiography of India: A Nineteenth-Century Agenda and its Implications* (Calcutta, 1988) 5–11.
14. Walter Kelly Firminger, ed., *The Fifth Report . . . on the Affairs of the East India Company . . . 1912*, 3 vols (Calcutta, 1917) ii. 159, cited in Guha, 5.
15. Garland Cannon, ed., *The Letters of Sir William Jones*, 2 vols (Oxford, 1970) 797, cited in Rosane Rocher, *Orientalism, Poetry and the Millenium: The Chequered Life of Nathaniel Brassey Halhed 1751–1850* (Delhi, 1983) 51.
16. J. Duncan M. Derrett, *Religion, Law and the State in India* (London, 1968) 250.
17. Bernard Cohn, 'The Command of Language and the Language of Command', *Subaltern Studies* IV. 293; Majeed, 19.

18. Lord Teignmouth, *Memoirs of the Life, Writings, and Correspondence of Sir William Jones* (London, 1804) 264.
19. See Cannon, *Letters* 720-1, 795; William Jones, *The Works of Sir William Jones*, 6 vols (London, 1799) iii. 469-70.
20. Jones, *Works*, iii. 14.
21. Ibid., 21.
22. Teignmouth, 325-6; Derrett, 245.
23. Homi Bhabha, *The Location of Culture* (London, 1994) 98.
24. Ibid., 98, 100.
25. Bernard Cohn, *An Anthropologist among the Historians and Other Essays* (Delhi, 1987) 477.
26. Majeed, 22.
27. Cannon, *Letters* 742.
28. Catherine Weinberger-Thomas, 'Les Yeux fertiles de la Mémoire. Exotisme Indien et représentations orientales' Collection Puruṣārtha xi (1988) 11.
29. Cannon, *Letters* 756, see also 780.
30. Ibid., 794; Cohn, 'Command of Language' 295.
31. Cannon, *Letters* 813.
32. Jones, *Works* iii. 62.
33. Ibid.
34. Majeed, 43; Jones, *Works* iii. 62.
35. Cannon, *Letters* 802.
36. Ibid., 923.
37. Ibid., 803, note.
38. Teignmouth, 314.
39. Derrett, 247-8.
40. Cannon, *Letters* 885.
41. On this point also see Tejaswini Niranjana, *Siting Translation: History, Post-Structuralism and the Colonial Context* (Berkeley, 1992).
42. Teignmouth, 400-1, note.
43. See for instance, Edward Moor, *A Narrative of the Operations of Captain Little's Detachment . . . during the late Confederacy in India, against the Nawab Tippoo Sultan Bahadur* (London, 1794) 118-19, Alexander Dow, *The History of Indostan*, i. iv, and James Browne, trans., 'An Account of the Battle of Paniput', *Asiatick Researches* iii. 134, note.
44. Nigel Leask, *British Romantic Writers and the East: Anxieties of Empire* (Cambridge, 1992) 9.
45. *Asiatick Researches* iv. 183.
46. Teignmouth, 400.
47. Hayley, 1.
48. Ibid., 35.
49. Ibid., 16.
50. David Irwin, *John Flaxman 1755-1826: Sculptor Illustrator Designer* (London, 1979) 140.
51. See James Hall, *Dictionary of Subjects and Symbols in Art* (London, 1974) for

this interpretation of the significance of the *caduceus*, rather than the more common medical symbol.
52. Hayley, 4.
53. Teignmouth, 267.
54. For reviews see Drew, 76.
55. Majeed, 23.
56. Mukherjee, 43; Drew, 73; Majeed, 48. William Jones, *Poems, consisting chiefly of Translations from the Asiatick Languages*, 2nd edn (London, 1777) 189, 190.
57. Jones, *Works*, vi. 338.
58. Ibid., 345–6.
59. Ibid., 348.
60. *Monthly Review* lxxvi (May 1787) 418; lxxxi (Appendix 1789) 653.
61. Majeed, 37.
62. Ibid.
63. Ibid., 38.
64. Ibid., 36.
65. James Boswell, *Life of Johnson*, ed. R. W. Chapman, new ed. J. D. Fleeman (Oxford, 1970) 159–60.
66. Cannon, *Letters* 755–6.
67. *Asiatick Researches* i. 224.
68. Ibid., 256, 262, 265.
69. See Jones, *Works* vi. 313, 337, 345, 355, 375.
70. Ibid., 313.
71. Ibid., 315–16. See also 'The Hymn to Durga', Jones, *Works* vi. 325.
72. Ibid., 340.
73. Ibid., 348, 350–1, 353.
74. Ibid., 358.
75. Jones's debt to Milton, Pope and Gray has been mentioned in passing by V. de Sola Pinto, 'Sir William Jones and English Literature', *Bulletin of the School of Oriental and African Studies* xi (1943–6) 692, and the influence of Gray, Collins and Milton has been briefly noted by R. M. Hewitt, 'Harmonious Jones', *Essays and Studies* xxviii (1942): 49–50.
76. Jones, *Works* vi. 314.
77. Ibid., 316; John Milton, *L'Allegro* 11–13.
78. Jones, *Works* vi. 325.
79. A. Jonston, ' "The Purple Year" in Pope and Gray', *Review of English Studies* xiv (1963) 389–93.
80. Drew, 75.
81. Ibid., 73.
82. Ibid., 45–82.
83. Ibid., 58–9.
84. Jones, *Works* vi. 369; Milton, *Paradise Lost* III: 8–9.
85. Jones, *Works* vi. 369; Milton, *Paradise Lost* III: 10–21.
86. Jones, *Works* vi. 369.
87. Milton, *Paradise Lost* III: 373–7, 380.

88. Jones, *Works* vi. 333.
89. Milton, Paradise Lost I: 19–22.
90. *Asiatick Researches* i. 244.
91. Jones, *Works* vi. 321, 386.
92. Ibid., 350; Thomas Gray, *The Poems of Mr Gray. To which are prefixed Memoirs of his Life and Writings by W. Mason* (York, 1775) 382.
93. Thanks to Andrew Topsfield for this point.
94. Jones, *Works* vi. 203.
95. Ibid., 203–4.
96. A. Leslie Wilson, *A Mythical Image: the Ideal of India in German Romanticism* (Durham N. C., 1964) 69-79; Raymond Schwab, *The Oriental Renaissance: Europe's Rediscovery of India and the East, 1680–1880*, trans. Gene Patterson-Black, Victor Reinking (New York, 1984) 57–64.
97. Schwab, 59.
98. August Wilhelm Schlegel, *A Course of Lectures on Dramatic Art and Literature*, trans. John Black, 2 vols (London, 1815) i. 25.
99. Jones, *Works* vi. 205.
100. Ibid., 204.
101. *Critical Review* i (2nd series) (January 1791) 25.
102. Jones, *Works* vi. 227.
103. William Jones, *Sacontala*, MS Sansk. *c.* 37, Bodleian Library, Oxford, 121.
104. Shakespeare, *The Taming of the Shrew* IV. i. 1–5.
105. Jones, *Works* vi. 228, 239.
106. Jones MS, 128 v.
107. Jones MS, 130, Jones, *Works* vi. 244.
108. Jones MS, 39, 131; Jones, *Works* vi. 245. See Cannon, *Life and Mind of Oriental Jones*, 312 for a similar point.
109. Jones, *Works* vi. 246.
110. Jones MS, 131.
111. *Annual Register* (1791) 'Account of Books' 194; *Analytical Review* (Aug 1790) 373.
112. Alf Hiltebeitel, *The Cult of Draupadi* (Chicago, 1988) 288.
113. *Lettres édifiantes* 2nd edn, 26 vols (Paris, 1781) xi. 38–41.
114. Ibid., xi. 40.
115. Jones, *Works* vi. 185.
116. Ibid., 181–2.
117. Ibid., 197–8.
118. Ibid., 198–9.
119. Ibid., 356.
120. Charles Wilkins, *The Bhagvat Geeta* (London, 1785) 13.
121. Jones, *Works* vi. 357.
122. Ibid., 365.
123. Ibid., 365.
124. John Horsford, *A Collection of Poems written in the East Indies* (Calcutta, 1797) 25.

228 / *India Inscribed*

125. Eyles Irwin, *Eastern Eclogues* (London, 1780) 25.
126. Ibid., 24–5.
127. Ibid., 25, note.
128. John Scott, *Poetical Works* (London, 1782) 152.
129. Jones, *Works* vi. 383.
130. Ibid., 391.
131. Ibid., 392.
132. Niranjana, 19.
133. Cannon, *Letters* 813; *Asiatick Researches* iv. 8; Jones, *Works* vi. 674.
134. For a similar point, see Niranjana, 19.
135. A. L. Basham, Foreward, Kejariwal, x.
136. Jones, *Works* vi. 353.

CHAPTER SEVEN

'Vocabularies of Vile Epithets': British Representations of the Sultans of Mysore

The names of Haidar Ali and Tipu Sultan enjoyed an extraordinary notoriety in late-eighteenth-century Britain. Company rule in South India was menaced by the armies of Mysore sporadically for over thirty years, and the two sultans came to embody the most threatening aspects of native power. The First Mysore War of 1767–9 brought Haidar to the walls of Madras, the Second of 1780–4 saw the alliance of Mysore with the French, the defeat of British forces at Pollilur (1780) and Bednur (1783) and the capture and imprisonment of significant numbers of British troops. Hostilities recommenced in 1790 with a triple alliance formed between the Marathas, the nizam of Hyderabad and the British against Tipu, who was forced to concede defeat at Seringapatam in 1792 and, famously, obliged to hand over two of his sons as hostages for the performance of the ensuing treaty. In the following years Tipu was suspected of attempting to revenge himself on the British by forging alliances at Hyderabad and Poona and sending embassies to Afghanistan and Mauritius. When a French force actually landed in Mysore, the British took decisive action; in 1799 they stormed Seringapatam and put an end both to the war and Tipu Sultan's life.

The four Mysore Wars were more extensively chronicled than any preceding Indian campaign.[1] Numerous military journals, narratives of captivity and histories were published during the 1780s and '90s and accounts continued to appear in the first decades of the nineteenth century. This body of writing reveals an enduring preoccupation with the figures of Haidar and Tipu; while greater attention is paid to Tipu, the characters of father and son are repeatedly assessed and contrasted over a number of years. The texts return with equal insistence to the topic of British imprisonment under the sultans, focusing on the mental and physical privations suffered by the captives, many of whom were forcibly converted to Islam, circumcised and drafted into slave batallions. The narratives of anxiety generated by the power of Mysore form the object of analysis in what follows. How do British texts attempt to describe and contain the threat of Mysore? In what ways do the circumcised bodies of the captives, marked with the sign of the Other, compromise a sense of national identity? I shall examine how such fears are stilled by the eventual defeat of Tipu. The death of the tiger of Mysore provides a form of narrative closure both for the first phase of colonial rule in India, and for this book.

THE SULTANS OF MYSORE

Discussions of Haidar and Tipu fall into one of two categories during the period; the rulers are generally depicted as cruel tyrants, but occasionally they feature as able, ambitious politicians.[2] The two images stand in opposition to each other, the second, as we shall see, designed to counter the first. Haidar's reputation for cruelty is based on accounts such as the anonymous 'Narrative of the Captivity and Sufferings of the Officers, Soldiers, and Sepoys, who fell into the Hands of Hyder Ally', appended to William Thomson's *Memoirs of the late War in Asia*, published anonymously in 1788 as the work of an officer of Colonel Baillie's detachment. After the defeat of the British under Munro at the battle of Pollilur, Haidar is depicted in 'barbarous triumph', seated in his tent with wounded British prisoners prostrate before him, while the 'heads of their unfortunate friends were, from time to time, presented to the conqueror; some of them even by English officers, who were forced to perform that inhuman service'.[3] Although Haidar, 'touched with a latent spark of humanity', subsequently ordered an end to the macabre parade, this theatrical tableau of the sultan's triumphant ease and British humiliation carried considerable emotive force and was reproduced in later accounts.[4]

Haidar appears in a quite different guise in an article which served as his obituary in the *Annual Register* for 1783 (and was later incorporated, with minor alterations, into the anonymous *Authentic Memoirs of Tippoo Sultaun* of 1799).[5] The tone of this description suggests the influence, perhaps the authorship, of Edmund Burke who was closely associated with the periodical. As Marshall has observed, Burke saw in Haidar's Mysore all the strengths of an independent Indian regime, free from the

Company's pernicious touch.[6] In the *Annual Register*, the sultan is lifted out of the category of cruel Eastern conquerors, where the Haidar of the earlier description would have happily sat, to be ranked among world rulers:

> Nor was he more redoubtable as a warrior than as a statesman; and if his actions, and the chain and motives of his conduct, had not been too remote from observation, to be thoroughly known and comprehended, he might possibly have been considered as one of the first politicians of his day, whether in Europe or Asia. He was so far from being naturally cruel, that he differed in that respect from all the eastern conquerors of whom we have any knowledge . . .[7]

This new Haidar, an actor on the contemporary political stage, is an altogether more reasonable opponent. In his 1785 speech on the nawab of Arcot's debts, Burke blamed the outbreak of the second Mysore War on the Madras Council which had provoked Haidar, through its duplicity and incompetence, to massive retaliation in 1780.[8] The *Annual Register* asserts that 'He [Haidar] had been, greatly through their own fault, and partly through their interference with his designs, a bitter, and very nearly fatal enemy, to the English East India company; but it would be disgraceful and mean, on that account, to suppress his virtues, or endeavour to conceal his great qualities.'[9] For all the assertions of judicious balance, this generous portrait of Haidar is also intimately linked to assessments of East India Company policy: if the British are in some way to blame, it follows that the sultan is less of a tyrant.

This relation between the depiction of ruler and political interest is equally apparent in representations of Tipu. His reputation, always worse than his father's, reaches a particularly low point in a work published in 1788 by J. Moodie, *Remarks on the most Important Military Operations of the English Forces on the Western side of the Peninsula of Hindostan*. Dubbed 'that disgrace to the human form', Tipu is here the incarnation of oriental brutality: 'He, among other moderns of the same character, may be said to be a living example of Eastern barbarity. Even his father, the implacable Hyder Ali Khân, has been exceeded by him in acts of the most unparalelled [sic] cruelty; his savage manners yielding only to the baseness and malignity of his heart.'[10] Tipu is here relegated to the ranks of Eastern barbarians because Moodie's pamphlet attempts to vindicate a British commander and his army: if the sultan is tyrannical, the British must be blameless.

Moodie's pamphlet is a polemical reply to an account of Brigadier-General Mathews' 1783 capture of Bednur and the storming of the neighbouring fort of Anantpur attributed to John Charles Sheen, an ensign in Mathews' army. Published in full as an appendix to Henry Oakes's *Authentic Narrative of the treatment of the English, who were Taken Prisoner on the Reduction of Bednore by Tippoo Saib* of 1785, Sheen's letter accuses Mathews of unscrupulous pillage, and charges the army with inhuman massacre and rape at Anantpur. The letter was first cited in the 1783 article in the *Annual Register* which praised Haidar at his death; the allegations were repeated the following year in the *New Annual Register* (a rival periodical which closely copied the *Annual Register's* format); and they reappeared in two works published in 1799—the *Authentic Memoirs of Tippoo Sultaun*, and the *View of Hindoostan*, a compilation of earlier works by the naturalist, Thomas Pennant.[11] In Sheen's letter, the condemnation of British conduct reaches its climax with the description of the scene at Anantpur: 'A most dreadful sight then presented itself: above four hundred beautiful women either killed or wounded with the bayonet, expiring in one another's arms, while the private soldiers were committing every kind of outrage, and plundering them of their jewels, the officers not being able to restrain them.'[12] Here the European construct of the seductive oriental harem is turned into a monstrous orgy of death. The lower ranks of the army, alarmingly out of control, indulge those base passions associated both with their own social origins and with oriental tyranny. The account suggests an unsettling association between the undisciplined lower classes and Eastern cruelty and lust. Such extravagant brutality provokes Tipu to equal ferocity and Tipu's recapture of Bednur, his harsh treatment of British prisoners and execution of Mathews, were 'evidently founded upon Principles of Retaliation; and Candor must acknowledge that the unjustifiable Behavior of the Company's Army goes a considerable Way in Justification of that of the Enemy'.[13] British misconduct refashions Tipu into a reasonable opponent, or at least one whose motives and actions are understandable.

As Denys Forrest has noted, Sheen's allegations were comprehensively refuted by a pamphlet which the directors of the East India Company ordered to be printed in 1787, *A Vindication of the Conduct of the English Forces employed in the late war, under the Command of Brigadier-General Mathews, against the Nabob Tippoo Sultaun.*[14] The *Vindication* was signed by Major J. S. Toriano and fifty-three officers, including Henry Oakes, the author of the *Narrative* to which Sheen's letter was appended. It also included a personal retraction by Sheen: 'The business of Annanpour is greatly exaggerated, and contrary to what I wrote home, together with the whole of the Appendix. As I never commented upon it myself, it is impossible that I can be accountable for what the printer chose to publish without my knowledge or consent.'[15] Such a public recantation suggests something of the political repercussions of Sheen's letter; indeed on 9 March 1791 a motion was passed in the House of Commons calling for the *Vindication* to be produced as evidence to clear the reputation of General Mathews and his army.[16] The *Vindication* was widely circulated and reprinted in the popular *Gentleman's Magazine* in 1788, but, according to Mark Wilks who was the first British resident of Mysore and author of the three-volumed *Historical Sketches of the South of India* (1810–17), the original allegations were still widely credited thirty years later. Wilks terms Sheen 'a silly young man, whose amende honorable [the public recantation] for dressing his adventures into a romantic tale, is not so generally known as the historical record of that supposed event in the respectable pages of the Annual Register.'[17]

Wilks's distrust of the historical record raises questions, familiar from our earlier discussion of Hastings's trial, about the status of representations of India. Whenever accounts compete against each other, such issues are likely to come to the fore. What is perhaps more striking is that discussions of the character and government of both Hastings and Tipu share a central term—that of 'oriental despotism'.

Essentially, discussions of Tipu's character, whatever their position, are based on a similar premise: they are constructed around the figure of the oriental despot and are intended either to substantiate or discredit this stereotype. In most accounts, Tipu oppresses his subjects with cruelty and intolerance, in a few he inspires loyalty and encourages prosperity through firm government.[18] Burke seems to move opportunistically between these two positions, from a more positive to a more negative assessment of Tipu. In 1783 he published Sheen's allegations in the *Annual Register* as part of his attack against the Company. But by 1790, as we have seen in Chapter Five, he ridiculed the evidence of Colonel Macleod, a defence witness in the impeachment of Hastings, who claimed that Tipu thought highly of the former governor-general. During the Third Mysore War Burke was privately critical of British policy, but he was too reliant on the government for the continuance of Hastings's trial to voice his objections publicly.[19]

In tyrannical guise—by far his most frequent manifestation—Tipu is neatly contained within the traditional role. Moodie, as we have seen, terms him 'a living example of Eastern barbarity', the incarnation of the Oriental menace which had loomed over Europe for centuries. If Tipu is representative of the timeless, generic Eastern threat, then authors generally attempt to bring him convincingly to life, to authenticate the cruel excesses which are written into the oriental despot's part. This is largely the function of the accounts of ex-prisoners. The authority of ten years' captivity and suffering informs the writings of both James Bristow and James Scurry, whose own status as survivors is of course heightened by the inhuman representation of their captor. These texts belong to the tradition which Mary Louise Pratt has termed 'survival literature—first-person stories of shipwrecks, castaways, mutinies, abandonments, and . . . captivities'; popular, sensational tales of overseas adventure which originated in the first phase of European expansion, during the fifteenth century.[20] As Pratt has noted, these narratives were often written to generate funds to set the survivors up again. Bristow's memoirs were first published by subscription in Calcutta in 1792, the year that the British celebrated the triumphant conclusion of the Third Mysore War. Announcing the subscription, the *Calcutta Gazette* reported that the book would be for 'the sole benefit of James Bristow and his family; and in order to make the subscription as general as possible', it would be issued at different prices 'printed on the best paper and . . . printed on inferior paper'.[21] The sufferings of ex-captives turned them into deserving objects of charity; in 1784 the same newspaper had informed readers of the establishment of a fund for the relief of 'all Europeans of the lower class' who had been held by Tipu.[22]

Both Bristow and Scurry served as low-ranking soldiers during the Second Mysore War and their accounts figure among the first works on India not written by members of the educated élite. Scurry's narrative, which was published posthumously in 1824, a quarter of a century after Tipu's death, gives some indication of the life-span of British interest in Tipu. The 1820s saw the growth of evangelical and utilitarian belief in Indian degeneracy, and Scurry's account of his *Captivity, Sufferings and Escape* would have served to confirm these views.[23] Scurry's social origins are used by his publisher as a guarantee of the authenticity of his narrative:

> No flowery words adorn this artless tale,
> Here simple truth alone is to be found

reads the epigraph on the title page. The humble style of low-class travellers had functioned as a guarantee of the reliability of their testimony since the Renaissance.[24] But the preface to Scurry's account points to the actual physical condition of ex-captives for further substantiation: 'Of their [Haidar and Tipu's] unexampled barbarities, many accounts have been published in England; and the enormities which these narratives record would have staggered credulity itself, had not the few mutilated wretches who have escaped their tyranny, furnished evidence by their appearance, that a faithful detail of facts could leave but little room for exaggeration.'[25] This reference to the enforced circumcision of conscripts in Tipu's cheyla or slave battalions is offered as proof of the tyranny of the sultans of Mysore. The bodies of the survivors, inscribed with the signs of despotism, endorse both the accounts and the stereotype.

A more scholarly method of authentication is offered through translation. In 1788 the *Gentleman's Magazine* printed a number of Tipu's proclamations in English translation, prefaced by the claim that they provided irrefutable evidence of the tyrannical image: 'From whence . . . can we so well learn the opinions of the despot as from authentic copies of edicts which he published uncontrouled? They are a faithful mirror. A number of them collected and carefully compared would certainly furnish an excellent clue to the real character.'[26] The confidence in translation as a medium that directly reflects reality is shared by William Kirkpatrick who, in 1811, published the *Select Letters of Tippoo Sultaun*, the kind of collection of documents envisaged by the *Gentleman's Magazine*. Kirkpatrick was one of the commissioners who oversaw the partition of Mysore after 1799. The letters, discovered in Tipu's palace at the fall of Seringapatam, were selected and translated, Kirkpatrick writes in his preface, to allow the sultan to represent himself directly:

[Tipu] is here successively and repeatedly delineated, in colors from his own pencil, as the cruel and relentless enemy; the intolerant bigot or furious fanatic; the oppressive and unjust ruler; the harsh and rigid master; the sanguinary tyrant; the perfidious negociator; the frivolous and capricious innovator; the mean and minute economist; the peddling trader; and even the retail shop-keeper. The painter will not be suspected of overcharging the unfavourable traits of the picture, when it is considered that the picture is his own.[27]

Kirkpatrick describes Tipu's epistolary self-portrait in terms drawn largely from the vocabulary of despotism: the cruel enemy, intolerant fanatic, oppressive ruler, harsh master, the sanguinary and perfidious tyrant. A sense of more specific characterization is only introduced with the four final personae, all of which relate to Tipu's less significant role (in this context) as domestic administrator, and which attempt progressively to deflate the ruler's status by associating him with the pettiness and mean-mindedness attributed to the trading classes. The sultan's own letters place him within the familiar category of oriental despot. In fact Kirkpatrick's sustained metaphor of painting and the long list of characteristic poses, which unfolds like a procession of stock figures, foregrounds the process by which the despotic image is produced. The final sentence, which leaves much inferred rather than stated, suggests that Kirkpatrick is attempting to answer those few writers who depict the sultan in reasonable guise and dismiss the tyrannical image as exaggeration.

One such advocate of Tipu is Edward Moor, who served as an officer in the Third Mysore War and in 1794, at the age of 23, published *A Narrative of the Operations of Captain Little's Detachment, and of the Mahratta Army . . . during the late Confederacy in India, against the Nawab Tippoo Sultan Bahadur*. In later years Moor was to publish The *Hindu Pantheon*, a study which would remain the standard text on Hinduism for the first half of the nineteenth century. Already displaying a scholarly disdain for the popular, Moor inveighs against the general view of Tipu:

> Of late years, indeed, our language has been ransacked for terms in which well disposed persons were desirous to express their detestation of his name and character; vocabularies of vile epithets have been exhausted, and doubtless many have lamented that the English language is not copious enough to furnish terms of obloquy sufficiently expressive of the ignominy, wherewith they in justice deem his memory deserves to be branded. It is not therefore, at all a matter of surprize, that the generality of people, particularly in parts so remote as England, should have the most unfavourable ideas of this prince's character . . .[28]

Moor parodies the excesses of Tipu's detractors with his own rhetorical extravagance. That 'the generality of people' should be convinced, far from endorsing these texts, condemns them further. Moor appeals to discerning readers to distinguish themselves from the less well-educated:

> Those . . . who do not choose to be carried away by the torrent of popular opinion, but, in preference to thinking by proxy, venture to think for themselves, can find the same excuse for the restlessness of Tippoo, as for that of any other ambitious sovereign; and on the subject of his cruelties, venture to express a doubt whether they may not possibly have been exaggerated.[29]

Moor is probably responding here to the extensive press coverage of the Third Mysore War which, Marshall has argued, convinced the British public that war with Mysore was a national rather than a local Indian concern and earned Tipu 'a unique place in British-Indian demonology'.[30] The popular tyrannical image (which we have seen projected by such writers as Bristow, a common soldier, whose account was widely available in a cheap edition) is attributed by Moor to 'the confined prejudices of contracted minds'; such an image must necessarily be rejected by 'the MAN who views events with philosophic liberality'.[31] Moor sets up an opposition between the popular view of Tipu and the élite view: an unreasonable despot for the unthinking lower classes and a reasonable monarch for the educated man.

While Moor encourages readers to step back in order to evaluate accounts of Tipu 'with philosophic liberality' and place the sultan in a wider historical context, Kirkpatrick offers an alternative, close-up scholarly view:

> My principal object, in this work, being to present as striking a likeness of Tippoo, as the nature of my materials, and the extent of my ability to employ them advantageously, would admit ... what I wished, but cannot hope to have attained, is, that the reader, losing sight entirely of the translator, should fancy himself in the presence of the *Sultan*, listening to the latter, while dictating to one or other of the different secretaries by whom he was usually attended.[32]

Kirkpatrick would like to grant the reader unmediated access to Tipu himself: the text should reveal the man. But for all his declared aspirations to editorial invisibility, Kirkpatrick's voice frequently intervenes in commentaries on the letters throughout the collection. Not only does he explain obscurities, he also endeavours to guide the reader's response quite openly; of one letter, for instance, he observes that the 'sanguinary and ferocious disposition of Tippoo Sultan is here displayed in the most glaring and odious colours'.[33] The same editorial tone intrudes in the letters themselves, in the form of italicization, when Kirkpatrick wishes to emphasize one of the sultan's orders which appears particularly cruel or treacherous.[34] Tipu's letters are thus framed to conform to expectations of despotism, even as they are offered as first-hand evidence of the sultan's character. This fiction of unmediated authenticity is conveyed by the conceit of the reader as an eye-witness in Tipu's palace. The same figure could stand as a convenient emblem for the reading public's voyeuristic preoccupation with Tipu. Kirkpatrick had previously translated passages from Tipu's secret writings, which appeared as an appendix to Alexander Beatson's *View of the Origin and Conduct of the War with Tippoo Sultan* of 1800. These included an account of a vision reported to the sultan and a record and interpretation of Tipu's dreams which, according to Beatson, 'the Sultaun always manifested peculiar anxiety to conceal' and showed that 'war and conquest, and the destruction of the Kaufers (infidels), were not less the subjects of his sleeping, than of his waking thoughts'.[35]

This fascination with the workings of Tipu's mind is a new and significant phenomenon: no previous Indian ruler had excited comparable interest in the British public. Of course, British authors had never before been granted equal access to materials relating to an Indian enemy as that furnished by the fall of Seringapatam, nor had they possessed the linguistic skills necessary to understand them. But the issue seems more complex. Tipu's private papers and letters are presented as documentary evidence of his religious fanaticism, his enmity to the British and cruelty to his subjects; they offer tangible proof of the sultan's tyrannical nature. The techniques of historical scholarship—the investigation of archival sources—are used to fix the role of the eastern despot firmly on Tipu. Why should British authors be so fascinated by this stereotype? Partly, of course, because it vindicates British military action against Mysore; but also, as I hope to show, because it contains and limits the menace posed by the sultan.

The real threat represented by Tipu resulted from his blurring of distinctions between East and West in his appropriation of European ideas, tactics and individuals. The Mysore army, actively supported by France from 1780 to 1784, derived its strength from contemporary European military principles: both Haidar and his son were quick to adopt the strategies and technology of their British enemies. The construct of oriental tyranny, with all its traditional overtones, to some extent obscured the westernized efficiency of the Mysore army. Bayly has recently argued that the sultans employed European techniques not only in military but also in commercial matters. Haidar and Tipu tried to defend their trade by enforcing monopolies and introducing strict revenue management in precisely the manner of the East India Company:

> [the sultans of Mysore] put themselves into the demonology of British imperial rhetoric by trying to exclude European trade and by acting as universal monopolists. They were examples of 'oriental despotism', 'Muslim tyranny' or the spirit of self-sufficiency'. Their policies were virtually a provocation in themselves at a period when free-trade rhetoric was being used to disguise the Company's own relentless drive for a monopoly of force, labour and revenue in the sub-continent. By the early 1790s it had become clear that the Company could never coexist with such more vigorous Indian régimes which sought to face down European power with its own weapons, exclusion of rivals from trade and a strong mobile army.[36]

Bayly argues that it was the implementation of tactics which mirrored the Company's own that incensed the British against Mysore. By erecting a wall of difference between East and West, the rhetoric of oriental despotism helped to conceal the similarities between the two powers' policies: the British were freed from the recognition of disturbing correspondences with their enemy. For such a recognition would reveal an ambivalence which, as Homi Bhabha argues, threatens the authority of colonial command. To contain this threat, the other is termed a despot: 'For despite its connotations of death, repetition and servitude, the despotic configuration is a monocausal system that relates all differences and discourses to the absolute, undivided, boundless body of the despot. It is this image of India as a primordial fixity—as a narcissistic inverted other—that satisfies the self-fulfilling prophecy of Western progress.'[37] British authors focus repeatedly on Tipu's person, on his despotic will and whims, on his letters, secret writings and dreams, in an attempt to deny the alarming modernity of Mysore's tactics.

To suggest any relation between the policies of Mysore and those of Britain it was therefore necessary first to remove the sultans from the context of Eastern barbarity. In a rare instance of praise, Thomson distinguishes Haidar and Tipu from their oriental origins and represents them as eager students of European learning:

Though it is education and example chiefly that form the characters of nations and men, yet among the human race there are strong marks of distinction, originally impressed on the frame of the body and mind by the hand of Nature. In the very bosom of luxury, and before the very throne of barbarian bigotry, a family has arisen in our times, who, uniting the greatest valour with the most profound sagacity, and the loftiest ambition, have laboured with success to learn the European arts, that they might thereby be enabled to oppose and overturn European, and particularly the English dominion in Asia.[38]

Hand-picked by Nature, the sultans transcend their barbarian context to acknowledge the superiority of European achievement (a flatteringly eurocentric concept of natural genius). The challenge posed to Britain by the rulers of Mysore is framed in terms of an attempt by precociously talented pupils to oust their teacher. Haidar employs foreign artisans to build up a fleet of battleships designed to weather the voyage to Britain; the ships were 'exceedingly strong and thick in the planks, being intended to encounter the European seas, the water of which, he had heard, was very *strong* and *thick*: a confused notion of ice'.[39] This childlike conception of European maritime conditions undercuts the earlier assertions of Haidar's 'profound sagacity', as does the outlandish nature of the scheme to invade Britain and the final abandonment of the project in 1782–3 when the British destroyed Haidar's fleet.[40] Tipu is likewise portrayed as an avid student of Western science, but Thomson implies the limitations of Tipu's knowledge by focusing on an unsuccessful attempt to extract information on European military tactics:

He learned the Elements of Mathematics, and was familiarly conversant with the principles of gunnery, and military architecture and tacticks. With the baggage of the [British] Officers that fell into his hands ... there was found, Sime's Military Guide, a book belonging to Ensign Spottiswood. This book was carried to Tippoo by some of his people, who, according to their superstitious notions, supposed that the draughts which it contained, related in some mysterious manner to arts of incantation. The Sultan, who instantly discovered its nature, began to shew great civility to Mr. Spottiswood, by sending cloth to him and other presents. At last a person from the Sultan requested him to translate the Treatise into the Moor's language, which he spoke fluently. But Mr. Spottiswood politely excused himself, saying, that he could not answer for translating a military book, without orders from his Commander.[41]

The mock courtesy of Ensign Spottiswood's refusal to translate the text helps to allay the fear that Tipu might corrupt his British prisoners by forcing them to collaborate. In fact this story addresses a particularly sensitive issue, for the sultans' treatment of their captives was represented as a threatening erosion of distinctions between the West and the East.

'EUROPEAN MUSSELMEN' AND LOYAL SEPOYS

Of all the British soldiers taken captive during the Second Mysore War, the fate of none excited greater British indignation than that of the seamen whom the French admiral Suffren handed over to his Mysore allies. Suffren's act was regarded as one of complete betrayal, a breach of European solidarity which, to borrow a phrase from Moodie, was 'Contrary to the instinct of humanity, the spirit of Christianity, and the honour of a soldier'.[42] The French admiral delivered the prisoners into a captivity which threatened their religious, personal and national identity. The most potent symbol of this violation of identity was the enforced circumcision of prisoners chosen for service in cheyla or slave battalions. These 'European Musselmen', as represented in the *Memoirs of the Late War in Asia*, belong to neither Mysore nor Britain and are alternately reviled by their Muslim commanders or pitied by the other captives.[43] The British cheylas, marked with the stigma of Muslim difference but otherwise unconverted to Islam, were stranded in a doctrinal no man's land, and the texts reveal their sense of marginalization.

Writers attempting a precise definition of the condition of circumcized prisoners tend to run into difficulties. James Bristow's account of his ten years' captivity in Mysore, published first in Calcutta in 1792, then in London in 1793, displays some of these problems of definition. In the first edition, he describes his own circumcision and then continues: 'After they had made, what they termed Musselmen of us'; in the second, the same sentence begins: 'After we had been made what was termed Musselmen'.[44] Perhaps prompted by stylistic considerations, this revision is nonetheless suggestive: the shifts between active and passive voices, and the change in designation of subject and object, point to a fundamental anxiety about what, if anything, had happened to their religious identity. This is brought out when Bristow explores the prisoners' anger at their loss of agency:

> we neglected no opportunity of evincing our contempt for the religion of our tormentors, and the cruel force they had employed against us, by catching dogs, and *bandicoots* (a species of large rats) and circumcising them publicly. This operation never failed to exasperate them, particularly as the dog is held a very impure animal, and it cannot be doubted but we very often owed some additional ill usage to these insults on one of their most sacred rites . . .[45]

In an attempt to re-establish some sense of difference between their Muslim captors and themselves, the prisoners enact parody circumcisions. Deliberately intended to insult, these blasphemous rites provoke the guards to retaliation. But the act of defiance is also an exercise in self-degradation, for the mock circumcisions imply an analogy between the prisoners' own state and that of dogs and rats. A similar sense of debasement is expressed in religious terms: Bristow, among others, defines circumcision as 'this diabolical ceremony'.[46]

Circumcision also refashions the prisoners' sense of personal identity. Cheylas were given Muslim names. The *Calcutta Gazette* for December 1791 and the *London Gazette* for 18 May 1792 lists some of these 'Country Names' in an attempt to establish which of the British soldiers survived and which died in captivity 'with a View to facilitate the Enquiry and Recovery of those who are still alive'.[47] The publication of the Muslim names seems admissible only under such pressing circumstances. They are scarcely referred to in other accounts and their absence seems significant—an act of deliberate omission, a denial of Mysore's power to translate British identity.

Service in a cheyla battalion, deemed a fate worse than death by the *Calcutta Gazette*, inevitably brought issues of national allegiance to the fore.[48] Bristow, forced to drill slave troops, writes of the sense of alienation induced by membership of the Mysore army:

> The task imposed upon us, (those who refused being cruelly flogged,) was to instruct these *Chaylahs* in the manual exercise. Our situation consequently became worse than before; we were obliged to perform an office, which, however small the benefit we took care the practitioners should derive from it, could not but cause the deepest affliction, when we reflected they were the detested enemies of our country whom we were compelled to instruct in that very art which would prove destructive to our countrymen.[49]

242 / *India Inscribed*

In mitigation of the captives' conduct, Bristow presents the reader with a series of excuses: the threat of flogging, the deliberately inadequate instruction, the mental anguish endured. He evidently feels that the prisoners must be defended from the charge of desertion, of aiding the enemy—the crime which Ensign Spottiswood avoided when he refused to translate the military guide in the exemplary tale considered earlier. In response to the ambiguities inherent in their position, Bristow clearly lays out the captives' loyalties, reiterating their affinity with Britain: 'our country' and 'our countrymen'.

A related sense of the captives' compromised national identity prompts James Scurry to observe:

> we were all young, yet none of us dared sing 'Rule Britannia,' or even hum it with impunity. We prohibited it between ourselves, under the impression of bitterness, and the idea of every hope being marred of ever seeing our country or friends again.
>
> The taunts and insolence of the guards were no small addition to our misery. We had the feelings of Englishmen, and we suffered from their insults more severely than from their punishments.[50]

The explanation supplied by Scurry for the self-imposed banning of the patriotic song—to prevent an outbreak of homesickness and despair—masks the implication that the proud claims of the anthem were invalidated by the captives' situation. Scurry's subsequent assertion that the prisoners 'had the feelings of Englishmen' has an edge of defensiveness, as if the cheylas' condition might have robbed them of proper English pride.

The place of 'Rule Britannia' in the captives' musical repertoire may have been supplied by one of the songs printed as an appendix to the *Memoirs of the Late War in Asia*. Composed, we are told, by one Lieutenant Thewlis, a young soldier who died in captivity, the 'Prison Song in Seringapatam' undermines any sense of British identity. Verse XI runs:

> You'd think we were far gone
> To hear but the jargon
> Of nations so strangely combin'd;
> We've Danes and we've Dutchmen,
> You scarce have seen such men,
> And scarcely again will you find:
> We've Sawneys and Paddies,
> And braw Highland laddies,
> Free Britons in here too they ramm;
> The Swiss and the Frenchman,
> The leek-loving Welchman,
> All chain'd in Seringapatam.[51]

The prison argot reflects the mixture of nationalities caught up in the Mysore wars. The jail's population, presented as an amalgam of national stereotypes, possesses a kind of composite European identity which seems to deny the possibility of patriotism.

The loss of national identity is most fully demonstrated by the case of James Scurry. Scurry's own narrative concludes with his escape and return to Britain, but the editor of the text continues the account with a description of the ex-prisoner's appearance and reception in England. After ten years' captivity, Scurry has almost forgotten English customs and 'the delicate refinements of his native land'.[52] When he first returns, he dislikes wearing European clothes, finds it hard to sit in a chair or handle a knife and fork; his English is 'broken and confused, having lost nearly all its vernacular idiom' and his skin colour 'nearly resembled the swarthy complexion of the negroes'.[53] Scurry's imprisonment in Mysore has transformed him in manner, language and appearance. Potentially a disturbing symbol of alienation, Scurry is rehabilitated through humour: he becomes an object of ridicule. Scurry's uncouth table manners furnish the subject of an anecdote about a meal at an inn, soon after his return, where he astonishes the owners by flinging bones and leftovers on the floor, leaving them to conclude 'that he was either deranged, or some foreigner totally unacquainted with the refinements of civilized life'.[54] The very form of the narrative serves to contain the threat of Scurry's confused cultural affiliations. Pratt argues that 'survival literature' provides a 'safe' context to explore taboo issues and transgressive plots such as the enslavement of Europeans by non-Europeans 'since the very existence of texts presupposed the imperially correct outcome: the survivor survived, and sought reintegration into the home society. The tale was always told from the viewpoint of the European who returned'.[55]

While the ex-captive author eventually returns to the domestic fold, the figure of the deserter remains unredeemed. Unwilling 'European Musselmen' can reassure themselves by measuring their own conduct against that of an unambiguous traitor. The deserter who voluntarily transfers his allegiance from Britain to Mysore embodies that appropriation of the West by the East which constitutes the most threatening aspect of the sultans' rule. In the narratives one man frequently appears in this transgressive role. John Dempster, formerly sergeant-major in the Bengal Artillery, supervises the selection of prisoners for circumcision—the most treacherous of all duties—in both Bristow's and Scurry's accounts. Bristow writes that 'every one of us [captives] were highly exasperated against him [Dempster], and it was fortunate for him that he was protected by the guards', while Scurry characterizes him as an insinuating hypocrite whose 'persuasive artillery, ... artifice and address' is deployed to convince the prisoners to submit to the rite.[56] Later in the narrative, Scurry blames Dempster for the cruel treatment which the British captives suffered over the period of a year.[57]

Interestingly, Dempster does not exclusively feature as an object of hate. In the *Memoirs of the Late War in Asia*, he appears as a secret correspondent of the inmates of the Seringapatam jail. This Dempster deplores his position in the Mysore army, claiming that he was himself forcibly circumcised and constrained to enter Haidar's service.[58] While he accepts the name given to him, it fills him with self-loathing: 'the title of Deserter is almost insupportable to any one tinctured with the smallest atom of spirit'.[59] The traitor, overcome with remorse, attempts to make amends by promising the prisoners all possible assistance and agreeing to deliver a letter to Madras to inform relatives of their fate. Given the central role played by the figure of the deserter in the alignment of East and West, it is certainly idle to speculate which, if any, of the versions of Dempster is authentic; however it is interesting to note that the *London Gazette* of 18 May 1792, lists Dempster as a deserter and records his execution at Seringapatam on charges of 'Correspondence'.[60]

If the figure of the impenitent deserter elicits nothing but contempt, that of the loyal sepoy commands universal respect. Fears of Mysore's powers to appropriate British citizens are allayed by a figure that represents the British ability to win over the East. At the end of his *Life of Hyder Ally*, published in 1786, Francis Robson adds *A genuine Narrative of the Sufferings of the British Prisoners of War, taken by his son, Tippoo Saib*. The narrative is all that its title promises: a heart-rending account of the humiliation of British captives. The power of Mysore may have successfully overwhelmed a British force, but Robson can at least celebrate the fact that British sepoys remained loyal. The captured sepoys, sentenced to hard labour, resist the threats and inducements offered by their captors to serve in Tipu Sultan's army:

our sepoys disregarded their threats, and told them, with firm resolution, that not a man of them would enter their service, that they would sooner die working as coolies, and that they well knew none of the European officers had taken, or would take service; this pleasing news of the fortitude and fidelity of our brave sepoys, who were labouring under such cruel hardships, gave us the utmost satisfaction, and considerably lightened the burden of our sufferings.[61]

The loyalty of the sepoys is such a source of comfort because it demonstrates that the British, though deprived of actual power, can still maintain control over Indians. The sepoys' faithfulness acts as a kind of emblem for the continuance of British authority. The respect with which the sepoys treat their British commanders, even in captivity, represents the durability of the former status quo:

> One circumstance... so much redounds to the honour of the sepoys, that it cannot pass unnoticed. In some of the prisons where the Europeans and sepoys were confined together, the latter saved money out of their daily allowance, and purchased meat for the former, at the same time telling them, that they well knew the customs of Europeans, and that they could not do without it; also when on the march, they would not suffer them to carry knapsacks, but the sepoys took them, and carried them themselves; telling the Europeans, that they were better able to bear the heat of the sun than they were, the climate being natural to them.[62]

Robson praises the sepoys for their acknowledgement of the British need to be served. He stresses the spontaneity of their selfless gestures, not so much as evidence of their charity, but more as proof of their voluntary subordination to the British.

One sepoy officer, Sayyad Ibrahim, features in both the *Memoirs of the late War* (as 'Sid Abram') and in Wilks's *Historical Sketches*. Imprisoned with the British officers at Seringapatam, Sayyad Ibrahim, a 'truly good man', repeatedly resists commands to enter Tipu's service, explaining his refusal in terms of affection for the British: 'he had, from his boyish days, been brought up amongst the English, had met with every attention and encouragement that a soldier merited'.[63] His loyal conduct prevents him from ever seeing his family again and he is removed from the British jail 'for farther torture'.[64] After his death and the fall of Seringapatam, Sayyad Ibrahim becomes an exemplary figure, a useful symbol of Indian fidelity. Wilks notes that a mausoleum was built over his remains and endowed by Lord Clive, governor of Madras, on behalf of the East India Company 'with a view to perpetuate the remembrance of his virtues, and the benefit of his example'.[65]

The Company-financed commemoration of Sayyad Ibrahim is a measure of the significance which the British attached to the issue of Indian loyalty. If such sponsorship was considered worthwhile, it was because the example of Sayyad Ibrahim provided an opportunity to convey the idea of an absolute transference of allegiance from India to the Company. A similar occasion for British self-congratulation was provided by an episode in the Third Mysore War, related by Roderick Mackenzie in his *Sketch of the War with Tippoo Sultaun* of 1793. Hindu sepoys had abandoned traditional concepts of religious pollution, by agreeing to travel by sea to aid the British war effort. Mackenzie comments: 'The soothing principle, that by conciliating the affections of the sepoys, overcame many of their most obstinate prejudices and in particular, the almost hitherto insurmountable aversion to expeditions by sea produced a conspicuous instance of the unlimited confidence reposed by that people in the wisdom of their ruler as well as in the established superiority of Great Britain.'[66] The renunciation of religious principles is construed as an acknowledgment of the moral, intellectual and political dominance of Britain. Of course, a force of faithful and increasingly westernized sepoys also represented a powerful bulwark against the threat of Tipu.

Indian Allies and British Triumphs

The Third Mysore War introduced another element into the narratives associated with the Anglo-Mysore conflict. The tripartite alliance between the British, the Marathas and the Nizam of Hyderabad presented authors with the question of how to depict the Eastern powers that were acting in concert against Tipu. The alliance was dictated by the demands of expediency and undermined by distrust. Accounts of the campaign typically distinguish Britain from her Indian allies in an attempt to guard against the dangers of oriental corruption. Wilks describes how British forces—the upholders of military order—spend much of their energy defending inhabitants from the depredations of the wild and unruly Marathas.[67] Generally characterized as unreliable, ill-disciplined, and superstitious, the allied forces were thought to hinder rather than help the campaign: the credit for the reduction of Tipu was reserved for British troops and loyal sepoys alone.[68]

The allies' military inefficiency is often characterized by means of theatrical or fictional metaphors. In his *Narrative of the Campaign in India* of 1793, Alexander Dirom, deputy-adjutant-general of crown forces in India, depicts the exercises of troops of both allied armies. Describing the processions of cavalry and infantry, with their banners and bands, elephants and camels, Dirom comments that 'A spectacle so wild and irregular, yet so grand and interesting, resembled more the visions of romance, than any assemblage that can be supposed to have existence in real life!'[69] These observations are closely echoed by Wilks in his later portrayal of the Nizam's cavalry, equipped with a haphazard collection of archaic armour and weaponry, 'scampering among each other in wild confusion': 'The whole exhibition presented to the mind an imagery scarcely more allied to previous impressions of reality, than the fictions of an eastern tale, or the picturesque disorder of a dramatic scene.'[70] All sense of military power evaporates under the influence of these metaphors: the allied armies inhabit an insubstantial, fictional realm, far removed from the actuality of armed confrontation. This self-contained, fanciful world presents itself as a diverting spectacle to a European audience; an image of Eastern power which is both ineffectual and non-threatening and that in no way compromises the British—the very antithesis of the power of Mysore.

The care taken to guard against oriental contamination, this time in the form of Eastern cruelty, is evident in the emphasis which almost all the authors place on the humanity of the British forces engaged in the conflict with Mysore. The single exception to this practice is Sheen's letter, which we considered earlier, accusing General Mathews' army of rape, massacre and pillage at Anantpur and Bednur. One of the elements which Sheen's detractors found most offensive in his account was the implication that British forces were adopting similar methods to those of the armies of Mysore. In his refutation of the letter, Moodie asks if Sheen has not represented Mathews' forces 'as tyrants; and in some respects, more cruelly oppressive than the instruments of Turkish despotism?'.[71] Understanding 'Turkish' here as a synonym for 'Muslim' or 'barbaric', we can see that Sheen stands accused of dismantling the distinctions between East and West, of transforming the British into oriental despots. In an attempt to re-erect the barriers of difference, Moodie constantly asserts the restraint and humanity of the British army. Subsequent authors follow suit. Mackenzie describes the perfect equanimity of the inhabitants of Mysore as British troops march through the country during the campaign of 1790:

On the advance of Colonel MAXWELL into the Barahmahl valley, the fields covered with plentiful crops, were nowhere abandoned by the peaceful cultivators; the herdsman, as if conscious of the invader's honour and the mildness of his supremacy, attended his numerous flocks; the weaver continued at his web, regardless of the calamities that the restlessness of its ruler had brought upon the state; and the avaricious Bazar-man exposed his whole stores to the soldiery without apprehension of injustice or deceit.[72]

Mackenzie chooses representative figures from the spheres of agriculture, manufacture and commerce and draws on various Indian stereotypes: the cultivators are 'peaceful'—an example of the gentle, inoffensive Indian; the weaver cares little for matters of state—a typically passive subject of despotic rule; and the Bazar-man is 'avaricious'—the familiar image of an

248 / *India Inscribed*

Indian trader, motivated by greed alone. This yoking together of sundry stock figures seems an attempt to assert the indisputability of British humanity by situating it in an essentially Indian context.

The end of the Third Mysore War provided the occasion for the most celebrated instance of British benevolence to emerge from the whole period of conflict. By the terms of the treaty of 1792, two of Tipu's sons were handed over to the British as a guarantee of Mysore's cession of territory and payment of a large cash indemnity. As Marshall has pointed out, the narrative of Cornwallis's kind reception of the young hostage princes, which originated in a report in the *Madras Courier*, was extensively reprinted both in periodical and book form, and was illustrated by numerous artists and engravers.[73] The narrative's characteristic elements are readily displayed in Alexander Dirom's version of the story. The princes are presented to Cornwallis by Tipu's vakil or appointed representative:

> the head vakeel, addressed his Lordship as follows. 'These children were this morning the sons of the Sultan my master; their situation is now changed, and they must look up to your Lordship as their father.'
>
> Lord Cornwallis, who had received the boys as if they had been his own sons, anxiously assured the vakeel and the young Princes themselves, that every attention possible would be shewn to them, and the greatest care taken of their persons. Their little faces brightened up; the scene became highly interesting; and not only their attendants, but all the spectators were delighted to see that any fears they might have harboured were removed, and that they would soon be reconciled to their change of situation, and their new friends.
>
> The Princes were dressed in long white muslin gowns, and red turbans. They had several rows of large pearls round their necks, from which was suspended an ornament consisting of a ruby and an emerald of considerable size, surrounded by large brilliants; and in their turbans, each had a sprig of rich pearls. Bred from their infancy with infinite care, and instructed in their manners to imitate the reserve and politeness of age, it astonished all present to see the correctness and propriety of their conduct.[74]

This scene effectively inverts descriptions of British captivity in Mysore; benevolence and courtesy take the place of the cruelty and humiliation which characterize accounts of British imprisonment: the transposition marks the establishment of British control. The description hinges on the transfer of paternity: Cornwallis accepts Tipu's sons as his own in a ceremonial enactment of the British appropriation of the East. The princes' willing acquiescence is strongly reminiscent of the account by Edward Ives, considered in Chapter Four, concerning the six-year-old son of the defeated pirate chief Tulaji Angria, who entrusts himself to Admiral

Watson's paternal care. Like Ives's narrative, the story of Tipu's sons reaffirms the beneficence of Company rule; an affirmation which is emphasized, in this case, by the contrast with the popular idea of Mysore's despotic government.

The generally accepted view of Tipu the tyrant is offset by the representation of his sons as decorous and self-controlled; in the *Authentic Memoirs of Tipoo Sultaun* the eldest prince is described as 'mild, courteous, and generous—in short, for affability and sentiment, he was the contrast of his ancestors'.[75] Scions of a notoriously aggressive family, the princes can now be praised because, as hostages, they embody the concept of a subdued Mysore. The detailed description of their bejewelled appearance introduces a new note of appreciative wonder into representations of Mysore: once tamed and under British control, Mysore can be transformed into a gorgeous eastern spectacle. Dirom's account continues with a description of a formal visit which Cornwallis paid to the princes: 'The tent in which the Princes received Lord Cornwallis, was lined with fine chintz, and the floor covered with white cloth. The attendants sprinkled rose water during the audience; and there was a degree of state, order, and magnificence in every thing, much superior to what had been seen amongst our allies.'[76] In its reduced condition Mysore becomes the seat of oriental splendour. The elements of eastern ceremonial and luxury are presented as an exotic show for British consumption. This idea of Mysore as a diverting exhibition persisted throughout the period that the princes were held hostage: Tipu's sons were lionized by Madras society, they sat for portraits and were even invited to a ball thrown in Cornwallis's honour.[77]

This production of a gorgeous image for Mysore is particularly apparent in visual representations of the hostage-reception scene. Mildred Archer has traced a large number of paintings and engravings on this theme in her authorative study, *India and British Portraiture, 1770–1825*. I have selected Robert Home's painting of the scene as representative of the genre (Fig. 9). Backed by the magnificent panoply of an elephant train, the princes, diminutive and graceful in their long robes, are greeted by Cornwallis at the centre of the painting. The artist expresses Cornwallis's benevolence through the gesture of an extended hand, and the youngest prince looks smilingly up at him. Home directs the viewer's attention on the reception scene by directing the gaze of most of the bystanders—both Indian and British—towards the central encounter. Here Mysore and Britain meet, as if the relationship between the two powers is structured around the framework of British paternal dominance and Mysore's childlike dependence. The scene became emblematic of Cornwallis's

250 / *India Inscribed*

Fig. 9: Painting of the reception of Tipu Sultan's sons as hostages by Robert Home (1793–4), National Army Museum, London.

achievement. The *Calcutta Gazette* announced on 5 January 1792 that the East India Company had commissioned a statue of Cornwallis standing on a pedestal with a bas-relief 'expressing the surrender of the sons of Tippoo to the British Hero'.[78]

This modification of the popular image of Mysore—the young princes under British guardianship replacing the tyrannical figure of their father—signals a wider change in attitudes towards the sultanate that originated in the British military successes of the Third and Fouth Mysore Wars. Not surprisingly, the literature relating to these campaigns tends to diminish the threatening reputation of Tipu, and emphasize instead the inevitability of the obliteration of Mysore's power by the British. On 30 August 1792 the *Calcutta Gazette* printed an anonymous poem, 'The Prophecy of Hyder'. This featured Haidar's ghost issuing from his tomb to deliver a warning to his son of the direful consequences of his overweening pride and ambition:

> Yet one short moment, and avengeful fate
>   The high blown bubble of thy power shall break;
> Shall dissipate thy dazzling dreams of state,
>   And leave thy pageant glories but a wreck.
> Yet one short moment, and thy boasted name
>   Shall from its giddy height of pride be thrust;
> Thy wild ambition shall be turn'd to shame,
>   And with repentant sorrow kiss the dust.[79]

The insubstantial nature of Tipu's power and its easy overthrow are also noted by Dirom in his account of the Third Mysore War. The British capture of the fort of Savandurga is considered a notable victory, not for any display of military skill (the defenders flee at the sight of the storming party), but because the fortress, like Tipu himself, enjoys a daunting but evidently unfounded reputation:

This stupendous fortress, so difficult of approach, is no less famed for its noxious atmosphere, occasioned by the surrounding hills and woods, than for its wonderful size and strength; and is said to have derived its name of Savendroog, or the Rock of Death, from its fatal climate.

The Sultan, sensible of its advantages, was reported to have congratulated his army on the infatuation of the English in having engaged in an enterprize that must terminate in their disgrace; as half the Europeans, he was pleased to assert, would die of sickness, and the other half be killed in the attack.[80]

Tipu's boasts have a hubristic ring, for it is Britain rather than Mysore that proves invulnerable: 'in less than an hour, in open day, the stupendous and hitherto deemed impregnable fortress of Savendroog, was stormed without the loss of a man.'[81] Similar sentiments are attributed to the sultan in his final confrontation with the British, during the siege that preceded the fall of his capital. Alexander Beatson observes that Tipu 'appears to have laboured under an infatuation, that Seringapatam was impregnable' and adds the footnote 'The Sultaun's constant expression upon every occasion was, who can take Seringapatam!'—a rhetorical question which inevitably invites a rejoinder in favour of the British.[82]

After the fall of Seringapatam, Tipu's alliance with the French—one of the aspects of Tipu's power which most alarmed the British—lost much of its menace. François Ripaud, the captain of a French privateer and commander of a corps of fifty-nine soldiers stationed at Seringapatam, had founded a Jacobin club in Tipu's capital. Reports of the transactions of the club and 'the celebration of Revolutionary orgies' which culminated in the planting of a liberty tree and professions of loyalty to 'Citizen Tippoo', offered a ready target for satire.[83] The *Annual Register* for 1799 typically dismissed such activities as 'mummeries' or a 'jacobinical farce'.[84] Such theatrical metaphors clearly undermine any sense of real threat.

The final overthrow of Tipu provided the occasion for many triumphant assertions of British superiority, but the discovery of the sultan's body by General Baird, himself a former prisoner in Seringapatam, leaves Beatson meditating on the vicissitudes of life:

He who had left the palace in the morning a powerful imperious Sultaun, full of vast ambitious projects, was brought back a lump of clay, abandoned by the whole world, his kingdom overthrown, his capital taken, and his palace occupied by the very man, Major-general Baird, who, about fifteen years before, had been, with other victims of his cruelty and tyranny, released from near four years' of rigid confinement, in irons, in a prison scarce three hundred yards from the spot where the corpse of the Sultaun now lay.[85]

The description of Tipu's death, with its clear echo of Hamlet's 'Imperious Caesar, dead and turned to clay', assumes a tragic or mythic quality: the sudden reverse of fortunes recalls the familiar device of peripeteia, and the return of the victim to wreak revenge on his tormentor is equally indebted to dramatic or fictional convention. Tipu's final act has been played out, justice has been done and order re-established. It is of course perfectly fitting that a British ex-prisoner, one of those appropriated by Mysore, should in turn take possession of the sultanate. This dramatic emplotment of Tipu's career held an enduring appeal. When

W. B. Beatson, deputy-surgeon-general in Lahore and descendant of Alexander Beatson, published his 1902 essay, *Plassy and Seringapatam*, he reproduced without acknowledgement the earlier Beatson's account of Tipu's finale.[86] The satisfying symmetry and literary resonances impart a proper sense of closure to the Anglo-Mysore conflict.

The discovery of Tipu's body also lent itself to pictorial representation and the scene, if not painted as often as that of the hostage princes, merits some analysis. The sultan's corpse was found after nightfall, so the subject offered artists considerable scope for dramatic lighting effects. These were most skilfully harnessed by David Wilkie in his 1838 painting, commissioned by Lady Baird to commemorate her dead husband's greatest triumph, and displayed at the Royal Academy (Fig. 10). The lamps and torches carried by the members of Baird's party throw more light on the General than on the object of their search—the body of the sultan. The heightened illumination increases the impact of Baird's triumphant stance. Placed on a higher level than the corpse, his body wholly turned towards the viewer's gaze, legs apart, with one arm pointing towards Tipu and the other raised, Baird is the only upright, full-length figure in the painting. The composition deliberately emphasizes the contrast between the vertical commander and the horizontal sultan. The significance of the general's past experience is not lost on Wilkie: notes which accompanied the Royal Academy show point out that beneath Baird 'in the parapet wall, is a grating here introduced as giving light to a dungeon in which he had been for nearly four years immured by Hyder Ally and his son, the same Tippoo Sultaun, who, by a remarkable dispensation of Providence, he now finds prostrate at his feet, bereft of his crown, his kingdom and his life'.[87] With a degree of artistic licence, Wilkie compresses Seringapatam's topography to situate Baird directly above his former prison; the barred window a reminder both of the general's suffering and Tipu's power. The painting thus asserts the British triumph over the perils of imprisonment. Any fears that Mysore could threaten or compromise the identity of its captives are decisively banished.

The exhibition notes suggest that Providence played a central role in Tipu's demise. This acknowledgement of divine assistance conveys something of the importance attached to the final overthrow of the sultan. Mark Wilks also enlists supernatural power in his representation of the sultan's end. Describing Tipu's funeral, he observes: 'Peals of thunder terrific and extraordinary even in this district, burst over the Island of Seringapatam immediately after the funeral; and the wanderings of a

FIG. 10: Mezzotint engraving by John Burnet (1843) after David Wilkie's painting of the discovery of Tipu Sultan's body (1838), India Office Library and Records, London.

pious imagination might innocently deem this awful close intended to mark the termination of the ceremony, and the memory of the scene.'[88]

The heavens note the passing of the sultan: as one era ends, another is portentously announced. Equally charged with significance is the official victory parade held at Fort St George when Mysore's standard was presented to Lord Wellesley. The *Calcutta Gazette* for 20–7 June 1800 reports the occasion: 'the Governor General, advancing a few steps, with a dignity not easily to be described laid his hand on the Standard of the once haughty and perfidious Mysorean, and by a firm and instant pressure bent it towards the earth.'[89] Wellesley's symbolic gesture, a controlled and decisive exercise of power, humbles the sultanate at a single stroke. The ceremony enacts the annihilation of the complex, troubling threat of Mysore. The standard is brought low, and the Indian stage is cleared for the unchallenged exercise of British power.

The following month Wellesley, writing to the Court of Directors of the East India Company in London, makes the implications of the ceremony quite clear: 'The glorious termination of the late war in Mysore . . . [has] established the ascendancy of the British power over all the States of India': from now on, it would be essential 'to consider the extensive and valuable possessions to the government of which the Company have succeeded, as a great Empire'.[90] This sense of the victory at Seringapatam as an epoch-making event is echoed by W. B. Beatson, over a century later. Beatson sees the eighteenth-century British as 'instruments in the hands of the Almighty Ruler of the Universe' and regards the two battles of Plassey and Seringapatam as founding acts of British India: 'the decisive victory, won at Seringapatam, advanced towards perfection the work begun by the English in India on the field of Plassy'.[91]

The defeat of Tipu not only puts the East in its place, it also refashions Company rule: the new century heralds the adoption of an explicitly imperial role for Britain in India. The East India Company emerges from the uncertain initial decades of government in India with new confidence. This book has examined the ways that India was inscribed by British and European writers in the seventeenth and eighteenth centuries. A close analysis of a wide range of texts has shown that this discourse is not monolithic; that it is possible to trace the multiple insecurities and conflicts running through and between accounts. These anxieties and contests are increasingly pushed to the margins of later texts of imperialism—until 1857 at least. After the fall of Mysore, the imperial pen re-inscribes India with greater assurance, and a firmer hand.

NOTES

1. Peter Marshall has noted the increased press coverage of the Third Mysore War in ' "Cornwallis Triumphant": War in India and the British Public in the Late Eighteenth Century', in *War, Strategy and International Politics*, eds Lawrence Freedman, Paul Hayes and Robert O'Neill (Oxford, 1992) 58.
2. Asok Sen has also noticed two contrasting versions of Tipu in 'A Pre-British Economic Formation in India of the late Eighteenth Century: Tipu Sultan's Mysore', in Barun De, ed., *Perspectives in Social Sciences* (Calcutta, 1977) i. 46–8.
3. William Thomson, *Memoirs of the Late War in Asia. With a Narrative of the imprisonment and sufferings of our officers and soldiers*, 2 vols (London, 1788) ii. 3, 4.
4. Thomson, ii. 3; for later accounts see Innes Munro, *A Narrative of Military Operations, on the Coromandel Coast* (London, 1789) 160; James Scurry, *The Captivity, Sufferings, and Escape of James Scurry* (London, 1824) 93–4.
5. *Annual Register* (1783) 'History of Europe' 88–90; *Authentic Memoirs of Tippoo Sultaun* (London, 1799) 28–9.
6. *The Writings and Speeches of Edmund Burke* v. 15.
7. *Annual Register* (1783) 'History of Europe', 89.
8. *The Writings and Speeches of Edmund Burke* v. 518.
9. *Annual Register* (1783) 'History of Europe', 89–90.
10. J. Moodie, *Remarks on the most Important Military Operations of the English Forces on the Western Side of the Penninsula of Hindoostan* (London, 1788) 56–7.
11. *Annual Register* (1783) 'History of Europe' 91–2; *New Annual Register* (1784) 'British and Foreign History' 96–8; *Authentic Memoirs*, 36; Thomas Pennant, *The View of Hindoostan*, 2 vols (London, 1798) i. 121–2. Pennant did not actually travel in India as the entry in H. K. Kaul's *Travels in South Asia* (Delhi, 1979) suggests. Pennant compiled his work from earlier accounts.
12. Henry Oakes, *An Authentic Narrative of the treatment of the English, who were taken prisoners on the reduction of Bednore, by Tippoo Saib* (London, 1785) 87.
13. Oakes, ii.
14. Denys Forrest, *Tiger of Mysore: The Life and Death of Tipu Sultan* (London, 1970) 67–8.
15. *Gentleman's Magazine* lviii, part i. (1788) 67.
16. Ibid., lxi, part i. (1791) 341.
17. Mark Wilks, *Historical Sketches of the South of India* 2 vols, 2nd edn (Madras, 1869) ii. 57.
18. For negative images of Tipu, see James Bristow, *A Narrative of the sufferings of James Bristow*, 2nd edn (London, 1794) 95–7, 108–9, 207–9; Scurry, 109–18. For positive images, see Edward Moor, *A Narrative of the Operations of Captain Little's Detachment* (London, 1794) 193–203; Alexander Dirom, *A Narrative of the Campaign in India* (London, 1793) 249–50.
19. Marshall, 'Cornwallis Triumphant', 61.

20. Mary Louise Pratt, *Imperial Eyes: Travel Writing and Transculturation* (London, 1992) 86.
21. Walter Scott Seton-Karr, ed., *Selections from Calcutta Gazettes*, 5 vols (London, 1864–9) ii. 536.
22. Ibid., i. 43.
23. Eric Stokes, *The English Utilitarians and India* (1959; rpt Delhi, 1989) 25–80.
24. Stephen Greenblatt, *Marvelous Possessions: The Wonder of the New World* (Oxford, 1991) 146–8.
25. Scurry, Preface, n. s.
26. *Gentleman's Magazine* lviii, part ii (1788) 685.
27. William Kirkpatrick, *Select Letters of Tippoo Sultaun* (London, 1811) x.
28. Moor, 193.
29. Ibid.
30. Marshall, 'Cornwallis Triumphant', 67, 74.
31. Moor, 198.
32. Kirkpatrick, xi.
33. Ibid., 114.
34. Ibid., 123, 128, 193.
35. Alexander Beatson, *A View of the Origin and Conduct of the War with Tippoo Sultaun* (London, 1800) 197.
36. C. A. Bayly, *Imperial Meridian: The British Empire and the World 1780–1830* (London, 1989) 59–60.
37. Homi Bhabha, *The Location of Culture* (London, 1994) 98.
38. Thomson, i. 505–6.
39. Ibid., 506.
40. Ibid., 506–7.
41. Ibid., 507–8.
42. Moodie, 58.
43. Thomson, ii. 163, 169.
44. Bristow (1792) 15; Bristow, 2nd edn (London, 1793) 42.
45. Ibid. (1793) 42.
46. Ibid., 41.
47. *Selections from Calcutta Gazettes* ii. 316; *London Gazette* (1792) 310.
48. *Selections from Calcutta Gazettes* i. 15.
49. Bristow (1793) 41–2.
50. Scurry, 165–6.
51. Thomson, ii. 294.
52. Scurry, 252.
53. Ibid., 252–3, 253.
54. Ibid., 254–5.
55. Pratt, 87.
56. Bristow (1793) 40; Scurry, 62.
57. Scurry, 68.
58. Thomson, ii. 54–5, 109–20.
59. Ibid., 114–15.
60. *London Gazette* (1792) 311.

61. Francis Robson, *The Life of Hyder Ally* (London, 1786) 201.
62. Ibid., 214–15.
63. Thomson, ii. 178, 191.
64. Wilks, ii. 97.
65. Ibid.
66. Roderick Mackenzie, *A Sketch of the War with Tippoo Sultaun*, 2 vols (Calcutta, 1793) i. 216–17.
67. Wilks, ii. 209.
68. For images of the allies' armies, see Moor, 32, Dirom, 12–13, Wilks, ii. 196.
69. Dirom, 24.
70. Wilks, ii. 195.
71. Moodie, 52.
72. Mackenzie, i. 164.
73. Marshall, 'Cornwallis Triumphant', 59–60; for illustrations, see Mildred Archer, *India and British Portraiture, 1770–1825* (London, 1979) 421–4.
74. Dirom, 229.
75. *Authentic Memoirs*, 146.
76. Dirom, 231.
77. *Selections from Calcutta Gazettes* ii. 338–9, *Gentleman's Magazine* lxiii, part i (1793) 272; Forrest, 194.
78. *Selections from Calcutta Gazettes* ii. 462.
79. Ibid., 348.
80. Dirom, 69.
81. Ibid., 72.
82. Beatson, 151.
83. *Annual Register* (1799) 'History of Europe', 118, 120.
84. Ibid., 120.
85. Beatson, ciii–civ.
86. W. B. Beatson, *Plassy and Seringapatam: A Comparison* (Eastbourne, 1902) 22.
87. Quoted in Archer, 435.
88. Wilks, ii. 374.
89. *Calcutta Gazette* 20–7 June 1800, quoted in *Vestiges of Old Madras, 1640–1800*, ed. H. Davison Love, 3 vols (London, 1913) iii. 461.
90. *The Despatches, Minutes, and Correspondence, of the Marquess Wellesley*, ed. Montgomery Martin, 5 vols (London, 1836) ii. 320, 312. Cited in P. J. Marshall and Glyndwr Williams, *The Great Map of Mankind: British Perceptions of the World in the Age of Enlightenment* (London, 1982) 155.
91. W. B. Beatson, 24.

Bibliography

PRIMARY SOURCES

Manuscripts
Jones, William, *Sacontala*, MS Sansk. c. 37, Bodleian Library, Oxford.

Periodicals
Analytical Review (1790).
Annual Register (1771).
Annual Register (1783).
Annual Register (1788).
Annual Register (1791).
Annual Register (1793).
Annual Register (1799).
Asiatic Annual Register i (1798–9).
Asiatick Researches i–vi (1788–99).
Critical Review (2nd series) i (1791).
Gentleman's Magazine xli (1771).
Gentleman's Magazine xlii (1772).
Gentleman's Magazine l (1780).
Gentleman's Magazine lvii (1788).
Gentleman's Magazine lxi (1791).
Gentleman's Magazine lxiii (1793).
Gentleman's Magazine lxv (1795).
London Gazette (1792).
London Magazine (1771).
Monthly Review lxvii (1782).
Monthly Review lxxvi (1787).
Monthly Review lxxxi (1789).
Monthly Review (New series) xxiii (1797).

New Annual Register (1784).
Philosophical Transactions i (1665–6).

Printed Works

Authentic Memoirs of Tippoo Sultaun (London, 1799).
Bacon, Francis, *The Advancement of Learning and New Atlantis* (Oxford: Oxford University Press, 1974).
Baldaeus, Philip, 'A true and Exact Description of the Most Celebrated *East-India* Coasts of Malabar and Coromandel', *A Collection of Voyages and Travels*, ed. A. and J. Churchill, 6 vols (London, 1732) iii. 501–822.
Beatson, Alexander, *A View of the Origin and Conduct of the War with Tippoo Sultaun* (London, 1800).
Beatson, W. B., *Plassy and Seringapatam: A Comparison* (Eastbourne: Farncombe & Co., 1902).
Bernier, François, *The History of the Late Revolution of the Empire of the Great Mogul*, 6 parts (London, 1671).
Bolts, William, *Considerations on Indian Affairs; particularly respecting the present state of Bengal and its dependencies* (London, 1772).
Bond, Edward, *The Speeches of the Managers and Counsel in the Trial of Warren Hastings*, 4 vols (London: Longman, 1861).
Boswell, James, *Life of Johnson*, ed. R. W. Chapman, new edn J. D. Fleeman (Oxford: Oxford University Press, 1970).
Bristow, James, *A Narrative of the sufferings of James Bristow, belonging to the Bengal Artillery, during Ten Years Captivity with Hyder Ally and Tippoo Saheb*, 2nd edn (1792, London, 1794).
Burke, Edmund, *India: Madras and Bengal 1774–85: The Writings and Speeches of Edmund Burke*, V, ed. P. J. Marshall (Oxford: Oxford University Press, 1981).
Burke, Edmund, *India: The Launching of the Hastings Impeachment 1786–88: The Writings and Speeches of Edmund Burke*, VI, ed. P. J. Marshall (Oxford: Oxford University Press, 1991).
Cambridge, Richard Owen, *An Account of the War in India, between the English and French, on the Coast of Coromandel, From the Year 1750 to the Year 1760* (London, 1761).
Campbell, Donald, *A Narrative of the extraordinary adventures, and sufferings by Shipwreck & Imprisonment, of Donald Campbell*, 4th edn (1798, London: T. N. Longman and O. Rees, 1801).
Catrou, F. F., *The General History of the Mogol Empire, From its Founda-*

tion by Tamerlane, to the Late Emperor Orangzeb. Extracted from the Memoirs of M. Manouchi (London, 1709).

Clarke, Richard, *The Nabob: or, Asiatic Pluderers* (London, 1773).

Cope, Captain, *A New History of the East-Indies* (London, 1754).

Copies of the Several Testimonials transmitted from Bengal by the Governor General and Council, Relative to Warren Hastings Esq. (London, 1789).

Craufurd, Quintin, *Sketches relating to the History, Learning, and Manners, of the Hindoos* (London, 1790).

Dellon, Charles, *A Voyage to the East-Indies* (London, 1698).

Dirom, Alexander, *A Narrative of the Campaign in India, which terminated the War with Tippoo Sultaun in 1792* (London, 1793).

Dow, Alexander, *The History of Indostan*, 2 vols (London, 1768); 3rd vol. (London, 1772).

Dryden, John, *Aureng-Zebe*, ed. Frederick M. Link (London: Edward Arnold, 1972).

Dryden, John, *The Works of John Dryden*, eds E. N. Hooker, H. T. Swedenberg *et al.*, 19 vols (Berkeley, University of California Press, 1956–) xvii.

Euripides, trans. Arthur S. Way, 4 vols (1912, London: Heinemann, 1962) iii. 'Suppliants'.

Fay, Eliza, *Original Letters from India (1779–1815)*, eds E. M. Forster and M. M. Kaye (London: Chatto & Windus, 1986).

Foote, Samuel, *The Nabob* (London, 1778).

Forster, George, *A Journey from Bengal to England, through the Northern part of India, Kashmire, Afghanistan, and Persia, and into Russia, by the Caspian Sea*, 2 vols (London, 1798).

Foxe, John, *Foxe's Book of Martyrs*, ed. A. Clarke (London: Ward, Lock and Co., 1888).

Fryer, John, *A New Account of East India and Persia*, ed. William Crooke, 2 vols (London: Hakluyt Society, 1909–15).

Gilchrist, John, *The Oriental Linguist* (Calcutta, 1798).

Gray, Thomas, *The Poems of Mr Gray. To which are prefixed Memoirs of his Life and Writings by W. Mason* (York, 1775).

Grose, John-Henry, *A Voyage to the East Indies* (London, 1757).

Guyon, Claude Marie, *A New History of the East-Indies, Ancient and Modern*, 2 vols (London, 1757).

Hadley, George, *A Compendious Grammar of the Corrupt Dialect of the Jargon of Hindostan*, 4th edn (London, 1796).

262 / Bibliography

Hakluyt, Richard, *The Principle Navigations Voyages Traffiques & Discoveries of the English Nation Made by Sea or Over-land to the Remote and Farthest Distant Quarters of the Earth at any time within the compasse of these 1600 Yeeres*, 12 vols (Glasgow: James Maclehouse and Sons, 1904).

Hamilton, Alexander, *A New Account of the East Indies*, 2 vols (Edinburgh, 1727).

Hamilton, Elizabeth, *Translation of the Letters of a Hindoo Rajah*, 2 vols (London, 1796).

Hartly House, Calcutta (Dublin, 1789).

Hayley, William, *An Elegy on the Death of The Honourable Sir William Jones* (London, 1795).

Head, Richard, *The English Rogue*, 3 parts (London, 1666).

Herbert, Thomas, *A Relation of Some Yeares Travaile* (London, 1634).

Herbert, Thomas, *Some yeares Travels*, 2nd edn (London, 1638).

The History of the Trial of Warren Hastings, 5 parts (London, 1796).

Hodges, William, *Travels in India, during the Years 1780, 1781, 1782, & 1783* (London, 1793).

Holwell, J. Z., *A Genuine Narrative of the Deplorable Deaths of the English Gentlemen and Others, who were suffocated in the Black-Hole in Fort-William, at Calcutta* (London, 1758).

Holwell, J. Z., *Interesting Historical Events, Relative to the Province of Bengal, and the Empire of Indostan*, 2nd edn (London, 1766).

Homer, *The Odyssey*, trans. E. V. Rieu (1946; rpt Harmondsworth: Penguin, 1981).

Horsford, John, *A Collection of Poems written in the East Indies* (Calcutta, 1797).

Irwin, Eyles, *Eastern Eclogues; Written during a Tour through Arabia, Egypt, and other Parts of Asia and Africa in the year MDCCLXXVII* (London, 1780).

Ives, Edward, *A Voyage from England to India, in the Year MDCCLIV, and an Historical Narrative of the Operations of the Squadron and Army in India* (London, 1773).

Jones, William, *The Works of Sir William Jones*, 6 vols (London, 1799).

Jones, William, *Poems, consisting chiefly of Translations from the Asiatick Languages*, 2nd edn (1772, London, 1777).

Journals of the House of Commons xli.

Kindersley, Jemima, *Letters from the Island of Teneriffe, Brazil, The Cape of Good Hope, and the East Indies* (London, 1777).

Kipling, Rudyard, *The Day's Work* (London: Macmillan, 1898).

Kipling, Rudyard, *Kim* (Harmondsworth: Penguin, 1987).
Kircher, Athanasius, *La Chine d'Athanase Kircher* (Amsterdam, 1670).
Kirkpatrick, William, trans., *Select Letters of Tippoo Sultaun to various Public Functionaries* (London, 1811).
La Boullaye le Gouz, François, *Les Vôyages et Observations dv Sievr de la Bovllaye Le-Gouz* (1653; rpt Paris, 1657).
La Croze, Mathurin Veyssière de, *Histoire du Christianisme des Indes* (La Haye, 1724).
La Mothe le Vayer, François, *Oeuvres*, 7 vols (Dresden, 1756–9).
Le Moyne, Pierre, *La Gallerie des Femmes Fortes* (Lyon, 1667).
Lettres Edifiantes et Curieuses Ecrites des Missions Etrangers par quelques Missionnaires de la Compagnie de Jesus, 34 vols (Paris, 1707–76).
Lettres Edifiantes et Curieuses, 2nd edn, 26 vols (Paris, 1781).
Lockman, J., *Travels of the Jesuits*, 2 vols (London, 1743).
Linschoten, John Huighen Van, *Discours of Voyages into the Easte and West Indies*, 4 vols (London, 1598).
Lord, Henry, *A discouerie of the Sect of the Banians* (London, 1630).
Mackenzie, Roderick, *A Sketch of the War with Tippoo Sultaun*, 2 vols (Calcutta, 1793).
Mackintosh, William, *Travels in Europe, Asia, and Africa*, 2 vols (London, 1782).
Mandelslo, John Albert de, 'The Voyages & Travels of J. Albert de Mandelslo', *The Voyages & Travels of the Ambassadors sent by Frederick Duke of Holstein, to the Great Duke of Muscovy, and the King of Persia*, trans. John Davis (London, 1662).
Marlowe, Christopher, *The Jew of Malta*, ed. N. W. Bawcutt (Manchester: Manchester University Press, 1978).
Marlowe, Christopher, *Tamburlaine the Great*, Parts I and II, ed. John D. Jump (London: Edward Arnold, 1967).
Memoirs of a Gentleman, who resided several years in the East Indies during the late Revolutions, and most Important events in that part of the world (London, 1774).
Milton, John, *Paradise Lost*, ed. Alastair Fowler (London: Longman, 1968).
Montaigne, Michel de, *The Essayes of Michel Lord of Montaigne*, trans. John Florio, ed. Thomas Seccombe (London: Grant Richards, 1908).
Moodie, J., *Remarks on the most Important Military Operations of the English Forces on the Western Side of the Penninsula of Hindoostan in 1783, and 1784, in which the Conduct of the Army under the command of Brigadier General Matthews is Vindicated, from the illiberal Mis-*

representations, contained in a late Narrative, signed John Charles Sheen (London, 1788).

Moor, Edward, *A Narrative of the Operations of Captain Little's Detachment, and of the Mahratta Army, commanded by Purseram Bhow; during the late confederacy in India, against the Nawab Tippoo Sultan Bahadur* (London, 1794).

Munro, Innes, *A Narrative of the Military Operations, on the Coromandel Coast, against the combined forces of the French, Dutch, and Hyder Ally Cawn* (London, 1789).

Niecamp, Jean Lucas, *Histoire de la Mission Danoise dans les Indes Orientales*, 3 vols (Geneva, 1745).

Oakes, Henry, *An Authentic Narrative of the treatment of the English, who were taken prisoners on the reduction of Bednore, by Tippoo Saib* (London, 1788).

Orme, Robert, *A History of the Military Transactions of the British Nation in Indostan*, 2 vols (London, 1763).

Ovington, John, *A Voyage to Suratt* (London 1696).

Pennant, Thomas, *The View of Hindoostan*, 2 vols (London, 1798).

Polo, Marco, *The most noble and famous travels of Marcus Paulus* (London, 1579).

Price, Joseph, *Some Observations and Remarks on a late Publication, intitled, Travels in Europe, Asia, and Africa*, 2nd edn (London, 1782).

Price, Joseph, *The Saddle put on the Right Horse; or, an Enquiry into the Reason Why certain Persons have been denominated Nabobs; With an Arrangement of those Gentlemen into their proper Classes, of Real, Spurious, Reputed, or Mushroom, Nabobs* (London, 1783).

Propagation of the Gospel in the East: being an Account of the Success of two Danish Missionaries, Lately sent to the East-Indies, for the Conversion of the Heathens in Malabar (London, 1709).

Purchas, Samuel, *Hakluytus Posthumus or Purchas his Pilgrimes Contayning a History of the World in Sea Voyages and Lande Travells by Englishmen and others*, 20 vols (Glasgow: James Maclehouse and Sons, 1905–7).

Pyrard de Laval, François, *Voyage de François Pyrard de Laual*, 2 vols (1611; rpt Paris, 1619).

Raynal, Abbé Guillaume, *A Philosophical and Political History of the Settlements and Trade of the Europeans in the East and West Indies*, trans. J. Justamond, 5 vols, 3rd edn (London, 1777).

Robson, Francis, *The Life of Hyder Ally: With an Account of his Usurpation of the Kingdom of Mysore, and other contiguous Provinces. To which is annexed, a genuine Narrative of the Sufferings of the British Prisoners of War, taken by his son, Tippoo Saib (London, 1786).

Roger, Abraham, *La Porte Ouverte Pour Parvenir à la Connoissance du Paganisme Caché* (Amsterdam, 1670).

Schlegel, August Wilhelm, *A Course of Lectures on Dramatic Art and Literature*, trans. John Black, 2 vols (London: Baldwin, Cradock, and Joy, 1815).

Scott, John, *The Poetical Works* (London, 1782).

Scrafton, Luke, *Reflections on the Government of Indostan* (1763; rpt London, 1770).

Scurry, James, *The Captivity, Sufferings, and Escape of James Scurry, who was detained a prisoner during ten years, in the dominions of Hyder Ali and Tippoo Saib* (London: Henry Fisher, 1824).

Seton-Karr, Walter Scott, ed., *Selections from Calcutta Gazettes*, vols i–ii (London: Longmans, Green, Reader and Dyer, 1864–5).

Shore, John (Lord Teignmouth), *Memoirs of the Life, Writings, and Correspondence of Sir William Jones* (London: Hatchard, 1804).

Short History of English Transactions in the East Indies (Cambridge, 1776).

Short Review of the British Government in India (London, 1790).

Solvyns, F. Baltazard, *Les Hindous, ou Description de leurs moeurs, coutumes et cérémonies*, 4 vols (Paris: H. Nicolle, 1808–12).

Spenser, Edmund, *The Fairie Queene*, eds Thomas P. Roche and Patrick O'Donnell (Harmondsworth: Penguin, 1978).

Sterne, Laurence, *A Sentimental Journey* (Oxford, Oxford University Press, 1984).

Sym, John, *Lifes preservative against self-killing* (London, 1637).

Tavernier, Jean-Baptiste, *The Six Voyages of Jean Baptista Tavernier*, 2 vols (London, 1678).

Tavernier, Jean-Baptiste, *Travels in India*, ed. William Crooke, 2 vols (Oxford: Oxford University Press, 1925).

Tennant, William, *Indian recreations: consisting chiefly of Strictures on the Domestic and Rural Economy of the Mahometans & Hindoos*, 3 vols (1802; rpt London: Longman, Hurst, Rees, Orme, 1804).

Terry, Edward, *A Voyage to East India*, 2nd edn (London, 1655).

Thévenot, Jean de, *Indian Travels of Thevenot and Careri*, ed. Surendraneth Sen (New Delhi: National Archives of India, 1949).

Thomson, William, *Memoirs of the Late War in Asia. With a Narrative of the imprisonment and sufferings of our officers and soldiers: By an Officer of Colonel Baillie's Detachment*, 2 vols (London, 1788).

266 / Bibliography

Thirty four Conferences between the Danish Missionaries and the Malabarian Bramans, trans. Jenkin Philipps (London, 1719).

Touchstone, Timothy (pseud.), *Tea and Sugar, or the Nabob and the Creole; A Poem in two Cantos* (London, 1792).

Valle, Pietro della, *The Travels of Pietro della Valle in India*, ed. Edward Grey (London: Hakluyt Society, 1892).

Varthema, Ludovico di, *The Travels of Ludovico di Varthema*, trans. George Percy Badger (London: Hakluyt Society, 1863).

Verelst, Henry, *A View of the Rise, Progress, and Present State of the English Government in Bengal: Including a reply to the Misrepresentations of Mr Bolts and other Writers* (London, 1772).

Wesley, John, *Thoughts upon Slavery*, 3rd edn (London, 1724).

Wilkins, Charles, *The Bhagvat-Geeta, or Dialogues of Kreeshna and Arjoon* (London, 1785).

Wilks, Mark, *Historical Sketches of the South of India*, 2 vols, 2nd edn (1810–17, Madras: Higginbotham & Co., 1869).

SECONDARY SOURCES

Unpublished

Burke, Peter, 'Bernier's Orient: an Occidentalist's Perspective', unpublished seminar paper.

Mani, Lata, 'The Production of Colonial Discourse: *Sati* in Early Nineteenth-Century Bengal', Dissertation, University of California, Santa Cruz, 1983.

Padel, Felix, 'British Rule and the Konds of Orissa: A Study of Tribal Administration and its legitmating Discourse', D. Phil thesis, Oxford, 1987 (forthcoming as *The Sacrifice of Human Being*, Delhi, Oxford University Press, 1995).

Trautmann, Thomas, 'The Lives of Asiatick Jones', unpublished seminar paper, delivered to the Commonwealth History Seminar, Oxford University, 18 January 1991.

Printed Works

Adams, Percy G., *Travellers and Travel Liars: 1600–1800* (Berkeley: University of California Press, 1962).

Adams, Percy G., *Travel Literature and the Evolution of the Novel* (Kentucky: University of Kentucky Press, 1983).

Arberry, A. J., *Asiatic Jones: The Life and Influence of Sir William Jones (1746–1794) Pioneer of Indian Studies* (London: Longman, 1946).

Archer, Mildred, 'Baltazard Solvyns and the Indian Picturesque', *The Connoisseur* clxx (Jan.–April 1969) 12–18.

Archer, Mildred, *India and British Portraiture, 1770–1825* (London: Sotheby Parke Bennet, 1979).

Ballhatchet, Kenneth, *Race, Sex and Class under the Raj: Imperial Attitudes and Policies and their Critics, 1793–1905* (London: Weidenfeld and Nicolson, 1980).

Barker, Francis, Peter Hulme, Margaret Iversen and Diana Loxley, eds, *Europe and its Others*, i. (Colchester: University of Essex, 1985).

Barrell, John, *The Infection of Thomas De Quincey: A Psychopathology of Imperialism* (New Haven: Yale University Press, 1991).

Basham, A. L., 'Sophia and the Bramin', *East India Company Studies Papers presented to Professor Sir Cyril Philips*, eds Kenneth Ballhatchet and John Harrison (Hong Kong: Asian Research Service, 1986) 13–30.

Bayly, C. A., *Indian Society and the Making of the British Empire. New Cambridge History of India*, ii, 1 (Cambridge: Cambridge University Press, 1988).

Bayly, C. A., *Imperial Meridian: The British Empire and the World, 1780–1830* (London: Longman, 1989).

Bayly, C. A., ed, *The Raj: India and the British 1600–1947* (London: National Portrait Gallery, 1990).

Bearce, George D., *British Attitudes towards India 1784–1858* (Oxford: Oxford University Press, 1961).

Bhabha, Homi K., *The Location of Culture* (London: Routledge, 1994).

Brown, Leslie, *The Indian Christians of St Thomas: An Account of the Ancient Syrian Church of Malabar* (Cambridge: Cambridge University Press, 1956).

Cannon, Garland, ed., *The Letters of Sir William Jones*, 2 vols (Oxford: Oxford University Press, 1970).

Cannon, Garland, *The Life and Mind of Oriental Jones: Sir William Jones, the Father of Modern Linguistics* (Cambridge: Cambridge University Press, 1990).

Carnall, Geoffrey and Colin Nicholson, eds, *The Impeachment of Warren Hastings: Papers from a Bicentenary Commemoration* (Edinburgh: Edinburgh University Press, 1989).

Clifford, James and George Marcus, eds, *Writing Culture: The Poetics and Politics of Ethnography* (Berkley: California University Press, 1986).

Clifford, James, *The Predicament of Culture: Twentieth-Century Ethno-*

graphy, Literature and Art (Cambridge, Mass.: Harvard University Press, 1988).
Cohn, Bernard S., 'Representing Authority in Victorian India', *The Invention of Tradition*, eds Eric Hobsbawm and Terence Ranger (Cambridge: Cambridge University Press, 1983).
Cohn, Bernard S., 'The Command of Language and the Language of Command', *Subaltern Studies* IV (1985) 276–329.
Cohn, Bernard S., *An Anthropologist among the Historians and Other Essays* (Delhi: Oxford University Press, 1987).
Davis, Natalie Zemon, *Fiction in the Archives: Pardon Tales and their Tellers in Sixteenth-Century France* (Cambridge: Polity Press, 1987).
Davison Love, H., ed., *Vestiges of Old Madras, 1640–1800*, 3 vols (London: John Murray, 1913).
De Bruyn, Frans, 'Edmund Burke's Gothic Romance: The Portrayal of Warren Hastings in Burke's Writings and Speeches on India', *Criticism* xxix. 4 (1987) 415–38.
De Certeau, Michel, *Heterologies: Discourse on the Other*, trans. Brian Massumi (Manchester: Manchester University Press, 1986).
Derrett, J. Duncan M., *Religion, Law and the State in India* (London: Faber and Faber, 1968).
Drew, John, *India and the Romantic Imagination* (Delhi: Oxford University Press, 1987).
Duchet, Michel, *Anthropologie et Histoire au Siécle des Lumiéres, Buffon, Voltaire, Rousseau, Helvétius, Diderot* (Paris: Maspero, 1971).
Dyson, Ketaki Kushari, *A Various Universe: A Study of the Journals and Memoirs of British Men and Women in the Indian Subcontinent, 1765–1856* (Delhi: Oxford University Press, 1978).
Fabian, Johannes, *Time and the Other: How Anthropology makes its Object* (New York: Columbia University Press, 1983).
Forrest, Denys, *Tiger of Mysore: The Life and Death of Tipu Sultan* (London: Chatto & Windus, 1970).
Foster, William, *Early Travels in India 1593–1619* (Oxford: Oxford University Press, 1921).
Foucault, Michel, *The Order of Things: An Archeology of the Human Sciences* (London: Tavistock Publications, 1970).
Foucault, Michel, *The Archaeology of Knowledge*, trans. A. M. Sheridan Smith (London: Tavistock Publications, 1972).
Foucault, Michel, *Discipline and Punish: The Birth of the Prison*, trans. Alan Sheridan (Harmondsworth: Penguin, 1977).

Foucault, Michel, *Power/Knowledge: Selected Interviews and other Writings 1972–1977*, ed. Colin Gordon (Brighton: Harvester Press, 1980).
Fraser, Antonia, *The Weaker Vessel: Woman's Lot in Seventeenth-Century England* (1984; rpt London: Octopus, 1989).
Geertz, Clifford, *Works and Lives: The Anthropologist as Author* (Cambridge: Polity, 1988).
Ghosh, Suresh Chandra, *The Social Condition of the British Community in Bengal, 1757–1800* (Leiden: E. J. Brill, 1970).
Greenblatt, Stephen, *Marvelous Possessions: The Wonder of the New World* (Oxford: Oxford University Press, 1991).
Greenblatt, Stephen, ed., *New World Encounters* (Berkeley: University of California Press, 1993).
Guest, Harriet, 'The Great Distinction. Figures of the Exotic in the Work of William Hodges', *Oxford Art Journal* xii. 2 (1989) 36–58.
Guha, Ranajit, *A Rule of Property for Bengal: An Essay on the Idea of Permanent Settlement* (1963, New Delhi: Orient Longman, 1981).
Guha, Ranajit, *An Indian Historiography of India: A Nineteenth-Century Agenda and Its Implications* (Calcutta: Centre for Studies in Social Sciences, 1988).
Guha, Ranajit, 'Dominance Without Hegemony and its Historiography', *Subaltern Studies* VI (1989) 210–309.
Gupta, Brijen K., *Sirajuddaullah and the East India Company 1756–7* (Leiden: E. J. Brill, 1962).
Hacking, Ian, 'The Archaelogy of Foucault', *Foucault: A Critical Reader*, ed. David Couzens (Oxford: Blackwell, 1986).
Halbfass, Wilhelm, *India and Europe: An Essay in Understanding* (New York: State University of New York, 1988).
Hall, James, *Dictionary of Subjects and Symbols in Art* (London: John Murray, 1974).
Hartog, François, *The Mirror of Herodotus: The Representation of the Other in the Writing of History*, trans. Janet Lloyd (Berkeley: University of California Press, 1988).
Hewitt, R. M., 'Harmonious Jones', *Essays and Studies* xxviii (1942) 42–59.
Hiltebeitel, Alf, *The Cult of Draupadi* (Chicago: University of Chicago Press, 1988).
Hodgen, Margaret T., *Early Anthropology in the Sixteenth and Seventeenth Centuries* (Philadelphia: University of Pennsylvania Press, 1964).

Hughes, Derek, *Dryden's Heroic Plays* (London: Macmillan, 1981).
Hulme, Peter, *Colonial Encounters: Europe and the Native Caribbean, 1492–1797* (London: Methuen, 1986).
Inden, Ronald, *Imagining India* (Oxford: Blackwell, 1990).
Irwin, David, *John Flaxman 1755–1826: Sculptor, Illustrator, Designer* (London: Cassell, 1979).
Jardine, Lisa, *Still Harping on Daughters: Women and Drama in the Age of Shakespeare* (Hemel Hempstead: Harvester Wheatsheaf, 1983).
Jones, Mark Bence, *Clive of India* (London: Constable, 1974).
Jonston, A., ' "The Purple Year" in Pope and Gray', *Review of English Studies* xiv (1963) 389–93.
Kabbani, Rana, *Europe's Myths of Orient* (London: Pandora, 1986).
Kaul, H. K., *Travels in South Asia: A Selected and Annotated Bibliography of Guide-books and Travel Books on South Asia* (Delhi: Arnold-Heinemann, 1979).
Kejariwal, O. P., *The Asiatic Society of Bengal and the Discovery of India's Past* (New Delhi: Oxford University Press, 1988).
Kelly, Gary, *Women, Writing and Revolution, 1790–1827* (Oxford: Oxford University Press, 1993).
Kopf, David, *British Orientalism and the Bengal Renaissance: The Dynamics of Indian Modernization 1773–1835* (Berkely: University of California Press, 1969).
Lach, Donald F., *India in the Eyes of Europe: The Sixteenth Century* (Chicago: University of Chicago Press, 1968).
Leask, Nigel, *British Romantic Writers and the East: Anxieties of Empire* (Cambridge: Cambridge University Press, 1992).
Losty, J. P., *Calcutta: City of Palaces* (London: The British Library, 1990).
Lowe, Lisa, *Critical Terrains: French and British Orientalisms* (Ithaca, New York, Cornell University Press, 1991).
Lynam, Edward, ed., *Richard Hakluyt and his Successors* (London: Hakluyt Society, 1946).
Maclean, Ian, *Woman Triumphant: Feminism in French Literature 1610–1652* (Oxford: Oxford University Press, 1977).
Majeed, Javed, *Ungoverned Imaginings: James Mill's* The History of British India *and Orientalism* (Oxford: Oxford University Press, 1992).
Majumdar, R. C., ed., *Classical Accounts of India* (Calcutta: Firma K. L. Mukhopadhyay, 1960).
Mani, Lata, 'The Production of an Official Discourse on *Sati* in Early Nineteenth-Century Bengal', *Europe and its Others*, ed. Francis Barker *et al.* (Colchester: University of Essex, 1985) i. 107–27.

Mani, Lata and Ruth Frankenberg, 'The Challenge of *Orientalism*', *Economy and Society* xiv. 2 (1985) 175–91.
Mani, Lata, 'Contentious Traditions: The Debate on Sati in Colonial India', *Cultural Critique* (1987) 119–56.
Mani, Lata, 'Cultural Theory, Colonial Texts: Reading Eye-Witness Accounts of Widow Burning', *Cultural Studies*, eds Lawrence Grossberg, Cary Nelson and Paula Treichler (New York: Routledge, 1992) 392–405.
Manuel, Frank E., *The Eighteenth-Century confronts the Gods* (Cambridge, Mass.: Harvard University Press, 1959).
Marshall, P. J., *The Impeachment of Warren Hastings* (Oxford: Oxford University Press, 1965).
Marshall, P. J., *Problems of Empire: Britain and India 1757–1813* (London: George Allen Unwin, 1968).
Marshall, P. J., *The British Discovery of Hinduism in the Eighteenth Century* (Cambridge: Cambridge University Press, 1970).
Marshall, P. J., 'British Expansion in India in the Eighteenth Century: A Historical Revision', *History* lx (1 975) 28–43.
Marshall, P. J., *East Indian Fortunes: The British in Bengal in the Eighteenth Century* (Oxford: Oxford University Press, 1976).
Marshall, P. J., ' "A Free though Conquering People": Britain and Asia in the Eighteenth Century,' *Inaugural Lecture in the Rhodes Chair of Imperial History*, Kings College, London, 5 March 1981.
Marshall, P. J. and Glyndwr Williams, *The Great Map of Mankind: British Perceptions of the World in the Age of Enlightenment* (London: Dent, 1982).
Marshall, P. J., *Bengal: The British Bridgehead. Eastern India 1740–1828*, The New Cambridge History of India, ii. 2 (Cambridge: Cambridge University Press, 1987).
Marshall, P. J., ' "Cornwallis Triumphant": War in India and the British Public in the late Eighteenth Century', *War, Strategy and International Politics*, eds Lawrence Freedman, Paul Hayes and Robert O'Neill (Oxford: Oxford University Press, 1992) 57–74.
Mason, Philip, *The Men who Ruled India*, 2 vols (London: Jonathan Cape, 1954).
Mills, Sara, *Discourses of Difference: An Analysis of Women's Travel Writing and Colonialism* (London: Routledge, 1991).
Mitter, Partha, *Much Maligned Monsters: History of European Reactions to Indian Art* (Oxford: Oxford University Press, 1977).
Moseley, C. W. R. D., 'Richard Head's "English Rogue": A Modern Mandeville?', *Yearbook of English Studies* i (1971) 102–7.

Mukherjee, S. N., *Sir William Jones: A Study in Eighteenth-Century British Attitudes to India* (1968; London: Sangam Books, 1987)

Murr, Sylvia, 'Les Conditions d'emergence du discours sur l'Inde au Siècle des Lumières', *Purusartha*, VII (1983) 233–84.

Musselwhite, David, 'The Trial of Warren Hastings', *Literature, Politics and Theory, Papers from the Essex Conference 1976–84*, eds Francis Barker, Peter Hulme, Margaret Iversen and Diana Loxley (London: Methuen, 1986) 77–103.

Neill, Stephen, *A History of Christianity in India*, 2 vols (Cambridge, Cambridge University Press, 1984).

Neill, Stephen, *A History of Christian Missions*, 2nd edn (Harmondsworth: Penguin, 1986).

Ness, Gayl D., William Stahl, 'Western Imperialist Armies in Asia', *Comparative Studies in Society and History* ixx (1977) 2–79.

Niranjana, Tejaswini, *Siting Translation: History, Post-Structuralism and the Colonial Context* (Berkely: University of California Press, 1992).

O'Leary, Brendan, *The Asiatic Mode of Production* (Oxford: Blackwell, 1989).

Porter, Dennis, '*Orientalism* and its Problems', *The Politics of Theory*, ed. Francis Barker *et al.* (Colchester: University of Essex, 1983) 179–93.

Pratt, Mary Louise, *Imperial Eyes: Travel Writing and Transculturation* (London: Routledge, 1992).

Pratt, Mary Louise, 'Fieldwork in Common Places', *Writing Culture: The Poetics and Politics of Ethnography*, eds James Clifford and George D. Marcus (Berkeley: University of California Press, 1986) 27–50.

Rajan, Rajeswari Sunder, *Real and Imagined Women: Gender, Culture and Post-Colonialism* (London: Routledge, 1993).

Ray, Alok, ed., *Calcutta Keepsake* (Calcutta: Riddhi-India, 1978).

Robbins, Bruce, *The Servant's Hand: English Fiction from Below* (New York: Columbia University Press, 1986).

Rocher, Rosanne, *Orientalism, Poetry and the Millenium: The Chequered Life of Nathaniel Brassey Halhed 1751–1850* (Delhi: Motilal Banarsidass, 1983).

Rousseau, G. S. and Roy Porter, eds, *Exoticism in the Enlightenment* (Manchester: Manchester University Press, 1990).

Said, Edward W., *Orientalism* (1978; rpt Harmondsworth: Penguin, 1985).

Said, Edward W., 'Orientalism Reconsidered', *Europe and its Others*, ed. Francis Barker *et al.* (Colchester: University of Essex, 1985) i. 14–27.

Said, Edward W., *Culture and Imperialism* (London: Chatto and Windus, 1993).

Schwab, Raymond, *The Oriental Renaissance: Europe's Rediscovery of India and the East, 1680–1880*, trans. Gene Patterson-Black, Victor Reinking (New York: Columbia University Press, 1984).

Scott, James C., *Domination and the Arts of Resistance: Hidden Transcripts* (New Haven: Yale University Press, 1990).

Sen, Asok, 'A Pre-British Economic Formation in India of the late Eighteenth Century: Tipu Sultan's Mysore', ed. Barun De, *Perspectives in Social Sciences* (Calcutta: Oxford University Press, 1977) i. 46–119.

Sharpe, Jenny, *Allegories of Empire: The Figure of Woman in the Colonial Text* (Minneapolis: University of Minnesota Press, 1993).

Skalweit, Stephen, 'Political Thought', *The Ascendancy of France 1648–88. The New Cambridge Modern History*, v, ed. F. L. Carsten (Cambridge: Cambridge University Press, 1961) 96–121.

Sola Pinto, V. de, 'Sir William Jones and English Literature', *Bulletin of the School of Oriental and African Studies* xi (1943–6) 686–98.

Spear, Percival, *The Oxford History of Modern India, 1740–1975* (Delhi: Oxford University Press, 1978).

Spivak, Gayatri Chakravorty, 'The Rani of Sirmur', *Europe and its Others*, ed. Francis Barker *et al.* (Colchester: University of Essex, 1985) i. 128–51.

Spivak, Gayatri Chakravorty, 'Can the Subaltern Speak?', *Colonial Discourse and Post-Colonial Theory: A Reader*, eds Patrick Williams and Laura Chrisman (Hemel Hempstead: Harvester Wheatsheaf, 1993) 66–111.

Sprott, S. E., *The English Debate on Suicide from Donne to Hume* (La Salle: Open Court Publishing, 1961).

Stokes, Eric, *The English Utilitarians and India* (1959, Delhi: Oxford University Press, 1989).

Strachen, Michael, *Sir Thomas Roe, 1581–1644* (Salisbury: Michael Russell, 1989).

Suleri, Sara, *The Rhetoric of English India* (Chicago: University of Chicago Press, 1992).

Sutherland, Lucy S., *The East India Company in Eighteenth-Century Politics* (Oxford: Oxford University Press, 1952).

Teltscher, Kate, ' "The Fearful Name of the Black Hole": The Fashioning of an Imperial Myth', *Writing India, 1757-1990*, ed. Bart Moore-Gilbert (Manchester: Manchester University Press, 1996).

Tilley, M. P., *A Dictionary of Proverbs in England in the Sixteenth and Seventeenth Centuries* (Ann Arbor: University of Michigan Press, 1950).

Todorov, Tzvetan, *La Conquête de L'Amerique: La Question de L'Autre* (Paris: Seuil, 1982).

Venturi, Franco, 'Oriental Despotism', *Journal of the History of Ideas* xxiv (1963) 133–42.

Viswanathan, Gauri, *Masks of Conquest: Literary Study and British Rule in India* (London: Faber, 1989).

Walvin, James, *England, Slaves and Freedom, 1776–1838* (Basingstoke: Macmillan, 1986).

Weinberger-Thomas, Catherine, 'Les Mystères du Véda. Spéculations sur le texte sacré des anciens brames au Siècle des Lumières', *Purusartha*, VII (1983) 177–231.

Weinberger-Thomas, Catherine, ed., *L'Inde et L'imaginaire*, *Purusartha* xi (1988).

Whinney, Margaret and Robert Gunnis, *A Collection of Models by John Flaxman R. A. at University College London* (London: Athlone Press, 1967).

Wilhelm, Friedrich and H. G. Rawlinson, 'India and the Modern West', *A Cultural History of India*, ed. A. L. Basham (Oxford: Oxford University Press, 1975) 470–87.

Wilson, A. Leslie, *A Mythical Image: The Ideal of India in German Romanticism* (Durham N.C.: Duke University Press, 1964).

Young, Robert, *White Mythologies: Writing History and the West* (London: Routledge, 1990).

Yule, Henry and A. C. Burnell, eds, *Hobson-Jobson* (1886; rpt Calcutta: Rupa & Co., 1986).

Županov, Ines G. 'Aristocratic Analogies and Demotic Descriptions in the Seventeenth-Century Madurai Mission', *Representations* 41 (1993) 123–48.

Index

Agra 128
Anantpur 232–3, 247
André, Major John 178
Anglo-Mysore Wars 4, 9–10, 111, 119, 220, 229–55
Annual Register 120, 178, 183, 230–1, 232, 233, 252.
anti-slavery movement 172–4, 184
Archer, Mildred 249
Argens, Marquis d', *see* Boyer, Jean Baptiste de
Asiatic Society of Bengal 5, 129, 139, 141, 144, 192
  see also Asiatick Researches; Jones, Sir William, 'Anniversary Discourses'
Asiatick Miscellany 192, 202
Asiatick Researches 5, 123, 132, 142, 143, 193–4, 211
Aurangzeb, Emperor 31, 32, 42, 44–5

Bacon, Francis 14
Baird, General David 252, 253
Baldaeus, Philip 46
Barrell, John 169
Basham, A. L. 135, 137, 223
Bayly, C. A. 113, 238
Beatson, Alexander 237, 252
Beatson, W. B. 253, 255
Bengal 110, 114, 119, 121, 127–8
Bernier, François, 3, 14, 28–34, 42, 165
  and historiography 30–3
  and land tenure 29–30
  and sati 54, 60, 62, 65, 67
Bhabha, Homi 7, 118, 142, 144, 146, 157–8, 163, 197, 238–9
Bhagalpur 121, 128, 180–1
Bhagavad Gita 204, 211

Black Hole of Calcutta 120–1, 171
Bobbili 126–7
Bolts, William 158–60, 161, 163–4, 166, 174, 177, 184
Boswell, James 206
Bouchet, Père (Jesuit) 87, 89, 94, 95, 99, 216
Bourzes, Père de (Jesuit) 80–1
Boyer, Jean Baptiste de (Marquis d'Argens) 139
Brahmans
  and Jesuits 75, 94–5
  and Lutherans 96–8
  in novels 135–8, 140–1
  in poetry 219, 220–3
  and sati 54–6
  and Sir William Jones 196–7, 198, 199–202, 213, 221–2
Bristow, James 234, 236, 240–2, 243
Bruyn, Frans De 172
Burke, Edmund 5, 146, 158, 178, 221
  and Fox's East India Bill 177–8
  and Haidar Ali 230–1
  and impeachment of Hastings 9, 157, 165–8, 169–74, 176–7, 180–2, 184
  and Nawab of Arcot's Debts 171, 231
  and Rohilla War 185
  and Tipu Sultan 181–2, 233
Burke, William 158
Bussy, Charles de (Marquis) 126–7

Calcutta 120, 145, 160–3, 183
  Council of 158, 177
Calcutta Gazette 145, 234, 241, 251, 255

Calmette, Père (Jesuit) 94, 96, 99–100
Cambridge, Richard Owen 110–11, 117
Cannon, Garland 194
captives 234–5, 240–5
Carnall, Geoffrey 167
caste 75, 129, 130, 146–7, 177
Catholicism 23–4
 see also Jesuits
Catrou, F. F. 59, 165
Chait Singh 175, 179
Chapelain, Jean 29
Chapman, Charles 196
charity 77–87
Charles I, King 12
Charnock, Job 67–8
Clarke, Richard 174
Cleveland, Augustus 121–4, 128, 181, 201, 222
Clifford, James 7
Clive, Lord (Governor of Madras) 245
Clive, Robert (First Baron) 116–18, 124, 158, 164, 173, 175–6
 parliamentary enquiry into 111, 121, 125, 158, 168
Cohn, Bernard 20, 21, 150, 196, 197, 198
Colbert, Jean-Baptiste 29, 30
Colebrooke, H. T. 197
Collins, William 220
Cook, Captain James 121
Cope, Captain 153–4n
Cornwallis, Lord Charles 151, 182, 199, 248–51
Courtney, John 206
Crone, G. R. 3–4
Curzon, Lord George 120

Daneshmand Khan 29
Dara Shukoh, Prince 29, 33
Davis, Natalie Zemon 5–6
Dellon, Charles 66
Dempster, John 243–4
Derrett, J. D. M. 196, 200
Devi Singh 167–8, 172, 184
Devil's Advocate 1–2
Diderot, Denis 164
Dirom, Alexander 246, 248, 251

Dow, Alexander 5, 113–14, 115, 129, 164, 165, 174, 184
Drew, John 209
Dryden, John 60–1, 208, 209

East India Company 2, 12, 17, 47, 49, 76, 223, 251, 255
 attacks on Company rule 111, 121, 127, 157–86, 220–1, 231
 military power of 110, 115–19, 232–3
 rule in India 111, 121–8, 151, 157–8, 221–3
 trade 17–18, 67, 114–15, 127–8, 172–3, 238
Elizabeth I, Queen 12
Elliot, Sir Gilbert 178
Euripides 59–60
European Magazine 192

Fabian, Johannes 100
famine 85–6, 127, 165, 183–4, 221
Finch, William 16, 17–18, 23
Fitch, Ralph 15, 23
Flaxman, John 201–2
Foote, Samuel 168–9, 170
Forrest, Denys 232
Forster, George 132–4
Foucault, Michel 118, 129, 145
Fox, Charles James 157, 179
Foxe, John 65
France 4, 28–9, 30–1, 126–7
 alliance with Mysore 229, 238, 240, 252
Francis, Philip 158, 160, 161, 177, 178
Frederici, Caesar 15
Freud, Sigmund 167
Fryer, John 38, 42–4, 45, 50, 51

Gassendi, Pierre 29
Gentleman's Magazine 175, 178, 182–3, 233, 235
Gheria 125
Ghosh, Suresh Chandra 161, 162
Gilchrist, John 151
Goethe, Johann Wolfgang von 213
Goldsmith, Oliver 139

Gray, Thomas 176, 208, 209, 210, 220, 221
Greenblatt, Stephen 3, 6, 24, 27, 76, 79
Grey, Charles 157, 175, 176
Griselda 65
Grose, John-Henry 114, 115
Guha, Ranajit 5, 176–7, 195
Guyon, Claude Marie 90

Hadley, George 150–1
Haidar Ali 251
  as able ruler 231, 239
  as cruel tyrant 121, 230
  as threat to British 9, 119, 229
Hakluyt, Richard 12, 15–16, 17
Halbfass, Wilhelm 92
Halhed, Nathaniel 165, 196
Hamilton, Alexander 67–8
Hamilton, Charles 139
Hamilton, Elizabeth 5, 138–42, 176
harem 40–5
Hartog, Francois 24
Hartly House, Calcutta 5, 134–8
Hastings, Warren 195, 218
  impeachment of 5, 9, 111, 121, 157–8, 164–84, 192, 233
  as patron 121, 123, 131, 139
Hawkins, William 16, 59
Hayley, William 192–3, 201–2
Head, Richard 50–1, 68, 70–1nn
Henry, Prince 12
Herbert, Sir Thomas 46, 50, 52–3, 60, 63–4, 65, 70n
Herder, Johann Gottfried 213
Hiltebeitel, Alf 216
Hinduism 16–17, 23
  and female sexuality 45–7
  and missionaries 98–101
  and sentimentalism 136–7
  and Sir William Jones 202–11, 216–20
  see also Brahmans; sati
Hodgen, Margaret T. 100
Hodges, William 121–2, 127–8, 129, 131, 141, 176
Holwell, J. Z. 120–1, 129, 164
Home, Robert 249
Homer 43–4

Horsford, Sir John 220
Howe, Darcus 1–2
Hughes, Derek 60
Hunter, William 142–4
Hyderabad, Nizam of 229, 246–7

Impey, Sir Elijah 177, 178
Irwin, Eyles 220–1
Islam 17, 24, 26–7, 230, 240–1
Ives, Edward 125–6, 127, 149–50, 248–9

Jagannatha Tarkapanchanan 199
Jahangir, Emperor 20–1, 25–7, 42, 109–10, 111–12
Jai Singh, Raja 96
James I, King 12, 22, 25, 53
Jardine, Lisa 44, 65
Jemla, Emir 32
Jesuits 4, 8, 74–6, 87–8, 90–3
  and brahmans 94–5
  and conversion 94–6
  and converts 77–81, 84–7, 103–5
  and exorcism 94
  and famine 85–6
  and funds 77–81
  and Hinduism 98–100
  and miracles 93–4
  and sati 103–5
  and St Thomas Christians 89–90
Jones, Sir William 3, 9, 123, 129, 141, 150
  and brahmans 135, 196–202, 213, 218–20, 221–2
  legal researches 195–200, 222
  reputation of 192–5
  works of :
    Al Sirajiyyah 197
    'Anniversary Discourses' 127, 135, 193, 204, 207, 223
    Digest of Indian Laws 197, 199
    'The Enchanted Fruit' 216–18
    Hymns 5, 202–10, 216, 218–20, 221–4
    Institutes of Hindu Law 197, 198
    Sacontala 5, 211–15
Jonston, A. 209
Judaism 99

Kabbani, Rana 40
Kalidasa 5, 211–15
Kelly, Gary 139
Khurram, Sultan 21
Kindersley, Jemina 115, 119
Kipling, Rudyard 124, 131–2
Kircher, Athanasius 56
Kirkpatrick, William 235–6, 237

La Boullaye le Gouz, François 39–42
La Croze, Mathurin Veyssière de 89–90, 100–1
La Mothe le Vayer, François 29, 32
land tenure 25, 29–30
Lane, Edward William 132
language 150–1, 196
Law, Edward 176–7, 180–1
Le Moyne, Pierre 51–2, 63
Leask, Nigel 7, 139, 201
Lettres édifiantes 4, 74–6, 77–81, 84–8, 93–6, 98–100, 103–5, 211, 216
Linnaeus, Carl 129, 217
Linschoten, John Huighen Van 46, 50
Lockman, J. 90–2
London Gazette 241, 244
London Magazine 125, 183
Louis XIV, King 30
Louis XV, King 99
Lowe, Lisa 14, 30
Lucretia 65
Lutherans 8, 76–7
  and brahmans 96–8
  and conversion 96–8, 102–3
  and Hinduism 98–9, 100–1
  and funds 81–4
  and Jesuits 92–3
  and St Thomas Christians 88–9
  and Tamil Bible 101–2
luxury 160–3, 173

Mackenzie, Roderick 245–6, 247–8
Mackintosh, William 160–3, 169
Macleod, Colonel Norman 181–2
Macpherson, James 205
Macpherson, Sir John 196
Macrabie, Alexander 178
Madras, Council of 158, 231
Madras Courier 248

Mahabharata 216
Majeed, Javed 196, 197, 199, 204, 205
Mandelslo, John Albert de 49–50, 66
Mandeville, Sir John 16, 27, 50
Mani, Lata 62–3
Manucci, Niccolao 42, 44–5, 51
Marathas 125, 128, 229, 246
Marlowe, Christopher 17, 21–2
Marshall, P. J. 119, 168, 174
  on impeachment of Hastings 164, 165–6, 167, 172, 179,
  on Haidar Ali 230–1
  on Tipu Sultan 236, 248
Martin, Père (Jesuit) 87, 103–4
martyrdom 65–6
Marvell, Andrew 175–6
Marx, Karl 29, 30
Mason, Philip 124
Mathews, Brigadier-General Richard 232–3, 247
Memoirs of a Gentleman 148–9
Mill, James 194
Milton, John 208–10
missionaries 4, 8, 74–105
  see also Jesuits; Lutherans
Mitter, Partha 23
Molière 146
Montaigne, Michel de 22, 28
Montesquieu, Charles Louis de Secondat de 4, 29, 113, 139, 165
Monthly Review 192, 193–4
Moodie, J. 231, 233, 240, 247
Moor, Edward 140, 144–5, 236
Mughal empire
  court 7, 18, 20–2, 25–9, 42, 44–5, 109–10, 111–12
  decline of 111–13, 128
  land tenure 14, 25, 29–31
  military power of 115–17
Mulligan, Hugh 172
Munro, Major Hector 230
Munro, Captain Innes 146–8, 150
Murr, Sylvia 4, 74, 93
Musselwhite, David 158, 179
Mysore 9–10, 111, 119, 220, 229–55
  and alliance with France 229, 238, 240, 252
  and British captives 234–5, 240–4

see also Anglo-Mysore Wars; Haidar Ali; Tipu Sultan

Nandakumar, Raja 177–8
Niranjana, Tejaswini 222
Nobili, Roberto de 74

Oakes, Henry 232
O'Leary, Brendan 30
oriental despotism 29–31, 33, 113–14, 119, 163–72, 230–9
orientalism, *see* Said, Edward
Orme, Robert 112–13, 114–15, 116–17, 126–7, 129, 168
Ovington, John 47

Padel, Felix 122
Parnell, Thomas 209
Parsis 144–5
Parsons, John 192
Pennant, Thomas 232, 256n
Philipps, Jenkin 99
Philosophical Transactions 70n
Pigot, George 158
Pindar 210
Plassey, Battle of 255
Plumer, Thomas 181
Pollilur, Battle of 230
Polo, Marco 47
Pope, Alexander 162–3, 209, 216
Porter, Dennis 9
Porter, Roy 8
Portuguese 24, 48–9, 89
Pratt, Mary Louise 34n, 137–8, 234, 243
Price, Joseph 160, 161–2, 163, 170–1
Propertius 64
prostitution 48–50
Protestantism 24, 82–3, 88–9
  see also Lutherans; Society for Promoting Christian Knowledge
Pucci, Suzanne Rodin 39
Purchas, Samuel 12–28
Pyrard de Laval, François 48–9

Raghunath Hari (Subadar of Jhansi) 142–4
Rajan, Rajeswari Sunder 53–4, 72n

Rajmahal 121, 180–1
Ranga Rao 126–7
Raynal, Abbé Guillaume 164, 167
Robbins, Bruce 146
Robson, Francis 244–5
Roe, Sir Thomas 16
  and Jahangir's court 7, 20–2, 25–8, 42, 109–10, 111, 113
Roger, Abraham 53, 55, 56
Rousseau, G. S. 8

S. Hyacinthe, Madame de 79–80, 85
Said, Edward 28, 132
  East/West opposition 6, 7–8, 22, 26
  orientalism as unified discourse 9, 30, 33
  orientalist knowledge 32, 129, 194, 223
Saignes, Père (Jesuit) 85–6
Saint Vallier, M. Cochet de 80
sati 8, 51–68, 103–5, 140, 178
Savandurga 251–2
Sayyad Ibrahim 245
Schlegel, August Wilhelm 213
Schwab, Raymond 213
Scott, James 147, 148
Scott, John 220–1
Scrafton, Luke 112, 116, 117–18
Scurry, James 234–5, 242–4
sentimentalism 134, 137
sepoys 117–19, 121–2, 244–6
Seringapatam 229, 235, 238, 242, 244, 245, 252–5
servants 132–3, 146–50
Shah Jehan, Emperor 31–2, 33
Shakespeare, William 194, 213–14
Sharpe, Jenny 53
Shaw, Thomas 123–4, 181, 222
Sheen, John Charles 232–3, 247
Sheridan, Richard Brinsley 157
Shore, John (Lord Teignmouth) 122–3, 181, 196, 197, 200–1, 202–4
Short History of English Transactions 184–5
Siraj-ud Daula (Nawab of Bengal) 120–1, 124, 171
Skelton, R. A. 3
slavery 172–4, 184

280 / Index

Smith, Adam 164
Society for Promoting Christian Knowledge (SPCK) 76, 83
Solvyns, Baltazard 129–31
Soudé, Comtesse de 78, 80
SPCK, *see* Society for Promoting Christian Knowledge
Spencer, George John (2nd Earl) 198, 200, 206, 223
Spenser, Edmund 19–20, 218
Spivak, Gayatri Chakravorty 63, 67
Sprott, S. E. 56
St Thomas Christians 88–90
Suffren, Admiral Baille de 240
suicide 52, 56, 65
Suleri, Sara 7, 111, 129, 166–7
Sutherland, Lucy 164
Swift, Jonathan 146
Sym, John 52

Tanjore 158, 221
Tasso, Torquato 51
Tavernier, Jean-Baptiste 4, 46, 54–5, 61–2
Taylor, Jeremy 210
tea 173
Teignmouth, Lord, *see* Shore, John
Tennant, Rev. William 118
Terry, Edward 16–17, 18–20, 24–5, 26, 64–5
theatricality 20–2, 59–60, 62, 113, 127, 168, 252–3
Thévenot, Jean de 39
Thomson, James 208
Thomson, William 230, 239–40
Tipu Sultan
  as able ruler 181–2, 232, 233, 236–7, 239
  death of 252–5
  defeat of 220, 246, 248–55
  and military tactics 238–40
  as oriental despot 9–10, 121, 172, 182, 230, 231, 233–9, 249
  sons of 248–51
  as threat to British 9, 119, 229–30
  and trade 238
Todorov, Tzvetan 96
Touchstone, Timothy, *pseud.* 173
trade 17–18, 28, 114–15, 127–8, 172–3, 238
Tranquebar, *see* Lutherans
translation 5, 90–2, 180, 200–1, 211–15, 235–6, 237–8
Tulaji Angria 125–7, 248–9
Tully, Mark 1–2

Valle, Pietro della 59, 66–7
Varthema, Ludovico di 47–8
Venturi, Franco 113
Verelst, Henry 158–60, 161, 177
Villiputtur Alvar 216
Virgil 209
Viswanathan, Gauri 9

Wandiwash, battle of 126
Watson, Admiral Charles 124–7
Weinberger-Thomas, Catherine 198
Wellesley, Richard Colley (1st Marquess) 255
Wesley, John 184
widowhood 44, 51, 53–4
Wilberforce, William 172
Wilkie, David 253
Wilkins, Charles 204
Wilks, Mark 233, 245, 246–7, 253–5
witchcraft 45–6, 47
Withington, Nicholas 65–6
women 8, 37
  Hindu 38–40, 45–68, 80–1, 103–5, 130, 148
  Muslim 38–45, 148

Ziegenbalg, Bartholomew 92, 97, 98–9, 101
Županov, Ines 105–6n